Using Turbo Prolog™

Khin Maung Yin

with

David Solomon

Que™ Corporation
Indianapolis, Indiana

Using Turbo Prolog™

Library of Congress Catalog No.: 86-62537
ISBN 0-88022-270-0

90 89 88 87   8 7 6 5 4 3 2 1

Interpretation of the printing code: the rightmost double-digit number is the year of the book's printing; the rightmost single-digit number, the number of the book's printing. For example, a printing code of 87-4 shows that the fourth printing of the book occurred in 1987.

This book covers version 1.1 of Turbo Prolog.

Dedication

I am dedicating this book to my wife, Philippa, for her patience and support, and to my children, Jordan and Lori, for teaching me the logic of life.

K.M.Y.

Development Director
David P. Ewing, M.A.

Editorial Director
David F. Noble, Ph.D.

Managing Editor
Gregory Croy

Production Editor
Bill Nolan

Editor
Lois Sherman

Technical Editor
Chingmin Jim Lo

Production Foreman
Dennis Sheehan

Production
Kelly Currie
Joe Ramon
Peter Tocco
Lynne Tone

Composed by Que Corporation
in Weideman and Que Digital

—— About the Authors ——

Khin Maung Yin

Khin Yin earned his Ph.D. in applied physics from Kent State University, where he is an associate professor in computer science and technology. He teaches courses in computer science, business data processing, data electronics, microprocessor applications, and robotics. He also teaches programming courses and uses C, LISP, and PROLOG.

Dr. Yin is a consultant in computer graphics, database design and development, and artificial intelligence systems. The applications he develops range from programs for academic computing to data processing programs for business. His consulting activities also include the management and utilization of the Digital Equipment Corporation's computers.

Dr. Yin is the author of many articles for applied physics professional journals. He also writes articles and software reviews for *DEC Professional* and *Vax Professional*.

David Solomon

David Solomon is in charge of computer development for the technical services department of an international biomedical manufacturer. He deals with equipment ranging from dedicated word processors to superminicomputers. Currently he is working on artificial intelligence programs for fault analysis and other applications.

Table of Contents

8   Using Windows, Graphics, and Sound 269

9   Building Dynamic Databases 341

10   Creating Expert Systems

11   Processing Natural Language

Acknowledgments

I am grateful to faculty colleagues and students at Kent State University and to professional colleagues in the Artificial Intelligence Special Interest Group (AISIG) of the Digital Equipment Computer Users Society (DECUS) for stimulating discussions on many of the topics discussed in this work.

I want to thank the Technical Support Group of Borland International, and Albert Holt in particular, who answered many technical questions on Turbo Prolog.

The staff at Que Corporation have provided superb editorial support throughout the writing of this book. While I am aware that it takes many individuals behind the scenes to produce a completed work, I especially appreciate the guidance the staff provided throughout this project.

Finally, I want to thank my wife, Dr. Philippa Brown Yin, for many comments and suggestions during the writing of this book.

K.M.Y.

Trademark Acknowledgments

Introduction

Turbo Prolog is the most exciting artificial intelligence (AI) language on the market today. Just a few years ago, AI programming languages were available only for users of expensive mainframe computer systems. Now several implementations of Prolog are on the market, but none compares with Borland International's Turbo Prolog for speed and low cost. The availability of Turbo Prolog for IBM® PCs and compatibles encourages small businesses and individuals to reap the benefits of Turbo Prolog applications programs at affordable cost.

Why Use Turbo Prolog?

Turbo Prolog is a high-level, compiler-based language developed by Borland International for use in writing AI programs. As an AI language, Turbo Prolog is especially suited to the development of expert systems, dynamic databases, natural-language processing programs, and general problem-solving applications. Turbo Prolog also has facilities for producing user-friendly applications programs with multiple windows, colorful graphics and interactive input/output facilities.

Turbo Prolog's built-in predicates and enhancements also make it suitable for developing programs in many standard business applications, including programs for accounting, payrolls, and presentation graphics.

The popularity of Prolog has increased dramatically since it was chosen as the language of the Japanese Fifth Generation Project. The demand for AI applications programs for use in place of and along with traditional applications programs is increasing steadily. In this continued evolution of computer applications, there is an increasing need to develop Prolog applications programs. Turbo Prolog meets this need admirably.

In addition to Turbo Prolog, there are several other implementations of Prolog in the United States, including Arity Prolog, Prolog II, Wisdom Prolog and Micro Prolog. Unlike many other implementations of Prolog, Turbo Prolog comes with a superb full-screen editor, along with multiple-window facilities and interactive debugging. It supports color graphics on IBM PCs equipped with the Color/Graphic Adapter (CGA) and Enhanced Graphics Adapter (EGA). Graphics predicates and the turtle graphic system are both supported. File-handling facilities are included for sequential files, and random access files, and binary files.

Another reason for choosing Turbo Prolog over other implementations is that Turbo Prolog is a compiled language, in contrast to some other versions of Prolog that are interpreted. An interpreted language takes source code instructions one by one and executes them. A compiler, on the other hand, compiles the whole source code program into machine code. Turbo Prolog compiles source code extremely fast (fastest among all Prolog implementations available for the IBM PC). Making a stand-alone executable program in Turbo Prolog is easily done. Further, Turbo Prolog has a superb user interface for program development. In a nutshell, Turbo Prolog is the best buy on the market today.

What is Prolog?

The name *Prolog* is derived from the term *Pro*gramming in *Log*ic. Alain Colmerauer and other members of the *Groupe d'Intelligence Artificielle*, of the Universite d'Aix-Marseille in France, designed and created Prolog in 1973. Their main purpose was to make natural-language translation programs. Since 1973, several expansions and improvements to Prolog have been made, notably by groups at the University of Edinburgh, in Scotland. The Scottish implementation of Prolog is sometimes called "C & M Prolog" in reference to William F. Clocksin and Christopher S. Mellish, the authors of the classic work *Programming in Prolog*. Although there is no official standard for Prolog, the Clocksin and Mellish text defines what is usually regarded as an unofficial standard for the language.

Turbo Prolog differs in a few ways from C & M Prolog. Some C & M elements are absent from Turbo Prolog, but those elements generally are used only in very advanced and complex programs. One significant difference between Turbo Prolog and the unofficial C & M standard (as well as other implementations) is Turbo Prolog's strict typing of data elements. Most of these differences contribute to Turbo Prolog's speed of compilation and execution. And even though some programmers object to the differences, saying that Turbo Prolog is not a "pure" Prolog, still the language offers many enhancements, such as windows and graphics, that are unavailable in other implementations. Whether or not it is a pure Prolog, Turbo Prolog is a flexible, full-featured modern programming language.

Turbo Prolog and Other Languages

Languages such as Pascal, BASIC, and C are imperative languages. A program in an imperative language consists of chunks of instructions that specify the steps taken to achieve the purpose of the program. Unlike those languages, Prolog is a declarative language. A program in a declarative language consists of logical declarations specifying what the program is supposed to achieve.

Consequently, Prolog lacks "brute-force" control structures such as DO WHILE and IF . . . THEN. Rather than specifying the steps of program execution, the programmer declares the logical method for achieving the goal of the program. Powerful *internal unification routines* (whose workings are discussed in Chapter 2) then search for solutions to the program's goal.

Turbo Prolog's power resides in its searching and pattern matching capabilities. The internal unification routines relentlessly search through all possible combinations of the program's rules in attempting to satisfy the goal set by the programmer. Because Prolog is based on familiar logical ideas, you will find yourself drawn more and more to Prolog as you learn how to work with it.

Who Should Use this Book?

Using Turbo Prolog is written for anyone interested in Turbo Prolog programming, whether newcomer or professional programmer. You need not know programming in procedural languages such as BASIC, Pascal, or C, or in some other declarative language such as LISP, to benefit from *Using Turbo Prolog*. This book provides the needed background concepts and methods to write useful programs. This book helps you to think "prologically" so that your programs are developed efficiently and run smoothly.

If you do not yet own Turbo Prolog, this book is for you. You can benefit from reading *Using Turbo Prolog*, as it will help you to know what declarative programming is and how the programs are designed and built. The use of logic predicates and the building of rules are major programming tasks common to all implementations of Prolog.

If you own Turbo Prolog, you should also own this book. *Using Turbo Prolog* shows you how to design and build applications programs that suit your needs. *Using Turbo Prolog* goes beyond the *Turbo Prolog Owner's Handbook* in its development of complete programs to illustrate the uses of built-in predicates and rules for each topic addressed in this book.

If you are a Turbo Prolog programmer, *Using Turbo Prolog* will be a valuable asset. In addition to comprehensive treatments of Turbo Prolog predicates, this book shows the uses of structured design tools such as data flow diagrams and structure charts. These tools are useful as development aids in file-processing programs, dynamic databases, and expert systems.

What Is in This Book?

Using Turbo Prolog is presented in two parts. The first part, consisting of eight chapters, presents Turbo Prolog fundamentals and programming techniques. Short programs in each of these chapters illustrate the techniques presented. The second part of the book introduces the design and implementation of Turbo Prolog programs in four major areas of AI programming: expert systems, databases, natural-language processing, and games and puzzles. Each chapter in the second part culminates in a complete applications program. This part of the book will show you how to build programs methodically and efficiently. In addition, throughout the book you will find useful Self-Help Exercises that encourage hands-on work with the programs.

Chapter 1, "Getting Started in Turbo Prolog," introduces major Turbo Prolog programming features and presents complete instructions for installing Version 1.1 of Turbo Prolog on both hard-disk and dual-floppy-disk systems.

Chapter 2, "Turbo Prolog Concepts," introduces the logical basis of Turbo Prolog. Fundamental concepts such as matching, instantiation and binding, and backtracking, which will help you understand how Turbo Prolog's internal unification routines work toward the goals you define for your programs, are presented in this chapter.

Chapter 3, "Programming Fundamentals," describes the structure and syntax of Turbo Prolog programs. Taking a hands-on approach, this chapter offers many short example programs demonstrating fundamental programming techniques. In addition, two useful program-design tools, the domain-structure diagram and the predicate-structure diagram, are presented.

Chapter 4, "Repetition and Recursion," describes the basic techniques for performing iterative tasks. Two methods of repetition—Backtrack After Fail and Cut and Fail—and three recursive methods—Cut and Fail, User Defined Repeat, and the General Recursive Rule—are the principal topics of the chapter.

Chapter 5, "Using Lists," shows you how to create and manipulate lists, including finding a member of a list, splitting a list into two lists, and combining two lists into a single list. Again, short programs are presented to help you become familiar with these concepts and techniques.

Chapter 6, "Using Strings," covers Turbo Prolog's character set, strings, and string-manipulation operations. Example programs demonstrate splitting and combining strings, searching for a character or substring within a string, and other techniques.

Chapter 7, "Using Files," begins with a description of the IBM PC's possible device configurations. Creating data files, writing to files, and reading from files are discussed next. Example programs show how files are created, read, and written.

Chapter 8, "Using Windows, Graphics, and Sound," presents Turbo Prolog's exciting window facilities. Examples demonstrate the creation of multiple windows and the direction of input and output from window to window. Graphics modes and the means for using them are discussed and are demonstrated in programs that produce line graphs, bar graphs, and pie graphs. Other programs demonstrate turtle graphics, a popular graphic system available in Turbo Prolog. Turbo Prolog's sound predicates are introduced and used to create musical tags.

Chapter 9, "Building Dynamic Databases," is the first applications chapter. Here, many of the techniques learned in the earlier chapters are used in the creation and manipulation of a relational database management system. As you read and create the database you will see Turbo Prolog's powerful internal matching routines in action.

Chapter 10, "Building Expert Systems," describes the organization and creation of expert systems. The knowledge base, the inference engine, and the user-interface system are discussed in relation to Turbo Prolog's rule-based and logic-based systems. Three different expert system programs are presented. These programs give the user hands-on experience in this exciting field.

Chapter 11, "Natural-Language Processing," describes natural-language processing techniques and the prevailing methods of language analysis. The chapter shows how Turbo Prolog's facilities for manipulating strings and lists can be used in simple natural-language user interfaces. Programs illustrating these techniques give you opportunities to see the techniques at work and to adapt them for your own purposes.

Chapter 12, "Building Games and Puzzles," presents general methods for Turbo Prolog to create games and puzzles. These techniques are demonstrated in a number-guessing game, two versions of the 23 Matches Game, a pattern-matching game, and a game based on the famous Monkey and Bananas problem.

Using Turbo Prolog contains six appendixes. Appendix A is short tutorial on the use of the Turbo Prolog editor. Appendix B tells how to use Turbo Prolog system features that are not discussed elsewhere in the book. Appendix C is a short introduction to basic commands and functions of PC DOS and MS-DOS, the operating systems used in IBM PCs and compatible computers. Appendix D is a brief glossary of Turbo Prolog terms. Appendix E is a short descriptive bibliography of references for further reading. Appendix F gives additional Turbo Prolog commands and utilities, some of which are essential in building complex applications programs.

1

Getting Started with Turbo Prolog

Overview

Turbo Prolog is Borland International's fast, compiler-based implementation of the Prolog programming language. It is designed to give you responses it deduces from its powerful internal routines. Just a few lines of Turbo Prolog code can accomplish tasks that might require several pages of code in other programming languages. Because of its powerful pattern-matching capabilities, Turbo Prolog is well suited not only to applications in artificial intelligence and natural-language processing, but also to more conventional applications such as database management.

Turbo Prolog runs on the IBM PC and compatible machines. To use Turbo Prolog effectively, you need a basic understanding of your computer system and of Turbo Prolog's program characteristics. If you need an introduction to your computer's disk operating system (PC DOS or MS-DOS) and to frequently used DOS commands, read Appendix C before continuing with this chapter.

The first section of this chapter briefly describes Version 1.1 of Turbo Prolog and gives instructions for installing Turbo Prolog both on hard-disk and on dual-floppy-disk systems. The next sections describe procedures you will use in a Turbo Prolog programming session. By following these procedures, you will learn the Turbo Prolog setup and system commands you will use most frequently. Finally, this chapter presents the functions of Turbo Prolog's superb menu system.

The Turbo Prolog Package

The Turbo Prolog compiler package contains two distribution disks and a manual that is more than 200 pages long. One disk is labeled *PROGRAM DISK* and the other is labeled *LIBRARY & SAMPLE PROGRAMS*. Table 1.1 describes the files that are contained on the distribution disks.

——————————————— Table 1.1 ———————————————
Files on the Version 1.1 Distribution Disks

1. Contents of the PROGRAM DISK:

PROLOG.EXE	The main file of the Turbo Prolog system.
PROLOG.OVL	An overlay file used by the Turbo Prolog system at startup, when creating .EXE files, and when performing certain other functions.
PROLOG.SYS	A file containing information on the color, size, and location of windows in the Turbo Prolog system, as well as information on the directories used by the system.
PROLOG.ERR	A file containing Turbo Prolog error messages.
PROLOG.HLP	Text of the Turbo Prolog help messages (accessed by pressing F1 in the Turbo Prolog system).
GEOBASE.PRO and GEOBASE.INC	The GeoBase™ database program.
GEOBASE.DBA	Data used by the GeoBase program.
GEOBASE.HLP	Text of the GeoBase help messages.
README.COM	A program for displaying contents of the README file.
README	A text file containing supplementary information not included in the *Turbo Prolog Owner's Handbook*.

2. Contents of the LIBRARY AND SAMPLE PROGRAMS Disk:

PROLOG.LIB and INIT.OBJ	Files used by the Turbo Prolog system when creating program files.
EXAMPLES	A subdirectory containing programs used in the Tutorial section of the *Turbo Prolog Owner's Handbook*.
ANSWERS	A subdirectory containing answers to exercises in the *Turbo Prolog Owner's Handbook*.
PROGRAMS	A subdirectory containing some sample Turbo Prolog programs.

Turbo Prolog Version 1.1

The Turbo Prolog Version 1.1 package includes two distribution disks, the *Turbo Prolog Owner's Handbook*, and one or two booklets containing errata and updates for the handbook. Before continuing, you may want to verify that you have received all the parts of the package.

Turbo Prolog Version 1.1 Errata describes new features and predicates that were introduced in Version 1.1 of the program. The booklet also corrects certain parts of the handbook and provides a new index. *Turbo Prolog Version 1.1 Update Errata*, which also describes new features and provides a new index, applies only to certain printings of the handbook. If you received the *Update Errata*, you should follow the instructions printed on the first page to determine whether its corrections apply to your handbook.

Installing Turbo Prolog Version 1.1

Turbo Prolog can run on either a hard-disk or a dual-floppy-disk system. For either system, a minimum of 384K of RAM is required. In addition, you need to have PC DOS Version 2.0 or later as your operating system.

Before installing Turbo Prolog, you should use the DISKCOPY command to make working copies of the distribution disks. (If you are not familiar with this command, consult Appendix C.) To guard against accidental erasure of the distribution disks, you might want to put write-protect tabs on the distribution disks before you begin copying them. Be sure to label your copies and to store the original distribution disks in a safe place.

If you have a hard-disk system, read the following section for instructions on installing Turbo Prolog. If you have a floppy-disk system, skip ahead to the section "Installation on a Dual-Floppy-Disk System."

Installation on a Hard-Disk System

To install Turbo Prolog Version 1.1 on your hard-disk system, you need to create a directory structure and copy the files from the distribution disks to your hard disk. You should create the same directory structure on your hard disk that you find on the distribution disk.

The following instructions assume that your hard disk is drive C:. The system prompt therefore is *C>*.

1. Create directories for the Turbo Prolog files by entering

   ```
   MD \TBPROLOG
   MD \TBPROLOG\EXAMPLES
   MD \TBPROLOG\ANSWERS
   MD \TBPROLOG\PROGRAMS
   ```

2. Copy the files from the distribution disks to the Turbo Prolog directory structure on your hard disk:

   A. Place your working copy of the Program Disk in drive A:.

   B. Change to the directory \TBPROLOG by entering

      ```
      CD \TBPROLOG
      ```

   C. Copy the files from drive A: to the directory C:\TBPROLOG with the command

      ```
      COPY A:*.* C:/V
      ```

   D. Remove the Program Disk from drive A: and insert the Utilities and Examples disk.

   E. Copy the two system files PROLOG.LIB and INIT.OBJ to the TBPROLOG directory. The commands are

      ```
      COPY A:PROLOG.LIB C:/V
      ```

      and

      ```
      COPY A:INIT.OBJ C:/V
      ```

   F. Copy all the files from the subdirectories on the Utilities and Examples disk, in drive A:, to the subdirectories on the hard disk. The commands to do this are

COPY A: \EXAMPLES*.* C:\TBPROLOG\EXAMPLES/V
COPY A: \ANSWERS*.* C:\TBPROLOG\ANSWERS/V
COPY A: \PROGRAMS*.* C:\TBPROLOG\PROGRAMS/V

Now you have copied all the Turbo Prolog distribution files to your hard-disk system. Further, the directory structure you have is the same as that of the distribution disks. You can now look at the directory listings in all the directories using the CD and DIR commands described in Appendix C.

Installation on a Dual-Floppy-Disk System

To install Turbo Prolog Version 1.1 on your dual-floppy-disk system, follow these steps, which assume that the floppy-disk drives are A: and B:. Before you begin, make sure you have three blank disks.

1. Use the FORMAT command to format three disks (if you are not familiar with this command, consult Appendix C):

   A. Place your DOS disk in drive A: and a blank disk in drive B:, then enter

      FORMAT B: /S

      The */S* option causes operating-system files to be copied to the disk so that it can be used to start the computer. When the FORMAT program asks whether you want to format another disk, press *N*. (If you press *Y* and proceed to format the other two disks, the system files will be copied to those disks, as well.) Remove the disk from drive B: and label it *Turbo Prolog Startup Disk*.

   B. Put another blank disk in drive B: and enter

      FORMAT B:

      (without the */S*). This time, answer *Y* when asked whether you want to format another disk.

   C. Insert a third disk in the drive, and follow the instructions that appear on-screen. While the third disk is being formatted, you can label the second disk (the first one formatted without the */S* option) *Turbo Prolog Working Disk*. When the third disk is formatted, answer *N*, remove the disk from drive B:, and label it *Turbo Prolog Library Disk*.

2. Put your working copy of the Program Disk in drive A: and the disk you labeled *Turbo Prolog Startup Disk* in drive B:, then enter

   COPY A:PROLOG.* B: /V

   to copy the Prolog system files to the Startup Disk.

3. Now put the disk you labeled *Turbo Prolog Working Disk* in drive B: (leaving the Program Disk in drive A:), and enter

   COPY A:GEOBASE.* B: /V

   Remove the Program Disk from drive A: and insert your working copy of the Library and Sample Programs disk. Enter the command

   COPY A:EXAMPLES*.* B: /V

   Then remove both disks from the drives.

4. Put the DOS disk in drive A: and enter

   DISKCOPY A: B:

   When the DISKCOPY program prompts you to place the source disk in drive A: and the target disk in drive B:, remove the DOS disk from drive A: and insert your working copy of the Library and Sample Programs disk. Put the disk you labeled *Turbo Prolog Library* in drive B: and press Enter.

Now you have three disks for your working Turbo Prolog system: a Startup Disk, a Working Disk, and a Library Disk. In the section that follows you will see how to make them work for you.

Running Turbo Prolog

Once you have properly installed the Turbo Prolog system, you can bring it up by following a few short and simple steps. Refer to the appropriate section for your floppy-disk or hard-disk system.

Hard-Disk Systems: Bringing up the Turbo Prolog system involves bringing up the operating system, changing to the Turbo Prolog subdirectory, and starting the Turbo Prolog program. The steps are as follows.

1. Turn on the computer. When the system prompts you for the date and time, either enter them or simply press Enter. (Entering the date and time is a good idea, however.) Soon the system will display the system prompt *C>*, which indicates that DOS is up and running.

2. Change to the Turbo Prolog subdirectory by entering

   CD \TBPROLOG

   You may want to look at the directory to make sure you have followed the correct procedures. The command to do this is

   DIR

The system should display the directory header \TBPROLOG and a list of the Turbo Prolog files in the directory.

3. Invoke the Turbo Prolog system by entering

   PROLOG

   The computer then reads the Turbo Prolog system files and loads them into memory.

Floppy-Disk Systems: Bringing up the Turbo Prolog system involves two stages: booting DOS from a floppy disk and bringing up the Turbo Prolog system. The steps are as follows.

1. Insert the Turbo Prolog Startup Disk in drive A: and the Turbo Prolog Working Disk in drive B:, then turn on the computer. When the system prompts you for the date and time, either enter them or simply press Enter. (Entering the date and time is a good idea, however.) Soon the system will display the system prompt A>, which indicates that DOS is up and running.

2. Invoke the Turbo Prolog system by entering

   PROLOG

   The computer then reads the Turbo Prolog system files and loads them into memory.

The first thing you see is the Turbo Prolog logon display, as shown in figure 1.1.

The logon display has two interior windows. The text in the top window shows the Turbo Prolog copyright and version number. The lower window describes the Turbo Prolog system configuration. The first line tells the default name of your Turbo Prolog program file. The remaining lines tell the path names of the directories in which Turbo Prolog writes or reads program files (the PRO directory), object-code files (the OBJ directory), executable program files (the EXE directory), and files used by the Turbo Prolog system itself (the TURBO directory). (For information on path names, see Appendix C. For information on changing these defaults, see Appendix B.)

The logon display also prompts you to press the space bar. When you do so, the system displays the Turbo Prolog main menu, as shown in figure 1.2. Now you are ready to begin using Turbo Prolog.

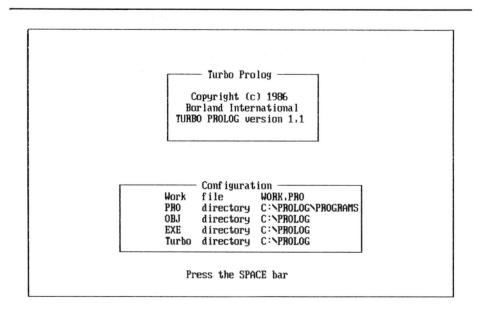

Fig. 1.1. *The Turbo Prolog Version 1.1 logon display.*

| Run | Compile | Edit | Options | Files | Setup | Quit |

```
┌──────────── Editor ────────────┐  ┌──────────── Dialog ────────────┐
│ Line 1    Col 1    Indent Insert WORK.P │  │                          │
│                                │  │                                │
│                                │  │                                │
│                                │  │                                │
│                                │  │                                │
│                                │  │                                │
│                                │  │                                │
│                                │  │                                │
│                                │  │                                │
└────────────────────────────────┘  └────────────────────────────────┘
┌─────── Message ───────┐  ┌─────────── Trace ───────────┐
│                       │  │                             │
│                       │  │                             │
└───────────────────────┘  └─────────────────────────────┘
```

Use first letter of option or select with -> or <-

Fig. 1.2. *The main menu.*

The Turbo Prolog Menu Display

The Turbo Prolog menu displays seven options at the top of the screen. If you have Turbo Prolog up and running on your computer, you'll notice that the first letter of each option is highlighted; the highlighting is not visible in the screen reproductions used in this book. The highlighting is a reminder that you can press the first letter to select an option.

These menu options are related to the seven functions of the Turbo Prolog system, which are

1. Running a program

2. Compiling a program

3. Editing a program

4. Selecting options

5. Manipulating files

6. Selecting setup features

7. Exiting the Turbo Prolog system

The Turbo Prolog menu system allows you to move easily and efficiently from one function to another.

There are two ways to select a menu option. The first way is to press the key character that corresponds to the command. To select *Edit*, for example, press *E*. (The letter can be either upper- or lowercase; you need not press the shift key.) To exit from the selected functional work area, press Esc. The second way is to press the ← or → key to place the highlighted cursor over the desired command word, then press Enter.

The main menu display has four windows. The Editor window is at the upper left, the Dialog window is at the upper right, the Message window is at the lower left, and the Trace window is at the lower right. If you use a color monitor, the default background colors of the windows are blue for the Editor window, red for the Dialog window, and black for the Trace and Message windows.

The top line in the Editor window gives the status of the program file (if any) that is loaded into the editor (refer to fig. 1.2). *Line 1* and *Col 1* mean that the editor's cursor is positioned at line 1 and column 1. These line and column indicators are updated as the cursor position changes. *Indent* indicates that the Turbo Prolog editor's automatic line-indent feature is on. *Insert* means that the editor's Insert/Overwrite function is in the Insert position. *WORK.PRO* is the default name for the currently active work file; .PRO is the default file extension for the Prolog program file. Note that if you type anything in the Editor window and save it without changing the file name, the Turbo Prolog system will save your text under the name WORK.PRO.

Running a Turbo Prolog Program

The program you are now going to write and run is designed to give you practice in using the Turbo Prolog menu and some of the basic editing commands. The program is called WELCOME.PRO. The commands you enter to create this program apply to both floppy- and hard-disk systems. If there is a difference at any point, you will be told how to proceed.

Use the → key to move the highlighted cursor across the menu to the *Edit* command and press Enter, or press *E*. Notice that the editor cursor, a "blinking dash," appears at the upper left corner of the Editor window. The Turbo Prolog editor is ready to accept text from the keyboard.

Now enter the following program text:

```
predicates
    hello

goal
    hello.

clauses
    hello :-
      write("Welcome to Turbo Prolog!"),
      nl.
```

When you come to the end of each line, press Enter to go to the next line. If you enter an incorrect character, press the backspace key to erase the character. Your screen display should look like the one in figure 1.3. But don't be concerned about making your program look exactly like the figure with regard to indentation; as in many other languages, indentation is used to increase readability and makes no difference in whether the program works.

Welcome to Turbo Prolog

You have now created your first Turbo Prolog program. To run it, you need to leave the editor; press Esc to do so. Then the editor cursor disappears and the main menu cursor is on the *Edit* command. Select the *Run* command, and notice the two lines that appear in the Message window as your program is compiled, as well as the program output in the Dialog window (see fig. 1.4).

The first line in the Message window indicates that Turbo Prolog has compiled the program. Compilation happens automatically when you select *Run*. You don't have to issue a separate command to perform this operation.

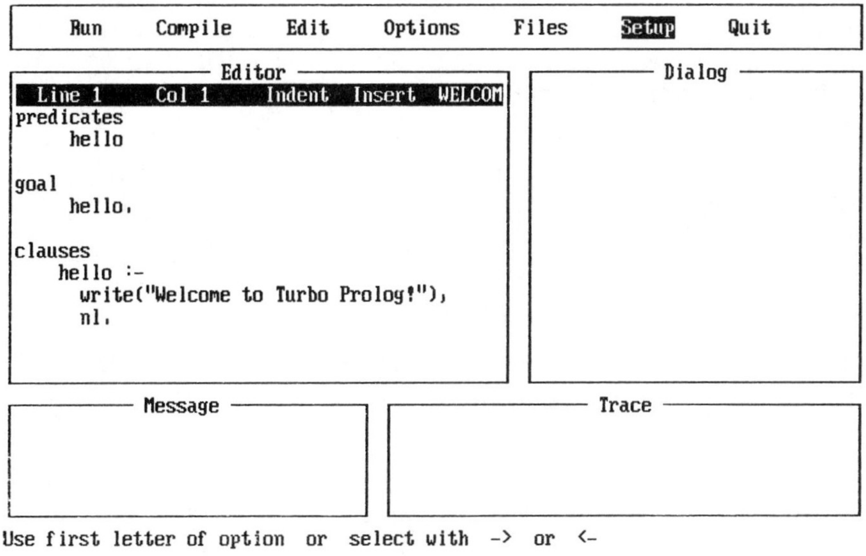

```
┌─────────────────────────────────────────────────────────────────┐
│   Run      Compile     Edit      Options     Files    ▐Setup▌   Quit │
├──────────────── Editor ─────────────────┬──────────── Dialog ──────┤
│▐Line 1      Col 1     Indent  Insert  WELCOM▌│                      │
│predicates                                │                          │
│     hello                                │                          │
│                                          │                          │
│goal                                      │                          │
│     hello.                               │                          │
│                                          │                          │
│clauses                                   │                          │
│    hello :-                              │                          │
│       write("Welcome to Turbo Prolog!"), │                          │
│       nl.                                │                          │
│                                          │                          │
├───────── Message ──────────┬──────────────── Trace ───────────────┤
│                            │                                        │
│                            │                                        │
│                            │                                        │
└────────────────────────────┴────────────────────────────────────────┘
   Use first letter of option  or  select with  ->  or  <-
```

Fig. 1.3. *The program WELCOME.PRO in the Editor window.*

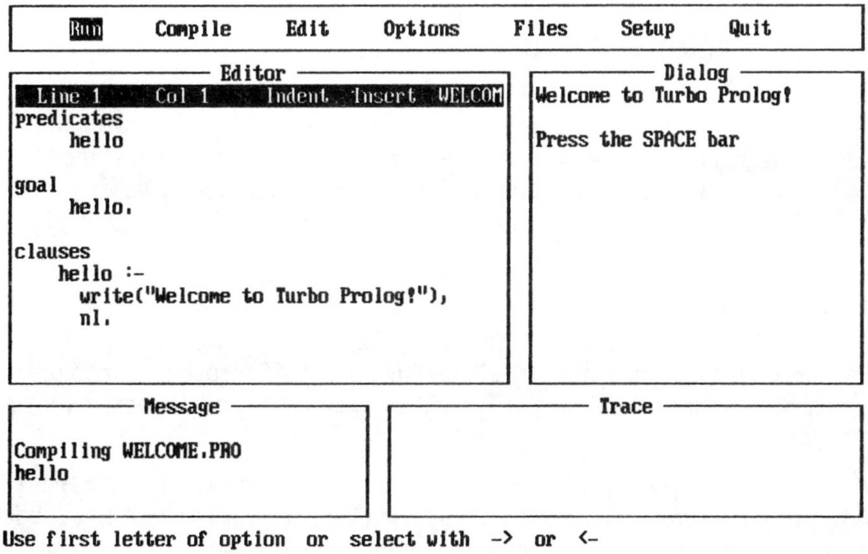

```
┌─────────────────────────────────────────────────────────────────┐
│  ▐Run▌    Compile     Edit      Options     Files    Setup     Quit │
├──────────────── Editor ─────────────────┬──────────── Dialog ──────┤
│▐Line 1      Col 1     Indent  Insert  WELCOM▌│Welcome to Turbo Prolog!│
│predicates                                │                          │
│     hello                                │Press the SPACE bar       │
│                                          │                          │
│goal                                      │                          │
│     hello.                               │                          │
│                                          │                          │
│clauses                                   │                          │
│    hello :-                              │                          │
│       write("Welcome to Turbo Prolog!"), │                          │
│       nl.                                │                          │
│                                          │                          │
├───────── Message ──────────┬──────────────── Trace ───────────────┤
│Compiling WELCOME.PRO       │                                        │
│hello                       │                                        │
│                            │                                        │
└────────────────────────────┴────────────────────────────────────────┘
   Use first letter of option  or  select with  ->  or  <-
```

Fig. 1.4. *The screen display after compiling and running a program.*

Turbo Prolog enables you to select compilation to disk or to memory. When you select *Run*, the program is compiled to memory. For now, you needn't be concerned with compiling to disk. But later, you may want to create object-code files for linking to other object modules, or executable "stand-alone" files that will run independently of the Turbo Prolog environment. When that time comes, you'll want to consult Appendix B of this book.

You will notice that Turbo Prolog compiles this small program very quickly—within a fraction of a second! The second line indicates that Turbo Prolog has compiled the predicate *hello*.

———————————————————————— **Exercise** ————————————————————————

1.1. Run the WELCOME program a couple of times and practice moving from one submenu to another until you are accustomed to the commands for changing windows and selecting options.

You can now exit the Turbo Prolog environment, if you want. To do so, select *Quit* from the main menu. If you have made any changes to the file in the editor since the last time you saved it, you are prompted to indicate whether the file should be saved. The prompt will appear now, because you have just entered the program. You can press *Y* to save the changed file before quitting. If this prompt appears because you have selected *Quit* by accident, you can press Esc to cancel the command.

Saving a Program File

To save your program, press Esc once if you are in the editor, and then select the *Files* option. From the submenu that appears, select *Save* (either press *S* or use ↑ and ↓ to highlight the option, then press Enter). A small window then displays either the default file name (such as WORK.PRO) or the name you have assigned to the file, as shown in figure 1.5. You can leave the file name unchanged, or you can edit the name. For this example, name the file WELCOME.PRO and press Enter.

If there is an existing file with the same name (whether or not the file is an earlier version of the current file), the extension of the existing file is changed to .BAK, indicating that it is a backup version of the current file. Remember to save any program in memory that you have been editing before you quit Turbo Prolog. Otherwise your modified program will be lost.

Saving files frequently is a good practice. In case of a mishap such as a power failure or a program "crash," you have the current working copy of your program saved. Some programmers save different steps of a program file under different names as they develop the program. These multiple "generations" of program files can also be useful for tracing the development of a program.

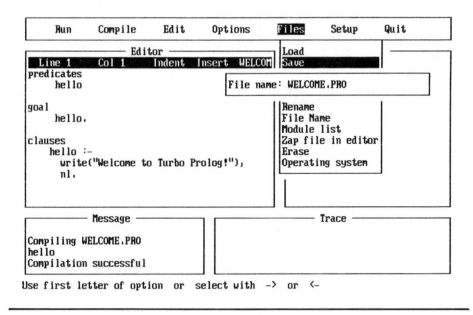

Fig. 1.5. *Saving a file.*

Displaying a File Directory

To display a listing of files, select *Files* from the main menu and then select *Directory* from the submenu. A small window displays the current .PRO directory path name. If necessary, you can edit the path name; press Enter when the path name is correct. Then you are prompted to enter a *File mask*. The default file mask is *.PRO. (See Appendix C for information on the wild-card characters * and ?, which are often used in file masks.) You can press Enter to accept that path, or you can edit it. After you press Enter, a window displays file names that match the path name and file mask. The directory display is shown in figure 1.6.

Loading and Editing a Program File

Turbo Prolog provides a very powerful screen editor with many features designed for your convenience in programming. This is an important difference between Turbo Prolog and some other implementations of Prolog: some of them do not provide an editor at all, and they require that you exit the Prolog system just to create or modify a file.

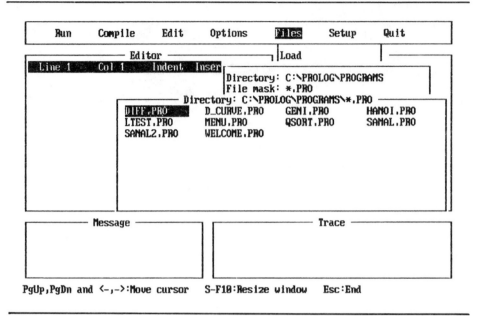

Fig. 1.6. Displaying a file directory.

Many of the Turbo Prolog editor commands are similar to those of the word-processing program WordStar®. If you are familiar with WordStar or other program editors such as the one provided with Turbo Pascal®, you'll find it easy to learn the commands of the Turbo Prolog editor. Appendix A provides details on the use of the Turbo Prolog editor. You are encouraged to read this appendix before you begin working on long Turbo Prolog programs.

To load an existing file into the editor, select *Files* from the main menu, then select *Load*. You are then prompted for the file name; if you just press Enter, a window displaying files in the .PRO directory appears. Then you can select a file by pressing ↑, ↓, ←, or → until the name of the file is highlighted, and then pressing Enter (see fig. 1.7). If you enter a file name, you need not enter the extension. By default, the extension is .PRO.

While using the Turbo Prolog editor, you can get information on the editor commands by pressing F1, the "help" key. This keystroke causes a small Help menu to appear, as shown in figure 1.8; selecting the first option causes the Help window to appear, as shown in figure 1.9. This window displays a useful summary of editor commands and other information about Turbo Prolog. By pressing Shift-F10, you can expand the Help window to full-screen size; pressing Shift-F10 again returns it to its original size (these keystrokes work for other windows as well). Other options on the Help menu give specific information on groups of editor commands.

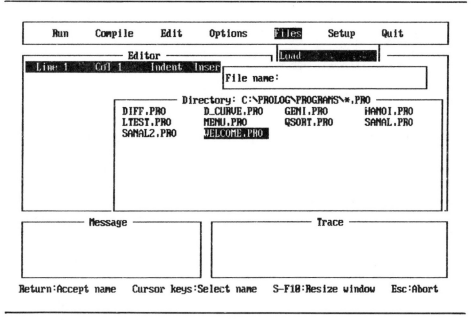

Fig. 1.7. *Loading a file into the editor.*

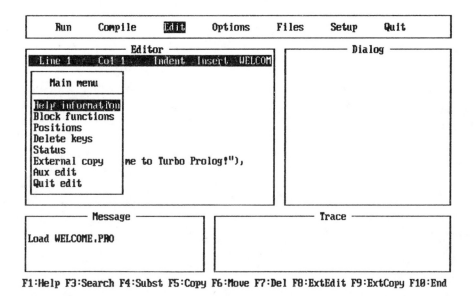

Fig. 1.8. *The Help menu.*

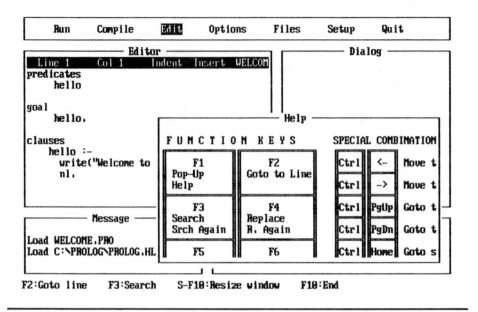

Fig. 1.9. The Help window.

If you want to create a new file and you have a file already in the editor, you need to erase the file in the editor. To do that, select the main-menu *Files* option, then select *Zap file in editor* from the submenu. Now a small window appears and you are prompted to verify that you want to "zap" the file. Press *Y* to do so. If you press *Y*, the text in the Editor window disappears.

Now a small window appears and you are prompted for a new file name for the new file you are about to create in the Editor window (see fig. 1.10). Type a new file name, if necessary, and press Enter. If you do not change the file name, the old file name is retained. After you press Enter, the small window disappears and the cursor is located at the *Files* command. Now, move the cursor to the *Edit* command and press Enter. At this stage, you can proceed to create or edit your program.

Exercise

1.2. Return to the Editor. Load the WELCOME program, and add the line

```
nl,write('Have a nice day.')
```

after the line

```
write("Welcome to Turbo Prolog!"),
```

Run the modified program a few times.

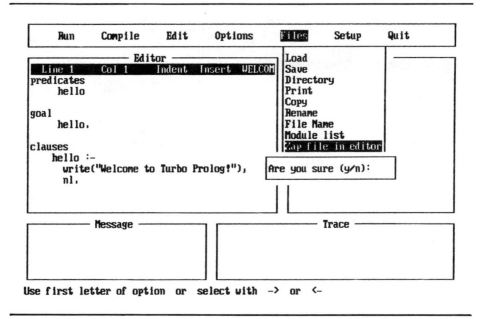

Fig. 1.10. *Zapping a file.*

Printing a File

The *Print* command, an option on the *Files* submenu, can be used to print the file that is currently in the editor. To use this command, first select *Files* and then select *Print* from the submenu. Figure 1.11 shows the screen just before a file is printed. Do not try this command unless a printer is connected to your computer.

Chapter Review

This short chapter has described some of Turbo Prolog's basic characteristics and has provided instructions for installing the program. In entering and running a short, simple program, you have "walked through" the basic steps of working with Turbo Prolog. The chapter has also provided a detailed description of Turbo Prolog's menu display system, which you will need to use routinely while you write programs in Turbo Prolog.

The information presented here, like that in many other parts of the book, is not intended to be read and memorized, but rather to be used as often as needed for reference and assistance.

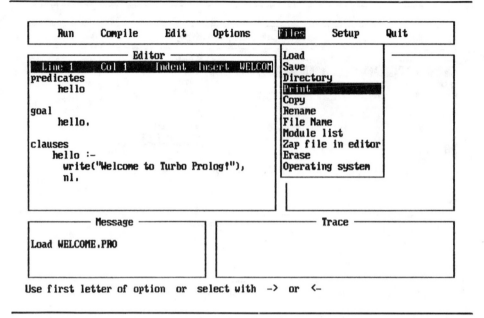

Fig. 1.11. Selecting the Print *command.*

2

Turbo Prolog Concepts

Overview

This chapter discusses Turbo Prolog from a conceptual point of view. Although many fundamentals of the language are presented, the purpose of this chapter is not to teach you Turbo Prolog's syntax and program construction. Instead, the purpose is to show why Turbo Prolog is called a *declarative language* and to show how declarative languages differ from imperative languages.

An important part of learning a new programming language is to learn how data is represented and how execution flows through a program. This chapter shows how Turbo Prolog's internal unification routines control program flow and the manipulation of data values. "Pseudo programs" and example code fragments will help you understand the fundamentals of using Turbo Prolog to solve problems.

Declarative and Imperative Languages

Perhaps the best way to understand the concept of a declarative language is to put it in the context of the evolution of computer languages. The earliest way to solve a problem with a computer was to write a program in the computer's "native tongue," or machine language. Having full control of the computer's memory and central processing unit (CPU), machine-language programmers could specify how the computer was to solve a problem by controlling the steps the computer took and how the computer arrived at values. Machine-language programs were *imperative*: they dictated the steps taken to solve a problem (the algorithm) and the ways in which values (data) were manipulated.

Machine-language programming is time consuming, and machine language is difficult for humans to read and write. Consequently, programs were developed to translate more readable and natural expressions of program algorithms into machine language. These translation programs take symbolic instructions and translate them into a sequence of machine-language instructions. These translation programs are known as compilers and interpreters. The symbolic instructions they translate are high-level languages such as FORTRAN and COBOL.

The development of high-level languages greatly increased the speed of program development and reduced the need for programmers to be intimately familiar with the architecture of the computer. But the programs written in those high-level languages were still imperative in nature: it was still necessary for programmers to specify the steps of processing and the manipulation of data values.

Most languages in use today are imperative. In the 1960s, however, non-imperative programming languages were developed that were based on declarative principles. These non-imperative languages, such as LISP and ISWIM, introduced methods of programming that blurred the distinction between the steps for solving a problem and the manipulation of the data values.

Prolog (for "Programming in Logic") was developed during that period. Prolog programs embody the programmer's expression, or "declaration," of the logic required to solve a problem. Languages that declare the logic by which the program solves a problem are called declarative languages. Programs written in such languages declare what effects should produce what outcomes. The programmer leaves to the language itself the burden of finding a solution to the problem.

For those who are used to programming in imperative languages, declarative languages can seem almost formless. Yet they often require much less code to solve a given problem than an imperative language would require. The purpose of most of the code in an imperative-language program is to control the steps the program takes and the manipulation of data values. In Prolog, however, much of the program flow is implied by the language itself or is declared in the logic of the program.

Programmers who are experienced in imperative languages sometimes feel at a loss when this absolute control is taken away. People who have never programmed at all may be able to learn declarative-language programming more quickly than can programmers with experience in imperative languages. If you have never programmed, then don't feel that learning Turbo Prolog will be hard because you don't know how to program in a language such as Pascal. If you have programmed in some imperative language such as C, BASIC, or Pascal, don't feel that you can jump right into Turbo Prolog and use everything you know. Learn to express the logic of the problem at hand and your Turbo Prolog programs will perform as you intend.

Predicate Logic

As you know by now, Turbo Prolog is a declarative language in which the logic of problem solving is declared in the program. The notation used to express the logic of a Turbo Prolog program is derived from predicate logic.

Predicate logic deals with the relations between statements and objects. Do not be intimidated by the term *predicate logic*. In all likelihood, the concepts (if not the terminology) of predicate logic are already familiar to you.

For example, consider this sentence:

Mary likes apples.

Just by reading the sentence, you know it is a fact that Mary likes apples. Now add another sentence to what you know:

Beth likes anything that Mary likes.

From these two sentences, you can conclude that Beth likes apples, too. In making that conclusion, you have used a simplified form of predicate logic to derive a new fact from two other statements.

Now look at the premises again, making some minor changes to one of the sentences:

Mary likes apples.
Beth likes something if Mary likes (the same) something.

The second sentence's wording, or syntax, has been changed, but the meaning is the same. In other words, the second sentence is semantically equivalent to

Beth likes anything that Mary likes.

Given the fact(s) about what Mary likes we still conclude that Beth likes apples.

Remember that predicate logic is concerned with the relations between statements and objects. In the premises "Mary likes apples" and "Beth likes something if Mary likes (the same) something," a relation exists between someone and something. The same thing is true in the concluded fact. The "someone" is Mary or Beth, and the "something" is apples. The relation between Mary or Beth and apples is the relation of liking. The objects of the relation are Mary, Beth, and apples.

Stripped of excess words, the relation in the first sentence looks like this:

Object	*Relation*	*Object*
Mary	likes	apples

Notice that the words standing for the relation and the objects appear in the order dictated by English syntax. We could, however, place the relation before the objects:

Relation	*Object*	*Object*
likes	Mary	apples

Despite the change of form, the meaning is the same; only the syntax has changed.

Now consider again the sentence

Beth likes something if Mary likes (the same) something.

and replace the word *something* with the pronoun *it*:

Beth likes it if Mary likes it.

Notice that this sentence expresses two *likes* relations. They are joined by a condition, which is expressed by the word *if*.

The *if* condition tests a premise to conclude a fact. Again, here are the relations:

Relation	Object	Object	Condition
likes	Mary	apples	
likes	Beth	it	if
likes	Mary	it	

As you probably know, *it* is a pronoun, and pronouns stand for other nouns. The pronoun *it* could stand for any noun, and what *it* stands for can change from sentence to sentence.

If a group of sentences does not indicate what noun the word *it* stands for in a particular sentence, then you don't know the exact meaning of the sentence. Because you do not know what *it* stands for in the sentence

Beth likes it if Mary likes it.

you cannot conclude any new facts.

But if you look again at the premises, you find

Mary likes apples.

Now you have a definite meaning for *it*: *apples*. For the time being, you can take for granted that *it* means *apples*, even though *it* may not always stand for *apples* because Mary may also start liking oranges or pears or popcorn.

With *it* equal in meaning to *apples*, the sentences can be restated as

likes Mary apples.
likes Beth it (apples) if likes Mary it (apples).

Now a new fact can be concluded: Beth likes apples. Earlier, the same thing was concluded in plain English. The next section shows how the same kind of reasoning is used in predicate logic.

Prolog and Predicate Logic

You understand the sentence *Mary likes apples* because the words appear in an order to which you are accustomed. The order of words, or *syntax*, helps to convey the meaning of the sentence. The same words in a different order would have a different meaning. However, if we agree that *Mary likes apples* and *likes Mary apples* have the same meaning, then we can use either word order version and still understand each other. Unfortunately, no one has yet developed a useful programming language that uses regular English syntax. But once you become accustomed to the syntax of Turbo Prolog, you'll find it quite natural.

You have already seen the form

| *Relation* | *Object* | *Object* |
| likes | Mary | apples |

The relation *likes* relates the objects *Mary* and *apples* in a meaningful way.

That relation *likes* can also be called a *predicate*:

| *Predicate* | *Object* | *Object* |
| likes | Mary | apples |

The same fact can be written

predicate(object1,object2)

or

likes(Mary,apples)

This syntactic form is very close to that of Turbo Prolog. However, words beginning with uppercase letters, like *Mary*, are variables in Prolog. Objects with known or constant values must begin with lowercase letters, unless the objects are numbers. (Strictly speaking, there are exceptions to that rule; later chapters will make them clear.) In Turbo Prolog syntax, then, this fact has the form:

likes(mary,apples).

Notice that this expression ends with a period. The period means, "Here is the end of this piece of information."

Remember that the English second sentence "Beth likes it if Mary likes it" is a conditional premise with *if* indicating the conditional relation. Also remember that the pronoun *it* can have a variable meaning from sentence to sentence. You won't be surprised to learn that the word *it* is the equivalent in English of a variable in Turbo Prolog. Turbo Prolog variables share some characteristics with pronouns. If you don't know what *it* stands for or what value the Prolog variable holds, you can't conclude any facts. If you do know the meaning of the word *it* or the value of the Prolog variable, then you can conclude new facts having a conditional relation to other facts which are already known.

Expressed in Turbo Prolog syntax, the second sentence is

| relation(object1,object2) | Condition | relation(object1,object2) |
| likes(beth,X) | if | likes(mary,X) |

In Turbo Prolog terminology, this sentence is a *rule*. As the name implies, a rule is used by Prolog to test the conditional conclusion of a new fact.

In Turbo Prolog syntax, all of the known relations about Mary, Beth, and apples are

likes(mary,apples).
likes(beth,X) if likes(mary,X).

The knowledge includes one fact, "Mary likes apples," and one rule, "Beth likes it if Mary likes it." You know at least one meaning for the variable *X* (or for the word *it*) because it is a known fact that Mary likes apples. The pronoun *it* stands for *apples*, so the variable *X* has the value *apples*.

Now you may wonder how Turbo Prolog knows to substitute *apples* for *X* in the rule. Remember that in declarative languages, the distinction between the program's data values and the steps the program takes to produce a solution is less distinct than in imperative languages such as C or Pascal. Turbo Prolog matches the facts it is given (about who likes what, in this case) with any rules from which new facts can be concluded.

Turbo Prolog has no provision for you, the programmer, to say, "Now compare *X* to apples and see if it fits any condition." Turbo Prolog is designed to attempt that matching on its own, using the principles of predicate logic. All you need to do is to describe, in Turbo Prolog syntax, which conditions will result in what conclusions. You state the logic, in other words, and the program uses your statements of logic to reach conclusions.

By now, you should be able to see some of the characteristics of Turbo Prolog as a declarative language and how Turbo Prolog uses the logical syntax of predicates to test facts. You'll learn more about the exact syntax and program structure of Turbo Prolog in the next chapter; for now, just concentrate on concepts and don't be concerned about how to construct a program.

You may find that writing Turbo Prolog facts and rules is a bit awkward, compared to writing facts and conditions in English. But in the simple examples of this chapter, you will probably be able to see similarities between English and predicate logic or Prolog syntactic structures. Because of these similarities, you'll soon find that the awkwardness has disappeared and you've become comfortable with "thinking in Prolog."

Controlling Program Flow

By now, you know that Turbo Prolog reaches conclusions based on the logic of the program. This section explains how the program input and the program logic work together to produce the program output.

A predicate construction called a *goal* is used to send the program into action. Turbo Prolog then attempts to match the goal with the facts and rules within the program. If the goal is a fact, such as *likes(mary,apples)*, Turbo Prolog responds *True* or *False*; if the goal contains variables, Turbo Prolog responds with values that constitute a solution, if one exists, or with the message *No solution*.

This discussion does not present all the elements of a Turbo Prolog program. Those are discussed in the next chapter. Instead, this section presents general concepts and knowledge that will be useful later, when you begin building your own programs.

Program Goals

A goal is a statement of the problem that the program is to solve. The goal also serves as the "trigger" to get the program started. Turbo Prolog uses both internal goals, which are embedded in the program, and external goals, which are entered from the keyboard after the program starts. Internal and external goals have more similarities than differences. External goals are used in this discussion, but most of what you will learn about external goals applies to internal goals as well.

When a Turbo Prolog program is started, it doesn't do anything meaningful until it encounters a goal statement. This example uses an external goal statement; Turbo Prolog therefore displays the prompt *Goal:*, as shown in figure 2.1.

A goal consists of a predicate relationship; its structure is the same as that of a fact or a rule. In the example of Mary, Beth, and apples, the relation (or predicate term) is *likes*. This same *likes* term can be used as a goal. The goal predicate is matched with the predicates in the program, so the goal for this example will have two objects, like the *likes* predicates discussed previously. The goal will have the form

    likes(beth,apples).

This goal says, in effect, that you want to know whether Beth likes apples, according to the information contained in the program.

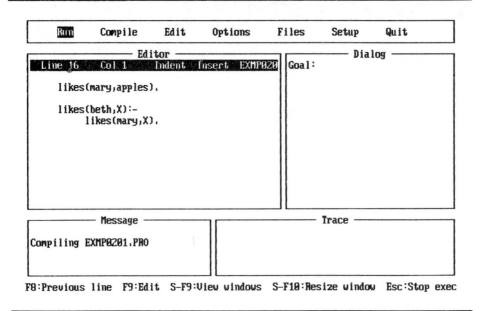

Fig. 2.1. The prompt for an external goal.

Solving the Problem

Assume that the Turbo Prolog program has the fact

    likes(mary,apples).

and the rule

    likes(beth,X) if likes(mary,X).

Also assume that the program has been started and has prompted you to enter a goal. You have entered

    likes(beth,apples).

as shown in figure 2.2. Now Turbo Prolog takes over to solve the problem posed in the goal. The facts and rules in the program are used to deduce a logical conclusion. Turbo Prolog accepts the goal statement and begins to search its program facts and rules for a match to the *likes* predicate.

The first match is the fact

    likes(mary,apples).

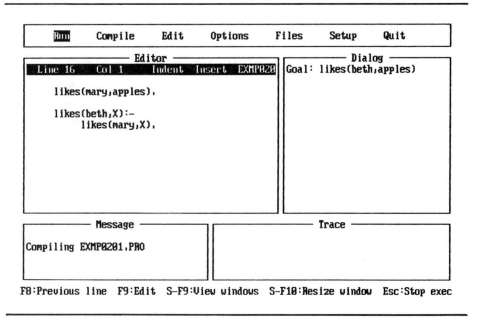

Fig. 2.2. *Entering an external goal.*

Clearly, the predicate term in the goal, *likes*, matches the one in the fact. Because the *likes* predicates match, Turbo Prolog then attempts to match the first object of the goal, *beth*, with the first object of the fact, *mary*. Turbo Prolog attempts the matching of terms from the left to the right until the match fails. Compare the goal and the fact:

```
likes(beth,apples).
likes(mary,apples).
```

The first objects, *beth* and *mary*, do not match. Consequently, the entire attempt to match the goal and the fact fails. Turbo Prolog does not attempt to match the second object of the goal with that of the rule, even though they do match.

Then Turbo Prolog searches the next entry in the program and finds the rule

```
likes(beth,X) if likes(mary,X).
```

The first part of this rule, *likes(beth,X)*, is called the *head* of the rule. Prolog attempts to match a goal with the head of a rule just as it tries to match a goal with a fact. If Turbo Prolog can match the predicate and all objects, it will attempt to match the part of the rule that follows the *if* condition (this part is known as the *body* of the rule).

Now Turbo Prolog is attempting to match the goal *likes(beth,apples)* and the rule head *likes(beth,X)*:

```
likes(beth,apples).
likes(beth,X).
```

The goal and the rule head have matching predicate terms and first objects. But literally, *apples* and *X* do not match. Before you conclude that the matching attempt has again failed, remember that *X* works like the pronoun *it*. Being a variable, *X* can match with anything.

In English, the meaning of *it* is determined by the context. The same principle applies to the "meaning" of variables such as *X*. Whenever Turbo Prolog encounters a variable while attempting to match objects, it attaches to the variable a meaning derived from the variable's context. Because the position of the object *X* in the rule head is the same as the position of *apples* in the goal, Turbo Prolog attaches the value *apples* to the variable *X*. Now *X* and *apples* mean the same thing to Turbo Prolog. This association continues either until the goal is satisfied or until no further matching can be done with this association.

Because *X* now means *apples*, the predicate *likes(beth,X)* now has the "meaning" *likes(beth,apples)*. Turbo Prolog has successfully matched the rule head and the goal by binding the value *apples* to the variable *X*.

Now Turbo Prolog tries to satisfy the condition *if likes(mary,X)*. Because the value *apples* is now bound to the variable *X*, Turbo Prolog must prove or disprove the condition "if Mary likes apples" in order to prove whether the rule head "Beth likes apples" is true. The new problem, then, is to see whether Mary likes apples. This "subproblem" or *subgoal* was created internally by Turbo Prolog as a step toward solving the problem posed by the goal.

The subgoal now is

```
likes(mary,apples).
```

Turbo Prolog attempts to satisfy this subgoal in order to prove or disprove the conclusion of the rule head *likes(beth,apples)*.

Examining the facts and rules in the program code, Turbo Prolog finds the fact

```
likes(mary,apples).
```

and attempts to match it from left to right with the subgoal:

```
likes(mary,apples).
```

As you can see, this fact matches the subgoal. The subgoal *likes(mary,apples)* therefore is successful. Consequently, the rule head *likes(beth,apples)* is factual. And because the rule head is factual, the goal *likes(beth,apples)* has been proven true; in other words, the goal has succeeded. A new fact has been successfully concluded even though that fact was never explicitly stated in the program.

The Output of a Goal Attempt

The goal *likes(beth,apples)* succeeds, and Turbo Prolog so indicates by displaying the message *True*, as shown in figure 2.3. If the goal had been *likes(beth,oranges)* and the same facts and rules were in the program, then the goal would not succeed; the response would be *False*.

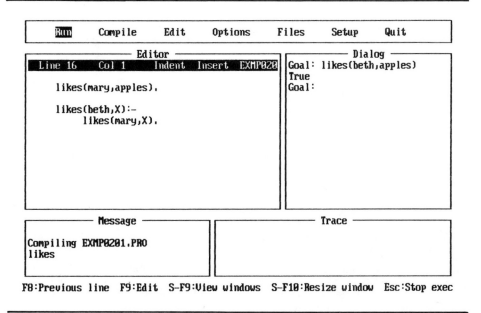

Fig. 2.3. *Turbo Prolog's response to an external goal.*

In this example, data manipulations and program flow were determined by facts and rules. In Turbo Prolog, facts and rules are called *clauses*. The fact

```
finds(john,gold).
```

is a clause. The rule

```
is(john,rich) if finds(john,gold).
```

is a clause, as well. Because the heads of rule clauses have the same form as facts, rules are referred to as facts. The distinction between facts and rules is important, however, and it is used in this book.

Clauses for the same predicate are grouped together in a Turbo Prolog program. You'll learn how in the next chapter.

Conjunctions and Other Symbols

A conclusion often requires more than one premise. An example is "John and Mary are married if John's wife is Mary and Mary's husband is John." In Turbo Prolog, this rule is written

```
married(john,mary) if
    wife(john,mary) and husband(mary,john).
```

Notice that this rule has two conditions joined by the word *and*. In Prolog terminology, this is a *conjunction* of the two conditions by means of the word *and*. The comma (,) is often used in Prolog to represent the word *and*. Turbo Prolog accepts the word *and*, but use of the comma increases readability. Prolog also uses a special symbol for the word *if*. The symbol is

```
:-
```

(a colon followed by a hyphen). When you read a Turbo Prolog program, the symbol *:–* is pronounced "if " and the comma is pronounced "and."

With these symbols used to represent *and* and *if*, the *married* relationship is written

```
married(john,mary) :-
    wife(john,mary),
    husband(mary,john).
```

Notice that the *:–* symbol follows the rule head of the clause, and that the two conditions are indented and separated by the comma. The indentation is not required; it is used to increase readability. Like all clauses, this one ends with a period.

The semicolon (;) is used to represent the conjunction *or*. As with the conjunction *and*, Turbo Prolog accepts either the word *or* or the symbol. The *or* conjunction is not often used in facts and rules. It has other uses, however, that you'll learn about in the following chapters.

Turbo Prolog ignores extra spaces and line breaks in most cases (you'll learn later about the exceptions). Even though the preceding clause seems to read from top to bottom, Turbo Prolog "reads" it as a left-to-right construction; the line breaks are ignored. The rule head is commonly called the *left side* of a rule, and the conditions following the *:–* are commonly called the *right side* of a rule. Left-to-right scanning is an important concept for you to visualize as this chapter continues to explore the inner workings of Turbo Prolog.

Goals and Subgoals

If you recall that goals, like facts and rules, are constructed from predicates, you should have no difficulty understanding that goals also can have conjunctions. Goals with conjunctions are said to have *subgoals*. The subgoals of a goal statement are separated by commas, just like the conditions of rules. When the goal is presented to a Turbo Prolog program, Turbo Prolog works from left to right through the subgoals, attempting to match the subgoals with facts and rules in the program. If any of the subgoals fails to produce a match, the entire goal fails. If all subgoals produce matches, the entire goal succeeds.

Suppose, for example, that a program has the following clauses:

```
likes(mary,apples).
color(apples,red).
```

Now we enter the goal

```
likes(mary,apples),color(apples,red).
```

Notice that the clauses end with periods; the clauses are independent facts. The subgoals, on the other hand, are separated by commas, and a period terminates the goal as a whole.

The leftmost subgoal, *likes(mary,apples)*, matches the clause *likes(mary,apples)*, so that subgoal succeeds. The next subgoal to the right then is matched with the clause *color(apples,red)*, and the entire goal succeeds. We are then informed on the screen that the goal is true. In English, the goal is "Mary likes apples and apples are red." Or you might state the goal as a question: "Does Mary like apples, and are apples red?" The facts support this goal.

In real programming situations, you would more likely ask for a confirmation of a question, such as "Does Mary like red apples?" This goal differs from the previous one. Before, you only needed to verify the facts that Mary likes apples and that apples are red. This time, you want to know whether Mary likes apples *and* whether the apples are red. Some apples are red, some are green, and some are yellow. But if Mary doesn't like apples *or* if she does like them and they are not red, you will get the answer *False*.

To enter these facts in the program, you remove the clause

```
likes(mary,apples).
```

and add the rule

```
likes(mary,apples):-
     color(apples,red).
```

In English, this rule reads, "Mary likes apples if they are red."

You want to know, "Does Mary like apples?" so you enter the goal

```
likes(mary,apples).
```

Turbo Prolog matches the goal with the rule head *likes(mary,apples)*. But this rule has the condition *color(apples,red)*. Thus the condition *color(apples,red)* must be proven before the goal can succeed.

Even though the goal itself has no subgoals, Turbo Prolog must match the rule-condition predicate with a corresponding clause. In effect, Turbo Prolog has created a subgoal. To prove the head of the rule, the conditions in the body of the rule must be proven, just as they are when the goal statement is made up of a conjunction of subgoals. Turbo Prolog succeeds in this subgoal by finding the fact *color(apples,red)* among the clauses. By proving this subgoal, Turbo Prolog proves that the rule head is factual. Because the rule head matches the goal, the goal succeeds.

One way to understand Turbo Prolog's internal generation of subgoals is to say that the conditions on the right side of the *if* (or *:–* symbol) become subgoals of the original goal when, in attempting to satisfy the goal, Turbo Prolog matches the goal with the rule head.

For simplicity, this section has presented clear, simple examples of the matching process. The examples were simplified so that you could easily see the logic of program flow in Turbo Prolog. You should be aware by now that matching is very important in Turbo Prolog.

Turbo Prolog's Internal Unification Routines

Turbo Prolog (like other implementations of Prolog) has internal routines that perform matching and related processes. These are integral parts of the language and are known as the *internal unification routines*. These routines perform the tasks of matching goals or subgoals against facts or rule heads in order to prove (or satisfy) goals or subgoals. These same routines also determine whether the right sides of rules have generated further subgoals. The programmer declares, in Turbo Prolog's logical syntax, which facts and rules are to produce what outcomes from what goals, and the internal unification routines do the rest of the work.

Data Representation in Facts and Rules

Data is represented in Turbo Prolog programs by facts and rules. Although a fact can be a predicate alone, most facts are written as predicates with one or more objects. Some examples are

```
likes(mary,apples).
employee(smith,john,1984).
gender(female).
```

When the object of a predicate begins with a lowercase letter, the object has a known constant value; in other words, the object is a *constant*. When Turbo Prolog is attempting to match two constants, the match succeeds only if the two constants are equal. Consequently, *mary* never can be matched with *beth*.

Assume that a program has the following facts:

```
likes(beth,apples).
likes(mary,pears).
likes(mary,oranges).
likes(mary,apples).
```

Now assume that you type in the external goal

```
likes(mary,apples).
```

As you remember, the goal has a structure like that of a fact or a rule. Both objects in this goal, *mary* and *apples*, are constants. In attempting to satisfy the goal, Turbo Prolog looks through the program from left to right, searching for a predicate with the same predicate term as the goal predicate. (Remember that what looks like "top to bottom" is really "left to right.") This is the first step performed by the internal unification routines.

In this example, the predicate term in the goal is *likes*. The first *likes* fact encountered in the program is *likes(beth,apples)*. Having matched predicate terms in the goal and the fact, the internal unification routines now attempt to match the first object of *likes* in the fact and the rule. Because *mary* does not match *beth*, the attempt fails.

The internal unification routines now attempt a match with the next *likes* predicate. This time, the matching succeeds because the constant *mary* in the goal matches the same constant in the rule. But to complete the match, the internal unification routines now must match the next object to the right. The constants *pears* and *apples* do not match. Because this attempt fails, the internal unification routines try again with the next *likes* predicate.

Each possible match is checked in left-to-right order. Of course, *likes(mary,apples)* does not match with *likes(mary,oranges)*.

The internal unification routines work from left to right throughout the entire program, trying each fact or rule for a match with the goal. Only predicates with corresponding objects are tested against the predicate in the goal. The last candidate for matching is the fact *likes(mary,apples)*. Both objects in this fact match with the corresponding objects in the goal predicate. The goal succeeds.

In viewing this example, you should understand that internal unification has worked from the top (or left) to the bottom (or right) of the relevant facts and rules. When a predicate match was found, the predicate's objects were matched from left to right until a match was successful, or the match failed. If the match failed, the next fact or rule was tested in turn until either a successful match occurred or until all relevant facts and rules had been tested and had failed.

When a constant is the object of a match against another constant, the two will match only if they are the same. In other words, a constant will always match itself.

Variables and Rules in Internal Unification

Variables in Turbo Prolog are analogous to pronouns in English. At some time, a variable may have a known value. At other times, it may not. You may have some understanding of the behavior of variables from some other programming language. If this is the case, pay particular attention to how Turbo Prolog variables behave. You may find some unusual differences.

This example includes some of what you have learned in the preceding section about the internal unification routine. The data value is the fact

```
likes(mary,apples).
```

You want to construct a goal to determine what (if anything) Mary likes. The form of the goal is

```
likes(mary,What).
```

Remember that in Turbo Prolog, an object beginning with an uppercase letter is a variable. The variable in this goal is *What*. When the internal unification routines attempt the matching of this goal to the facts and rules in the program, the variable *What* has no value; *What* is not zero and *What* is not blank. The variable does not even have a "garbage" value (whatever happens to be in the memory space allocated for the variable).

The variable *What* has no value because it is *unbound*, or *uninstantiated*; the two terms are used interchangeably. Unbound variables are also known as *free* variables. When the free variable *What* from the goal is matched with the corresponding object *apples*, the value of *What* becomes *apples*. The variable *What* is now bound (or instantiated) to *apples*; the variable, in other words, is no longer free.

While *What* is bound to *apples*, the variable "means" *apples* to Turbo Prolog. In fact, whenever an unbound variable is matched with a constant in Turbo Prolog, the variable becomes bound to the value of the constant. Turbo Prolog will report on the screen that *What=apples* and the internal unification routine has found all (the only) appropriate matches for your goal.

Now suppose that the program has these facts:

```
likes(mary,apples).
likes(mary,pears).
likes(mary,popcorn).
```

The same goal as before, *likes(mary,What)*, matches all of these facts, so Turbo Prolog reports all values of *What* that satisfy the goal, as shown in figure 2.4. External goals cause Turbo Prolog's internal unification routines to find all solutions to the goal. Internal goals, however, cause the internal unification routines to stop after the first successful match of the goal.

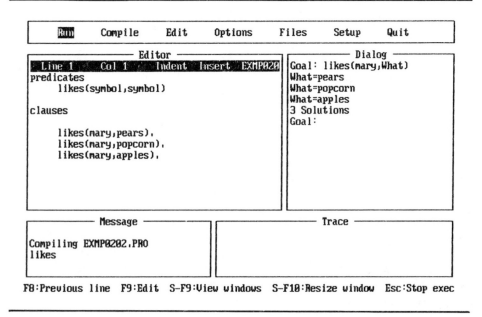

Fig. 2.4. *Multiple solutions to a goal.*

It may appear that the variable *What* is bound to *apples*, *pears*, and *popcorn* at the same time, but that is not the case. The internal unification routines bind a variable to a corresponding value during matching; the variable then is unbound if the match fails or if the goal succeeds.

Programmers with experience in imperative languages sometimes have difficulty understanding this "unbinding" or freeing of variables. Usually, in imperative languages, once a variable is assigned a value, the variable retains that value throughout its scope or until it is assigned a new value. These assignments are under strict control of the program code. In Turbo Prolog, however, the internal unification routines assign values to variables, and variables become unbound as soon as the internal unification routines no longer need to associate the value with the variable in order to prove a subgoal.

It may seem that a Prolog programmer has no control over the values assigned to variables. Indeed, the Prolog programmer has no "brute-force" control of values, just as the programmer has no brute-force control over program flow. But by understanding how the internal unification routines work, the programmer can use Turbo Prolog's logical syntax to declare what needs to be done and what data values are being sought. If this is not yet clear, don't worry. Examples will help you become familiar with the process. The rest of the chapters in this book contain hands-on examples to increase your understanding.

An example using the = operator will increase your understanding of binding and variables. In a programming language such as BASIC, the = operator can mean "Make these two terms have the same value," as in the expression *X=6*. In this usage, the = operator is an *assignment* operator. The result is to make *X* equal to 6, or, in other words, to assign the value of 6 to *X*. And in BASIC, the = operator has another use: to test the equality of two terms. This use of the = symbol is seen in conditional expressions, such as *IF X=6 GOSUB 3010*. Used in this manner, the = operator says "The two terms that I am between must be equal for the statement as a whole to be true." The = operator is interpreted as an assignment operator or a comparison operator according to the syntax of the language. (Some languages, however, use different symbols for assignment and comparison.)

Turbo Prolog also uses the = operator, but whether it serves as a comparison operator or an assignment operator is determined by whether the values or terms are free or bound.

For example, consider the expression

```
apples = apples
```

This expression could be a subgoal generated internally. Because both values are known, the = operator is a comparison operator. In this case, the comparison is true and the subgoal succeeds.

Now consider the expression

```
apples = oranges
```

Because the two terms have different values, the comparison fails.

Now consider an example that uses a variable:

```
X = apples
```

Again, this could be a subgoal generated internally at some point in Turbo Prolog's attempt to satisfy a goal. But the equal sign is not necessarily an assignment operator. This subgoal assigns (or binds) the value *apples* to the variable *X* only if *X* is not yet bound.

If *X* has already been bound to a value, however, then that value is known to the internal unification routines, and that value is compared to the constant *apples*. If the two values are the same, the subgoal succeeds; if they are different, the subgoal fails.

Turbo Prolog's interpretation of the = operator depends upon whether both values are known. If both values are known, then the operation is comparison, even if one or both values are variables. If one of the values is unknown, then that value will be bound to the value of the other value. It is not important to Turbo Prolog whether the known value is on the right or the left of the =; in either case, the unknown will take on the value of the known.

For example, suppose that the variable *Fruit* is unbound. The subgoal

```
apples = Fruit
```

causes the value *apples* to be bound to the variable *Fruit*. Now, suppose that the subgoal

```
Fruit = X
```

immediately follows the preceding one and that *X* is a free variable. The result of attempting this subgoal is that the value *apples* is bound to the variable *X*. You see that even when both of the terms *Fruit* and *X* are variables, Turbo Prolog assigns (or binds) the known value to the unbound variable. In many programming languages, assignment occurs only from the right term to the left. In Turbo Prolog, however, assignment can take place in either direction.

For a final example, consider the subgoal

```
X = oranges
```

The variable *X* is bound to *apples* from a previous instantiation. The constant *oranges* also has a known value. Because both values are known, Turbo Prolog checks them for equality. The resulting expression, *apples = oranges*, is false; consequently, this subgoal fails and the goal fails. Upon failure of the goal, both *Fruit* and *X* become unbound.

Studying the behavior of the = operator in comparison and assignment is useful for two reasons. First, the = operator is widely used in Turbo Prolog programs. Second, and more important, the = operator behaves in the same way that the internal unification routines behave when matching goals or subgoals to facts and rules in a program. Values can be bound to variables during attempts to satisfy goals, and values can be compared for equality. The results of bindings are carried forward to other subgoals that call for comparisons or assignments of the corresponding objects to which the variables are bound. If any subgoal fails, or if subsequent subgoals do not call for the use of the values that are bound to variables, the variables become unbound and are again free variables.

The next chapter gives more detail on the binding and freeing of variables. For now, just remember context determines how Turbo Prolog evaluates and assigns values.

Backtracking

Backtracking is the mechanism that Turbo Prolog uses to find additional facts or rules for satisfying a goal if the current attempt to satisfy that goal fails. An analogy will clarify the concept of backtracking. Suppose that your goal is to get to a friend's house, and that you don't know exactly how to get there. You do know that you are to turn right at a crossroads after leaving the highway. The friend lives in a house across the road from a park entrance.

When you leave the highway and turn right at the first intersection, you don't find the entrance to the park. You therefore backtrack to the crossroads and continue in your original direction until the next crossroads. There, you turn right again and look for the entrance to a park. If you fail to find the park entrance, you backtrack once again and try the next crossroads. You repeat this process until you succeed at your goal of finding the house, or you fail completely and give up.

This kind of searching would be tiresome for you, but Turbo Prolog is relentless in its search for all possible routes to a solution. Like you, Turbo Prolog employs backtracking to try new routes to the solution. And like you, Turbo Prolog uses that which is known to assist in determining an appropriate course of action.

A typical Turbo Prolog program has facts and rules based on different predicate relationships. The rules might each have several right-hand parts, all joined by conjunctions. The goal might consist of several subgoals, and variables could be the objects of the predicate relationships in both the clauses and the subgoals. In other words, typical programs are some combination of everything you've learned in this chapter so far.

Turbo Prolog attempts to satisfy goals by matching the predicate terms and objects in goals with those in facts and rule heads; the matching proceeds from left to right. Because some of the subgoals are likely to fail when matched against some of the facts or rules, Turbo Prolog needs a way to "remember" the points from which it can proceed in attempting alternative solutions. Before trying one possible solution of a subgoal, Turbo Prolog in effect places a "marker" in the program. This marker indicates a point to which Turbo Prolog can backtrack if the current attempt fails.

As Turbo Prolog succeeds in its left-to-right attempts to satisfy subgoals, backtracking markers are left at each point that might lead to a solution. If a subgoal fails, Turbo Prolog then backtracks to the left, stopping at the nearest backtracking marker. From that point Turbo Prolog attempts to find another solution for the failed subgoal.

Unless a subsequent subgoal succeeds at this level, Turbo Prolog will again backtrack to the left to the next backtracking marker. These attempts are performed by the internal unification routines and the backtracking mechanism. The ultimate outcome is either the success or the failure of the goal.

With a few additions, the facts and rules about Mary, Beth, and apples can be used to illustrate backtracking and internal unification. This example has variables, as well as facts and rules that are bypassed by the internal unification routine during matching.

These are the facts for the *likes* relation:

```
likes(mary,pears).
likes(mary,popcorn). /* These are the likes facts. */
likes(mary,apples).
```

These rules declare what can be concluded about what Beth likes:

```
likes(beth,X):-      /* Beth likes         */
     likes(mary,X), /* what Mary likes    */
     fruit(X),      /* if it is a fruit   */
     color(X,red).  /* and it is red      */

likes(beth,X):-      /* Beth likes         */
     likes(mary,X), /* what Mary likes    */
     X=popcorn.     /* if it is popcorn.  */
```

And these predicate clauses provide some background facts:

```
fruit(pears).
fruit(apples).

color(pears,yellow).
color(oranges,orange).
color(apples,yellow).
color(apples,red).
```

Note that these predicates alone do not constitute a complete program in Turbo Prolog. In the next chapter, you'll learn about the other parts that are necessary.

This goal statement is used to extract some information from the clauses:

```
likes(beth,X).
```

The goal means, "What does Beth like?"

To answer this question, Turbo Prolog's internal unification routines test for a fact or rule head matching the goal statement. This search starts with the first *likes* clauses, which are three facts about what Mary likes. Turbo Prolog tries these clauses from left to right (or top to bottom). Matching fails with all of them because the constant *beth* does not match the constant *mary*.

Turbo Prolog's internal unification routines proceed to the rule

```
likes(beth,X):-
     likes(mary,X),
     fruit(X),
     color(X,red).
```

The variables in the rule head and the goal are both unbound, so the goal and the rule head match. Because the head (the left side) of the first rule matches the goal, the facts on the right side of the rule become subgoals that Turbo Prolog must satisfy, proceeding from left to right. Remember that Turbo Prolog views terms separated by commas as being "side by side," even when they appear on separate lines.

Other *likes* clauses follow this rule, so Turbo Prolog places a backtracking marker at the beginning of the next *likes* rule. This point is labeled 1 in figure 2.5.

```
      likes(mary,pears).
   ②likes(mary,popcorn). /* These are the likes facts. */
   ④likes(mary,apples).

      likes(beth,X):-      /* Beth likes        */
           likes(mary,X), /* what Mary likes    */
           fruit(X),      /* if it is a fruit   */
           color(X,red).  /* and it is red      */

   ①likes(beth,X):-       /* Beth likes         */
           likes(mary,X), /* what Mary likes     */
           X=popcorn.     /* if it is popcorn.  */

      fruit(pears).
   ③fruit(apples).

      color(pears,yellow).
      color(oranges,orange).
      color(apples,yellow).
      color(apples,red).
```

Fig. 2.5. *Backtracking markers used by the internal unification routines.*

The first subgoal is *likes(mary,X)*. Because this is a new subgoal, Turbo Prolog starts again at the top of the *likes* predicates and finds *likes(mary,pears)*. This fact matches the subgoal *likes(mary,X)* because all the terms match when *X* becomes bound to *pears* by unification.

Now the subgoal *likes(mary,X)* is satisfied, but the rule that generated this subgoal has generated other subgoals which still must be proven. The internal unification routines therefore leave a place marker at the next *likes* fact. This point is labeled 2 in figure 2.5. This marker indicates that at least one other *likes* clause exists that might satisfy the current subgoal. In the event that a subsequent subgoal fails, the backtracking mechanism has a place from which to seek another candidate for satisfying the goal.

At this time, the goal *likes(beth,X)* has been matched with the rule head *likes(beth,X)*. Turbo Prolog's unification routines have left a backtracking marker at the next *likes(beth,X)* rule head and have begun attempting to satisfy the clauses on the right side of the rule. This attempt has generated the subgoal *likes(mary,X)*. In attempting to satisfy this subgoal, the unification routines have found the matching clause *likes(mary,pears)*. Now *X* is bound to *pears* and the value of the subgoal has become *likes(beth,pears)*. Because other clauses exist that might satisfy the subgoal, a backtracking marker has been placed at *likes(mary,popcorn)*.

The next subgoal to the right is *fruit(X)*. Because *X* is now bound to the value *pears*, the subgoal means *fruit(pears)*. The internal unification routines find a match with the first *fruit* clause. Another clause exists that might satisfy the subgoal, so another backtracking marker, labeled 3 in figure 2.5, is placed at this clause.

Now there are two backtracking markers indicating alternative routes to solution of the rule

```
likes(beth,X):-
     likes(mary,X),
     fruit(X),
     color(X,red).
```

These are points 2 and 3 in figure 2.5. (Point 1 is alternative path to solution of the main goal.) The last point marked is always the point from which an alternative solution will be sought.

The last subgoal of the rule is *color(X,red)*. Always scanning clauses from left to right, the internal unification routines attempt a match with the clause

```
color(pears,yellow).
```

But because *X* is bound to *pears*, the current subgoal is

```
color(pears,red).
```

All attempts to satisfy this subgoal fail, because the program does not contain the clause `color(pears,red)`. This subgoal has failed.

The internal unification routines cause backtracking to the last marker, which is at the *fruit(apples)*. This match fails so the backtracking mechanism retreats to the preceding closest marker, which is placed at *likes(mary,popcorn)*.

The variable *X* has become free again because of the failure of this subgoal in the last attempt with *pears*. At the backtracking marker, Turbo Prolog finds the fact *likes(mary,popcorn)*. A backtracking marker, labeled 4 in figure 2.5, is placed at the following *likes* clause. The variable *X* is bound to *popcorn*, so the subgoals now are equivalent to "Mary likes popcorn and popcorn is red fruit."

The subgoal *fruit(popcorn)* cannot be proven with the facts and rules present in the program, so once again the subgoal *likes(mary,X)* fails. The variable *X* is freed, and the subgoal *likes(mary,X)* in the rule *likes(beth,X)* has one more chance of success, because one more fact about what Mary likes has been marked for backtracking. The internal unification routines cause backtracking to point 4.

Now the subgoal is matched with *likes(mary,apples)*, and *X* becomes bound to *apples*. The next subgoal, *fruit(apples)*, is attempted. The first *fruit* clause has the object *pears*. The objects do not match, so the internal unification routines move on to the next fact, *fruit(apples)*, which matches the subgoal.

Finally, the last subgoal of the first rule is tested. Again, a match is attempted with a *color* fact; this time, the subgoal is *color(apples,red)*. Starting at the top of the *color* facts, the internal unification routines try to match this subgoal with the facts *color(pears,yellow)*, *color(oranges,orange)*, and *color(apples,yellow)*. On this last attempt, the object *apples* (bound to the variable *X*) does match the object *apples* in the fact, but the last objects, *red* and *yellow*, do not match, so the attempt fails. The final color fact is *color(apples,red)*, which matches the subgoal *color(apples,red)*.

The rule has been proven with the successful matching of the last subgoal. The variable *X*, being instantiated to *apples* on the left side, proves the right side of the rule.

The entire rule, with *X* instantiated to *apples*, looks like

```
likes(beth,apples) :-
    likes(mary,apples),
    fruit(apples),
    color(apples,red).
```

to the internal unification routines. By displaying the output *X=apples*, Turbo Prolog indicates that at least one solution to the goal has been found.

The last subgoal is tried again, this time with the value

```
color(apples,red)
```

Once more, all of the *color* clauses are tried in turn for a match to the new subgoal. A match is found in the last clause, *color(apples,red)*. Now all three subgoals of the rule have been proven. The variable *X* is bound to *apples*. Consequently, the head of the rule now is

    likes(beth,apples)

This rule head matches the goal statement

    likes(beth,X).

so the goal succeeds, and Turbo Prolog displays the message *X=apples*.

Because an external goal has been used with this "blackboard example" program, Turbo Prolog continues to look for other solutions to the goal. This goal has succeeded, so the variable *X* is freed and can be bound again by the internal unification routines.

The search for solutions begins again at the backtracking marker that is now the most recent. This is the marker at point 1 in figure 2.5; the marker at point 2 has been removed, because a solution was found at the end of the route.

The internal unification routines therefore begin searching with the rule

    likes(beth,X):-
        likes(mary,X),
        X=popcorn.

Once again, the first subgoal is *likes(mary,X)*, and the internal unification routines search the *likes* clauses for a match. The clause

    likes(mary,pears).

matches the subgoal, so *X* is bound to *pears*. A marker is left for backtracking to the next clause, *likes(mary,popcorn)*.

With the current subgoal satisfied and *X* bound to *pears*, Turbo Prolog attempts to satisfy the remaining subgoal, which is

    X=popcorn

As was explained earlier in this chapter, the = operator functions as a comparison operator because the values of both terms are known: the variable *X* is bound to *pears*, and *popcorn* is a constant. The comparison is

    pears = popcorn

Because these terms do not match, the subgoal fails, and *X* is freed once again.

The internal unification routines now cause backtracking to the last marker so that an alternative route to a solution can be attempted. The most recent backtracking marker is at the clause

    likes(mary,popcorn).

Because *X* has been freed, it is now bound to the value *popcorn*. After placing a back-tracking marker at the next clause, *likes(mary,apples)*, the internal unification routines attempt again to satisfy the subgoal *X=popcorn*. Internally, the terms are

```
popcorn = popcorn
```

The match succeeds, and the last subgoal of the rule is satisfied. The *X* in the rule head is bound to *popcorn*; thus the concluded fact is *likes(beth,popcorn)*. Turbo Prolog reports this fact by displaying *X=popcorn*.

Now two solutions have been found to the goal, and a backtracking marker remains at the clause

```
likes(mary,popcorn).
```

Turbo Prolog returns to that point and looks for another solution.

Remember that this route is an alternative for the second subgoal of the second *likes* rule. The subgoal therefore is again

```
likes(mary,X)
```

Because the variable *X* is again free, it is bound to *apples* and the subgoal succeeds again. Although no more facts remain among the *likes* clauses, two rules do remain, so a marker is placed at the fact *likes(mary,apples)*.

Returning to the next subgoal, Turbo Prolog compares

```
X=popcorn
```

or

```
apples = popcorn
```

and the subgoal fails. Again, the internal unification routines cause backtracking to the rule head *likes(beth,X)*. This rule head does not match with the subgoal controlling this alternative route attempt, *likes(mary,X)*, so unification tests the next rule head for a match. This rule head is also *likes(beth,X)*, so again, unable to match beth and mary, the match fails. Turbo Prolog has no more backtracking markers and the subgoal has failed.

The rule has failed to produce a conclusion this time, so the goal fails. We have only the previous two solutions to the goal. To show that the process is complete, Turbo Prolog displays the message *Two solutions*, as shown in figure 2.6.

Summary

This chapter has introduced Turbo Prolog from a conceptual point of view. Turbo Prolog, you have learned, is a declarative programming language based on predicate logic. Predicates generally indicate relations between objects.

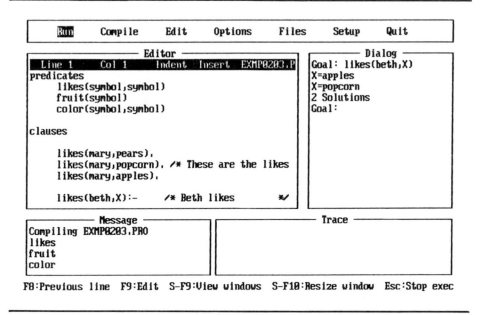

Fig. 2.6. *Multiple solutions to a goal.*

Facts and rules are clauses that make up the data values of a Turbo Prolog program. Rules have a left part (the head) and a right part (the body). The left part of a rule is true if the right part of the rule is true. Rules generate new facts when all of the clauses in the body are satisfied.

Goals are predicate constructions that declare what the Turbo Prolog program is to prove. Conjunctions are used to join the parts of rules and goals. Conjunctions in goals and rules cause subgoals to be generated as part of the goal-proving process.

The internal unification routines bind variables and values. Bound variables and constants have values that are "known" by Turbo Prolog. Free variables have no value.

Turbo Prolog uses backtracking to mark possible alternative routes to the satisfaction of a goal or subgoal. If a subgoal fails and backtracking markers have been placed, a previous subgoal will attempt to succeed from the backtracking point. The goal will succeed if all subgoals succeed; otherwise, the goal fails.

Understanding the behavior of variables, unification, and backtracking can be a challenge for beginners in Turbo Prolog. This chapter has provided several examples to demonstrate how variables, unification, and backtracking work together. As you proceed through the following chapters, you will become more comfortable with the underlying actions of programs written in Turbo Prolog.

3

Programming Fundamentals

Overview

Turbo Prolog syntax and program structure reflect many of the concepts of predicate logic that were introduced in Chapter 2. The syntax of Turbo Prolog and the structure of Turbo Prolog programs are introduced in this chapter.

After learning how to manipulate simple objects in Turbo Prolog, you'll learn how to use compound objects. In this chapter you'll be introduced to two design aids, the Domain Structure Diagram (DSD) and the Predicate Structure Diagram (PSD), both of which will help you design more logical and efficient programs.

To make the organization of facts and rules easier, Turbo Prolog supports compound domain structures. The building blocks of these domain structures are Turbo Prolog's basic domain types. This chapter discusses the use of the basic types to create compound objects and domain structures.

The final section of this chapter introduces the Turbo Prolog arithmetic operators that are essential to simple data manipulations.

Sample programs are provided to demonstrate new concepts and procedures, and the exercises give you opportunities to experiment with the programs. After this chapter, you will have a working knowledge of several useful Turbo Prolog programming techniques.

The Structure of a Turbo Prolog Program

A Turbo Prolog program consists of five divisions, as shown in figure 3.1. These are the domains division, the database division, the predicates division, the goal division, and the clauses division. The words *domains*, *database*, *predicates*, *goal*, and *clauses* mark the beginnings of the divisions.

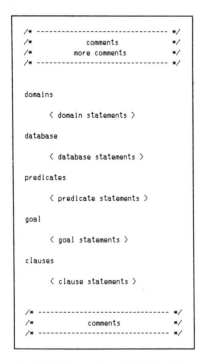

```
/* --------------------------------- */
/*              comments             */
/*           more comments           */
/* --------------------------------- */


domains

        < domain statements >

database

        < database statements >

predicates

        < predicate statements >

goal

        < goal statements >

clauses

        < clause statements >


/* --------------------------------- */
/*              comments             */
/* --------------------------------- */
```

Fig. 3.1. *The structure of a Turbo Prolog program.*

The contents of each section are as follows:

- The *domains* division contains domain declarations, which describe the different classes of objects used in the program.

- The *database* division contains database statements, which are predicates used in the dynamic database. If the program does not require a database, this division is absent from the program. Chapter 8 explores the use of Turbo Prolog's dynamic database capabilities.

- Entries in the *predicates* division are predicates defined and used in the program.

- The *goal* division of a program states its purpose in Turbo Prolog language. The entries in this division can be subgoals that form a single program goal.

- The entries in the *clauses* division are facts and rules, which are familiar to you by now. You can think of this as the data division of the program.

Many programs do not contain all five divisions, for reasons you will learn later in this chapter.

Turbo Prolog provides for the inclusion of comments in the program. Comments are preceded by the characters /* and followed by */, as in figure 3.1. Comments can be placed anywhere within the program; there is no practical limit to their length. To be useful, comments should include information about the program, the name of the file, the compiler, the databases, and the purposes of any predicates and rules whose purposes are not apparent.

Declaring Domains and Predicates

Chapter 2 had several examples using the predicate *likes*, as in

```
likes(mary,apples).
```

Recall that *likes* is the predicate (or predicate term), and *mary* and *apples* are objects of the predicate. Turbo Prolog requires that you indicate what kinds of objects will be used by all predicates in a program. Some objects are numeric data, for example, and others are alphanumeric string data. In the *predicates* division, you declare what objects will be used for each predicate.

To use the *likes* predicate in a program, for example, you would make the following declaration:

```
predicates
     likes(symbol, symbol)
```

This declaration means that both objects of the *likes* predicate are of the type *symbol*. That is one of Turbo Prolog's fundamental data types, which are explained in the next section.

In some programming situations, you will want to be able to indicate more about an object than its fundamental data type. The objects of the *likes* predicate, for example, can be thought of as "the person who likes [something]" and "the thing that is liked." Turbo Prolog enables you to construct your own data objects from the fundamental domain types. Suppose, for example, that you wanted to give the objects of *likes* the names *person* and *thing*. In the *domains* division of the program, you would make these declarations:

```
domains
     person, thing = symbol
predicates
     likes(person, thing)
```

The terms *person* and *thing* name collections (or domains) of values. In the examples in Chapter 2, the terms *mary* and *beth* are particular values belonging to the domain *person*, and *apple* is a particular value belonging to the domain *thing*.

Any value belonging to the domain can be instantiated to the object named by *person*. The same is true for any object belonging to the domain *thing*. For example, consider these three clauses:

```
likes(john, camera).
likes(tom, computer).
likes(kathy, computer).
```

The terms *john*, *tom*, and *kathy* belong to a domain whose name is *person*. The terms *camera* and *computer* belong to the domain with the name *thing*. All three clauses belong to the same predicate; they differ only in the values of the objects. These clauses, in other words, are variants of one another.

Declaring Domain Types

Turbo Prolog has six built-in domain types: characters, integer numbers, real numbers, strings, symbols, and files. The type of the domain must be indicated in the *domains* section of your Turbo Prolog program.

Table 3.1 shows the six standard domain types used in Turbo Prolog.

This predicate illustrates the use of different domain types:

```
payroll(employee_name, pay_rate, weekly_hours)
```

The domain types for this predicate are declared as follows:

```
employee_name = symbol
pay_category = integer
weekly_hours = real
```

The domain declaration for *employee_name* indicates that objects of the *employee_name* domain are symbols. Similarly, objects of the domain *pay_rate* are integers, and objects of the domain *weekly_hours* are real numbers. Possible clauses using this predicate are

```
payroll("John Walker", 16, 45.25).
payroll("Arthur Berman", 28, 32.50).
payroll("Sandy Taylor", 23, 40.00).
```

Declaring Predicates

In Turbo Prolog programs, predicates are used to represent data items as well as rules to manipulate the data. Predicates are declared in the *predicates* division of the program.

——————————————————— **Table 3.1.** ———————————————————
Turbo Prolog Standard Domain Types

Data type	Domain declaration	Range of values	Appearance in Turbo Prolog program
Characters	char	All possible characters	'a','b','#','B','%','\13'
Integer numbers	integer	−32768 to 32767	−63, 84, 2349, 32763
Real numbers	real	± 1e−307 to ± 1e308	−42769,8324,360,093 1.25e(23), 5.15e(−9)
Strings	string	Sequence of characters (up to 250)	"today", "123", "just_a_reminder"
Symbol	symbol	1. Sequence of letters, digits, and underscores, with first character in lowercase	pay_check, school_day, flower,
		2. Other characters enclosed in double quotation marks	"Stars and Stripes" "singing_in_the_rain"
File	file	valid DOS file name	mail.txt, BIRDS.DBA

A predicate term is a string of characters in which the first character is a lowercase letter. Predicates can take very simple forms, as in these examples:

```
go
do_menu
repeat
look_for_fruits
search_for_items
```

These predicate names are well suited for identifying rules and program goals. For example, the predicate *go* is indicative of starting a specific process. It is suitable for use as a goal. The predicate name *do_menu* is more specific; it is suitable for identifying a rule to create a menu. The preceding examples are known as "bare" predicates, because they have no objects.

In many cases, however, particularly when a rule is used as a subgoal of another rule, values from one rule need to be used in attempting to satisfy a second rule. You saw such a case in the preceding chapter. The rule

```
likes(beth,X) if
     likes(mary,X).
```

had to attempt the rule *likes(mary,X)*.

In cases like these, objects are specified when you declare the predicates in the *predicates* division of the program. Some examples are

```
predicates
     likes(symbol,symbol)
     book(symbol,symbol,integer)    /* author, title, pages */
     person(symbol,char,integer)    /* name, sex (m or f), age */
     do_search(integer)
     sum(real,real,real,real)
```

Notice that the lists of objects in these predicate names are placed within parentheses, and the objects are separated by commas. The predicate *likes* has two objects, which are both of the domain type *symbol*. This predicate may be used to construct clauses such as

```
likes(mary,peaches).
likes(john,plums).
likes(jack,oranges).
```

Because the terms *mary*, *peaches*, *john*, *plums*, and *oranges* all meet the requirements for objects of type *symbols*, these clauses are consistent with the domain types specified in the predicate declaration.

Because you are using the standard domain type names in the predicate name, you do not need to declare the domain for the objects in the clauses. However, you have the option of making domain type declarations and then using the declared domain names in the predicate name. For this case, you would make the following declarations in the *domains* and the *predicates* divisions.

```
domains
     name, fruit = symbol
predicates
     likes(name,fruit)
```

This kind of declaration is easy to work with because *name* suggests names of people and *fruit* suggests names of fruits. However, this predicate declaration does not prevent you from writing clauses such as *likes(mary,rain)*. Any object is acceptable so long as the object is of the type *symbol*, and *rain* is of that type. Confusion may result, then, because *rain* is not a *fruit*. A better choice of object name might be *thing* or *item*. Then both *peaches* and *rain* are logically consistent.

Suppose that you want to write a predicate for keeping track of your books. A *book* predicate might be written like this:

```
book("Tom Sawyer","Mark Twain",1855).

book("Man and Superman","Bernard Shaw",1905).
```

Notice that the first two objects of the predicate must be of the domain type *symbol* and the last object must be of type *integer*. You could declare the predicate like this:

```
book(symbol, symbol, integer)
```

An alternative declaration is

```
domains
    title, author = symbol
    year          = integer

predicates
    book(title,author,year)
```

Later in this chapter, you will learn about the advantages that come with using domain declarations.

Writing Turbo Prolog Terms

A Turbo Prolog term can have a maximum of 250 characters, and must begin with a lowercase letter (*a* through *z*). Spaces are not permitted within a term; the underscore character (_) can be used, however, to join the components of a term, as in these examples:

```
employee_name
color_of_box
wild_animal_kingdom
beginning_of_year_to_date_activities_report
```

Most Turbo Prolog programmers prefer names that are concise and definitive. Although the last term is valid, it is longer than normal. If you choose, terms can be as short as a single character:

```
domains
     a,b = symbol

predicates
     s(a,b)

clauses
     s(brave, daring).
```

Writing Predicates and Clauses

This section takes a hands-on approach to introducing the fundamentals of programming in Turbo Prolog. The programs presented here illustrate various basic features of the language.

Wordsmith, in listing 3.1, is a complete Turbo Prolog program that shows the uses of predicates and clauses. The goal of the program is to find and print a synonym for a word. For example, a synonym for *brave* is *daring*. A Prolog clause indicating the relationship between a word and its synonym is

```
synonym(brave, daring).
```

The predicate term is *synonym* and the objects are *brave* and *daring*. The predicate declaration for the clause is

```
synonym(word, syn)
```

Here, *word* and *syn* name the objects of the predicate *synonym*.

```
/* Program: Wordsmith    File: PROG0301.PRO */
/* Purpose. To show word associations by     */
/*            building a small thesaurus.     */

domains

   word, syn, ant = symbol

predicates

   synonym(word,syn)

   antonym(word,ant)
```

```
goal

    synonym(brave,X),
    write ("A synonym for 'brave' is "),
    nl,
    write ("' ",X,"' ."),
    nl.

clauses

    synonym(brave,daring).
    synonym(honest,truthful).
    synonym(modern,new).
    synonym(rare,uncommon).

    antonym(brave,cowardly).
    antonym(honest,dishonest).
    antonym(modern,ancient).
    antonym(rare,common).


/*****        end of program        *****/
```

The domain declaration for the predicate is

```
word, syn = symbol
```

This domain declaration indicates that all objects in of the predicate *synonymn* belong to the domain *symbol*.

The predicate *synonym* has four clauses:

```
synonym(brave,daring).
synonym(honest,truthful).
synonym(modern,new).
synonym(rare,uncommon).
```

Notice that each of these clauses has a word and its synonym as the first and second objects, respectively.

Using External and Internal Goals

Not every Turbo Prolog program contains a goal; some have external goals, which the user enters when the program starts. Turbo Prolog programs with external goals are interactive. The purpose of using external goals is to allow the user to have free rein when using the data; the program then is run as a "neutral" database. When a program has no internal goal, the whole *goal* division, including the division header, is not included in the program.

Internal Goals

The goal of the Wordsmith program is to find and print a synonym for a chosen word. The search is initiated within the program; Wordsmith therefore has an *internal goal*. The goal statement consists of five subgoal statements separated by commas. The first one is

```
synonym(brave, X)
```

Here, *X* is a free variable; it is "free" because no value has yet been bound to it. (Remember that in Turbo Prolog the name of a variable begins with an uppercase character.) In ordinary English the first goal statement means "Find a clause of the predicate *synonym* such that the first object is *brave*, and bind the variable *X* to the second object of the clause."

When you run the program, Turbo Prolog searches through the *synonym* clauses. If a match is found with the object *brave*, the variable *X* is bound to the value of the second object. In this case, the object is *daring*.

The second subgoal writes this character string on the screen:

```
A synonym for 'brave' is
```

This subgoal is performed by the *write* predicate, which is one of many built-in predicates provided by Turbo Prolog. You do not need to declare these built-in predicates in your programs; you can simply use them.

The built-in *write* predicate is entered in the program in the form

```
write("A synonym for 'brave' is ")
```

The double quotation marks are used to delimit the character string *A synonym for 'brave' is*. All string values must be enclosed in double quotation marks, as shown in this clause. The *write* predicate may also include variable names, which are not enclosed in double quotation marks. A simple example of this case is

```
write(X),
```

where *X* is a variable name. If *X* has the value *daring*, then the output of this *write* predicate is *daring*.

In both of these cases, the string values and the variable name are arguments of the *write* predicate. As for other predicates, the arguments for *write* are written as a list, with the elements separated by commas. The arguments may be mixed according to your needs, so long as the conventions described here are followed. The Turbo Prolog compiler will prompt you to correct missing quotation marks and other problems as it compiles your program.

An example of a mixed argument list is

```
write("Today is the ",N,"th day of ",M," a ",D,".").
```

This *write* predicate will produce the sentence

Today is the 19th day of August, a Tuesday.

if the variables *N*, *M*, and *D* are bound to the values 19, August, and Tuesday.

The third subgoal is another built-in predicate: *nl*. This predicate moves the cursor to the beginning of the next line. The fourth subgoal writes the three objects that are enclosed within the parentheses. The first object is a single quotation mark ('). The second object, referenced by the name *X*, is *dare*. The third object is a string composed of a single quotation mark (') and the period (.). The fifth subgoal, another *nl* predicate, moves the cursor to the beginning of the next line. Notice that the goal statement ends with a period; the Turbo Prolog compiler will issue an error message if you omit the period, and your program will not be compiled.

The subgoals, working together, create the screen output shown in figure 3.2.

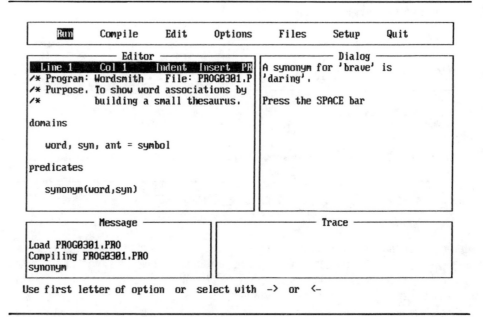

Fig. 3.2. *The output of the Wordsmith program.*

External Goals

When you run a program without an internal goal, Turbo Prolog prompts you to enter a goal. If you delete the entire *goal* division of the Wordsmith program and run it, and you'll see that Turbo Prolog shows the prompt *Goal:* in the Dialog window.

Now suppose that you want to ask the question, "What is a synonym for the word *modern*?" As with the internal goal, here a variable is used to represent the value that Turbo Prolog is to "fill in" by matching your goal with a clause in the database. For this purpose, we'll use the variable Q. The goal you enter is

```
synonym(modern, Q).
```

The result of entering this goal is shown in figure 3.3.

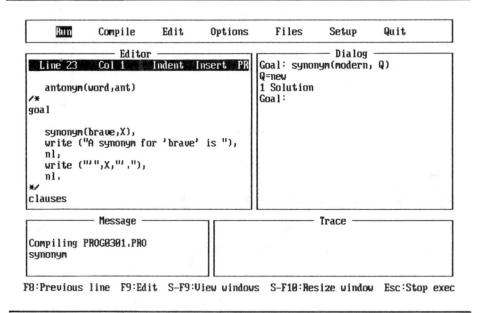

Fig. 3.3. *The output of the Wordsmith program with an external goal.*

Program execution does not end when the program has attempted to satisfy an external goal. Instead, Turbo Prolog prompts you to enter another goal. Thus you can enter as many goals as you wish, and press Esc at the *Goal:* prompt when you want to halt the program. A typical program run is shown in figure 3.4.

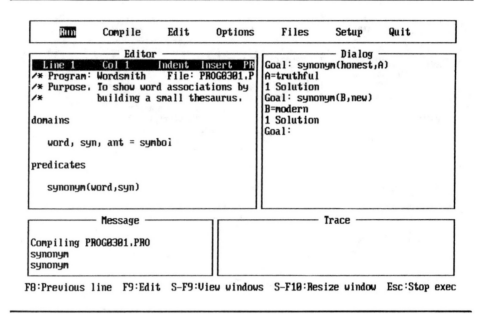

Fig. 3.4. *The output of Wordsmith with another external goal.*

You are not limited to the use of a single variable in the external goals you enter. If you use two variables, for example, your program displays all possible combinations of values that match the variables, as in figure 3.5.

The external goal is useful for short goal statements and for getting all possible answers to the goal. Another advantage of using external goals is that they permit "free-form" querying of the database.

Exercise

3.1 Design and write a program that uses the predicate

`capital(state, city).`

Include clauses for your state and for three states near yours. Do not include an internal goal; you will query the program interactively. Remember that all predicate terms must begin with lowercase letters; so must all object terms, unless you enclose them in quotation marks.

Then run your program and enter goals corresponding to these questions:

What is the capital city of <your state>?

What is the name of the state whose capital is Columbus?

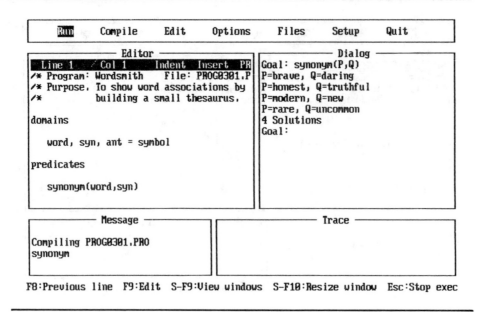

| Run | Compile | Edit | Options | Files | Setup | Quit |

```
---- Editor ----
Line 1    Col 1    Indent  Insert  PR
/* Program: Wordsmith    File: PROG0301.P
/* Purpose. To show word associations by
/*          building a small thesaurus.

domains

   word, syn, ant = symbol

predicates

   synonym(word,syn)
```

```
---- Dialog ----
Goal: synonym(P,Q)
P=brave, Q=daring
P=honest, Q=truthful
P=modern, Q=new
P=rare, Q=uncommon
4 Solutions
Goal:
```

```
---- Message ----
Compiling PROG0301.PRO
synonym
```

```
---- Trace ----
```

```
F8:Previous line  F9:Edit  S-F9:View windows  S-F10:Resize window  Esc:Stop exec
```

Fig. 3.5. *Using two variables with an external goal.*

Higher Arity Predicates and Clauses

As you've learned from the preceding chapter, Turbo Prolog attempts to match clauses in terms of the predicate name, the total number of objects in a clause and the domain type of the objects. The term *arity* refers to the total number of objects in a clause. The clause *likes(mary,apples)* has an arity of 2.

Most Turbo Prolog programs have several different clauses. Examples would be *likes(mary,apples)*, *runs(john,6.3)*, and *drinks(beth,tea,coke)*, to name just a few. If a query is *watches(john,cats)*, Turbo Prolog first tries to find a match in the *watches* predicate; all other predicates are "ignored" for the time being. The matching process initiates a search through all clauses of the *watches* predicate. When the matching predicate term is found, Turbo Prolog looks for clauses having the same total number of objects. The clause *watches* has two objects, *john* and *cats*. The number of objects in the specified query predicate and the clauses in the program body must be the same; otherwise the matching process fails.

When clauses have the same predicate term and the same number of objects, Turbo Prolog then checks the domain type of the objects. In the clause *watches(john,cats)*, both *john* and *cats* are of the type symbol. If the query clause specifies objects of a type that is different from those in the clause, the attempt at matching fails.

Consider the following predicates with different arities:

```
go_home
female(person)
father(person, person)
owns(person, book, book)
europe(country, country, country, country)
```

The objects in these predicates are *person, book* and *country*. The following clauses use these predicates; the arity is given in the right-most column.

Predicate	Clauses	Arity
go_home	go_home	0
female(person)	female(betty) female(kathy)	1
father(person, person)	father(john, kathy) father(john, tom)	2
owns(person, book, book)	owns(sam, "Hobbit", "Lord of the Rings")	3
europe(country, country, country, country)	europe("France", "Germany", "Spain", "Italy")	4

The first predicate, *go_home,* has no object. Because its arity is zero, it is called a "headless predicate." Headless predicates are often used to build rules, as in these examples:

```
go_home if condition(sickness)
go_home if (condition(sickness) and
     transportation(bus))
```

Predicates with arity 1 are useful for putting objects in domain categories. In the above examples, *betty* is a member of the female population (domain). Similarly, *john* is a member of the male population (domain).

Predicates with arity 2 are useful for establishing relationships between two objects. The predicate

```
father(person, person)
```

and the corresponding clause

```
father(john, kathy)
```

can stand for the fact that *john* is the father of *kathy*. Notice that this clause could also be written

```
father(kathy, john)
```

and "translated" as "The father of Kathy is John." The order of objects is unimportant as long as it is consistent throughout your program.

Predicates with arity greater than 2 are useful for relating several objects that have some common attributes. In the clause

```
europe("France", "Germany", "Spain", "Italy")
```

the values *France*, *Germany*, *Spain*, and *Italy* all belong to the domain *country*. The common attribute of the four values is that they are all countries of Europe.

The Thesaurus program, shown in listing 3.2, is an extension of the Wordsmith program. Now, the predicate *synonym* contains four objects: a word and three synonyms. The program also declares a predicate for antonyms. That, too, has four objects. As an example of a small thesaurus program, this one is more realistic than the Wordsmith program.

```
/* Program: Thesaurus    File: PROG0302.PRO */
/* Purpose. To show word associations by     */
/*          building a small thesaurus.       */

domains

    word,
    syn1, syn2, syn3,
    ant1, ant2, ant3 = symbol

predicates

    synonym(word,syn1,syn2,syn3)

    antonym(word,ant1,ant2,ant3)

goal

    synonym(brave,S1,S2,S3) and
      write ("The synonyms for 'brave' are")
      and nl and
      write (S1,", ",S2,", ",S3,".") and nl
```

```
and

antonym(rare,A1,A2,A3) and
    write ("The antonyms for 'rare' are")
    and nl and
    write (A1,", ",A2,", ",A3,".") and nl.

clauses

    synonym(brave,daring,defiant,courageous).
    synonym(honest,truthful,open,sincere).
    synonym(modern,new,novel,recent).
    synonym(rare,uncommon,scarce,infrequent).

    antonym(brave,cowardly,fearful,timid).
    antonym(honest,dishonest,crooked,deceitful).
    antonym(modern,ancient,old,obsolete).
    antonym(rare,common,ordinary,ubiquitous).


/*****         end of program         *****/
```

The internal goal of Thesaurus is composed of two subgoals. The purpose of the first subgoal is to display the three synonyms for *brave*. The purpose of the second subgoal is to display the three antonyms of *rare*.

Notice that the goal statement uses the word *and* to separate the subgoals. The *and* in the goal of the Thesaurus program is equivalent to the , (comma) in the goal of the Wordsmith program. The output of the program is shown in figure 3.6.

───────────────────────── **Exercise** ─────────────────────────

3.2. Modify the program you wrote in exercise 3.1 so that it uses the predicate

```
cities_of_state(state, city1, city2, city3, city4).
```

Write more clauses so that your program includes five states and their cities. Run the program, and enter an external goal that will cause the program to display the four cities in one of the states.

The Presidents program, in listing 3.3, demonstrates the use of mixed object types. The clauses of this program contain facts on six presidents of the United States. The predicate

```
president(name, party, state, birth_year, year_in, year_out)
```

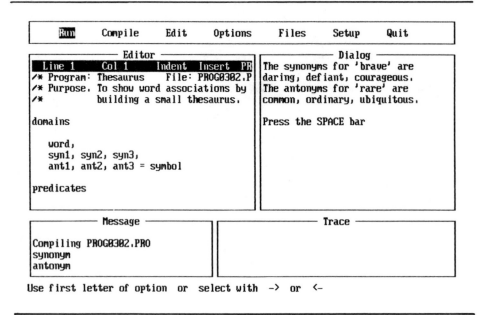

| Run | Compile | Edit | Options | Files | Setup | Quit |

——————— Editor ———————
```
Line 1     Col 1      Indent  Insert  PR
/* Program: Thesaurus    File: PROG0302.P
/* Purpose. To show word associations by
/*          building a small thesaurus.

domains

   word,
   syn1, syn2, syn3,
   ant1, ant2, ant3 = symbol

predicates
```

——————— Dialog ———————
```
The synonyms for 'brave' are
daring, defiant, courageous.
The antonyms for 'rare' are
common, ordinary, ubiquitous.

Press the SPACE bar
```

——————— Message ———————
```
Compiling PROG0302.PRO
synonym
antonym
```

——————— Trace ———————

Use first letter of option or select with -> or <-

Fig. 3.6. *The output of the Thesaurus program.*

has objects of type *symbol* and type *integer*, as you can see in the *domains* section of
the program.

```
/* Program: Presidents   File: PROG0303.PRO */
/* Purpose: To show relations (predicates)  */
/*          and to extract information.      */

domains

   name,party,state = symbol
   birth_year,year_in,year_out = integer

predicates

   president(name,party,state,
             birth_year,year_in,year_out)
```

```
goal

    president(X,democrat,S,Yb,Yi,Yo),nl,
    write(X," -  democrat"),nl,
    write("State  -  ",S),nl,
    write("Birth year  -  ",Yb),nl,
    write("Year-in  -  ",Yi),nl,
    write("Year-out  -  ",Yo),nl,nl.

clauses

    president(eisenhower,republican,texas,
            1890,1953,1961).
    president(kennedy,democrat,massachusetts,
            1917,1961,1963).
    president(johnson,democrat,texas,
            1908,1963,1969).
    president(nixon,republican,california,
            1913,1969,1974).
    president(ford,republican,nebraska,
            1913,1974,1977).
    president(carter,democrat,georgia,
            1924,1977,1981).



    /*****          end of program          *****/
```

The last three objects in the predicate *president* are integers with the domain names *birth_year,* year_in, and *year_out*. The declaration of these integers in the domains division is simple:

```
birth_year, year_in, year_out = integer
```

The comma (,) serves as a separator for multiple domain names of the same type.

In English, the goal of the program is "Name the state of birth, year of birth, and initial and final year in office for all presidents who are Democrats."

The first subgoal contains the free variables X, S, Yb, Yi, Yo, and the value of the object *democrat*. (Notice that some of the variable names give a clue to the meaning of the objects. For example, Yb is "year of birth.") During the program run, the free variables are instantiated to the corresponding values in the second clause. The next five subgoals include *write* predicates to display the instantiated values in separate lines. The program output is shown in figure 3.7.

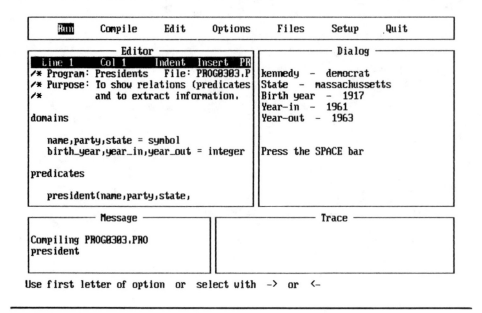

```
─────────── Editor ───────────      ─────────── Dialog ───────────
Line 1    Col 1    Indent  Insert  PR
/* Program: Presidents   File: PROG0303.P   kennedy  -  democrat
/* Purpose: To show relations (predicates   State  -  massachussetts
/*          and to extract information.      Birth year  -  1917
                                             Year-in  -  1961
domains                                      Year-out  -  1963

   name,party,state = symbol
   birth_year,year_in,year_out = integer    Press the SPACE bar

predicates

   president(name,party,state,
```

```
─────────── Message ───────────      ─────────── Trace ───────────
Compiling PROG0303.PRO
president
```

Use first letter of option or select with -> or <-

Fig. 3.7. *The output of the Presidents program.*

This program can also be used with an external goal. In that case the goal division of the program would be omitted. A possible run-time dialogue with the program is shown in figure 3.8.

As you see, the program gives all possible answers to the question.

——————————— Exercise ———————————

3.3. Enter the Presidents program, then run it to make sure it gives the results shown in figure 3.7. Modify the program so that it will respond to the following external goal, then run the program again:

    president(X, republican, S, Yb, Yi, Yo).

You should get all the data responses that were not given when the program was run for the presidents who were Democrats.

Using Rules in Queries

In the previous sample programs, you have used goal statements containing clauses having the same structure as clauses in the program. Such goal statements provide one means for querying the program.

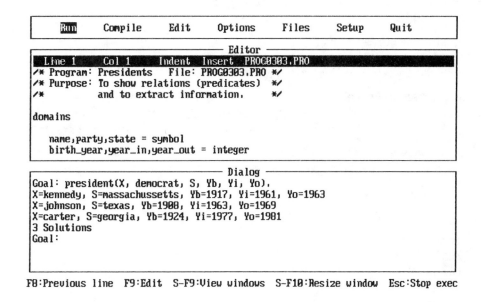

```
   Run      Compile     Edit     Options     Files     Setup     Quit
┌───────────────────────────── Editor ──────────────────────────────┐
│ Line 1      Col 1      Indent   Insert   PROG0303.PRO              │
│ /* Program: Presidents    File: PROG0303.PRO */                    │
│ /* Purpose: To show relations (predicates)  */                    │
│ /*          and to extract information.      */                    │
│                                                                     │
│ domains                                                            │
│                                                                     │
│    name,party,state = symbol                                       │
│    birth_year,year_in,year_out = integer                          │
└─────────────────────────────────────────────────────────────────┘
┌───────────────────────────── Dialog ──────────────────────────────┐
│ Goal: president(X, democrat, S, Yb, Yi, Yo).                      │
│ X=kennedy, S=massachussetts, Yb=1917, Yi=1961, Yo=1963            │
│ X=johnson, S=texas, Yb=1908, Yi=1963, Yo=1969                     │
│ X=carter, S=georgia, Yb=1924, Yi=1977, Yo=1981                    │
│ 3 Solutions                                                        │
│ Goal:                                                              │
└─────────────────────────────────────────────────────────────────┘
 F8:Previous line  F9:Edit  S-F9:View windows  S-F10:Resize window  Esc:Stop exec
```

Fig. 3.8. *Using an external goal with the Presidents program.*

Queries are built from predicates that include conditions to limit the inquiry to the desired results. When you want to ask the same query many times, repeating the query conditions often becomes tedious. It would be useful to be able to draw conclusions from the databases without putting facts from the databases in the query statements.

In Turbo Prolog, you do this by constructing rules without data values in them—rules, in other words, whose heads have arity zero. In this way your task is reduced to writing abbreviated queries. You can see how this is done in the following example.

Consider a hypothetical family:

Frank and Mary are married. They have a
son named Sam and a daughter named Debbie.

Here is a dialogue on the family relationships:

Question: How are Debbie and Sam related?
Answer: Debbie is the sister of Sam.
Question: How do you arrive at that answer?
Answer: Well, Debbie and Sam have the same parents, and Debbie is female. So Debbie is the sister of Sam.

The second answer is a colloquial statement of a rule used for answering the question. A rephrased statement of this rule is

> Debbie is the sister of Sam if
>   Debbie is female and
>   the parents of Debbie are the parents of Sam.

The rephrased statement includes an *if* that makes a logical connection between the clauses on either side of it. The sentence on the left side (before the *if* is a conclusion, or *consequent*, and the sentence on the right-hand side is an assumption, or *premise*.

Predicate expressions are the building blocks of Prolog rules. The facts describing the family relationships between Frank, Mary, Sam, and Debbie can be stated in these Turbo Prolog clauses:

```
male("Frank").
male("Sam").
female("Mary").
female("Debbie").
parents("Sam", "Frank", "Mary").
parents("Debbie", "Frank", "Mary").
```

With these clauses, all that's needed is a rule to establish the sister-brother relationship:

```
sister(Sister, Brother) if
    female(Sister),
    parents(Sister, Father, Mother),
    parents(Brother, Father, Mother).
```

Note that there are no data values in the rule statement; the objects *Sister*, *Brother*, *Father*, and *Mother* all are variables. The two *parents* predicates make the logical connection between *Sister* and *Brother*. The *female* predicate selects the female child of the parents.

The three predicates in the assumption statement of the rule are sufficient to make the desired conclusion. The Relatives program, in listing 3.4, is a complete Turbo Prolog program showing the use of these facts and the *sister* rule.

```
/* Program: Relatives    File: PROG0304.PRO */
/* Purpose: To show rule construction.      */

domains

  person = symbol
```

```
predicates

    male(person)
    female(person)
    parents(person,person,person)
    sister(person,person)
    who_is_the_sister

goal

    who_is_the_sister.

clauses

    /* facts */

    male("Frank").
    male("Sam").
    female("Mary").
    female("Debbie").
    parents("Sam","Frank","Mary").
    parents("Debbie","Frank","Mary").

    /* rules */

    who_is_the_sister if
        sister(Sister,Brother),
        write(Sister,
            " is the sister of ",
            Brother,
            "."),
        nl.

    sister(Sister,Brother) if
        female(Sister),
        parents(Sister,Father,Mother),
        parents(Brother,Father,Mother).


    /*            end of program            */
```

The Relatives program also contains another rule: the predicate *who_is_the_sister*. The goal of the program is *who_is_the_sister*, a single goal statement. It is a rule, and it is defined in the *clauses* division of the program. Because the goal is defined as a rule, the entry in the *goal* division of the program is merely a single goal statement with no subgoals. This body of this rule contains two subrules. The first subrule is itself a rule, *sister*. The other assumption is a predicate to write the result obtained from the *sister* rule. This way of writing the goal is desirable because it simplifies the goal statements. Goal simplification is very helpful when you program has many subgoals for distinct tasks, which may involve fairly complex operations. From the user's point of view, a simple (uncluttered) goal statement facilitates use of the program.

The screen output of this program is shown in figure 3.9.

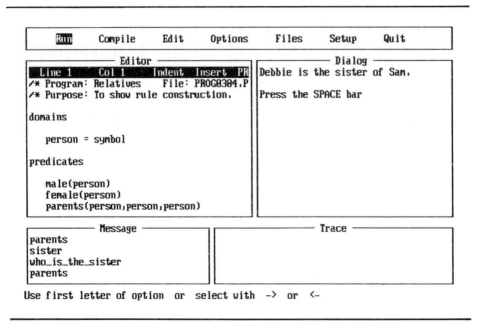

Fig. 3.9. *The output of the Relatives program.*

In Turbo Prolog, rules are written in the clauses division. A Prolog program may have many rules to draw many different conclusions. The effect is the same as that of having many clauses (facts) in the program. In the Relatives program, for example, you might put more rules in the *clauses* division. Suppose that you want to know the name of the son. This rule would determine the answer:

```
who_is_the_son :-
    parents(Son,_,_),
    male(Son),
    write("The son is ",Son,"."),nl.
```

You can put this rule in the *clauses* division and replace the goal with this new rule. Then, when the program is run, this rule will be attempted, and the program will show the result *The son is Sam.*

In similar fashion, many rules can be written and placed in the program. Rules can be selectively activated by "attaching" them to the goal. Being able to select the desired rules in Turbo Prolog makes the programs more flexible and powerful. An important direct application is writing queries to databases in the form of rules and "storing" them in the program for specified uses. You will be introduced to examples of these applications in chapters 9 and 10.

—————————————————— **Exercise** ——————————————————

3.4 Enter the Relatives program, and run it to make sure you have entered the program accurately. Then modify the program by writing a rule to search for the brother. The desired screen output will tell you that Sam is the brother of Debbie.

Simple Databases

The DateMatch program, in listing 3.5, demonstrates the use of rules to get information resulting from searching and pattern matching through a collection of facts. The program is a simple prototype of a dating-service program. The program contains facts on seven men and three attributes: height, hair color, and kind of car. The single domain is *man*.

```
/* Program: DateMatch    File: PROG0305.PRO */
/* Purpose: To show rule construction.      */

domains

    man = symbol

predicates

    choice(man)
    short_height(man)
    medium_height(man)
```

```
        tall_height(man)
        black_hair(man)
        brown_hair(man)
        blond_hair(man)
        old_car(man)
        new_car(man)
        sports_car(man)

        kathy_choice(man)
        who_is_the_choice

goal

        who_is_the_choice.

clauses

        /* facts */

        choice(bill).
        choice(jim).
        choice(mark).
        choice(robert).
        choice(willy).
        choice(tom).
        choice(frank).

        short_height(mark).
        short_height(willy).

        medium_height(bill).
        medium_height(tom).

        tall_height(jim).
        tall_height(robert).
        tall_height(frank).

        black_hair(bill).
        black_hair(willy).

        brown_hair(jim).
        brown_hair(tom).
```

```
blond_hair(mark).
blond_hair(robert).
blond_hair(frank).

new_car(bill).
new_car(willy).
new_car(frank).

old_car(mark).
old_car(tom).

sports_car(jim).
sports_car(robert).

/* rules */

who_is_the_choice :-
        kathy_choice(Choice),
        write("Kathy's choice is ",Choice,"."),
        nl.

kathy_choice(Choice) :-
        choice(Choice),
        tall_height(Choice),
        blond_hair(Choice),
        sports_car(Choice).


/*****        end of program        *****/
```

In the *clauses* division, seven *choice* clauses hold the names *bill, jim, mark, robert, willy, tom,* and *frank*. The clauses *short_height, medium_height, tall_height, black_hair, brown_hair, blond_hair, new_car, old_car,* and *sports_car* also hold men's names. The goal of the program is to find a name of a man who has the attributes Kathy desires: *tall_height, blond_hair,* and *sports_car*. The program should then print the name of the man. The rule to find the man is

```
kathy_choice(Choice) :-
    choice(Choice),
    tall_height(Choice),
    blond_hair(Choice),
    sports_car(Choice).
```

The purpose of this rule is to find at least one object of the *choice* clause that is also an object of the four attribute clauses *choice*, *tall_height*, *blond_hair*, and *sports_car*.

First, the rule binds the variable *Choice* to one object of the clause *choice*. You'll recall from the discussion of the *likes* clause that Turbo Prolog searches the clauses from first to last; consequently, on the first attempt, the variable *Choice* is bound to the value *bill*. Then the rule attempts to match this value with the object of the first attribute clause, *tall_height*. No match is found, so Turbo Prolog backtracks to the next *choice* clause and makes another attempt. This time, *Choice* is bound to the value *jim*. This value satisfies Kathy's specification of a tall man, so Turbo Prolog attempts to match *jim* against the clause *blond_hair*. This attempt fails, so the process is repeated with the third *choice* clause. This process repeats until a value of *Choice* is found that satisfies the three subgoals

```
tall_height(Choice),
blond_hair(Choice),
sports_car(Choice).
```

You can probably tell who Kathy's choice is just by examining the clauses in the program.

—————————————— **Exercise** ——————————————

3.5. Modify the DateMatch program. Write a rule to find a man who is tall, who has blond hair, and whose car is new.

Negation

Besides belonging to the same domain, some objects may have further common attributes. For example, some European countries have common borders, and some do not. A predicate to represent this relationship is

```
border(country,country)
```

The statement "France and Germany have a common border" can be represented in the clause

```
border( "France", "Germany").
```

France and Germany have a common border, as do France and Spain and France and Italy.

Six clauses can therefore represent all possible pairs of the four countries:

```
euro_pair("France", "Germany").
euro_pair("France", "Spain").
euro_pair("France", "Italy").
euro_pair("Germany", "Spain").
euro_pair("Germany", "Italy").
euro_pair("Spain,", "Italy").
```

The clauses for countries with common borders are

```
border("France", "Germany").
border("France", "Spain").
border("France", "Italy").
```

Now suppose that you want to find which countries do *not* have a common border. Rather than list all the countries with common borders and then figure out which countries are not on the list, you can use a simple and effective method of determining which countries do not share a border. The negation of the border predicate is written with the *not* predicate:

```
not(border(Country_1, Country_2)).
```

This predicate selects all the non-bordering pairs. The Europair program, in listing 3.6, is a complete Turbo Prolog program to solve the problem. The output of the program is shown in figure 3.10.

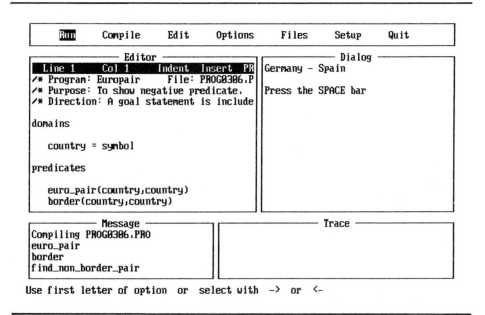

Fig. 3.10. *The output of the Europair program.*

```
/* Program: Europair    File: PROG0306.PRO */
/* Purpose: To show negative predicate.    */
/* Direction: A goal statement is included. */
```

```
domains

    country = symbol

predicates

    euro_pair(country,country)
    border(country,country)
    find_non_border_pair

goal

    find_non_border_pair.

clauses

    /* facts */

    euro_pair("France","Germany").
    euro_pair("France","Spain").
    euro_pair("France","Italy").
    euro_pair("Germany","Spain").
    euro_pair("Germany","Italy").
    euro_pair("Spain","Italy").

    border("France","Germany").
    border("France","Spain").
    border("France","Italy").

    /* rules */

    find_non_border_pair :-
            euro_pair(X,Y),
            not(border(X,Y)),
            write(X," - ",Y), nl.


/*            end of program               */
```

In Prolog programming, negative conditions are sometimes convenient for inferring facts from the existing data in the database. Using the *not* predicate in a rule often gives smoother logic. For example, a negative query can be used to determine whether two countries have a common border. Suppose that you want to learn whether Germany and Spain have a common border. The query is

```
not(border("Germany","Spain")).
```

The response to this query is *True* because, according to the database, these two countries have no common border. Now consider another query,

```
not(border("France","Italy")).
```

The response to this query is *False*, because these two countries do have a common border.

—————————————————— **Exercise** ——————————————————

3.6. Modify the Europair program for use with external goals. At the *Goal:* prompt, enter

```
not(border("Spain", "Italy")).
```

What is the response?

Using Compound Objects

The objects of clauses represent data; simple objects are limited to the six domain types. Consider this example of a clause:

```
owner("Mary", "Garfield").
```

The first object, *Mary*, has no further structure; the object *Mary* represents itself. Similarly, the object *Garfield* represents itself. Any object that represents itself is called a *simple object*. Likewise, a structure made up of simple objects is called a *simple structure*.

The *owner* clause represents the fact that Mary owns "Garfield," which could be the name of either a pet or a book. To suggest this distinction, you may wish to write the clause in a form that makes the object more specific:

```
owner("Mary", pet("Garfield")).
owner("Mary", book("Garfield")).
```

An object that represents another object or a collection of objects is called a *compound object*. These *owner* predicates are called *compound structures* because they are made up of compound objects. In the examples, *pet* represents *Garfield* in the first clause, while *book* represents *Garfield* in the second clause. The terms *pet* and *book* are compound objects. Notice that the objects they represent are enclosed in parentheses.

The clause

```
likes("Tom", apple, orange, banana).
```

states that Tom likes to eat three kinds of fruit: apples, oranges and bananas. You can put the three fruits together in a separate structure, like this:

```
fruits(apple, orange, banana).
```

The result is a compound object that clarifies the relationships:

```
likes("Tom", fruits(apple, orange, banana)).
```

(Note the double parentheses at the end.) The term *fruits* in this predicate statement is called a *functor*. A functor is the first term of a compound object; the functor of a compound object is a predicate in its own right, even though the compound object is embedded within another predicate. The predicate *likes* is the main functor.

To facilitate writing clauses and predicates in this form, Turbo Prolog allows you to declare compound objects in the *domains* division of the program. The declarations for this example are

```
domains
    personal_liking = fruits(type1, type2, type3)
    type1, type2, type3    = symbol
```

The domain name *personal_liking* is a name for the compound object created by the use of the *fruits* functor. The name *fruits* represents both the compound object and the functor.

If a structure's objects are all of the same domain type, it is called a *single-domain structure*. A structure with the objects *apples*, *peaches* and *oranges*, which all are declared as domain type *symbol*, constitutes a single-domain structure.

If a structure has objects of different domain types, it is called a *multiple-domain structure*. An example is a collection of *apples*, *r* and *16*. Here, *apples* is of domain type symbol, *r* is of type char, and *16* is of type integer. Thus, a compound object is one particular domain structure. Each domain structure implies a particular representation of facts in the data base. They provide a means of putting objects into categories. You make reference to the domain structure by using the functor name.

Functors and Domain Structures

The Library program, in listing 3.7, demonstrates the use of a domain structure whose name is *personal_library*. This domain structure contains data about a few books in several personal book collections.

```
/* Program: Library            File: PROG0307.PRO */
/* Purpose: To show compound object construction  */
/*          at a single level.                     */

domains

    personal_library = book(title,author,publisher,year)
    collector, title, author, publisher = symbol
    year = integer

predicates

    collection(collector,personal_library)

clauses

    collection(kahn,
            book("The Computer and the Brain",
                "von Neumann",
                "Yale University Press",1958)).
    collection(kahn,
            book("Symbolic Logic",
                "Lewis Carroll",
                "Dover Publications",1958)).
    collection(johnson,
            book("Database: A Primer",
                "C.J. Date",
                "Addison-Wesley",1983)).
    collection(johnson,
            book("Problem-Solving Methods in AI",
                "Nils Nilsson",
                "McGraw-Hill",1971)).
    collection(smith,
            book("Alice in Wonderland",
                "Lewis Carroll",
                "The New American Library",1960)).
    collection(smith,
            book("Fables of Aesop",
                "Aesop-Calder",
                "Dover Publications",1967)).


/*****          end of program          *****/
```

The functor name for the domain structure *personal_library* is *book*. The domain declaration is

```
personal_library = book(title, author, publisher, year)
     title, author, publisher = symbol
     year = integer
```

The predicate declaration uses the domain structure *personal_library*:

```
collection(collector, personal_library).
```

The predicate *collection* includes two object names. The first name stands for a single object, and the second name stands for a domain structure consisting of multiple objects.

The use of the domain structure simplifies the predicate structure. If it did not use domain structures, this program would need a predicate of the form

```
collection(collector,title,author,publisher,year)
```

in the *predicates* division. In this predicate, the last four objects stand for the properties (or attributes) of a book. A rule to manipulate the personal library would need to treat the last four objects as separate entities, and the code would be more complicated.

This program uses an external goal. To find out, for example, which books belong to Smith, you can enter the goal

```
collection(smith, Books).
```

The object *smith* is a specific value of the domain *collector*, and *Books* is a free variable. The goal is to find all the books that belong to *smith*. The output of the program when presented with this goal is shown in figure 3.11.

Now suppose that you want to know collectors' names and book titles for the books published in 1967. The goal for finding that information is

```
collection(Collector, book(Title,_,_, 1967)).
```

In this goal, *Collector* and *Title* are free variables. The underscore (_) indicates that you have no interest in seeing the values corresponding to the two object names *author* and *publisher*. (Remember that the underscore symbol stands for an anonymous variable.) The screen output of the program is shown in figure 3.12.

The exercises that follow will familiarize you with using different kinds of goal statements.

——————————————— **Exercises** ———————————————

3.7 You wish to ask this question:

What is the name of a collector who owns a book with the title *Database: A Primer*?

```
┌─────────────────────────────────────────────────────────────────┐
│   Run    Compile    Edit    Options    Files    Setup    Quit     │
├─────────────────────────────────────────────────────────────────┤
│ ──────── Editor ────────  │ ──────── Dialog ────────              │
│ Line 1   Col 1   Indent  Insert  PR│Goal: collection(smith,Books) │
│ /* Program: Library      File: PROG│Books=book("Alice in Wonderland","L│
│ /* Purpose: To show compound object const│ewis Carroll","The New American Lib│
│ /*          at a single level.    │rary",1960)                    │
│                                   │Books=book("Fables of Aesop","Aesop│
│ domains                           │-Calder","Dover Publications",1967)│
│                                   │                               │
│   personal_library = book(title,author,p│2 Solutions              │
│   collector, title, author, publisher =│Goal:                    │
│   year = integer                  │                               │
│                                   │                               │
│ predicates                        │                               │
│                                                                   │
│ ──────── Message ────────  │ ──────── Trace ────────              │
│ Compiling PROG0307.PRO            │                               │
│ collection                        │                               │
│                                                                   │
└─────────────────────────────────────────────────────────────────┘
 F8:Previous line  F9:Edit  S-F9:View windows  S-F10:Resize window  Esc:Stop exec
```

Fig. 3.11. *A dialogue with the Library program.*

```
┌─────────────────────────────────────────────────────────────────┐
│   Run    Compile    Edit    Options    Files    Setup    Quit     │
├─────────────────────────────────────────────────────────────────┤
│ ──────── Editor ────────  │ ──────── Dialog ────────              │
│ Line 1   Col 1   Indent   │Goal: collection(Collector, book(Title,_,_,19│
│ /* Program: Library       │67))                           │
│ /* Purpose: To show compound ob│Collector=smith, Title=Fables of Aesop│
│ /*          at a single level.  │1 Solution                   │
│                                 │Goal:                        │
│ domains                         │                               │
│                                 │                               │
│   personal_library = book(titl  │                               │
│   collector, title, author, pu  │                               │
│   year = integer                │                               │
│                                 │                               │
│ predicates                      │                               │
│                                                                   │
│ ──────── Message ────────  │ ──────── Trace ────────              │
│ Compiling PROG0307.PRO          │                               │
│ collection                      │                               │
│                                                                   │
└─────────────────────────────────────────────────────────────────┘
 F8:Previous line  F9:Edit  S-F9:View windows  S-F10:Resize window  Esc:Stop exec
```

Fig. 3.12. *Querying the database for objects of a functor.*

The goal statement you enter is

```
collection(Collector, Book("Database: A Primer",
                _,_,_)).
```

What is the screen output?

3.8 You wish to ask another question:

What are the titles of the books that were published after the year 1980?

The goal statement is

```
collection(collector, book(Title,_,_, Year),
Year > 1980
```

What is the screen output?

Structure Diagrams

Diagrams can help you see or plan the components of compound structures. Figure 3.13 shows a domain-structure diagram (DSD) for the Library program. The domain is **personal_library**; the structure name is *book*. This structure has four objects: *title*, *author*, *publisher*, and *year*.

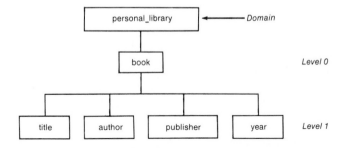

Fig. 3.13. *The domain-structure diagram for the Library program.*

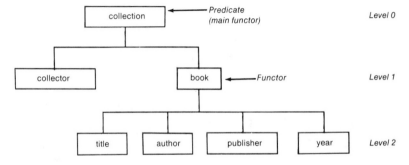

Fig. 3.14. *The predicate-structure diagram for the Library program.*

Figure 3.14 shows the predicate-structure diagram (PSD) for the Library program. Notice that the DSD is a component of the PSD. Here *book* is a functor. There are 3 levels in the PSD.

These diagrams clearly show the organization of the domains and predicates. Diagrams like these are useful for showing the components of the structures. The top levels show the general features of the structures, and the lower levels show more detail.

The DSD and PSD are useful tools in Turbo Prolog program design and documentation. They can also serve as resources to guide you in writing effective rules. Later in this book, you'll become familiar with two other tools, the data-flow diagram and the structure chart, that can be useful in planning your programs.

The program MoreLibrary, in listing 3.8, shows the construction of a three-level domain structure and a four-level predicate structure.

```
/* Program: MoreLibrary        File: PROG0308.PRO */
/* Purpose: To show compound object construction  */
/*          at two levels.                         */

domains

    personal_library = book(title,author,publication)
    publication = publication(publisher,year)
    collector, title, author, publisher = symbol
    year = integer

predicates

    collection(collector,personal_library)

clauses

    collection("Kahn",
              book("The Computer and the Brain",
                  "von Neumann",
                  publication("Yale University Press",
                              1958))).
    collection("Kahn",
              book("Symbolic Logic",
                  "Lewis Carroll",
                  publication("Dover Publications",
                              1958))).
```

```
collection("Johnson",
          book("Database:A Primer",
               "C.J. Date",
               publication("Addison-Wesley",
                           1983))).
collection("Johnson",
          book("Problem-Solving Methods in AI",
               "Nils Nilsson",
               publication("McGraw-Hill",
                           1971))).
collection("Smith",
          book("Alice in Wonderland",
               "Lewis Carroll",
               publication("The New American Library",
                           1960))).
collection("Smith",
          book("Fables of Aesop",
               "Aesop-Calder",
               publication("Dover Publications",
                           1967))).


/*****          end of program          *****/
```

MoreLibrary uses the same data as in the Library program. In this program, however, the objects *publisher* and *year* are objects of the third-level functor *publication*. The domain declarations are

```
personal_library = book(title, author, publication)
publication = publication(publisher, year)
collector, title, author, publisher = symbol
year = integer
```

The predicate declarations and the clauses are the same as in the previous program. The two programs differ only in their domain structures.

The DSD and PSD for this program are shown in figures 3.15 and 3.16. Notice that the DSD has three levels and the PSD has four levels. Both *book* and *publication* are functors; *publication* is a component of the *book* functor. The effort and time that you put into designing the predicate and domain structures will reward you with databases that are easier to use. The more functors, the more specifically you can query the database; of course, specific queries are usually most desirable.

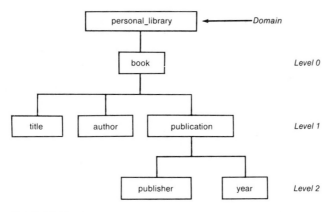

Fig. 3.15. *The domain-structure diagram for the program MoreLibrary.*

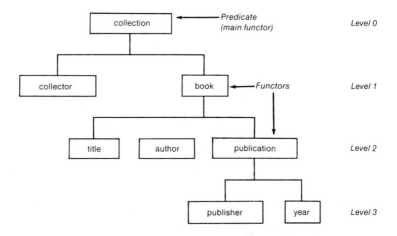

Fig. 3.16. *The predicate-structure diagram for the program MoreLibrary.*

Exercises

3.9. Run the MoreLibrary program, and enter external goals such as

    collection(smith, Books)

or

    collection(Collector,book(Title,_,publication(_,1967)

Can you find Kahn's books?

3.10. Modify the domain structure of the program MoreLibrary. Put the two domain objects *title* and *author* in a subdomain under the name *volume*. The domain declaration is

```
volume = volume(author, title)
```

Remember to change the clauses to conform to the modified predicate structure. Run the modified program. Now you should be able to query your data base in other ways. Try this goal, for example:

```
collection(_, Book(Volume,_)).
```

Does the screen output provide a list of all the authors and works? If not, review your domain declaration statements.

Using Alternative Domains

Data representation often requires many domain structures. In a Turbo Prolog program, these domain structures can require numerous declarations. Furthermore, keeping track of predicates using numerous domain structures can be difficult. To lessen this burden, Turbo Prolog offers alternative domain declarations. The Things program, in listing 3.9, uses alternative domain declarations.

```
/* Program: Things       File: PROG0309.PRO */
/* Purpose: To show the use of alternative  */
/*          domain constructions            */

domains

    thing = misc_thing(whatever)     ;
            book(author,title)       ;
            record(artist,album,type)

            person,
            whatever,
            author, title,
            artist, album, type = symbol

predicates

    owns(person,thing)
```

```
clauses

    /* facts */

    /* Miscellaneous things */

    owns("Bill",
        misc_thing("sail boat")).
    owns("Bill",
        misc_thing("sports car")).
    owns("Jack",
        misc_thing("motor cycle")).
    owns("Jack",
        misc_thing("house trailer")).
    owns("Beth",
        misc_thing("Chevy wagon")).
    owns("Beth",
        misc_thing("Piano")).
    owns("Linda",
        misc_thing("motor boat")).


    /* books */

    owns("Bill",
        book("J.R.R. Tolkien",
            "Return of the Ring")).
    owns("Bill",
        book("James A. Michener",
            "Space")).
    owns("Jack",
        book("Manuel Puig",
            "Kiss of the Spider Woman")).
    owns("Beth",
        book("Frank Herbert",
            "Dune")).
    owns("Beth",
        book("Tom Clancy",
            "The Hunt for Red October")).
    owns("Linda",
        book("Garrison Keillor",
            "Lake Wobegon Days")).
```

```
/* records */

owns("Bill",
     record("Elton John",
            "Ice on Fire",
            "popular")).
owns("Bill",
     record("Michael Jackson - Lionel Richie",
            "We are the World",
            "popular")).
owns("Jack",
     record("Bruce Springsteen",
            "Born to Run",
            "popular")).
owns("Jack",
     record("Benny Goodman",
            "The King of Swing",
            "jazz")).
owns("Beth",
     record("Madonna",
            "Madonna",
            "popular")).



/*            end of program                */
```

This code fragment shows how the program would have to be written if Turbo Prolog did not support alternate domain declarations:

```
domains

    person,whatever,author,title = symbol
    artist,album,type            = symbol
        misc_thing = misc_thing(whatever)
        book_library = book(author,title)
        record_library = record(artist,album,type)

predicates

    personal_thing(person,misc_thing)
    personal_books(person,book_library)
    personal_records(person,record_library)
```

```
clauses

    personal_thing("Bill",misc_thing("sail boat")).
    personal_books("Bill",book("J.R.R. Tolkien",
        "Return of the Ring")).
    personal_records("Bill",record("Elton John",
        "Ice on Fire","popular")).
```

The Things program uses three domain structures. The first one is *misc_thing*, which has a single object called *whatever*. The second domain structure is *book*, whose objects are *author* and *title*. The third domain structure is *record*, which is composed of three objects: *artist, album*, and *type.*

The objects of all three domain structures are of type *symbol*. These three domain structures have the common domain name *things*. The domain declaration is

```
things = misc_thing(whatever) ;
         book(author, title) ;
         record(artist, album, type)
```

Note the use of the semicolon (;) to separate alternative domains.

A simple predicate serves to associate a person with his or her possessions:

```
owns(person, things)
```

The use of alternative domains enables you to use this single *owns* predicate to write clauses for all the different kinds of possessions. Without alternative domains, you would need the three predicate declarations shown previously.

Try this goal with the Things program:

```
owns(P, misc_thing(T)).
```

The translation of this query is "List all the miscellaneous things owned by all persons." Other goals you might want to try are *owns(_,book(A,T))* and *owns(P,record(_,A,_)).*

Notice that the terms *misc_thing*, *book* and *record* are domain structure names. But those terms also appear in the predicate expression; these terms therefore are also functor names. Turbo Prolog does not distinguish between functors and domain structures. This is an intended feature of Turbo Prolog in particular. It is a convenient feature for programming in a declarative language.

——————————————————— **Exercises** ———————————————————

3.11. Run the Things program, and enter this external goal:

```
owns(_, book(_,T)).
```

What is the screen output? Translate the goal into ordinary language. (*Hint:* The question begins, "Who owns . . .".)

3.12. Run the Things program again, and enter this external goal:

```
owns(P, record(_, A, _).
```

What is the screen output? Translate this goal into ordinary language.

The MoreThings program, in listing 3.10, is an altered version of the Things program.

```
/* Program: MoreThings   File: PROG0310.PRO */
/* Purpose: To show the use of alternative  */
/*          domain constructions            */

domains

    things = misc_thing(whatever)     ;
             book(author,title)       ;
             record(artist,album,type)

             person,
             whatever,
             author, title,
             artist, album, type = symbol

predicates

    owns(person,things)

    show_misc_things
    show_books
    show_records

goal

    write("Here are the books:"), nl, nl,
    show_books.
```

```
clauses

    /* facts */

    /* Miscellaneous things */

    owns("Bill",
        misc_thing("sail boat")).
    owns("Bill",
        misc_thing("sports car")).
    owns("Jack",
        misc_thing("motor cycle")).
    owns("Jack",
        misc_thing("house trailer")).
    owns("Beth",
        misc_thing("Chevy wagon")).
    owns("Beth",
        misc_thing("Piano")).
    owns("Linda",
        misc_thing("motor boat")).


    /* books */

    owns("Bill",
        book("J.R.R. Tolkien",
            "Return of the Ring")).
    owns("Bill",
        book("James A. Michener",
            "Space")).
    owns("Jack",
        book("Manuel Puig",
            "Kiss of the Spider Woman")).
    owns("Beth",
        book("Frank Herbert",
            "Dune")).
    owns("Beth",
        book("Tom Clancy",
            "The Hunt for Red October")).
    owns("Linda",
        book("Garrison Keillor",
            "Lake Wobegon Days")).
```

```
/* records */

owns("Bill",
     record("Elton John",
            "Ice on Fire",
            "popular")).
owns("Bill",
     record("Michael Jackson - Lionel Richie",
            "We are the World",
            "popular")).
owns("Jack",
     record("Bruce Springsteen",
            "Born to Run",
            "popular")).
owns("Jack",
     record("Benny Goodman",
            "The King of Swing",
            "jazz")).
owns("Beth",
     record("Madonna",
            "Madonna",
            "popular")).

/* rules */

show_misc_things :-
     owns(Owner, misc_thing(Whatever)),
     write(Owner,"    ",Whatever), nl,
     fail.
show_misc_things.

show_books :-
     owns(_,book(_,Title)),
     write("   ",Title), nl,
     fail.
  show_books.
```

```
show_records :-
     owns(Owner,record(_,Album,_)),
     write("   ",Owner," ",Album), nl,
     fail.
show_records.
```

```
/*****          end of program          *****/
```

As you can see, the program has three rules. Each of them can be used as part of an internal goal. (As shown in listing 3.10, the program uses the rule *show_books* in the internal goal. You can change it if you wish.)

The first rule is

```
show_misc_things :-
     owns(Owner, misc_thing(Whatever)),
     write(Owner, "   ", Whatever),nl,
     fail.
```

This rule translates into the query, "List all the miscellaneous things owned by various persons."

The second rule is

```
show_books :-
     owns(Owner, book(_, Title)),
     write(" ", Title),nl,
     fail.
```

The "translation" is "List all book titles in the database."

The third rule is

```
show_records :-
     owns(Owner, record(_, Album, -)),
     write(" ", Owner, "  ", Album),nl,
     fail.
```

The query in plain English is, "List the names of the owners and their record album names."

In each of these cases, using alternate domains makes the task manageable and the programming more efficient.

——————————— **Exercise** ———————————

3.13. Consider this query:

List all the names of "popular" music records along with the names of the artists.

Build a Prolog rule to achieve this goal. Include your version of the rule in the program, and run it. What is the screen output?

Arithmetic Applications

Turbo Prolog has two numeric domain types: integers and real numbers. The four basic arithmetic operations are addition, subtraction, multiplication and division. In Turbo Prolog, predicates are used to perform these operations. The program Numbers, in listing 3.11, shows how to perform mathematical operations with predicates.

```
/* Program: Numbers    File: PROG0311.PRO */

/* Purpose: To show simple arithmetic.    */

predicates

    add(integer,integer).
    subtract(integer,integer).
    multiply(integer,integer).
    divide(integer,integer).
    fadd(real,real).
    fsubtract(real,real).
    fmultiply(real,real).
    fdivide(real,real).

goal

    write("          Results"), nl, nl,
    add(44,23),
    subtract(44,23),
    multiply(44,23),
    divide(44,23),
    fadd(12.65,7.3),
    fsubtract(12.65,7.3),
```

```
        fmultiply(12.65,7.3),
        fdivide(12.65,7.3), nl,
        write("          All done, bye!").

    clauses

        add(X,Y):-
            Z = X + Y, write("Sum = ",Z), nl.
        subtract(X,Y):-
            Z = X - Y, write("Diff = ",Z), nl.
        multiply(X,Y):-
            Z = X * Y, write("Prod = ",Z), nl.
        divide(X,Y):-
            Z = X / Y, write("Quo = ",Z), nl.
        fadd(P,Q):-
            R = P + Q, write("Fsum = ",R), nl.
        fsubtract(P,Q):-
            R = P - Q, write("Fdiff = ",R), nl.
        fmultiply(P,Q):-
            R = P * Q, write("Fpro = ",R), nl.
        fdivide(P,Q):-
            R = P / Q, write("Fguo = ",R), nl.



    /*****       end of program           *****/
```

The rules for addition, subtraction, multiplication and division of integers are

```
    add(X, Y) :- Z = X + Y, write("Sum = ",Z), nl.
    subtract(X, Y) :- Z = X - Y, write("Diff = ",Z), nl.
    multiply(X, Y) :- Z = X * Y, write("Prod = ",Z), nl.
    divide(X, Y) :- Z = X/Y, write("Quo = ",Z), nl.
```

The four rules for addition, subtraction, multiplication and division involving real numbers are

```
    fadd(P, Q) :- R = P + Q, write("Fsum = ",R), nl.
    fsubtract(P, Q) :- R = P - Q, write("Fdiff = ",R), nl.
    fmultiply(P, Q) :- R = P * Q, write("Fpro = ",R), nl.
    fdivide(P, Q) :- R = P/Q, write("Fguo = ",R), nl.
```

The internal goal is a sequence of subgoal statements using these rules. The subgoals include values that are passed to the rules. It is important to match the data types with the predicate types. This program produces the screen output shown in figure 3.17.

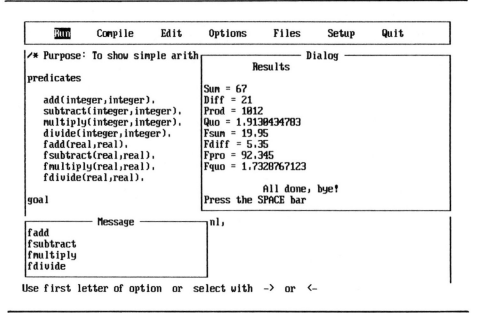

Fig. 3.17. *Output of the program Numbers.*

Note that division of an integer by an integer often yields a decimal number. The decimal numbers are correct up to 10 decimal places.

Exercises

3.14 You wish to add four decimal numbers. The predicate declaration is

    sum(real, real, real, real, real)

Write a rule to add the numbers. Incorporate the predicate and the rule into the Numbers program.

3.15 Run the Numbers program, and enter this external goal:

    sum(3.9,4.6,2.6,9.7,Z).

What is the screen output?

Chapter Review

This chapter has introduced the fundamental concepts of programming in Turbo Prolog. You have learned the uses of fundamental entities such as predicates, clauses, and domain types.

You have also learned much about the structure and organization of Turbo Prolog programs. In doing so, you learned to use both internal goals and external goals. A number of techniques for building Turbo Prolog rules and writing simple queries for databases have been discussed. You have seen these techniques illustrated in programs presented for these specific purposes, and you have learned to modify the programs to serve your own needs.

The formation of compound objects to form hierarchical domain structures was also presented, and you have learned the connection between domain structures and functors. You have also learned to appreciate and use the Domain Structure Diagram (DSD) and the Predicate Structure Diagram (PSD) as tools for program design and documentation.

And finally, you have learned to write Turbo Prolog rules to manipulate numbers.

4

Repetition and Recursion

Overview

Programs often need to perform the same task repeatedly. In Turbo Prolog programming, repetitive operations are usually performed by rules that use backtracking and recursion. Iterative rules, recursive rules, and general techniques for implementing them are discussed in this chapter.

Four important methods are introduced in this chapter: the Backtrack After Fail method, the Cut and Fail method, the User-Defined Repeat Rule, and the General Recursive Rule. Simple programs using these methods of rule construction will increase your understanding of those techniques so that you can readily use them in your own programs.

Repetitive and recursive rules must be controlled if they are to be useful. Turbo Prolog's built-in *fail* and *cut* predicates are used to control backtracking, and exit conditions are used to control recursion. Those topics are introduced here, with graphic examples to increase your understanding.

Performing Repetitive Tasks

Goals direct Turbo Prolog programs to perform specific sets of tasks. As you have already learned, goals can contain subgoals, and goals (or subgoals) can contain rules. You also have learned that rules often need to perform certain tasks repeatedly, such as looking for data items in the database or writing data values to the screen.

There are two ways of implementing rules that perform repetitive tasks. One method is *repetition* and the other is *recursion*. In Turbo Prolog, repetition rules use backtracking; recursive rules call themselves.

The form of a repetition rule is

```
repetitive_rule :-
    <predicates and rules>,
    fail.
```

In the rule body, *<predicates and rules>* represents predicates with multiple clauses and rules that are defined in the program. The built-in predicate *fail* causes backtracking so that the predicates and rules are attempted again.

The form of a recursive rule is

```
recursive_rule :-
    <predicates,rules>,
    recursive_rule.
```

Notice that the last rule in the rule body is the rule itself, *recursive_rule*. A recursive rule includes itself in the rule body.

Both repetitive rules and recursive rules can produce the same output. However, the manner in which the two rules work is different; each has advantages in different programming situations.

Recursion can make heavier demands on system resources. Each time a rule calls itself recursively, new copies of values used in the rule are placed on the stack, which is a memory area used for passing values among rules and for other purposes. These values are not reclaimed until the rule ultimately succeeds or fails. This use of the stack can be useful in some programming situations, when temporary values need to be stored in a certain order for later use. In the next chapter, you will see what a prominent part the the stack plays in rules for processing lists.

Although Turbo Prolog has features that can eliminate this stack "consumption," repetitive rules (which employ backtracking) do not increase stack usage. The programs in this chapter do not try to indicate the correct choice between repetitive and recursive programming methods. What the programs do show is the method for employing both techniques. Later chapters will include programs that make use of repetition and recursion in appropriate ways. What you will learn now is the method of using each of these programming techniques.

Repetition and Backtracking

The goal of a Turbo Prolog program usually contains one or more subgoals, which can be either facts or rules. A fact can be satisfied immediately; the result is either a success or a failure, depending on whether a fact in the program matches the fact in the rule. A rule, being a conjunction of subrules, is satisfied by satisfying its subrules. If a subrule cannot be satisfied, Turbo Prolog will backtrack in the search for other possible ways of satisfying the subrules.

To review the idea of backtracking, consider a simple game database containing these clauses:

```
plays(tom,football).
plays(john,soccer).
plays(john,volleyball).
plays(tom,basketball).
plays(tom,volleyball).
plays(john,baseball).
```

The task of the program is to determine which game is played by both John and Tom. The goal statement is

```
plays(john,G),plays(tom,G).
```

Notice that this goal is a conjunction of two subgoals. Each subgoal contains the variable G. The task is to find the value of G that satisfies both subgoals.

Figure 4.1 illustrates the backtracking process. To satisfy the first subgoal, *plays(john, G)*, Turbo Prolog looks for a matching clause in the database. The first object of the clause *plays(john,soccer)* matches the first object of the subgoal, so the subgoal succeeds and the variable G is instantiated to *soccer*. Other *plays* clauses exist that may satisfy this subgoal, and Turbo Prolog needs to keep track of those clauses in case the goal fails with G instantiated to *soccer*. Turbo Prolog's internal routines therefore place a backtracking marker at the point labeled 1 in the figure. The purpose of the backtracking marker is to indicate the point from which further efforts to satisfy the first subgoal can proceed.

Now, Turbo Prolog tries to satisfy the second subgoal. Because G is instantiated to *soccer*, the subgoal is *plays(tom,soccer)*. Turbo Prolog searches the database for a clause matching this subgoal. No matching clause exists, so the subgoal fails.

Because the second subgoal has failed, Turbo Prolog must begin again with the first subgoal. The variable G is freed because this attempt to satisfy the goal has failed, and Turbo Prolog again begins searching for a clause to satisfy the first subgoal, *plays(john, G)*.

The search begins at backtracking marker 1. The next matching clause is *plays(john,volleyball)*. The variable G is instantiated to *volleyball*. Again, a backtracking marker (labeled 2 in fig. 4.1) is placed at the following clause. Then Turbo Prolog attempts to satisfy the second subgoal, *plays(tom,volleyball)*. On this attempt, a matching clause is found; the instantiation of G to *volleyball* is successful. Both subgoals are satisfied. Because there are no further subgoals, the entire goal is satisfied.

If the goal for this example were an internal goal, the process of goal-satisfaction would stop after the first satisfaction of the goal. Because the goal is external, however, the process is repeated and all possible satisfactions of the goal are found. But given the data contained in the clauses, only one possible instantiation of G exists that satisfies both subgoals; the result of satisfying the goal is G = *volleyball*.

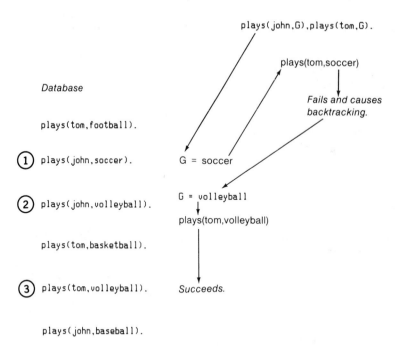

Fig. 4.1. *Backtracking to multiple goal solutions.*

Backtracking is an automatic process that is initiated unless otherwise controlled. Turbo Prolog provides two built-in predicates to control the backtracking process. They are the *fail* predicate and the *cut* predicate. The uses of these predicates are discussed in the sections on the Backtrack After Fail (BAF) method and the Cut and Fail (CAF) method.

In running a program, Turbo Prolog creates the necessary internal data structures (such as lists and trees) for manipulation of values. The manipulation involves such processes as searching, pattern matching, instantiation, variable binding and unbinding, and backtracking. You will recall from Chapter 2 that these processes are performed by internal parts of the language, which are called the internal unification routines. Remember that the internal unification routines are always at work in a running Turbo Prolog program. You will encounter frequent references to these unification routines in explanations of the programs in this book.

Methods for Repetition

Remember that an external goal statement causes variables to be bound to all possible values, one after another. (You can review this idea in chapters 2 and 3.) If the number of the instantiated values is small (say, less than 10), the display of these values on the computer screen is a convenient feature. If the number is larger, however, the display scrolls off the video screen. It is difficult, if not impossible, to read all of them.

But if the goal is internal to the program, then Turbo Prolog's internal unification routines stop the search for successful instantiations after the first satisfaction of the goal. Thus only the first solution is shown. If other values can be successfully instantiated to the variables in the goals, these values are not accessed unless the program forces the internal unification routines to repeatedly search for solutions.

In the following sections, you will learn two methods of implementing repetition in Turbo Prolog. The Backtrack After Fail method and the Cut and Fail method are very useful in programming.

The Backtrack After Fail Method

In this section you will see how the Backtrack After Fail (BAF) method can be used with an internal goal to find all the possible solutions to the goal. The BAF method uses the *fail* predicate. The Cities program, in listing 4.1, illustrates a simple use of this predicate.

```
/* Program: Cities      File: PROG0401.PRO */
/* Purpose: To show the use of "fail"      */
/*          predicate and the BAF Method.  */

domains

    name = symbol

predicates

    cities(name)
    show_cities

goal

    write("Here are the cities:"),nl,
    show_cities.

clauses

    cities("ANN ARBOR").
    cities("ATLANTA").
    cities("NEW HAVEN").
    cities("INDIANAPOLIS").
    cities("BOSTON").
    cities("MESA").
    cities("MINNEAPOLIS").
```

```
cities("SAN ANTONIO").
cities("SAN DIEGO").
cities("TAMPA").

show_cities :-
    cities(City),
    write("     ",City), nl,
    fail.
```

The purpose of the Cities program is to list the names of ten U.S. cities. The output of the program is shown in figure 4.2.

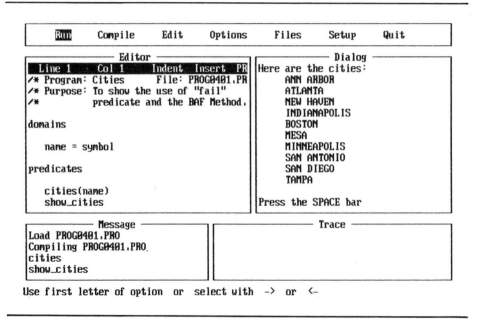

Fig. 4.2. *Output of the program Cities.*

The first subgoal statement displays the heading *Here are the cities:*. The second subgoal is a rule to list the names of the cities. The subrule *cities(City)* instantiates the variable *City* with the name of a city. This value then is written to the screen. The *fail* predicate causes backtracking to the next clause that might satisfy the goal.

Figure 4.3 shows how the Cities program works. The figure shows 10 predicates, each of which is a variant clause of the predicate *cities(name)*. When the program's goal is attempted, Turbo Prolog's internal unification routines instantiate the variable *City* with the object of the first clause, which is *ANN ARBOR*. Because other clauses exist that can satisfy the subgoal *cities(City)*, a backtracking marker is left at the point marked 1 in the figure. The value *ANN ARBOR* is written to the screen.

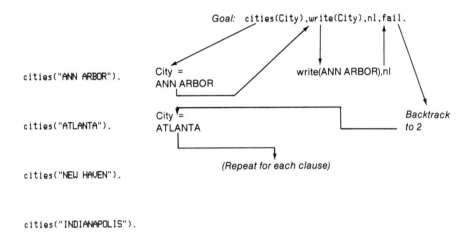

Fig. 4.3. *The working of the Cities program.*

The *fail* predicate causes the rule to fail, and Turbo Prolog's internal unification routines cause backtracking to point 1, and the process is repeated for all of the *cities* predicates. This process continues until the last clause is processed.

—————————————— **Exercises** ——————————————

4.1. Modify the Cities program so that the outputs on the screen are the integers 66, 46, 32, 93, 44, 98, 37, 21, 16, 12. Write one integer per line.

4.2. What modification is needed to write the integers on the same line with each number separated by two spaces?

Using the BAF method as illustrated in the Cities program allows you to retrieve data from every clause in the database. If there are 10 variant clauses, there are 10 output lines. The data from every clause is retrieved because each variant clause satisfies the subgoal *cities(City)*. But by imposing a condition on one or more values of the object variables in the predicate, you can retrieve data from selected clauses. The Employees program, in listing 4.2, demonstrates this method.

```
/* Program: Employees    File: PROG0402.PRO */
/* Purpose: To show the use of selective    */
/*          rules using BAF method.          */

domains

   name, sex, department = symbol
   pay_rate              = real

predicates

   employee(name,sex,department,pay_rate)
   show_male_part_time
   show_data_proc_dept

goal

   write(" Male Part Time Employees"),
   nl, nl,
   show_male_part_time.

clauses

   employee("John Walker    ","M","ACCT",3.50).
   employee("Tom Sellack    ","M","OPER",4.50).
   employee("Betty Lue      ","F","DATA",5.00).
   employee("Jack Hunter    ","M","ADVE",4.50).
   employee("Sam Ray        ","M","DATA",6.00).
   employee("Sheila Burton ","F","ADVE",5.00).
   employee("Kelly Smith    ","F","ACCT",5.00).
   employee("Diana Prince  ","F","DATA",5.00).

   /* rule to create a list of male */
   /*          employees            */

   show_male_part_time :-
       employee(Name,"M",Dept,Pay_rate),
       write(Name,Dept,"  $ ",Pay_rate), nl,
       fail.

   /* rule to create a list of employees */
   /*    in data-processing department    */
```

```
show_data_proc_dept :-
    employee(Name,_,"DATA",Pay_rate),
    write(Name,"   $ ",Pay_rate), nl,
    fail.
```

The clauses in the Employees program contain data about a company's part-time employees. The database predicate is

```
employee(name, sex, department, pay_rate)
```

This is a rule to write the contents of the whole database:

```
show_all_part_time_employees :-
    employee(Name, Sex, Dept, Pay_rate),
    write(Name, " ", Sex, " ", Dept, " ", Pay_rate),nl,
    fail.
```

The variables *Name*, *Sex*, *Dept*, and *Pay_rate* are unbound, so they are all instantiable. If this rule were the goal for the program, the output of the program would be a list of all part-time employees.

Suppose, however, that you want to create an output list showing data for male employees only. This requires that the matching process for the *sex* values take place only for clauses that contain *M* in the second object position. You will recall from Chapter 2 that a constant only matches itself. The constant value *M* only matches *M* during internal unification. Any other constant value bound to the variable *sex* will not match *M*. Here is a rule for imposing such a condition on the data that is retrieved:

```
show_male_part_time :-
    employee(Name, "M", Dept, Rate),
    write(Name, Dept, " $", Rate),
    nl,
    fail.
```

An alternative form of the sex-selection condition is the equality predicate: *Sex* = *M*. Using this equality predicate, you can construct a different rule having the same output:

```
show_male_part_time :-
    employee(Name, Sex, Dept, Rate),
    Sex = "M",
    write(Name, Dept, " $", Rate),nl,
    fail.
```

Notice that some subgoals fail both of these rules due to failure to match the *sex* condition. Backtracking then occurs before the information contained in the fact can be written to the screen. The *fail* predicate will not be needed in the case of failure to match the rule's conditions because the subgoal fails on its own. The *fail* predicate is included in the rule to force backtracking when the rule's conditions are met and the rule succeeds.

The screen output for this program is shown in figure 4.4.

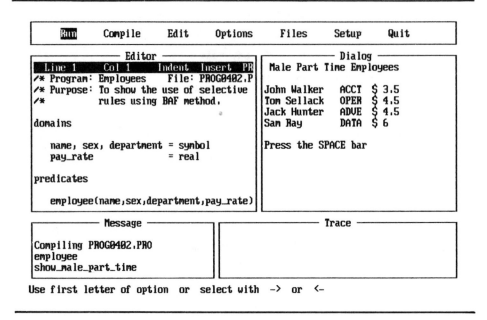

Fig. 4.4. *The output of the Employees program.*

Now suppose that you want to create a list of part-time employees who work in the Data Processing department. In this case, the condition to be imposed on the object variable *department* is that its value be *DATA*. Two rules that would achieve that result are

```
show_list_data_proc :-
    employee(Name, Sex, "DATA", Rate),
    write(Name, Sex, "   $ ", Rate),nl,
    fail.

show_list_data_proc :-
    employee(Name, Sex, Dept, Rate),
    Dept = "DATA",
    write(Name, Sex, "   $ ", Rate),nl,
    fail.
```

The BAF method is useful in Turbo Prolog programming for business data processing applications. Maintaining a payroll database, computing pay using data in the database, and creating a payroll report are typical data processing examples. The Payroll program, in listing 4.3, is an expansion of the Employees program.

```
/* Program: Payroll      File: PROG0403.PRO */
/* Purpose: To show rule construction and   */
/*          making report using BAF method. */

domains

   name, sex, department     = symbol
   pay_rate, hours, gross_pay = real

predicates

   employee(name,sex,department,
            pay_rate,hours)
   make_pay_roll_report
   compute_gross_pay(pay_rate,
                     hours,
                     gross_pay)

goal

   write(" Employees Payroll Report"),
   nl, nl,
   make_pay_roll_report.

clauses

   employee("John Walker   ","M","ACCT",3.50,40.00).
   employee("Tom Sellack   ","M","OPER",4.50,36.00).
   employee("Betty Lue     ","F","DATA",5.50,40.00).
   employee("Jack Hunter   ","M","ADVE",4.50,25.50).
   employee("Sam Ray       ","M","DATA",6.50,30.00).
   employee("Sheila Burton ","F","ADVE",5.50,32.50).
   employee("Kelly Smith   ","F","ACCT",5.50,25.50).
   employee("Diana Prince  ","F","DATA",5.50,20.50).
```

```
make_pay_roll_report :-
    employee(Name,_,Dept, Pay_rate,Hours),
    compute_gross_pay(Pay_rate,Hours,Gross_pay),
    write(Name,Dept," $ ",Gross_pay), nl,
    fail.

compute_gross_pay(Pay_rate,Hours,Gross_pay) :-
            Gross_pay = Pay_rate * Hours.
```

In the Payroll program, the predicate *employee* has five objects:

```
employee(name, sex, department, pay_rate, hours)
```

Because the objects *pay_rate*, *hours*, and *gross_pay* are of domain type real, decimal arithmetic operations can be performed on them. The rule to compute *gross_pay* is simple:

```
compute_gross_pay(Pay_rate, Hours, Gross_pay) :-
    Gross_pay = Pay_rate * Hours.
```

The purpose of the rule *make_pay_roll_report* is to create the report. It calls the rule *compute_gross_pay* for computing the gross pay. The output of the program is shown in figure 4.5.

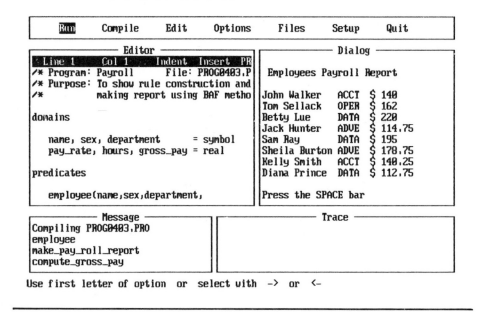

Fig. 4.5. *The output of the Payroll program.*

—————————————— **Exercises** ——————————————

4.3. For the Employees program, write a rule to create screen output listing all female part-time employees.

4.4. For the same program, write a rule to create a listing of all employees whose hourly rate is $5.00.

4.5. A shoe store records the number of shoes sold in a day. The sales data includes the item number, the sales price, the quantity of each shoe type sold, and the size. Design and develop a Turbo Prolog program that creates a sales report. Include tax in the gross sales amount, and assume that the tax rate is 6.5 percent.

The Cut and Fail (CAF) Method

In some programming situations, you need to access only a portion of a database. This might be the case when, for example, parts are inventoried as soon as they are received, or when orders are picked up in a random sequence. The Cut and Fail (CAF) method can be used to place limitations on the data that is extracted from database predicates.

The usefulness of this method becomes more obvious as more conditions are applied to the selection. For example, the CAF method makes it possible to list all orders that were picked up on June 18 or 19, that had B in the invoice number, and that were picked up before clerk Elaine Lark came on duty. By using the clerk's initials as a condition, the other information will be applied continually up to that time.

You've already seen how the *fail* predicate can cause backtracking to other possible solutions of a goal or subgoal. To place conditions on the data extracted from the database, you need to be able to control backtracking. Turbo Prolog has a built-in predicate, called *cut*, for that purpose. The symbol for the cut predicate is the exclamation point (!). This predicate, which always succeeds, causes the internal unification routines to "forget" any backtracking markers that have been placed during attempts to satisfy the current subgoal.

In other words, the cut predicate "puts up a barrier," preventing any backtracking to alternative solutions of the current subgoal. Subsequent subgoals may generate more backtracking markers and therefore opportunities to backtrack to more solutions; the cut will not prevent these subsequent backtrackings. However, if all later goals fail, the barrier put in place by the cut will cause the backtracking mechanism to take a short cut past the cut solutions by retreating immediately to some other possible solutions marked before the cut.

The Cut and Fail method uses the *fail* predicate to cause failure and backtracking until a specified condition is met; the cut predicate then serves to eliminate any further backtracking.

To see an illustration of the Cut and Fail method, consider a simple programming situation in which your database predicates contain several names, as do the *child* predicates of the Names program (listing 4.4). Suppose that you want to write a list of names up to and including the name Diana.

```
/* Program: Names        File: PROG0404.PRO   */
/* Purpose: To show the use of 'cut' predicate */
/*          (!) and the CAF Method.            */

domains

   person = symbol

predicates

   child(person)
   show_some_of_them
   make_cut(person)

goal

   write(" Boys and Girls "), nl,nl,
   show_some_of_them.

clauses

   child("Tom    ").
   child("Beth   ").
   child("Jeff   ").
   child("Sarah ").
   child("Larry ").
   child("Peter ").
   child("Diana ").
   child("Judy   ").
   child("Sandy ").

   show_some_of_them :-
        child(Name),
        write("    ",Name), nl,
        make_cut(Name), !.

   make_cut(Name) :-
        Name = "Diana ".
```

The *cut* predicate will make the cut at the specified place. To continue backtracking and accessing the database sequentially until you arrive at the name Diana, you use the *fail* predicate. Thus, a proper combination of the cut element and the *fail* predicate achieves the goal. This combination method is known as the *Cut and Fail (CAF) method*. The Names program illustrates this method.

In the Names program, the database predicate is *child(person)*. There are 9 variant clauses for this predicate. A rule to list all the names (not just some of them) looks like this:

```
show_all_of_them:-
    child(Name),
    write("   ", Name), nl,
    fail.
```

You will recognize that this rule is based on the BAF method. To introduce a cut, you need to define a condition. To understand the Cut and Fail method, it is important that you realize that the condition can be simple, as in this example, or quite complex. In this case, the simple condition *Name = Diana* will do. The rule to specify the condition is

```
make_cut(Name):-
    Name = "Diana".
```

This rule followed by the cut predicate (!) constitutes the *make_cut* rule. Now the program will fail and backtrack repeatedly until Name equals Diana. At this time the *make_cut* predicate will succeed, causing the cut predicate to be attempted. Thus, by combining the cut rule and the BAF method, you get the CAF rule:

```
show_some_of_them :-
    child(Name),
    write("   ",Name),nl,
    make_cut(Name),!.

make_cut(Name) :-
    Name = "Diana ".
```

The Names program incorporates the CAF rule. The working of this program is shown in figure 4.6, and the program output is shown in figure 4.7.

You can change the output listing by changing the value of the object name in the cut condition. For example, *Name = Beth* creates a listing up to and including the name Beth. This way of using the CAF method is known as *range cutting*.

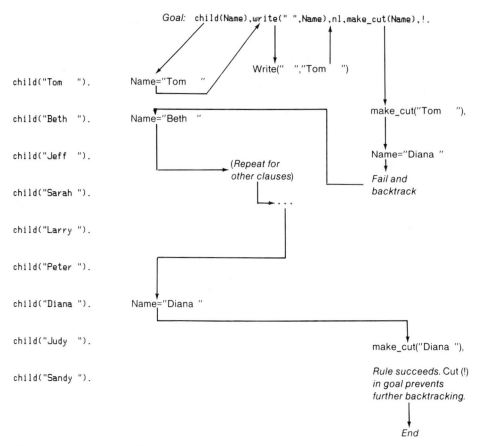

Fig. 4.6. *A diagram of the Names program.*

————————————————— **Exercise** —————————————————

4.6. Modify the *make_cut* rule in the Names program to create an output list of names including Peter.

You can use the CAF method in other ways. One way is to apply the rule to the processing of selected items. The program MoreNames, in listing 4.5, illustrates the use of the CAF method for creation of a list containing selected items from the database.

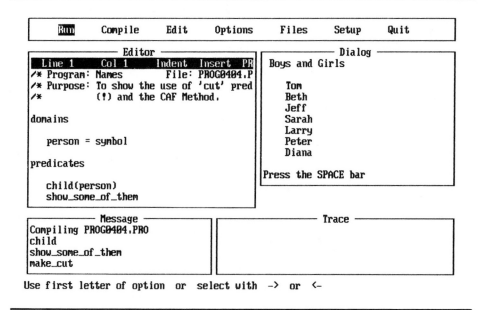

Fig. 4.7. *The output of the Names program.*

```
/* Program: MoreNames    File: PROG0405.PRO    */
/* Purpose: To show the use of 'cut' predicate */
/*          (!) and the CAF Method.            */

domains

   name = symbol

predicates

   child(name)
   go_and_get_them

goal

   go_and_get_them.
```

```
clauses

    child("Tom").
    child("Alice").
    child("Diana").
    child("Alice").
    child("Beth").
    child("Lee").
    child("Alice").


    go_and_get_them :-
        write(" Here is the list."),
        nl, nl,
        child(Name),
        Name = "Alice",
        write("  ",Name), nl,
        fail.
```

As in the program Names, the predicate *child(name)* in this program is a database predicate for a list of names. There are seven variant clauses for this predicate. Three of these clauses contain the name *Alice*. The rule that selects and writes the name *Alice* is the BAF-based rule:

```
get_alice :-
    child(Name),
    Name = "Alice",
    write("   ", Name),nl,
    fail.
```

Because the name Alice occurs three times in the database, the output of this rule is a list of three identical names, as shown in figure 4.8.

The *get_alice* rule finds all three possible instantiations of the *Name* variable. This is an application of the BAF method. Suppose that you wish to write only the first instance of the *Name* variable. To achieve this, you introduce a cut in the selective rule:

```
get_first_alice :-
    child(Name),
    Name = "Alice",
    write("   ", Name),nl,
    !,
    fail.
```

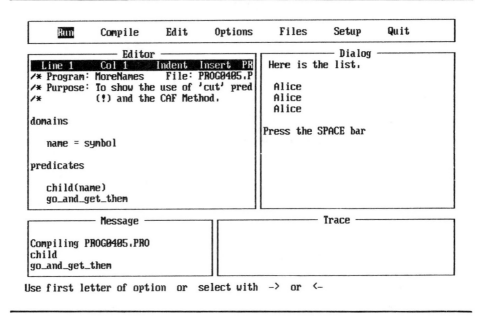

Fig. 4.8. The output of the MoreNames program.

The output of this rule is a list with a single *Alice*. The goal (rule) statement in the example program includes the elements of the rule *get_first_alice*. This rule can be used as an internal or external goal.

If you examine this rule closely, you will notice that the *fail* predicate is attempted only once. At the time it is allowed to work, the cut has already eliminated any backtracking. The result is a rather useless *fail* predicate. Bear in mind, however, that these backtracking and cutting techniques could be used in a variety of situations, so the rules are presented in a general form. You may find the general forms easy to modify for your specific needs when you employ these techniques in your own programs.

——————————————— **Exercise** ———————————————

4.7. For the program MoreNames:

A. Introduce a predicate that includes both first names and last names of some children. Use this predicate format:

```
child(first_name, last_name)
```

B. Extend the clauses to include the first and last names for all children.

    C. Write a rule to print the names of children whose last name is Smith.

    D. Write a rule to print the full name where the first name is Alice.

    E. Run your modified programs.

The User-Defined Repeat (UDR) Method

Like the CAF method, the UDR method also uses backtracking. The UDR method, however, makes backtracking always possible instead of forcing failure and subsequent backtracking. The General Recursive Rule method extends the same principles to a more complex structure.

The form of the user-defined repeat rule is

```
repeat.
repeat :- repeat.
```

The first *repeat* is a statement that establishes *repeat* as a valid predicate. Because the first *repeat* generates no subgoals, the rule always succeeds; because a variant of the rule exists, a backtracking marker is left at the first *repeat*. The second *repeat* is a rule that uses itself as the component (the third *repeat*). When the second *repeat* calls the third *repeat*, it succeeds because the first *repeat* satisfies the subgoal *repeat*. Consequently, the *repeat* rule always succeeds. Each time it is reached by backtracking, *repeat* will succeed by using the fact in the rule to satisfy all the subgoals of the program. This implies that *repeat* is a never-failing recursive rule.

The usefulness of the *repeat* rule is that it can be included as a component in other rules. As an example, consider the program Echoes, in listing 4.6. This program accepts string data from the keyboard and echoes it on the screen. When the user types *stop*, the program terminates.

```
/* Program: Echoes       File: PROG0406.PRO */
/* Purpose: To show the User Defined Repeat */
/*              (UDR) Method.                */
/* Remark: Repeatedly echo entered names.   */

domains
        name = symbol

predicates
        write_message
        repeat
        do_echo
        check(name)
```

```
goal
        write_message,
        do_echo.

clauses

        repeat.
        repeat :- repeat.

        write_message :-
                nl, write("Please enter names."), nl,
                write("I shall repeat them."), nl,
                write("To stop me, enter 'stop'."), nl, nl.

        do_echo :-
                repeat,
                readln(Name),
                write(Name), nl,
                check(Name),!.

        check(stop) :-
                nl,
                write("    - OK, bye !").

        check(_) :- fail.
```

The *repeat* rule is the first rule in the *clauses* division of the Echoes program. The second rule writes instructions for the user. The third rule, *do_echo*, is a user-defined repeat (UDR) rule; its first component is *repeat*:

```
do_echo :-
    repeat,
    readln(Name),
    write(Name),nl,
    check(Name),!
```

The presence of *repeat* causes all the following components of *do_echo* to be repeated. The predicate *readln(Name)* accepts string data from the keyboard. Then *write(Name)* writes (or "echoes") the strings to the screen.

The last subrule, *check(Name)*, has two possible meanings. One is specified by

```
check(stop) :-
    nl,write("    -OK, bye!").
```

If the string the user enters has the value *stop*, this rule succeeds; it moves the cursor to the beginning of the next line, writes the message *OK, bye!*, and stops the repeat process. Notice the cut symbol (!). It serves to stop backtracking when the *check* condition is met.

The other meaning of *check(Name)* is specified by this subrule:

```
check(Name) :-  fail.
```

This rule fails if the string has a value other than *stop*. The failure of this rule causes backtracking to the *repeat* rule. Thus, the *do_echo* is a finite repeat rule. It has an exit condition defined in the *check* predicate. By virtue of having a *repeat* rule as a component, *do_echo* becomes a finite repeat rule.

The output of this program is a dialogue between the running program and the user. A typical dialogue with the program is shown in figure 4.9.

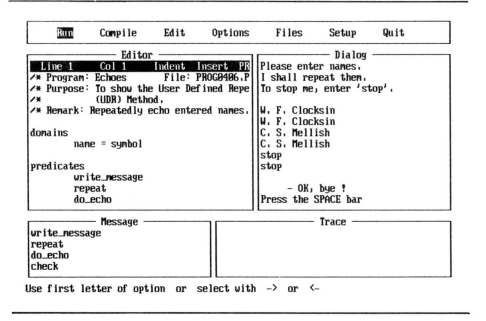

Fig. 4.9. *A dialogue with the Echoes program.*

In the Echoes program, the repeat rule is the first component of the *do_echo* rule. The repeat rule is very flexible in Turbo Prolog programming. You will see other uses of the *repeat* rule in later chapters of this book. By virtue of the repeat rule, the whole rule will repeat its defined repeat functions.

Also, you can use more than one repeat rule in a UDR rule. Here is a UDR using two repeat rules:

```
do_two_things :-
     repeat1,
     <repeating body>,
     <exit condition>,!,
     repeat2,
     <repeating body>,
     <exit condition>,!.

repeat1.
repeat1 :- repeat1.

repeat2.
repeat2 :- repeat2.

<rule for exit condition1>.

<rule for exit condition2>.
```

In defining the repeat rules, you may choose a rule name other than *repeat*. Here are a few good candidates for repeat rule examples:

```
loop.
loop :- loop.

loop1.
loop1 :- loop1.

loop2.
loop2 :- loop2.

iterate.
iterate :- iterate.

recurse.
recurse :- recurse.
```

The UDR method is useful in applications such as accessing data from databases and data files on disks. It is also used for screen outputs and menu constructions. You will see these applications in later chapters.

—————————————— **Exercises** ——————————————

4.8. Modify the Echoes program so that it accepts integer numbers from the keyboard and echoes them on the screen. Write your repeat rule so that the program terminates when the number 0 (zero) is entered. (The Turbo Prolog built-in predicate for reading integers from the keyboard is

```
readint(Number)
```

where *number* is the variable name for integers.)

4.9. Now modify the Echoes program so that it accepts two decimal numbers from the keyboard and echoes them to the screen. As a further modification, make the program compute the sum of the two entered decimal numbers and write the sum on the screen. Write your rule so that the program terminates when one of the numbers is 0 (zero). (The Turbo Prolog built-in predicate for reading decimal numbers from the keyboard is

```
readreal(number)
```

where *number* is the variable name for decimal numbers.) A rule to add two decimal numbers can be written as

```
sum(X, Y, Z):-
    Z = X + Y.
```

where *X, Y, Z* are variable names for decimal numbers.

Methods for Recursion

Building recursive rules without using repeat rules as components provides for a more generalized use of recursion in Turbo Prolog programming, for applications ranging from file handling to mathematical computations.

Simple Recursion

If a rule contains itself as a component, the rule is said to be *recursive*. Like repetitive rules, recursive rules provide means of performing tasks repeatedly. For example, they are useful in construction of queries for manipulating databases. And certain domain structures, such as lists, are best handled by recursive rules. Chapter 5 discusses Turbo Prolog lists and recursion.

Here is an example of a recursive rule:

```
write_string :-
    write("WE ARE THE WORLD"),
    nl,
    write_string.
```

This rule has three components. The first two components write the string *WE ARE THE WORLD* and move the cursor to the beginning of the next line. The third component is the rule itself. Because it contains itself, the rule *write_string* must satisfy itself in order to succeed. That calls again for writing the string and moving the cursor to the next line. This process goes on infinitely; the result is that the string is written an infinite number of times.

When infinite recursion occurs, the data items used by the recursive processes continue to grow. The stack will eventually overflow and an error message will be displayed. You would not want this overflow to happen during a program run, as valuable data could be lost in the process. Use the *Miscellaneous settings* option on the *Setup* menu to increase the size of the stack to accommodate extra demand due to recursion.

If the recursive rule generates no backtracking markers and the last subgoal of the rule is the recursive call to the rule itself, Turbo Prolog will eliminate the extra overhead caused by recursion. This process is known as eliminating tail recursion.

To avoid infinite recursion, you need to include a terminating predicate. This terminating predicate must contain what is known as an *exit condition*. An English statement of an exit condition for the *write_string* rule would be, "Keep on printing the string until the print count exceeds 7. Then terminate the process." Devising exit conditions and incorporating them into recursive rules are very important parts of Prolog programming.

The program ComeAgain, in listing 4.7, illustrates another simple recursive rule. In this program, the recursive rule has an exit condition.

```
/* Program: ComeAgain   File: PROG0407.PRO */
/* Purpose: To show building of a recursive */
/* predicate to read and write characters.  */

domains

   Char_data = char

predicates

   write_prompt
   read_a_character

goal

   write_prompt,
   read_a_character.
```

```
clauses

    write_prompt :-
        write("Please enter characters."), nl,
        write("To terminate, enter '#'."), nl, nl.


    read_a_character :-
            readchar(Char_data),
            Char_data <> '#',
            write(Char_data),
            read_a_character.
```

This program repeatedly accepts a character entered by the user. If the character is not #, it is written to the screen. If the character is #, the program terminates. The recursive rule is

```
read_a_character :-
    readchar(Char_data),
    Char_data <> '#',
    write(Char_data),
    read_a_character.
```

The first component of the rule is the built-in Turbo Prolog predicate to read a character. The character value is bound to the variable *Char_data*. The next subrule checks to see whether the character is #. If not, then the subrule succeeds, the character is written to the screen, and *read_a_character* is called recursively. This process will continue until the internal test finds the invalid # character. At this point the processing stops, and the program terminates.

———————————————— **Exercise** ————————————————

4.10. Run the program ComeAgain. At the *Goal:* prompt, enter this sequence of characters:

```
The early bird gets the worm.#
```

The General Recursive Rule (GRR) Method

A general recursive rule is, as you will recall, a rule that includes itself in the rule body. For finite recursion, it also includes an exit condition to ensure proper termination of the rule. The rule body may contain clauses and rules that specify the tasks to be performed by the rule.

The following rule shows symbolically the general form of a recursive rule:

<recursive rule name> :–
    <predicate list>,   (1)
    <exit condition predicate>,   (2)
    <predicate list>,   (3)
    <recursive rule name>,   (4)
    <predicate list>.   (5)

Although this rule structure is more complex than the simple recursive rules you examined in the last section, the same principles are applicable in this rule.

This recursive rule has five components. The first is a group of predicates. The success or failure of any one of these predicates does not cause recursion. The second component is an exit-condition predicate. The success or failure of this predicate either allows the recursion to go on or causes it to stop. The third component is another list of predicates. Again, the success or failure of these predicates does not influence the recursion. The fourth group is the recursive rule itself. The success of this rule involves recursion. The fifth group is a list of predicates, whose success or failure does not influence the recursion. The fifth group also receives values (if any) pushed onto the stack during the time that recursion was taking place.

Remember that the recursive rule must contain an exit condition. Otherwise, the recursion is infinite and the rule is not useful. It is your responsibility as a programmer to make sure that a recursive rule has an exit and that the rule terminates correctly. Rules constructed in this way are General Recursive Rules (GRR); this method is called the GRR method.

For example, suppose that you want a rule to write the integers starting with 1 and ending with 7. Let the rule name be

`write_number(Number).`

The first component in the general form of a recursive rule is not used in this example. The second component, an exit-condition predicate, is *Number* < 8. When the value of *Number* is 8, the rule succeeds and the program terminates.

The third component of this rule manipulates the number. In this case, the number is written and then incremented by 1. This incremented value will have a new variable name, *Next_number*. The fourth component is the recursive rule itself, *write_number(Next_number)*. The fifth group discussed in the general case is again not involved.

The WriteSeries program, in listing 4.8, uses this recursive rule:

```
write_number(8).
write_number(Number) :-
    Number < 8,
    write(Number),nl,
    Next_number = Number + 1,
    write_number(Next_number).
```

The program begins by trying to satisfy the subgoal *write_number(1)*. First the program matches the subgoal with the first rule, *write_number(8)*. Because 1 is not equal to 8, the matching fails. Then the program attempts to match the subgoal again, this time with the rule head *write_number(Number)*. This time the match succeeds, binding *Number* to 1. Then the program compares this value to 8; this is the exit condition. Because 1 is less than 8, the subrule succeeds. The next predicate writes the instantiated value of *Number*. The variable *Next_number* is instantiated to 2, the value of Number incremented by 1.

```
/* Program: WriteSeries    File: PROG0408.PRO  */
/* Purpose: To show recursion for writing a    */
/* sequence of numbers in ascending order.     */

domains
        number = integer

predicates
        write_number(number)

goal
        write("   Here are the numbers: "),
        nl, nl,
        write_number(1),
        nl, nl,
        write("          All done, bye!").

clauses

        write_number(8).
        write_number(Number) :-
                Number < 8,
                write("            ", Number), nl,
                Next_number = Number + 1,
                write_number(Next_number).
```

At this point, the rule *write_number* calls itself with the new value of the parameter, 2, instantiated to *Next_number*. Notice that it is not necessary to call the rule using the same variable name as appears in the rule head. It is the position in the parameter list that matters when values are passed. In fact, without sending the new variable *Next_number*, the incrementing of the central number of the program could not occur. On the recursive call to the rule head, the program again tries to satisfy the subgoal *write_number(8)*. The program completes cycles of matching, instantiation, and writing values of *Number* until the value of Number is 8. At this point, the subgoals are satisfied, the rule succeeds, and the program terminates after writing All done, bye!.

The output of this program is a list of integers displayed on the screen, as shown in figure 4.10.

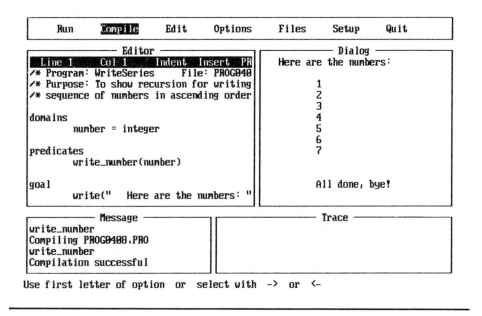

Fig. 4.10. *The output of the WriteSeries program.*

Exercises

4.11. Modify the program WriteSeries to produce an output of all integers from 53 to 62.

4.12. Modify the subgoal and the recursive rule so that the output of the program is a display of integers from 1 to 7 in descending order.

An important feature of the recursive rule is that it is expandable. For example, it can be expanded to compute the sum of a series of integers.

The program SumSeries1, in listing 4.9, uses a recursive rule to compute the sum of a series of integer numbers from 1 to 7:

$S(7) = 1 + 2 + 3 + 4 + 5 + 6 + 7 = 28$

or

$S(7) = 7 + 6 + 5 + 4 + 3 + 2 + 1 = 28$

The recursive rule in the program carries out the computation in a longhand addition format:

1	*Starting value*
+2	*Next value*
—	
3	*Partial Sum*
+3	*Next value*
—	
6	*Partial Sum*
. . .	

The recursive rule is

```
sum_series(1,1).
sum_series(Number, Sum) :-
    Number > 0,
    Next_number = Number - 1,
    sum_series(Next_number, Partial_Sum),
    Sum = Number + Partial_Sum.
```

This rule has four components and one auxiliary nonrecursive rule. Notice that the last component of the recursive rule is the *Sum* rule with *Partial_Sum* as a variable. This *Sum* rule cannot be satisfied until *Partial_Sum* is instantiated to some value.

```
/* Program: SumSeries1  File: PROG0409.PRO  */
/* Purpose: To show building of a recursive */
/* predicate to find sum of a series S,     */
/* S(N), where N is a positive integer.     */
/* Example:   S(7) = 7+6+5+4+3+2+1 = 28     */
/* Direction: Run the program. A goal       */
/*            statement is included.         */
```

```
domains

    number, sum = integer

predicates

    sum_series(number, sum)

goal

    sum_series(7, Sum),
    write(" Here is the sum:"), nl, nl,
    write("      S(7) = ", Sum), nl.

clauses

    sum_series(1,1).
    sum_series(Number,Sum) :-
        Number > 0 ,
        Next_number = Number - 1 ,
        sum_series(Next_number,Partial_Sum),
        Sum = Number + Partial_Sum.
```

The program SumSeries1 begins by attempting to satisfy the subgoal *sum_series(7,Sum)*. First, the program tries to match the subgoal with the subrule *sum_series(1,1)*. The matching fails. Then, it attempts to match the subgoal with *sum_series(Number,Sum)*. This time the match succeeds, instantiating *Number* to 7. Then, the program compares the value of *Number*, which is 7, to 0, the exit condition. Since 7 is greater than 0, the matching succeeds, and the program goes to the next subrule.

For this rule, the variable *Next_number* is instantiated to 6, the value of *Number* – 1. Next, the rule calls itself, in the form *sum_series(6,Partial_Sum)*. The next subrule is the *Sum* rule, which contains a free variable, *Partial_Sum*. Because the recursion process has already been invoked, the *Sum* rule cannot be satisfied.

The program now attempts to match the fixed rule *sum_series(1,1)* with *sum_series(6,Partial_Sum)*. This matching process fails, because neither parameter matches. So, it goes to match the latter rule with the rule head *sum_series(Number,Sum)*, instantiating *Number* to 6.

The cyclic matching process continues until *sum_series(1,Partial_Sum)* is obtained. This rule now matches *sum_series(1,1)*, instantiating *Partial_Sum* to 1. On matching the rule to the rule head, the variable *Sum* is instantiated to 1. As the matching continues further, the variable *Next_number* is instantiated to 0 (1 − 1). On the next matching cycle, the variable *Number* is instantiated to 0. On matching with the exit condition, the rule fails and the matching "jumps" to the *Sum* rule.

During the matching processes in which the variable *Partial_Sum* is free, the program stores the values of *Number* for later use. The rule continues to instantiate the *Sum* rule, giving the Sum the successive values 1, 3, 6, 10, 15, 21, and 28. The final value of *Sum* therefore is 28. The output of the program is shown in figure 4.11.

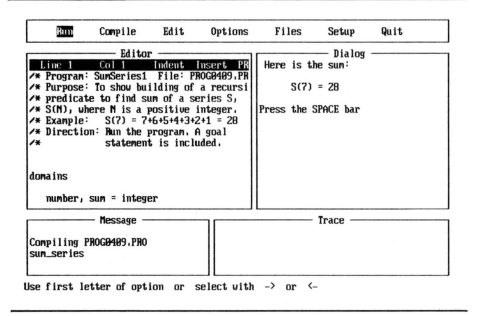

Fig. 4.11. *The output of the program SumSeries1.*

Exercises

4.13. Modify the program SumSeries1 so that its output is the sum of this odd series:

S(15) = 1 + 3 + 5 + ... + 15

4.14. Develop a table of entries for the program SumSeries1, showing the working of the recursive rule.

The program SumSeries2, shown in listing 4.10, is a modification of SumSeries1. The modification is accomplished by removing the exit condition *Number > 0* and inserting the rule

```
sum_series(1,1) :-!.
```

in place of the rule *sum_series(1,1).*

```
/* Program: SumSeries2  File: PROG0410.PRO  */
/* Purpose: To show building of a recursive */
/* predicate to find sum of a series S,     */
/* S(N), where N is a positive integer.     */
/* Example:   S(7) = 7+6+5+4+3+2+1 = 28     */

domains

    number, sum = integer

predicates

    sum_series(number,sum)

goal

    sum_series(7,Sum),
    write(" Here is the sum:"), nl, nl,
    write("      S(7) = ", Sum), nl.

clauses

    sum_series(1,1) :- !.
    sum_series(Number,Sum) :-
        Next_number = Number - 1 ,
        sum_series(Next_number,Partial_Sum),
        Sum = Number + Partial_Sum.
```

Compare the recursive rule from the preceding program to the modified recursive rule in SumSeries2:

SumSeries1 Recursive Rule

```
sum_series(1,1).
sum_series(Number, Sum) :-
    Number > 0,
    Next_number = Number - 1,
    sum_series(Next_Number, Partial_Sum).
```

SumSeries2 Recursive Rule

```
sum_series(1, 1,) :- !.
sum_series(Number, Sum) :-
    Next_number = Number - 1,
    sum_series(Number, Partial_sum).
```

The outputs of the two recursive rules are the same. The use of cut (!), as in SumSeries2, does not improve the working of the recursive rule. The two rules should be regarded as alternative forms of one another.

—————————————————— **Exercises** ——————————————————

4.15. Modify the program *SumSeries2* so that it computes the sum of this series of even integers:

$$S(16) = 2 + 4 + 6 + 8 + 10 + 12 + 14 + 16.$$

4.16. Make a table of entries for the preceding program, showing the working of the recursive rule.

The Factorial! program, in listing 4.11, uses a recursive rule to compute and print the factorial of an integer number. (The factorial of a number N is written as N!. The exclamation point is conventional notation for the factorial and should not be confused with the symbol for the cut.) N! is the product of all integer numbers between 1 and N:

$$N! = N * (N–1) * (N–2) * . . . 2 * 1$$

```
/* Program: Factorial!  File: PROG0411.PRO  */
/* Purpose: To show recursion, by showing a */
/* procedure to find factorial of a         */
/* positive integer N, N!. The procedure    */
/* uses a "cut" to prevent backtracking.     */
/*    Example: 7! = 7*6*5*4*3*2*1 = 5040     */

domains

    number, product = integer

predicates

    factorial(number,product)
```

```
goal

    factorial(7,Result), nl,
    write("   7! = ", Result), nl.

clauses

    factorial(1,1) :-  !.
    factorial(Number,Result) :-
      Next_number = Number - 1 ,
      factorial(Next_number,Partial_factorial),
      Result = Number * Partial_factorial.
```

Here are examples:

```
1! = 1
2! = 2 × 1 = 2
3! = 3 × 2 × 1 = 6
4! = 4 × 3 × 2 × 1 = 24
5! = 5 × 4 × 3 × 2 × 1 = 120
6! = 6 × 5 × 4 × 3 × 2 × 1 = 720
7! = 7 × 6 × 5 × 4 × 3 × 2 × 1 = 5040
```

The fundamental structure of the recursive rule to compute the factorial of a number is the same as that of the recursive rule in the preceding program. For the summation of a series, you use a continued sum. This summing is carried on throughout the recursion. For factorial computation, you use a continued product (the result of a multiplication). This value is developed when values are returned from the stack as parameter lists to the last subrule after recursion has stopped. The recursive rule for factorial computation is

```
factorial(1, 1) :- !.
factorial(Number, Result) :-
    Next_number = Number - 1,
    factorial(Next_number, Partial_factorial),
    Result = Number * Partial_factorial.
```

The output of the program is 7! = 5040.

—————————————————— **Exercise** ——————————————————

4.17. Modify the Factorial! program so that it computes and displays the factorial of 10. The factorial of 10 is 3,628,800. *Hint:* Use the real number domain for computation. The result is too large to be stored in a variable of type *integer*. Turbo Prolog places the upper limit of the integer domain at 32767.

Chapter Review

In this chapter four methods of building rules were discussed: the Backtrack After Fail (BAF) method, the Cut and Fail (CAF) method, the User-Defined Repeat (UDR) method, and the General Recursive Rule (GRR) method.

With the BAF method, you learned to use the built-in *fail* predicate to control Turbo Prolog's backtracking mechanism. You learned by examining example programs as well as graphical representations of the workings of the rule.

The introduction to the CAF method showed the use of the cut element (!), which is a built-in feature of Turbo Prolog. And in discussion of the UDR method, you saw how Turbo Prolog's inherent ability to perform recursion works in the user-defined recursive rule. You also learned how to call this rule from within other rules.

Finally, the GRR method of building recursive rules was presented. The discussion included applications of these rules in typical programming situations. The examples included printing sequences of integer numbers, summation of series, and finding factorials of integer numbers. You will find that you will utilize these methods of building rules from this point on. They are powerful tools that you will use frequently in constructing your programs.

5

Using Lists

Overview

In Chapter 3, you worked with a basic framework for data representation in Turbo Prolog. This framework consists of clauses, whose objects are data values. Turbo Prolog also supports related objects called *lists*. A list is an ordered set of objects in sequence. The objects in a list are linked internally so that they can be accessed as a group (the list as a whole) or as individual objects (the elements of the list).

Turbo Prolog enables you to perform several operations on lists. These operations include

- accessing the objects in a list

- discovering whether an object is a member of a list

- splitting one list into two lists

- combining two lists into a single list

- sorting elements of a list into ascending or descending order

Lists are useful in building knowledge bases (databases), expert systems, and symbol dictionaries, to name just a few uses. This chapter presents the structures, organization, and representation of lists and shows you some methods that you'll find useful in writing your own Turbo Prolog programs.

Lists and Turbo Prolog

A list is an ordered set of objects that are all of the same domain type. Objects in a list can be integers, real numbers, characters, symbols, or structures. The order is a distinctive part of the list; the same elements in a different order constitute a distinct list. This order is important in matching.

Turbo Prolog also allows lists whose elements are structures; if alternative domains are declared for the structures, then the domains can be of different types. Such lists have special uses and will not be discussed in this book.

A list is written with square brackets ([ ]) enclosing the object values and with commas separating the elements. These are examples of lists:

```
[1, 2, 3, 6, 9, 3, 4]
[3.2, 4.6, 1.1, 2.64, 100.2]
["YESTERDAY","TODAY","TOMORROW"]
```

The elements of the first list are integers. The second list is a list of real numbers. The third list is a list of symbols. The objects in the third list are strings; that is, the values are characters. Any printable ASCII character is legal in this type of list. (See Chapter 6 for more information on ASCII characters.)

Attributes of Lists

The objects in a list are called the *elements* of the list. A list can have any number of elements, limited only by available system memory.

Turbo Prolog requires that all the elements of a list be of the same domain type. In other words, the elements must be all integers, or all real numbers, or all characters, or all symbols. A list such as

```
["JOHN WALKER", 3.50, 45.50]
```

is not legal in Turbo Prolog because it has elements of different types. Lists of structures are exceptions to this rule.

The number of elements in a list is its length. The length of the list *["MA-DONNA","AND","CHILD"]* is 3. The length of the list *[4.50, 3.50, 6.25, 2.9, 100.15]* is 5.

A list can also contain a single element or no elements at all:

```
["SUMMER"]
[]
```

A list with no elements is called an *empty list* or *null list*. Later in this chapter, you'll see the usefulness of the empty list.

A non-empty list can be viewed as consisting of two parts: (1) the first element of the list, which is called the *head*; and (2) the remaining part of the list, which is called the *tail*. The head is an element of a list, and the tail is another list. The head is an individual value, which cannot be broken down further. The tail, however, is a list, consisting of what is left when the original list is decomposed into a head and a tail. This list often can be broken down into yet another list. A list with one element decomposes into a head consisting of that one element and a tail consisting of an empty list.

In the list

    [4.50,3.50,6.25,2.9,100.15]

for example, the head is the value 4.50; the tail is the list

    [3.50,6.25,2.9,100.15]

This list, too, has a head and a tail. The head is 3.50, and the tail is *[6.25,2.9,100.15]*.

Table 5.1 shows the heads and tails for several lists.

—————————————— **Table 5.1** ——————————————
List Heads and Tails

List	Head	Tail
[1,2,3,4,5]	1	[2,3,4,5]
[6.9,4.3,8.4,1.2]	6.9	[4.3,8.4,1.2]
[cat,dog,horse]	cat	[dog, horse]
['S','K','Y']	'S'	['K','Y']
["PIG"]	"PIG"	[]
[]	(Undefined)	(Undefined)

Graphic Representations of Lists

Graphic representations of lists are useful visual aids for the design of domain structures and databases in your Turbo Prolog programs. They are also used in program and software system documentation. This section discusses two ways to represent lists graphically.

The first type of list representation is the linear graph. Look at the following clause:

    number([66,84,12,32]).

The object of the *number* predicate is a four-element list. The head of the list is 66, and the tail is *[84,12,32]*. The order of the list proceeds from the head of the list on the left to the last element, 32, on the right. Figures 5.1 and 5.2 show graphic representations of this list.

Figure 5.1 represents the list of four integers as a directed linear graph of the order in which the elements of the list are linked together. The direction indicates the order in which the elements are accessed. This graphic representation is useful in visualizing the ordering of the elements within the list.

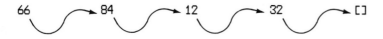

Fig. 5.1. *A directed linear graph of a list.*

Figure 5.2 is a binary tree graph (or simply a *binary tree*) representing the same list of four integers. The list functor, *number*, is the root of the tree. The root has two *branches*. The left branch terminates at a *leaf* with the value 66. The right branch terminates at a junction, called a *node*. This node has left and right branches. The left branch has a leaf with the value 84, and the right branch terminates at another node. This node has two branches. The left branch has a leaf with the value 12, and the right branch ends at another node. Again, the node has two branches. The left branch has a leaf with the value 32, and the right branch terminates at an empty list.

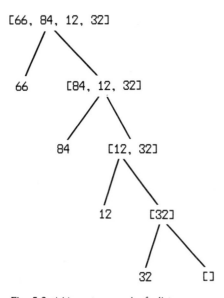

Fig. 5.2. *A binary-tree graph of a list.*

The order in which the elements are linked begins at the root position. The first element (leaf) on the left branch is linked next. The linkage then proceeds to the right branch where, at the node, another left branch goes to the next element, 4. This process continues until the last element, 32, is linked. There are no more elements to be linked, so the tree terminates by branching to a null list.

Turbo Prolog's internal unification routines follow the direction indicated by the graphs in figures 5.1 and 5.2. Turbo Prolog attempts to match the first element to a "head" element and then proceeds in a specific direction. The binary tree representation is particularly useful in visualizing Turbo Prolog's backtracking process as it moves along the branches of the tree.

—————————— **Exercises** ——————————

5.1. For the list

    games([football, soccer, tennis, baseball])

    A. Draw a linear graph. Use arrows to indicate the direction of linkage.

    B. Draw a binary tree. How many nodes does it have? Include the root.

5.2. Write a list whose elements are the names of as many of Snow White's dwarfs as you can remember. What is the length of the list?

5.3. Write a list whose elements are the names of 10 popular American sports.

5.4. Are these two lists the same? Why or why not?

    [63, 29, 24, 27, 86]
    [63, 24, 29, 27, 86]

5.5. Is the following named list "legal"? Why or why not?

    score(["Kennedy High School", 6, 3, 8, 9, 6.2])

5.6. Is the following named list "legal"? Why or why not?

    symbols(["*", "+", "-", "?", "#", "&"])

Using Lists in Your Programs

In order to use a list in a program, you need to declare a *list predicate*. Here are the preceding examples with list predicates:

```
num([1,2,3,6,9,3,4])
realnum([3.2, 4.6, 1.1, 2.64, 100.2])
time(["YESTERDAY","TODAY","TOMORROW"])
```

In these expressions, *num*, *realnum* and *time* are all list predicates. List predicates customarily are given meaningful names that indicate a characteristic either of the element type (such as *num*) or of the data (*junesales*).

To declare a list in a Turbo Prolog program, you need to make entries in three of the program divisions. The list domain must be declared in the *domains* division, and the the predicate that will have the list as an object must be declared in the *predicates* division. Finally, the list must be made accessible; in other words, the list itself must appear somewhere in the program. The list can appear either in a clause or in part of a goal statement. This section will show you how to create and use lists in your programs.

In the following list, each element is a bird name:

```
birds(["sparrow","robin","mockingbird","thunderbird",
    "bald eagle"])
```

If you use such a list in a Turbo Prolog program, you will want to use a logical, descriptive name such as *bird_name* for the domain of the list elements. As you know by now, the list may have many elements, one element, or none.

A list domain is declared in Turbo Prolog by placing an asterisk (*) after the domain name of the list elements. The notation

```
bird_name*
```

indicates that the domain is a list whose elements are *bird_name*. You can think of the *bird_name* notation as meaning "list of bird_name."

The declaration in the domains division, then, is

```
bird_list = bird_name*
bird_name = symbol
```

or

```
bird_list = symbol*
```

The domain *bird_list* is the domain for a list of symbols (your list of birds).

In the *predicates* division, the decalration consists of the predicate name followed by the domain name in parentheses:

```
birds(bird_list)
```

By now you are familiar with this form of predicate declaration; you can see that the declaration of a list predicate is no different from that of any other predicate.

The list itself appears in the *clauses* division of the program:

```
birds(["sparrow","robin","mockingbird","thunderbird",
    bald eagle"]).
```

Later in this chapter, you'll see how to use lists in the *goal* section of a program.

In addition to showing the creation of a list of birds, the Lists program, in listing 5.1, also includes the creation of a list of seven integers with the list variable name *number_list* and the predicate *score*.

```
/* Program: Lists  File: PROG0501.PRO */
/* Purpose: To manipulate lists      */
/* of objects.                       */

domains

    bird_list = bird_name *
                bird_name = symbol

    number_list = number *
                  number = integer

predicates

    birds(bird_list)
    score(number_list)

clauses

    birds(["sparrow",
           "robin",
           "mockingbird",
           "thunderbird",
           "bald eagle"]).

    score([56,87,63,89,91,62,85]).
```

The program has been constructed to accept external goals such as these:

```
birds(All).
birds([_,_,_,B,_]).
birds([B1,B2,_,_,_]).
score(All).
score([F,S,T,_,_,_,_]).
```

The following paragraphs will discuss the result of attempting each of these goals to clarify the way the lists are manipulated in Turbo Prolog programs.

The results with the goal *birds(All)* and other goals are shown in figure 5.3. Notice that the free variable *All* is bound to the list as a whole. The list is considered as a unit, and the elements are presented as parts of a whole.

For the second goal, *birds([_, _, _,B,_])*, the matching starts with the first element. The first three variables in the goal are anonymous, however, so the matching overlooks

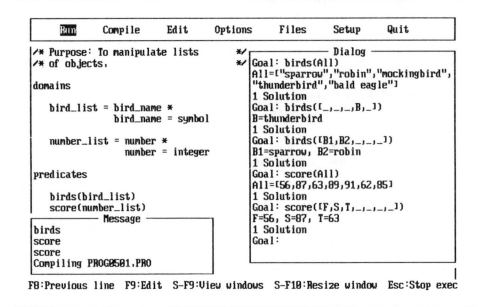

```
   Run     Compile     Edit     Options     Files     Setup     Quit

/* Purpose: To manipulate lists    */ ————— Dialog —————
/* of objects.                     */ Goal: birds(All)
                                      All=["sparrow","robin","mockingbird",
domains                               "thunderbird","bald eagle"]
                                      1 Solution
   bird_list = bird_name *           Goal: birds([_,_,_,B,_])
             bird_name = symbol       B=thunderbird
                                      1 Solution
   number_list = number *            Goal: birds([B1,B2,_,_,_])
             number = integer         B1=sparrow, B2=robin
                                      1 Solution
predicates                            Goal: score(All)
                                      All=[56,87,63,89,91,62,85]
   birds(bird_list)                   1 Solution
   score(number_list)                 Goal: score([F,S,T,_,_,_,_])
————— Message —————                   F=56, S=87, T=63
birds                                 1 Solution
score                                 Goal:
score
Compiling PROG0501.PRO
```

F8:Previous line   F9:Edit   S-F9:View windows   S-F10:Resize window   Esc:Stop exec

Fig. 5.3. Results of running the program Lists with several goals.

these. The variable *B* is instantiated to the value *mockingbird*. The internal linkage of list elements is used in this process. The result of this goal-satisfying process is *B = thunderbird*.

The third goal, *birds([B1,B2,_,_,_])*, commands two elements in the specific order shown. The output is B1=sparrow, B2=robin, the first and second elements in the list.

Now look at the second part of the program, which deals with lists of integers. The goal *score(All)* binds the whole list of integers to the variable *All*. The output is

    All=[56,87,63,89,91,62,85].

The fifth goal is *score([S1,_,_,S4,_,S6,_])*. The output is *S1=56, S4=89, S6=62*. As with the third goal, the elements, linked internally, are displayed selectively and in the order of their position in the list.

————————— **Exercises** —————————

5.7. Draw a linear graph of the list

    birds(bird_list).

5.8. Draw a tree graph of the list

score(number_list).

5.9. Run the Lists program, and enter the external goal statement

birds([S,R,M,T,B]).

What is the output? How does this output differ from the output of the goal *Birds(All)?*

Using the Head-Tail Method

In the Lists program, external goals were used to access elements of two lists. Entering a goal such as *birds(All)* caused an entire list to be bound to a variable. The goal *birds([_,_,_,B,_])* caused one element of the list to be bound to a variable. Notice that in order to access one element of the list by means of the goal *birds([_,_,_,B,_])*, you have to know the number of elements in the list that is the object of the predicate *birds*. If you enter the goal *birds([B1,B2,B3])*, the goal fails because the number of variables in the goal does not match the number in the list.

However, Turbo Prolog enables you to separate the first element from a list and process that element separately; this method works regardless of the number of elements in the list, as long as the list is not an empty (or null) list. The method for accessing the head of a list is called the Head-Tail Method.

Figure 5.4 shows the repeated separation of list heads and tails. In the list *[4, −9, 5, 3]*, the head is the element 4 and the tail is the list *[−9, 5, 3]*. The head of the tail is −9, and the tail of the tail is the list *[5, 3]*. This tail has the head 5 and the tail *[3]*. Finally, the head of this list is 3 and the tail is the null list, *[]*. Soon, you'll learn that the repeated separation of heads and tails is an important technique in Turbo Prolog programming.

The vertical bar symbol (|) separates the head and the tail, as in

[Head|Tail].

Head is a variable name for the head of the list. *Tail* is a variable name for the tail of the list. (Any legal Turbo Prolog name can be used for the head and tail variables.)

The program Head-Tail, in listing 5.2, illustrates the use of the Head-Tail Method. This program has declarations for two lists. The first is a list of integers, with the domain name *number_list*. The second list is a list of symbols, with the domain name *animal_list*. The rule *print_list* is used to access elements of both lists.

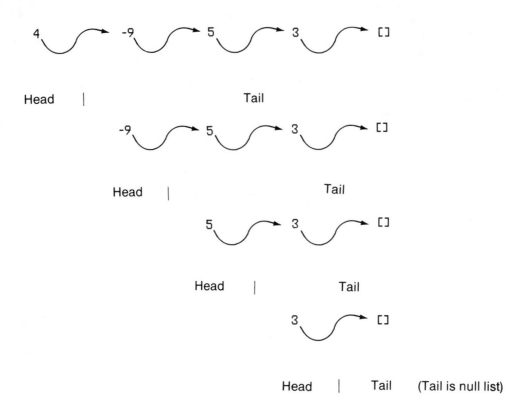

Head | Tail

Head | Tail

Head | Tail

Head | Tail   (Tail is null list)

Fig. 5.4. *The repeated separation of heads and tails.*

```
/* Program: Head-Tail   File: PROG0502.PRO */
/* Purpose: To manipulate and display lists */
/* with the Head/Tail Method.             */

domains

   number_list = integer *
   animal_list = symbol *

predicates

   print_list(number_list)
   print_list(animal_list)
```

```
clauses

    print_list([]).
    print_list([Head|Tail]) :-
            write(Head), nl,
            print_list(Tail).
```

The Head-Tail program uses the rule

```
    print_list([]).
    print_list([Head|Tail]) :-
        write(Head),nl,
        print_list(Tail).
```

to access the elements of the lists. Because the predicate *print_list* is declared for objects of both domains, the rule can be used for both kinds of lists.

When the rule *print_list* is attempted with the goal

```
    print_list([4, -9, 5, 3])
```

the first variant of the rule, *print_list([])*, fails because the object of that rule is the empty list. However, the list presented in the goal does match the object in the head of the second variant, *print_list([Head|Tail])*. The variable *Head* therefore is bound to the first element, 4; the variable *Tail* is bound to the rest of the list, *[-9, 5, 3]*.

Now that the first element of the list has been accessed, it can be processed just like any other simple object:

```
    write(Head),nl,
```

Because the tail of a list is a list, the value bound to *Tail* can be used as the object of a recursive call to *printlist*:

```
    print_list(Tail)
```

When this subrule is attempted, *Tail* is bound to the list *[-9, 5, 3]*. Again the first variant fails and matching occurs with the second variant. The value of the first element, -9, is bound to *Head* and then written to the screen. This process is repeated for the tail *[5, 3]*.

Finally, when the last element, 3, is bound to *Head*, *Tail* is bound to the a null list. Now the object presented in the recursive call matches the object of the rule

```
    print_list([])
```

Because this variant has no recursive call, the goal succeeds. Thus this variant rule defines the terminating condition for the recursion of *print_list*. The variant enables *print_list* to succeed when repeated recursion has emptied the list.

A similar process occurs with the goal

```
print_list(["cat","dog","horse","cow"])
```

First, *cat* is bound to the variable *Head* and is written to the screen, and *Tail* is bound to *[dog, horse, cow]*. On successive recursions, the values *dog*, *horse*, and *cow* are written. Again, when *Head* is bound to the last symbol, *cow*, Tail is bound to the null list. The variant

```
print_list([])
```

succeeds, ending the recursion.

The results of running Head-Tail with the goals

```
print_list(["cat","dog","horse","cow"])
```

and

```
print_list([4, -9, 5, 3])
```

are shown in figure 5.5.

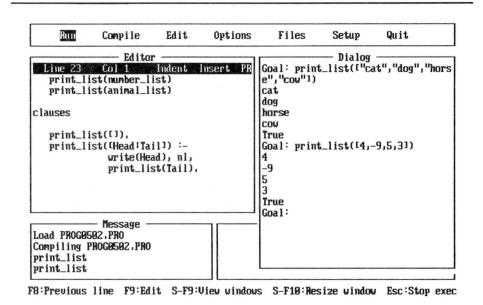

Fig. 5.5. *Output of the program Head-Tail.*

Recursive rules for accessing lists are simple, but very important. They can be used in many kinds of programs.

—————————————— **Exercises** ——————————————

5.10. For the list

["Boston", "Philadelphia", "Seattle", "Chicago"]

A. Draw a list-accessing diagram for the Head-Tail Method.

B. Write the successive values of the head? Write them down.

C. Write a recursive rule that writes each element of a list to the screen with two spaces between elements.

List Manipulations

The manipulations that can be performed on data items in lists include searching for an element in a list, splitting one list into two lists, appending a list to another list, sorting lists and collecting data from a database into a list. This section introduces programming techniques for those operations.

Searching in Lists

Often you will want to search for an element in a list. Searching a list entails looking for a match between a data item (the *search object*) and an element in a target list. If a match is found, the search succeeds; otherwise, the search fails. The result of a search, like the result of other Turbo Prolog operations based on the unification of terms, is always either a success or a failure.

To associate a candidate search element with the target list, you need a predicate whose objects are the search object and the list, such as

```
find_it(3,[1,2,3,4,5]).
```

The first object, 3, is the search object. The second object is the list *[1,2,3,4,5]*.

The Head-Tail method can be used to access an element of a target list and compare it to the search object. The search strategy is to recursively access the heads of the list and to compare each head with the search element.

As in the Head-Tail program, on each recursion, the tail becomes a new list whose head is bound to a variable for comparison with the search object.

A search rule must compare the search object and the head of the current list. The comparison can be written as

```
find_it(Head,[Head|_]).
```

This fact implies a match between the search object and the head of the list. Notice that the tail of the list is bound to an anonymous variable. Because you are trying for a match between the search element and the head of the list, you are not concerned at this time with the contents of the tail. If the search object and the head do match, the result is a success. If not, the result is a failure. In other words, this clause succeeds if the search object matches the head of the list. If those two items are different, then this attempt will fail, and Turbo Prolog will backtrack, looking for another fact or rule with which it can attempt a match.

In case the search object and the head don't match, we need a rule that will take the next element in the list and make it available for comparison. Because the next item after the current head is the first item of the tail, we can present the current tail of the list as a new list, whose head is to be compared with the search object:

```
find_it(Head,[Head|_].
find_it(Head,[_|Rest]) :-
       find_it(Head,Rest).
```

If the rule *find_it(Head,[Head|_])* does not succeed, then backtracking occurs, and the second variant of *find_it* is attempted.

On this second occurrence of the predicate *find_it*, Turbo Prolog will unify terms with the rule head *find_it(Head,[_|Rest])*. Notice that now, the head of the list is matched with an anonymous variable. We're not concerned with the value of the head, because this rule would not be attempted if the head had matched the search object in the previous attempt with *find_it(Head,[Head|_])*. Now, we want to bind the tail of the list, not the head, to a variable so that Turbo Prolog can again attempt a match between the search object and the head of this new list. An attempt to satisfy the recursive subrule *find_it(Head,Rest)* causes Turbo Prolog to present the tail of the current list as the new current list.

Again, the list bound to the variable *Rest* is split into a head and a tail by the clause *find_it(Head,[Head|_])*. The process repeats until this clause either succeeds because a match is found or fails because the list is exhausted.

The Members program, in listing 5.3, illustrates the list-searching method. Because the predicate *find_it* is declared for both integer lists and symbol lists, this program works for both kinds of lists.

```
/* Program: Members  File: PROG0503.PRO */
/* Purpose: To search for a          */
/* member in a list.                 */
```

```
domains

    number_list = number *
                  number = integer
    member_list = member *
                  member = symbol

predicates

    find_it(number, number_list)
    find_it(member, member_list)

clauses

    find_it(Head, [Head|_]).
    find_it(Head, [_|Tail]) :-
                find_it(Head, Tail).
```

With the goal

```
find_it(3,[1,2,3,4,5]).
```

the first variant of the rule attempts to match the head of the list, 1, with the search element, 3. Because 1 is not equal to 3, the rule fails. The matching proceeds to the next head of the list, 2, which also fails. On the next matching of the search element, 3, with the head of the list, now also 3, the matching succeeds. **True** appears on the screen, indicating the success of the matching process, that there is a 3 in the list.

Figure 5.6 shows a search diagram for the first external goal. As you have seen, there is only one match for this list.

The goal

```
find_it(1,[2,3,4,5]).
```

fails because the element 1 is not in the target list. The goal

```
find_it("Alice",["Diana","Peter","Paul","Mary","Alice"]).
```

succeeds because the list contains the element *Alice*, and the goal

```
find_it("Toledo",["Cleveland","Dayton","Chardon",
                  "Youngstown","Cincinnati"]).
```

fails.

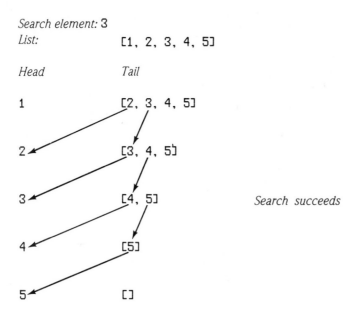

Search element: 3
List: [1, 2, 3, 4, 5]

Head   *Tail*

1   [2, 3, 4, 5]

2   [3, 4, 5]

3   [4, 5]   *Search succeeds*

4   [5]

5   []

Fig. 5.6. *A search diagram.*

————————————— **Exercise** —————————————

5.11. Draw a search diagram for this search using the following external goal:

    find_it(44,[11,22,33,44,11,22,33,44,11,22,33,44,55]).

In how many cases does the goal succeed?

Splitting Lists

Often you will need to split a list into two or more lists. Doing so might be necessary when only part of an original list is needed for the current processing task, for example, and the rest of the list is to be set aside for the time being. You'll find that splitting a list into two lists is very easy.

For this example, we'll consider an action predicate called *split*, whose arguments are one list element and three lists:

    split(Middle,L,L1,L2).

The element *Middle* is a comparator; *L* is the source list, and and *L2* are two sublists obtained by splitting *L*. If an element of the source list is less than or equal to *Middle*, the element is put into *L1*. If the element is greater than *Middle*, it is put in *L2*.

Assume that at the start, the variable M is bound to the value 40, the variable L is bound to the list *[30,50,20,25,65,95]*, and the variables *L1* and *L2* are originally unbound:

```
split(40,[30,50,20,25,65,95],L1,L2).
```

The splitting rule is to be written so that all the values of the source list that are less than or equal to *Middle* are to be placed in *L1*, and those that are greater than 40 are to be placed in *L2*.

The Head-Tail Method is used to access the first element of the list *L*, and this element is compared to the midvalue *Middle*. If the value of the element is less than or equal to the midvalue, the element is put in list *L1*. If the value of the element is greater than the midvalue, the element is put in *L2*. The tail of *L* becomes the new list *L*, and this process is repeated until all elements have been placed in *L1* or *L2*. Figure 5.7 shows the contents of the objects *Middle*, *L*, *L1*, and *L2* as the list *L* is being split.

Midvalue: **40**
L: [30, 50, 20, 25, 65, 95]
L1:   []
L2:   []

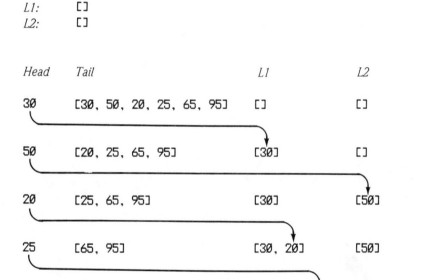

Fig. 5.7. A diagram of the list-splitting operation.

The output of the clause after splitting the list is

```
split(40,[],[30,20,25],[50,65,95]).
```

The resulting lists *L1* and *L2* therefore are *[30,20,25] and [50,65,95]*.

A Turbo Prolog rule to split a list is

```
split(Middle,[Head|Tail],[Head|L1],L2) :-
    Head <= Middle,
    split(Middle, Tail, L1, L2).
split(Middle,[Head|Tail],L1,[Head|L2]) :-
    split(Middle, Tail, L1, L2),
    Head > Middle.
split(_, [], [], []).
```

Notice that this rule uses the head-tail method both to split the source list and to combine elements in the output lists.

This list-splitting rule works for any legal data type in Turbo Prolog. If the list is an integer list, then the list elements and the value *Middle* are declared as integers. If the lists are symbol lists, then the list elements and *Middle* are declared as symbols.

The program SplitList, in listing 5.4, incorporates a list-splitting rule. Try this program with the external goal

split(40,[30,50,20,25,65,95],L1,L2).

The outputs of the program are shown in figure 5.8.

```
/* Program: SplitList    File: PROG0504.PRO */
/* Purpose: To split a list into two lists. */

domains

    middle = integer
    list = integer *

predicates

    split(middle,list,list,list)
```

```
clauses

    split(Middle,[Head|Tail],[Head|L1],L2) :-
        Head <= Middle,
        split(Middle, Tail, L1, L2).
    split(Middle,[Head|Tail],L1,[Head|L2]) :-
        split(Middle, Tail, L1, L2),
        Head > Middle.
    split(_, [], [], []).
```

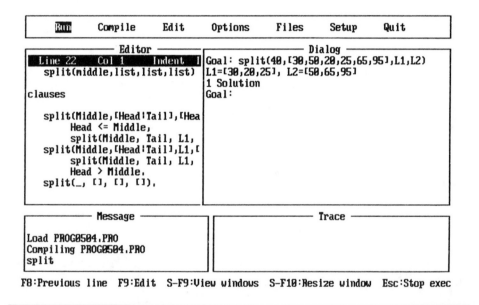

Fig. 5.8. *Output of the program SplitList.*

Exercise

5.12. For the program SplitList:

A. Enter this external goal:

split(12,[96,32,8,16,55,12],L1,L2).

Write down the elements of L1 and L2.

B. Draw a diagram showing the contents of the lists as source list is split (see figure 5.7).

Appending Lists

Combining two lists to form a third list is among the most useful of operations performed on lists. This process is known as *appending* one list to another. The method presented in this section is useful in applications such as database management systems. It is also useful in the construction of user interfaces. In fact, you'll find it useful in almost any Turbo Prolog program that requires manipulation of lists.

As an example, consider two list variables, *L1* and *L2*, which are bound to the values *[1,2,3]* and *[4,5]*. These are called the *input lists*. A predicate to append *L2* to *L1*, creating an output list *L3*, must move the elements of *L1* and *L2* to *L3*. The process can be performed as follows:

1. List *L3* is initially empty.

2. Move the elements of *L2* into *L3*, so that *L3* contains *[1,2,3]*.

3. Move the elements of *L1* into *L3*, so that *L3* contains *[1,2,3,4,5]*.

The rule to append lists in this manner has a simple structure:

```
append([],L,L).
append([NIL1],L2,[NIL3]) :-
     append(L1,L2,L3).
```

The following discussion will illustrate how this rule works for the case of the input lists *L1* and *L2*.

Turbo Prolog first attempts to satisfy the first variant of this rule,

```
append([],L,L).
```

To satisfy this rule, the first list must become a null list. The initial form of the *append* rule is

```
append([1,2,3],[4,5],_)
```

Notice that the third list, *L*, is represented as an anonymous variable in this form. Turbo Prolog's internal unification process makes the first list a null list, moving each successive element of the list to a stack. The stack, a logical data structure in the memory, provides temporary storage for these elements.

When the first list becomes a null list, the third list is instantiated to the values of the second list. This process can be seen in the two *append* steps shown, before and after instantiation:

```
append([],[4,5],_)
append([],[4,5],[4,5])
```

At this point, Turbo Prolog's unification routines have completely satisfied the first *append* rule.

Then Turbo Prolog attempts to satisfy the second *append* rule,

```
append([NIL1],L2,[N,L3]) :-
      append(L1,L2,L3).
```

Turbo Prolog does this by removing elements from stack storage and placing them, one by one, as Head for the first list and the third list. Note that the value of the element taken from the stack is concurrently bound to the variable "N" in [N|L1] and [N|L3]. The first steps in this process are

```
append([],[4,5],[4,5])
append([3],[4,5],[3,4,5])
append([2,3],[4,5],[2,3,4,5])
append([1,2,3],[4,5],[1,2,3,4,5])
```

This binding process continues recursively for each element on the stack until none are left. The result of this process is that *L*, the third list, is bound to elements from the first list and the second list, so that *L* contains *[1,2,3,4,5]*.

The program AppendList, in listing 5.5, demonstrates this method. In this program, *n_list* is the domain for a list of integers. The action predicate to append one list to another is:

```
append(n_list,n_list,n_list).
```

The *clauses* division includes the *append* rule. The external goal is:

```
append([1,2,3],[4,5],L).
```

The output is shown in figure 5.9.

```
/* Program: AppendList   File: PROG0505.PRO */
/* Purpose: To append one list to another   */

domains

   n_list = integer *

predicates

   append(n_list,n_list,n_list)

clauses

   append([],L,L).
   append([NIL1], L2, [NIL3]) :-
                append(L1,L2,L3).
```

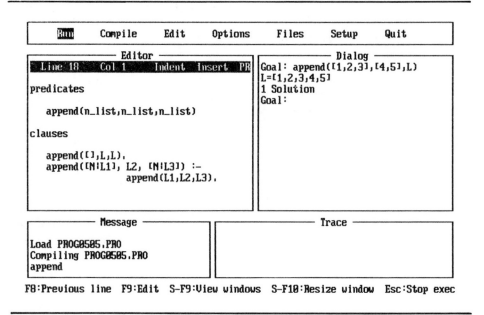

Fig. 5.9. Output of the program AppendList.

In this program, Turbo Prolog works very efficiently and relentlessly. Only a couple of program lines are required; in the background, Turbo Prolog creates the temporary lists and moves elements from one list to another. The beauty of this program is definitely behind the scenes. The programmer need not specify these tasks at all.

Rules for appending are important programming tools. The way they work can be confusing at first, so be sure to get some hands-on practice by doing the exercises.

—————— Exercises ——————

5.13. Run the program AppendList with this goal:

```
append([9,15,3,60,55],[15,2,21],L).
```

What is the output?

5.14. Draw a list-appending diagram for the preceding exercise.

Sorting Lists

Sorting is rearranging a set of list elements into a specific order. The purpose of sorting is to facilitate easy access to the sorted elements. Sorting is a fundamental activity in real life as well as in computer applications. Names are sorted in telephone books; Social Security account information is sorted in order by number; and mail is sorted by ZIP code, carrier route and house number.

Sorting data with computers is a routine but important activity. It is much easier and more efficient to search through a sorted list than through an unsorted list.

There are many ways of sorting a list. For example, consider a list of integers:

```
[51,23,84,17,11]
```

In this unsorted list, the elements are not arranged in any of the orders we commonly recognize. The same list, sorted in ascending order, is

```
[11,17,23,51,84].
```

A Turbo Prolog sorting rule accepts an unsorted list and produces a sorted list. The unsorted list is called the *source list*, and the sorted list is called the *target list*.

Three methods are most commonly used for sorting: the exchange sort, the insertion sort, and the selection sort. Sorting can be performed by one of these methods or a combination of them. The exchange sort entails repeatedly exchanging elements of the list until the whole list is in the desired order. The insertion sort is performed by repeatedly inserting elements into the list until the entire list is in the desired order. The selection sort involves repeated selection and placement of the elements of a list until the whole list is in the desired order.

The insertion sort is particularly easy to implement in Turbo Prolog. This section shows you how to implement a rule to perform an insertion sort.

Consider a list *[4,7,3,9]* of integers in random order. The desired list is *[3,4,7,9]*, in which the elements are placed in ascending order.

You can define the action predicate to do the insertion sort with this form:

```
insert_sort(source_list,target_list).
```

The external goal to do an insertion sort on the list *[4,7,3,9]* is

```
insert_sort([4,7,3,9],S).
```

In this goal statement, *S* is the variable name for the sorted list. To take advantage of the internal unification power of Turbo Prolog, you can do what is known as *tail sorting*. You will recall that a list can always be divided into a head and a tail. Before the first element of the list is bound to a head variable, the tail actually contains all the elements of the list. Sorting the tail therefore is the same as sorting the entire list.

Rules for this kind of insertion sort have the following structure:

```
insert_sort([],[]).
insert_sort([X|Tail],Sorted_list) :-
        insert_sort(Tail,Sorted_tail),
        insert(X,Sorted_Tail,Sorted_list).

insert(X,[Y|Sorted_list],[Y|Sorted_list]) :-
        asc_order(X,Y), !,
        insert(X,Sorted_list,Sorted_list1).
insert(X,Sorted_list,[X|Sorted_list]).

asc_order(X,Y) :- X > Y.
```

The following discussion will illustrate how this rule works for the source list *[4,7,3,9]*.

Turbo Prolog first specifies the *insert_sort* with the initial list. The target list is initially unbound:

```
insert_sort([4,7,3,9],_).
```

The first attempt is to satisfy the rule

```
insert_sort([],[]).
```

To satisfy this rule, the two lists must be null lists. The source list is treated as a head-tail combination. Turbo Prolog's unification routines will attempt to make the source list become a null list. The removal of the elements begins with the head of the list, and continues recursively.

The part of the rule that does the removal is

```
insert_sort([X|Tail],Sorted_list) :-

        insert_sort(Tail,Sorted_list).
```

As Turbo Prolog attempts to satisfy the first rule, *X* is bound to each successive element of the list, which is then placed on the stack. The source list is now a null list. The target list is then instantiated to a null list, giving the *insert_sort* rule the form

```
insert_sort([],[]).
```

When both lists become null lists, the first rule is satisfied.

Turbo Prolog attempts to satisfy the insertion process using the rule *insert*. On instantiating *X* to the value of the first element taken from the stack, 9, the insert rule assumes the form

```
insert(9,[],[9]).
```

On taking the next element from the stack, that is, 3, the internal unification process determines the order for insertion, using the ordering rule

```
asc_order(X,Y) :-
     X > Y.
```

The variable *X* is instantiated to 3, and *Y* is instantiated to 9. These instantiations give the rule the form

```
asc_order(3,9) :- 3 > 9.
```

This rule fails, because 3 is not greater than 9, and 3 is inserted on the left-hand side of 9 in the target list. The result is

```
insert(3,[9],[3,9]).
```

On returning to the *insert_sort* rule, the rule takes the form

```
insert_sort([3,9],[3,9]).
```

The next cycle of recursion inserts the element 7 from the stack. The rule states are

```
insert(7,[3,9],_)

asc_order(7,3) :- 7>3. (rule succeeds)
asc_order(7,9) :- 7>9. (rule fails)
```

The results of the matchings determine that 7 is inserted on the right side of 3 and to the left of 9. You will notice that this *insert* rule is also a recursive rule.

```
insert(7,[3,9],[3,7,9]).
```

The next cycle of recursion does insertion of the element 4 from the stack. The rule states are

```
insert(4,[3,7,9],_)

asc_order(4,3) :- 4 > 3. (rule succeeds)
asc_order(4,7) :- 4 > 7. (rule fails)
asc_order(4,9) :- 4 > 9. (rule fails)
```

The results of the matchings determine that 4 is inserted on the right side of 3 and on the left side of 7.

```
insert(4,[3,7,9],[3,4,7,9])
insert_sort([4,7,3,9],[3,4,7,9]).
```

Because there are no more elements for instantiation, the *insert_sort* recursion stops. The target list is now bound to the list *[3,4,7,9]*, and the goal is satisfied.

SortList, in listing 5.6, implements the insertion-sort rule for lists of integers. The program accepts external goals.

```
/* Program: SortList     File: PROG0506.PRO */
/* Book.                  Using Turbo PROLOG */
/* Purpose: To show sorting of a list of    */
/*          integers in ascending order,    */
/*          using an insertion sort rule.   */

domains

    number = integer
    list   = number *

predicates

    insert_sort(list,list)
    insert(number,list,list)
    asc_order(number,number)

clauses

        insert_sort([],[]).
        insert_sort([X|Tail],Sorted_list) :-
            insert_sort(Tail,Sorted_Tail),
            insert(X,Sorted_Tail,Sorted_list).

        insert(X,[Y|Sorted_list],[Y|Sorted_list1]) :-
            asc_order(X,Y), !,
            insert(X,Sorted_list,Sorted_list1).
        insert(X,Sorted_list,[X|Sorted_list]).

        asc_order(X,Y) :- X > Y.
```

Try this program with the external goals

```
insert_sort([4,7,3,9],S).
```

and

```
insert_sort([7,6,5,4,3,2,1],S).
```

The results of entering these goals are shown in figure 5.10.

```
        Run        Compile      Edit      Options      Files      Setup      Quit

 ──────────── Editor ────────────       ──────────── Dialog ────────────
  Line 1     Col 1     Indent  Insert  PR   Goal: insert_sort([4,7,3,9],S)
 /* Program: SortList     File: PROG0506.P    S=[3,4,7,9]
 /* Book.              Using Turbo PROL       1 Solution
 /* Purpose: To show sorting of a list of     Goal: insert_sort([7,6,5,4,3,2,1],S
 /*          integers in ascending order,     )
 /*          using an insertion sort rule.    S=[1,2,3,4,5,6,7]
                                              1 Solution
 domains                                      Goal:

   number = integer
   list   = number *

 predicates

 ──────────── Message ────────────       ──────────── Trace ────────────
 Compiling PROG0506.PRO
 insert_sort
 insert
 asc_order

 F8:Previous line  F9:Edit  S-F9:View windows  S-F10:Resize window  Esc:Stop exec
```

Fig. 5.10. Output of the program SortList.

─────────────────────────── **Exercises** ───────────────────────────

5.15. Run the SortList program. Enter this goal:

```
insert_sort([53,11,93,77,11],S).
```

What is the output?

5.16. Modify the SortList program so that you can sort the integers in descending order. Run your modified program. Enter this goal:

```
insert_sort([1,2,3,4,5,6,7],S).
```

What is the output?

Collecting Data into a List

Certain programming situations require that data from a database (variant data clauses) be collected for manipulation. Turbo Prolog provides a built-in predicate to do that task conveniently. It is the *findall* predicate. It creates a list as a bound variable which is one of its objects.

The *findall* predicate is predefined as

```
findall(Variable_name,Predicate_expression,List_name).
```

Variable_name denotes an object of the input predicate, which is represented by *Predicate_expression*. The object *List_name* is the variable name for the output list. *List_name* must belong to a user-defined list domain.

To make this concept more concrete, consider the database predicate

```
football(name,points)
```

This predicate has eight variant clauses:

```
football("Ohio State",116.0).
football("Michigan",121.0).
football("Michigan State",114.0).
football("Purdue",99.0).
football("UCLA",122.0).
```

These clauses constitute a database of team power-rating points.

You want to collect all the power-rating points and calculate the average. The specification for the *findall* predicate is

```
findall(Points,football(_,Points),Point_list).
```

The variable *Points* is a free variable for the power-rating points. *Point_list* is a list variable; its elements belong to the same domain as that of *Points*. In this case, the domain is *real*.

The built-in predicate *findall* does its work internally. In this example, it searches through the *football* clauses, starting with the first clause. The value of *Points* for this first clause, 116.0, is instantiated to the head of the list whose variable name is *Point_list*. Other *Points* values are placed at subsequent positions in the list. *Point_list* is bound to

```
[116.0,121.0,114.0,99.0,122.0]
```

when the *findall* predicate has completed its work.

A recursive rule is used to find the average of these values. The rule is

```
sum_list([],0,0).
sum_list([H|T], Sum, Number) :-
    sum_list (T,Sum1,Number1),
    Sum = H + Sum1,
    Number = Number1 + 1.
```

This rule resembles the *sum* rule in Chapter 4.

To get a sum of the values in the list *Score_list*, this rule is called by the subgoal

```
sum_list(Point_list, Sum, Number)
```

Turbo Prolog first matches the subgoal with the rule head *sum_list([H|T], Sum, Number)*. *Point_list* is matched with *[H|T]*, and the variables *Sum* and *Number* are not yet bound.

Then, Turbo Prolog attempts to satisfy the rule

```
sum_list([],0,0).
```

To accomplish this task, it makes the *Point_list* become a null list, moving each successive element of the list to a stack. Then, the variables *Sum* and *Number* are each instantiated to 0. Now, Turbo Prolog completely satisfies the first *sum_list* rule in the form shown above.

Turbo Prolog next attempts to satisfy the second *sum_list* rule. It does this by removing elements from the stack storage and placing them, one by one, as head of the list. In doing so, the variable *H* is instantiated to the element removed from the stack, the variable *Sum* is instantiated to the sum of the values of the head and a previous *Sum* value, and the variable *Number* is instantiated to the sum of 1 and the previous value of *Number*. These matching and instantiation cycles continue recursively, giving the results shown:

```
sum_list([122],122,1)

sum_list([99,122],221,1)

sum_list([114,99,122],335,3)

sum_list([121,114,99,122],456,4)

sum_list([116,121,114,99,122],572,5)
```

You will notice that at the termination of the *sum_list* rule, the variables *Sum* and *Number* are bound to 572 and 5, respectively.

The rule to find the average of the power ratings is simply

```
Average = Sum / Number
```

This *Average* rule is carried out first by passing the values of *Sum* and *Number* from the *Sum_list* rule to the *Average* rule. The *Average* rule performs the specified division operation and the variable *Average* is bound to the result, which is 114.4.

The program Points, in listing 5.7, uses the *findall* predicate to collect the points data from the database.

```
/* Program: Points      File: PROG0507.PRO */
/* Purpose: To show the use of "findall"    */
/*          predicate in computing average  */
/*          from data in a data base.       */

domains

  name    = string
  points  = real
  list    = points *

predicates

  football(name,points)
  sum_list(list,points,integer)
  report_average_football_score

goal

  report_average_football_score.

clauses

  /* facts (football data base) */

    football("Ohio State",116.0).
    football("Michigan",121.0).
    football("Michigan State",114.0).
    football("Purdue",99.0).
    football("UCLA",122.0).

  report_average_football_score :-
    findall(Points,football(_,Points),
          Point_list),
    sum_list(Point_list,Sum,Number),
    Average = Sum / Number,
    write("College Football Power Rating:"),
    nl,
    write("    Average Points = ",Average).
```

```
sum_list([],0,0).
sum_list([H|T], Sum, Number) :-
    sum_list(T,Sum1,Number1),
    Sum = H + Sum1,
    Number = Number1 + 1.
```

The Points program computes the sum and average of the point data. The internal goal is

`report_average_football_score`

This goal is used as a rule that contains the subgoals *findall*, *sum_list*, *Average* and predicates to write the average value in a "friendly" format.

To carry out the subgoals, the program begins by satisfying the *findall* subgoal, as described above. When this subgoal is satisfied, it continues to satisfy the *sum_list* and *Average* subgoals. At this stage, the value of *Average* is bound to 114.4, which is used in the *write* predicate. Because all subgoals are now satisfied, the goal succeeds and the program terminates. The output of the program is shown in figure 5.11.

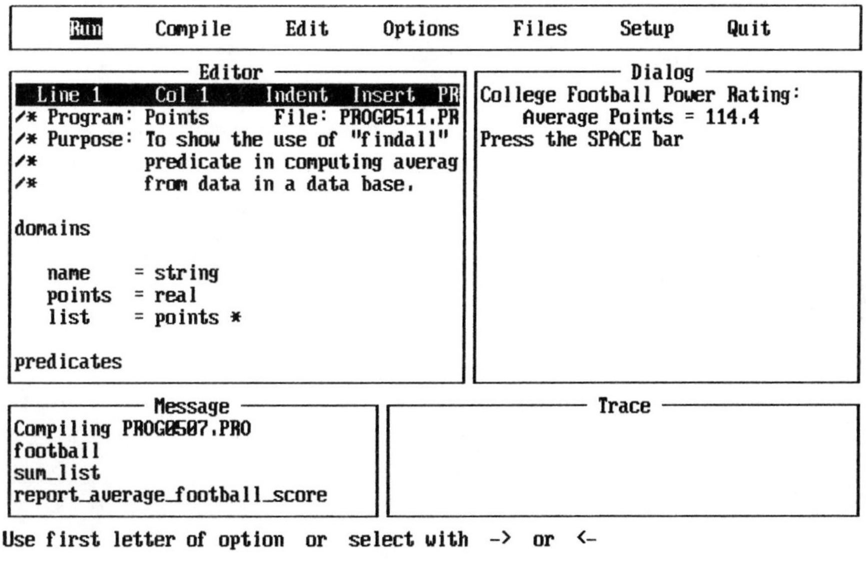

Fig. 5.11. *Output of the program Points.*

—————————————— **Exercise** ——————————————

5.17. Collect football scores for the most recent game of the Big Ten teams. Modify the Points program to include your database. Run the program. What is the calculated average of the scores?

Chapter Review

This chapter has introduced the structures and functions of Turbo Prolog lists, and has shown how to perform various operations on them. You have progressed from the creation and printing of lists through the Head-Tail method of accessing lists; to searching, splitting, and appending lists; to sorting lists; and to the use of the *findall* predicate to collect data from a database.

In reading this chapter, you have learned to build Turbo Prolog rules to accomplish your programming goals. You have learned to connect and translate natural-language rule statements into Turbo Prolog rules for your programming applications.

You are again encouraged to work through the exercises. They are designed to reinforce your understanding of the basic structures or techniques involved. They also help you in attempting to modify the example programs. The seven complete Turbo Prolog programs in this chapter illustrate the basic methods of list manipulation and specific features of Turbo Prolog. They are for you to modify or to use as patterns in constructing programs for your own purposes.

Be sure to review this chapter if your programming projects require list manipulations. The methods presented here are widely used in Turbo Prolog programming. You can use these methods without completely understanding how they work, but your proficiency as a programmer will be much enhanced if you understand them.

6

Using Strings

A string is a set of characters. For example, these words and sentences you are now reading—a set of characters—are strings to a computer. Included in the term *characters* are the letters of the English alphabet; digits; symbols such as +, @, and $; and computer control characters corresponding to keys such as Enter and Esc.

Strings are, in fact, the most common objects in computer programming. Examples of strings used in programming are the sequences of characters that you type at the keyboard to control the computer, such as *DIR A:*; program commands, such as *Print @25*; and data to be manipulated, such as *John Smith, Boston MA*.

Operations commonly performed on strings include

- Combining strings to form a new string

- Splitting a string to make two strings that each contain some of the original characters.

- Searching for a character or substring within a string

These and other string operations are both basic and important in Prolog programming.

For the convenience of programmers, Turbo Prolog provides several built-in predicates for use in building rules to manipulate strings. In this chapter you will work with strings and build Turbo Prolog rules to manipulate them.

The Turbo Prolog Character Set

Characters are represented in the computer by numbers. Most personal computers, including all IBM PCs and compatible machines, use the same system of numeric codes, which is known as the American Standard Code for Information Interchange (ASCII). The characters *A*, *B*, and *C*, for example, are represented by the ASCII numbers 65, 66, and 67. Lowercase letters are represented by numbers beginning 32 numbers higher. Thus, *a* is 97 (65 + 32).

The ASCII set includes these subgroups: the English alphabet characters, both upper- and lowercase; the digits from 0 to 9; special symbols such as +, –, $, *, and the punctuation symbols; and control characters such as Ctrl-C and Ctrl-Q. Table 6.1 lists the ASCII characters available for use in Turbo Prolog programming.

Using ASCII Numbers to "Write" Characters

In Turbo Prolog programming, characters can be "written" by means of their ASCII numbers. A backslash (\) immediately followed by the ASCII decimal number (N) of a character is recognized as that character. For a single-character representation, the \N must be enclosed in single quotation marks ('\N'). To make a string of characters, you place their ASCII representations side by side and enclose the whole string in double quotation marks ("\N\N\N").

As examples, consider the characters A, B and C, whose ASCII decimal numbers are 65, 66 and 67. In Turbo Prolog, you write the character A in its ASCII representation as '\65'. The ASCII representation of the string *ABC* is "\65\66\67". The decimal digit 4 is represented in ASCII code as '\52'. The decimal number 436.375 is written as a Turbo Prolog ASCII code string "\52\51\54\46\51\55\53".

In general, a backslash (\) immediately followed by the ASCII number of a character is recognized as that character. Some of the control characters are represented as graphics characters when output to the screen. The character '\10' is the linefeed character.

The program ASCIIprint, in listing 6.1, demonstrates the writing of characters by means of their ASCII number representations. The output of the program is shown in figure 6.1.

String Assignments

A character string can be assigned to a variable. Thus the assignments

   S = "\84\117\114\98\111\32\80\82\79\76\79\71"

and

   S = "Turbo PROLOG"

are equivalent.

ASCII number representations of character strings are long and bulky, and direct alphabetic representation is usually more effective. In machine-oriented languages such as an assembly language, however, the ASCII number notation for characters and strings is used. Applications that use ASCII number notation include writing compilers, operating systems, and communications device controllers. Although these are more complex topics than you will learn about in this book, you may come across modules that will use ASCII notation within a Turbo Prolog program.

```
/* Program: ASCIIPrint    File: PROG0601.PRO */
/* Purpose: To demonstrate uses of ASCII       */
/*          numbers for character printing.    */
/* Direction: Run the program. A goal is       */
/*            included.                         */

predicates

   print_by_ascii_numbers

goal

   print_by_ascii_numbers.

clauses

   print_by_ascii_numbers :-
      nl,
      write("Here are the numbers:"),
      nl, nl,
      write( 41,"   ", 42,"   ", 43),
      nl,
      write($41,"   ",$42,"   ",$43),
      nl, nl,
      write("Here are the strings:"),
      write('\10','\10'),
      write('\65',"    ",'\66',"    ",'\67'),
      write("\10\10"),
      write("\65\66\67"),
      nl,
      write("\84\117\114\98\111\32"),
      write("\80\82\79\76\79\71").
```

Table 6.1
The ASCII Character Set

Control characters

Character	Code	Effect
Ctrl-A	1	
Ctrl-B	2	
Ctrl-C	3	Halt program execution
Ctrl-D	4	
Ctrl-E	5	
Ctrl-F	6	
Ctrl-G	7	
Ctrl-H	8	Backspace
Ctrl-I	9	Tab
Ctrl-J	10	Line feed
Ctrl-K	11	
Ctrl-L	12	
Ctrl-M	13	Carriage Return
Ctrl-N	14	
Ctrl-O	15	
Ctrl-P	16	Send output to printer
Ctrl-Q	17	Continue execution (after Ctrl-S)
Ctrl-R	18	
Ctrl-S	19	Pause execution
Ctrl-T	20	Turn trace off and on
Ctrl-U	21	
Ctrl-V	22	
Ctrl-W	23	
Ctrl-X	24	
Ctrl-Y	25	
Ctrl-Z	26	End-of-file
Escape	27	

Special characters

Character	Code
(Space)	32
!	33
"	34
#	35
$	36
%	37
&	38
'	39
(	40
)	41
*	42
+	43
,	44
-	45
.	46
/	47
:	58
;	59
<	60
=	61
>	62
?	63
@	64
[	91
\	92
]	93
^	94
_	95
`	96
{	123
		144
}	125
~	126

Digits

Character	Code
0	48
1	49
2	50
3	51
4	52
5	53
6	54
7	55
8	56
9	57

Alphabetic Characters

Character	Code	Character	Code
A	65	a	97
B	66	b	98
C	67	c	99
D	68	d	100
E	69	e	101
F	70	f	102
G	71	g	103
H	72	h	104
I	73	i	105
J	74	j	106
K	75	k	107
L	76	l	108
M	77	m	109
N	78	n	110
O	79	o	111
P	80	p	112
Q	81	q	113
R	82	r	114
S	83	s	115
T	84	t	116
U	85	u	117
V	86	v	118
W	87	w	119
X	88	x	120
Y	89	y	121
Z	90	z	122

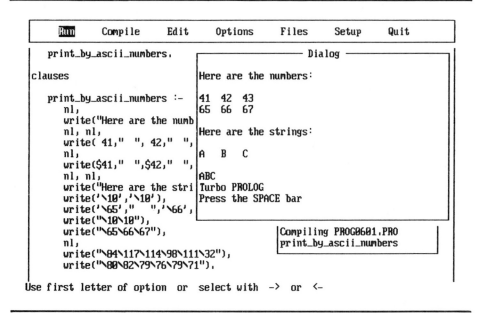

Fig. 6.1. Output of the program ASCIIprint.

The program TeamPrint1, in listing 6.2, uses a number of string assignments. The fixed string constants S1, S2, . . . S9 are declared in the *domains* division. The rule *print_ strings* includes the ten string assignment predicates as well as the ten string *write* statements. The equality symbol (=) is used as the symbol for establishing the relationship (predicate). This notation is the "infix" notation for relationship. The output of the program is shown in figure 6.3.

```
/* Program: TeamPrint1   File: PROG0602.PRO   */
/* Purpose: To demonstrate uses of Turbo       */
/*          Prolog Strings.                     */

predicates

   print_strings

goal

   print_strings.

clauses
```

```
print_strings :-
    nl,
    write(" Good luck to you all !"),
    nl, nl,

    S1 = "Cleveland Browns",
    S2 = "Cincinnati Bengals",
    S3 = "Dallas Cowboys",
    S4 = "Denver Broncos",
    S5 = "Indianapolis Colts",
    S6 = "New York Giants",
    S7 = "Los Angeles Raiders",
    S8 = "St. Louis Cardinals",
    S9 = "Tampa Bay Buccaneers",

    write(S1), nl,
    write(S2), nl,
    write(S3), nl,
    write(S4), nl,
    write(S5), nl,
    write(S6), nl,
    write(S7), nl,
    write(S8), nl,
    write(S9).
```

In the program TeamPrint1, the fixed strings are placed within the rule that prints them. It is also possible to place strings in rules and call these from other rules for manipulation. The program TeamPrint2, in listing 6.3, illustrates this method of string manipulation.

In this program, the rule *data_strings* contains the strings. The rule *print_strings* writes the strings. To pass the strings from the *data_strings* rule to the *print_strings* rule, you include the *data_strings* rule in the *print_strings* rule. In addition, you must pass the data strings to the calling rule by explicitly including the string symbols, S1,S2,S3 . . .S9, in the object list of the called rule.

The output of this program is the same as that of Program 6.2. This method of handling data strings is desirable when the number of data strings is not great. If the number of data strings is more than 20 or so, however, the process of passing the strings becomes cumbersome.

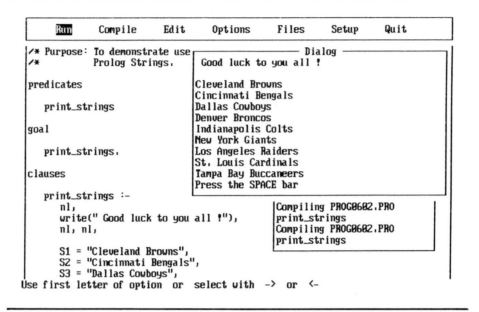

Fig. 6.2. Output of the program *TeamPrint1.*

```
/* Program: TeamPrint2     File: PROG0603.PRO */
/* Purpose: To demonstrate uses of Turbo       */
/*          Prolog Strings.                     */

domains

    s1,s2,s3,s4,s5,s6,s7,s8,s9 = string

predicates

    data_strings(s1,s2,s3,s4,s5,s6,s7,s8,s9)
    print_strings

goal

    print_strings.

clauses
```

```
data_strings(S1,S2,S3,S4,S5,S6,S7,S8,S9) :-

    S1 = "Cleveland Browns",
    S2 = "Cincinnati Bengals",
    S3 = "Dallas Cowboys",
    S4 = "Denver Broncos",
    S5 = "Indianapolis Colts",
    S6 = "New York Giants",
    S7 = "Los Angeles Raiders",
    S8 = "St. Louis Cardinals",
    S9 = "Tampa Bay Buccaneers".

print_strings :-
    nl,
    write(" Good luck to you all !"),
    nl, nl,
    data_strings(S1,S2,S3,S4,S5,S6,S7,S8,S9),
    write("        ",S1), nl,
    write("        ",S2), nl,
    write("        ",S3), nl,
    write("        ",S4), nl,
    write("        ",S5), nl,
    write("        ",S6), nl,
    write("        ",S7), nl,
    write("        ",S8), nl,
    write("        ",S9).
```

Lengths of Strings

The length of a string is the total number of characters in the string. Turbo Prolog pro-vides a built-in predicate, called *str_len*, that can be used to find the length of a string. The syntax of this predicate is

```
str_len(String_value, String_length).
```

In the clause

```
str_len("TODAY",L).
```

where L is not bound before the clause is attempted, the variable L is bound to the a value equal to the length of the string *TODAY*. This value is an integer number. If both variables are bound, then the predicate succeeds if the value of *String_length* is equal to the length of *String_value*. For example, if S is bound to *ABC* and L is bound to 3, the predicate *str_len(S,L)* succeeds. Otherwise, it fails.

The program ShowLength1, in listing 6.4, illustrates the use of an internal goal to find the length of the string *Turbo Prolog*. The output is shown in figure 6.3.

```
/* Program: ShowLength1  File: PROG0604.PRO */
/* Purpose: The use of the predicate        */
/*      str_len(string_value, string_length). */

predicates

    find_string_length

goal

    find_string_length.

clauses

    find_string_length :-

        str_len("Turbo Prolog", Length),
        nl, nl,
        write("    Turbo Prolog"),
        nl, nl,
        write("    Length = ", Length).
```

The program ShowLength2, in listing 6.5, demonstrates a simple application of the *str_len* predicate. The program shows the length of the objects of the database clauses. The rule to find the lengths of the strings is *find_length*. This rule contains *lin(S)*; the data line, *str_lin(S,L)* where S is the string variable name, and L is the length of the string; and a *write* predicate to write the lengths of the strings.

The output of the program is shown in figure 6.4. The numbers in parentheses are the lengths of the strings. Notice that the two "blank" lines are not blank at all; each has 27 space characters.

```
┌─────────────────────────────────────────────────────────────────┐
│    Run      Compile    Edit    Options    Files    Setup    Quit  │
├───────────────────────────────────────────────────────────────────┤
│ /*    str_len(string_value, string_length). *┌────── Dialog ──────┐│
│ predicates                                    │                    ││
│    find_string_length                         │    Turbo Prolog    ││
│                                               │    Length = 12     ││
│ goal                                          │ Press the SPACE bar││
│    find_string_length.                        └────────────────────┘│
│ clauses                                                            │
│    find_string_length :-                                           │
│        str_len("Turbo Prolog", Length),                            │
│        nl, nl,                                                      │
│        write("    Turbo Prolog"),                                  │
│        nl, nl,                                                      │
│        write("    Length = ", Length).                             │
│                                                                    │
└────────────────────────────────────────────────────────────────────┘
 Use first letter of option  or  select with  ->  or  <-
```

Fig. 6.3. *A dialogue with the program ShowLength1.*

```
/* Program-id. ShowLength2File: PROG0605.PRO */
/* Book.                  Using Turbo PROLOG */
/* Purpose: The use of the predicate        */
/*     str_len(string_value, string_length). */
/* Direction: Run the program. A goal is     */
/*            included.                       */

predicates

    lin(string)
    find_length

goal

    find_length.
```

```
clauses

    lin("       Discovery            ").
    lin("                            ").
    lin("It was a journey,           ").
    lin("- a journey into night,").
    lin("- a journey into day,").
    lin("- a journey into dream.").
    lin("When I came to the land").
    lin("I found myself.").
    lin("                       ").
    lin("              Khinzu   ").


    find_length :-
        lin(S),
        str_len(S,L),
        write(S," (",L,")"), nl,
        fail.
```

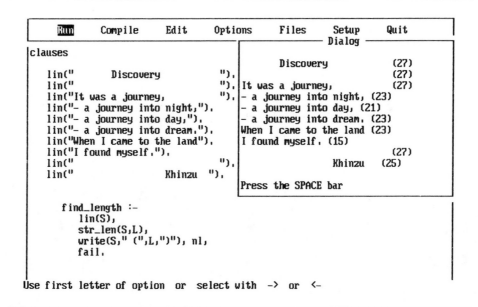

Fig. 6.4. *Output of the program ShowLength2.*

———————————————— **Exercises** ————————————————

6.1. Modify the ShowLength1 program so that it outputs the lengths of these strings:

"The father of an enemy of a friend of a man owes that man nothing."

"When I code without the pressure of a deadline, it's very relaxing."

6.2. Modify the ShowLength2 program, replacing the database clauses with clauses from your favorite poem. Then run the program.

String Concatenations

To *concatenate* two strings is to join them, forming a single string. For example, the result of concatenating the two strings

"one day"

"at a time"

can be either "one day at a time" or "at a time one day". The two resulting strings are different because the constituent strings are put together in different orders.

Turbo Prolog provides a built-in predicate named *concat*, which concatenates two strings. The syntax is

```
concat(Input_string1,Input_string2,Output_string).
```

The objects *Input_string1* and *Input_string2* are the two input strings. The object *Output_string* is the concatenated output string. For example,

```
concat("TODAY"," TOMORROW",S).
```

binds *S* to the string *"TODAY TOMORROW"*.

The program Concat1, in listing 6.6, demonstrates the concatenation of strings. This program uses an internal goal. The rule *print_strings* concatenates strings and prints the result of the concatenation. The program's output is shown in figure 6.5.

The program Concat2, in listing 6.7, is a variant of Concat1. In this program, input as well as output strings are represented by variables with single-character names: *R, S, T, U, V, W, X, Y, Z, A, B, C*. These variables are used as arguments of the *concat* predicate. This form of concatenation predicate entry is shorter and more convenient for repeated concatenations. The output of this program is the same as that of Concat1.

```
/* Program: Concat1      File: PROG0606.PRO */
/* Purpose: The use of the predicate        */
/*             concat(string1,string2,string3) */

predicates

   print_strings

goal

   print_strings.

clauses

   print_strings :-

      concat("Turbo Prolog"," is fast!",R),
      nl, nl, write(R),

      concat("Every body loves ",
             "somebody sometime.",S),
      nl, nl, write(S),

      concat("Artificial",
             " Intelligence.",T),
      nl, nl, write(T),

      concat("A thing of beauty ",
             "is a joy forever.",U),
      nl, nl, write(U), nl, nl.
```

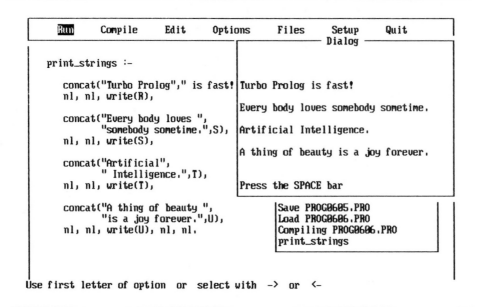

Fig. 6.5. *Output of the program Concat1.*

```
/* Program: Concat2      File: PROG0607.PRO */
/* Purpose: The use of the predicate        */
/*          concat(string1,string2,string3) */

predicates

    print_strings

goal

    print_strings.

clauses

    print_strings :-

        nl, nl,
```

```
O = "Turbo Prolog",
P = " is fast !",
concat(O,P,Q),
write(Q), nl, nl,

R = "Every body loves ",
S = "somebody sometime.",
concat(R,S,T),
write(T), nl, nl,

U = "Artificial",
V = " Intelligence",
concat(U,V,W),
write(W), nl, nl,

X = "A thing of beauty ",
Y = "is a joy forever.",
concat(X,Y,Z),
write(Z), nl, nl.
```

—— **Exercises** ——

6.3. Modify the Concat1 program so that it concatenates these four strings, taking two strings at a time:

1. "Logic puzzles me"
2. "Neither of us is old"
3. "What is difficult needs attention!"
4. "No riddles interest me if they can be solved"

The desired order of concatenation is 1, 3, 2, 4. Build the string in the shortest possible way.

6.4. Modify the Concat2 program to concatenate these strings:

"Thunderstorms"
"very strong winds"
"heavy rainfalls"
"and"
"hailstorms"
"are"
"all"
"destructive."

The output should be a sentence made up of those strings in the given order.

Creating Substrings

A substring is a string copied from part of another string. For example, two possible substrings of the string "Expert Systems" are "Expert " and "Systems". Turbo Prolog provides a built-in predicate to create substrings. The syntax is

```
frontstr(Number,Source_string,Substring1,Substring2).
```

The argument *Number* is the total number of characters to be copied to *Substring1* from *Source_string*, which is the original string; the remaining characters in *Source_string* are copied to *Substring2*. For example, the clause

```
frontstr(6,"Expert systems",String1,String2).
```

binds *String1* to "Expert" and *String2* to " Systems". Notice that the number 6 corresponds to the total number of characters in "Expert".

The program Substring, in listing 6.8, demonstrates the use of the *frontstr* predicate. The program finds two substrings for each input string. For example, the first input string is *Turbo Prolog is fast!* The *frontstr* predicate is applied to the first string in the form

```
frontstr(12,"Turbo Prolog is fast!",R1,R2).
```

The *print_strings* rule prints the resulting two strings on separate lines, giving the outputs shown in figure 6.6.

```
/* Program:    Substring  File: PROG0608.PRO */
/* Purpose: The use of the predicate         */
/*      frontstr(Num,string,string1,string2)  */

predicates

    print_strings

goal

    print_strings.

clauses

    print_strings :-
        nl, nl, nl,

        frontstr(12,
                "Turbo Prolog is fast!",
                R1,R2),
```

```
write(R1), nl,
write(R2), nl, nl,

frontstr(10,
        "Every body loves somebody",
        S1,S2),
write(S1), nl,
write(S2), nl, nl,

frontstr(10,
        "Artificial Intelligence",
        T1,T2),
write(T1), nl,
write(T2), nl, nl,

frontstr(17,
        "A thing of beauty is a joy.",
        U1,U2),
write(U1), nl,
write(U2).
```

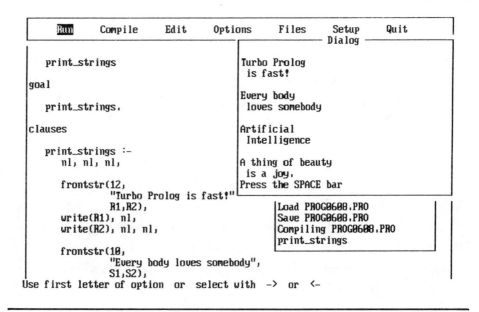

Fig. 6.6. *Output of the program Substring.*

—————————————— **Exercise** ——————————————

6.5. Modify the Substring program so that it produces the substrings in the right column from the input strings in the left column:

Input String	*Substrings*
"LOTUS 123"	"LOTUS"
	"123"
"Default Directory"	"Default"
	"Directory"
"Fifth Generation"	"Fifth"
	"Generation"
"Are they safe for my children?"	"Are they safe"
	"for my children?"

Now modify the program so that it extracts the output substrings in the right column from the input strings in the left column:

Input String	*Output Strings*
"Tom Shallack is an account."	"Tom Shallack"
	"accountant"
"Juniper tar is an anti-itch treatment for skin disorders"	"Juniper tar"
	"anti-itch"
	"skin disorders"

Data Conversions

Turbo Prolog provides built-in predicates to convert data from one type to another. These predicates are

upper_lower
str_char
str_int
str_real
char_int

These predicates are useful because some built-in predicates require objects of data types that may differ from those of objects in predicates you design.

For example, the *writef* predicate can cause the system to crash if it's passed an object of type *char*. If the character variable *Drive_ltr* is bound to the character 'a', then the predicate

```
writef("The current drive is %:",Drive_ltr_char)
```

causes a crash. (No compiler error or warning is given.) However, this problem can be avoided by using

```
str_char(Drive_ltr_str,Drive_letter),
writef("The current drive is%:",Drive_ltr_str).
```

Conversions are also necessary when a value of one data type must be instantiated to a variable of a different type.

The conversion predicates all take two objects. You've probably noticed that the names of the predicates indicate the kinds of conversions they perform. For example, *str_char* converts a one-character value of type *string* to a value of type *char*. The names of the predicates also indicate the order of the objects. The *string* object is the first object of *str_char*, for example, and the *char* object is the second.

These predicates have multiple flowpatterns. For example, if the variable *S1* is bound to the string *STARS AND STRIPES*, the predicate

```
upper_lower(S1,S2)
```

binds *S2* to the string *stars and stripes*. But if *S2* is bound and *S1* is unbound, *S1* becomes bound to *STARS AND STRIPES*. If both variables are bound, the predicate succeeds if one is the lowercase equivalent of the other.

The predicate *str_char* is used to convert objects of the type *string* to objects of type *char*. The predicate *str_int* is used to convert string representations of integer numbers to variables of type *integer*. The predicate *str_real* is used to convert real numbers to strings. The predicate *char_int* is used to bind the integer (ASCII number) of the character to the character.

The program Conversions1, in listing 6.9, shows examples of data conversions using built-in Turbo Prolog predicates. The program output is shown in figure 6.7.

```
/* Program: Conversions1     PROG0609.PRO */
/* Purpose: To demonstrate data type      */
/*          conversions                    */

predicates

    do_conversions

goal

    do_conversions.
```

```
clauses

  do_conversions :-

    upper_lower("STARS AND STRIPES",S1),
    write("STARS ANS STRIPES"), nl,
    write(S1), nl, nl,

    upper_lower(S2,"one day at a time"),
    write("one day at a time"), nl,
    write(S2), nl, nl,

    write("T"), nl,
    str_char("T",C1),
    write(C1), nl, nl,

    write("U"), nl,
    char_int('U',N1),
    write(N1), nl.
```

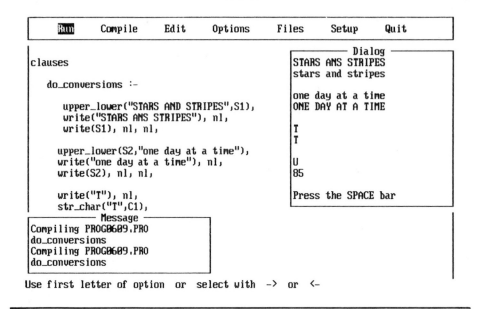

Fig. 6.7. *Output of the program Conversions1.*

—————————————— **Exercise** ——————————————

6.6. Write a program that performs the following conversions. Use an internal goal.

1. upper_lower("PREDICATE LOGIC",L).
2. upper_lower(V,"expert systems").
3. upper_lower("LOTUS123",S).
4. upper_lower("Oral_Cavity",Q).
5. str_char("A",C8).
6. str_char("Z",C9).
7. char_int('Q',N6).
8. char_int('#',N9).

User-Defined Conversions

The conversion of real numbers to integers or integers to real numbers is useful in mathematical computing. Converting strings into symbols is useful in preparing data for manipulation and storage. In this section you will see how to build rules to perform these conversions.

Consider the conversion of a real number into an integer. In this example, the integer value corresponding to the real number 5432.765 is 5432. The conversion rule is built with the equality symbol (=):

```
conv_real_int(R,N) :- R = N.
```

Here, *R* is the variable for real numbers and *N* is the variable for integers.

The declaration in the *predicates* division is

```
conv_real_int(r,n)
```

The rule attempts to find the value of R. In doing so, it checks to see whether the current value of R is a real number; if R is not real, the rule fails. On succeeding, the rule takes the integer part of the real number and binds it to the real variable N. Because integers in Turbo Prolog are limited to the range −32768 to 32767, this conversion rule will not work if the real value is less than −32768.0 or greater than 32767.0.

The rule for converting an integer to a real number is

```
conv_int_real(N,R) :- N = R.
```

Here, N is the integer variable and R is the real number variable. If N is bound to 1234, then R is bound to 1234 (a decimal point is implied but not written).

This rule attempts to find the value of N. If the current value of N is an integer, the rule succeeds; otherwise it fails. Upon succeeding, the rule takes the integer and binds it to R. Again, this conversion rule works only when the integer number is within the legal range.

The conversion of a string into a symbol is also effected by a simple rule:

```
conv_str_symb(S,Sb) :- S = Sb.
```

For example, if S = "TURBO PROLOG", then Sb = TURBO PROLOG. The object S is declared as type *string* and Sb is declared as type *symbol*.

The program Conversions2, in listing 6.10, implements the three preceding rules. The program output is shown in fig 6.8.

```
/* Program: Conversions2    PROG0610.PRO    */
/* Purpose: To demonstrate conversion of:   */
/*              (1) real into integer       */
/*              (2) integer into real       */
/*              (3) string into symbol      */

predicates

    conv_real_int(real,integer)
    conv_int_real(integer,real)
    conv_str_symb(string,symbol)

goal

    X1 = 5432.765,
    conv_real_int(X1,N1), nl, nl,

    N2 = 1234,
    conv_int_real(N2,X2), nl, nl,

    S = "TURBO PROLOG",
    conv_str_symb(S,Sb), nl.
```

```
clauses

    conv_real_int(R,N) :-
      R = N,
      write("Input real      - ",R), nl,
      write("Output integer - ",N).


    conv_int_real(N,R) :-
      N = R,
      write("Input integer  - ",N), nl,
      write("Output real     - ",R).


    conv_str_symb(S,Sb) :-
      S = Sb,
      write("Input string    - ", S), nl,
      write("Output symbol   - ", Sb).
```

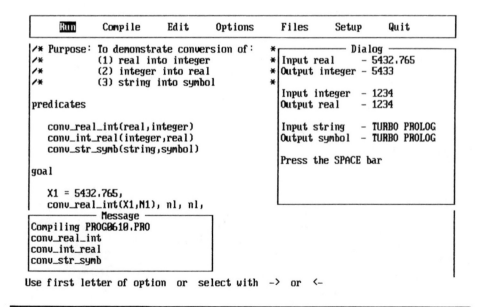

Fig. 6.8. *Output of the program Conversions2.*

————————————————— **Exercise** —————————————————

6.7. Write the outputs for these inputs, based on the rules in the Conversions2 program.

1. Input real number: 1697.43284
   Output iteger: _____

2. Input integer number: 3333
   Output real number: _____

3. Input string: "Turbo_Prolog_Compiler"
   Output symbol: _____

Character Prefixing

To "prefix" a character is to attach that character to the beginning of a string. For example, the prefixing of 'A' to "BCDEF" produces the string "ABCDEF". Turbo Prolog provides a built-in predicate named *frontchar* to accomplish this task:

```
frontchar(String,Char,Rest_of_string).
```

The object *String* is bound to a value consisting of *Char* and *Rest_of_string*.

An example is

```
frontchar(Str,'F',"OX").
```

This predicate binds *Str* to "FOX". Another example is seen in the predicate expression

```
frontchar("SPRING",C,"PRING").
```

This predicate binds the character variable *C* to 'S'.

In the expression

```
frontchar("dBASE",'d',X).
```

the predicate binds *X* to *BASE*.

The *frontchar* predicate is similar to the *concat* predicate except that the former appends a value of data type *char* to the front of the string; *frontchar* provides a way to append a value of type *char* to a string. Like the conversion predicates, *frontchar* has multiple flowpatterns.

The program Frontchar, in listing 6.11, shows the uses of the *frontchar* predicate. The output is shown in fig 6.9.

—————————————————— **Exercise** ——————————————————

6.8. Write a Turbo Prolog program that repeatedly prefixes characters to the string "POEM.TXT" so that the output is "type POEM.TXT".

```
/* Program: Frontchar File: PROG06011.PRO */
/* Purpose: The use of the predicate        */
/*          frontchar(string,fronchar,string).   */

predicates

    print_all

goal

    print_all.

clauses

    print_all :-
        frontchar(Str1,'A',"BCDEF"),
        nl, write(" Str1 = ",Str1),
        frontchar(Str2,'B'," is enough"),
        nl, write(" Str2 = ",Str2),
        frontchar(Str3,'?',"Show"),
        nl, write(" Str3 = ",Str3),
        frontchar(Str4,'#',"&%#!!!"),
        nl, write(" Str4 = ",Str4),
        frontchar(Str5,'1',"23LOTUS"),
        nl, write(" Str5 = ",Str5),
        frontchar(Str6,' ',"// "),
        nl, write(" Str6 = ",Str6).
```

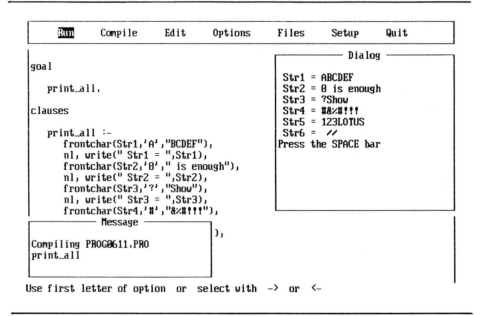

Fig. 6.9. *Output of the program Frontchar.*

Converting Strings to Character Lists

The *frontchar* predicate is useful in converting a string into a list of characters. Suppose, for example, that you want to convert the string *STARS* to the list *['S', 'T', 'A', 'R', 'S']*. The method used for the conversion is to use the *frontchar* predicate repeatedly to "extract" the front characters and put them into a list. The rule that will achieve this goal is

```
conver("",[]).
conver(Str,[Head|Tail]) :-
      frontchar(str,Head,Str1),
      conver(Str1,Tail).
```

In the *conver* rule, the first parameter is a string and the second parameter is a list. The *frontchar* predicate recursively extracts the front character from *Str* and puts it in the list.

The program CharList1, in listing 6.12, uses this rule. As you can see from the *domains* section, *char_list* is a list of characters and *str* is a string.

A run-time dialogue with the program is shown in figure 6.10. Notice that the second list is a list of digits. These digits constitute a string, however. They do not have numerical meaning; that is, arithmetic operations cannot be performed on them.

```
/* Program: Charlist1 File: PROG06012.PRO   */
/* Purpose: To show conversion of a string  */
/* into a list of characters, using the      */
/* predicate "frontchar".                     */

domains

    char_list = char *
    str       = string

predicates

    conver(str, char_list)

clauses

    conver("",[]).

    conver(Str,[Head|Tail]):-
            frontchar(Str,Head,Str1),
            conver(Str1,Tail).
```

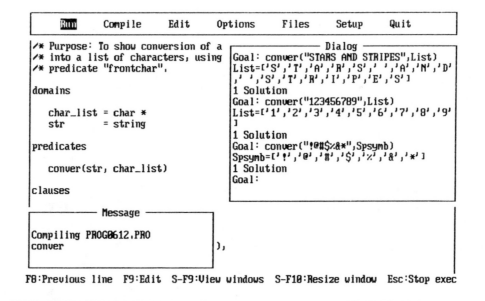

Fig. 6.10. *A dialogue with the program Charlist1.*

The program CharList2, in listing 6.13, is a variation of CharList1. This program has an internal goal, consisting of the rule *do_convert_and_print*. This rule uses the rule *conver* to convert the string "STARS AND STRIPES" to a list of characters. (You may recall the *print_list* rule from Chapter 5.) CharList2 then prints the list of numbers in a pleasing format, as shown in figure 6.11.

```
/* Program: Charlist2   File: PROG06013.PRO */
/* Purpose: To show conversion of a string  */
/* into a list of characters, using the     */
/* predicate "frontchar".                    */

domains

    char_list = char *
    str       = string

predicates

    conver(str,char_list)
    print_list(char_list)
    do_convert_and_print

goal

    do_convert_and_print.

clauses

    conver("",[]).
    conver(Str,[Head|Tail]):-
            frontchar(Str,Head,Str1),
            conver(Str1,Tail).

    print_list([]).
    print_list([Head|Tail]) :-
        write(Head," "),
        print_list(Tail).
```

```
do_convert_and_print :-
    nl, nl,
    write("STARS AND STRIPES"), nl, nl,
    conver("STARS AND STRIPES",List),
    print_list(List),
    nl, nl,
    write("          All done!"), nl.
```

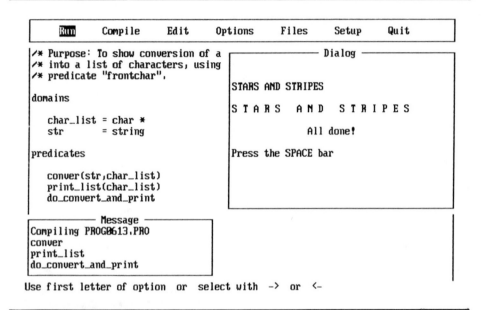

Fig. 6.11. *Output of the program Charlist2.*

——————————————————— **Exercises** ———————————————————

6.9. Run the program CharList1 and enter these goals:

1. conver("National Football League",B).

2. conver("Material Girl",G).

3. conver("phenylpropanolamine hydrochloride",M).

Note the output in each case.

6.10. Modify the program CharList2 so that each list element is printed on a different line.

Turbo Prolog-Specific Strings

So far, this chapter has discussed strings in general. Turbo Prolog defines and uses strings for specific purposes in programming. These strings are called *names*. Names are used to denote symbolic constants, domains, predicates, and variables. By definition, a Turbo Prolog-specific string has these five properties:

1. The string is made up of uppercase or lowercase characters, digits, and underscores.

2. No blank spaces occur between characters.

3. The string begins with a letter.

4. The string does not begin with any of the special characters shown in table 6.1.

5. The string does not contain any control characters.

These examples will help you to see more clearly the differences between general strings and Turbo Prolog names:

1. "A ROSE IS A ROSE IS A ROSE" is not a Turbo Prolog name, because it contains spaces.

   "A_ROSE_IS_A_ROSE_IS_A_ROSE" is a Turbo Prolog string.

2. "123LOTUS" is not a Turbo Prolog string, because it begins with a numeral. "LOTUS123" is a Turbo Prolog string. Reversing the order so the numerals follow makes it acceptable.

3. "_intelligence" is not a Turbo Prolog string because it begins with the special character "_". However, "artificial_" is a Turbo Prolog string; the underscore does not influence its "legality" because the underscore is not the first character.

4. Ctrl-P is not a Turbo Prolog string, because it is a control character.

Turbo Prolog provides a built-in predicate to test whether a string is a Turbo Prolog-specific string. The syntax of the predicate is

```
isname(String).
```

If *String* is a Turbo Prolog string, the predicate succeeds; otherwise, it fails.

The program Isname, in listing 6.14, uses the *isname* predicate to check whether a string is a Turbo Prolog string. A dialogue with the program is shown in figure 6.12.

```
/* Program: Isname        File: PROG06014.PRO   */
/* Purpose: The use of the built-in predicate */
/*          isname(string).                    */

predicates

    test_good_names
    test_bad_names

goal

    test_good_names,
    test_bad_names.

clauses

    test_good_names :-
        Name = "employee_ID",
        isname(Name),
        nl, write(Name," is a legal name.").

    test_bad_names :-
        Name = "$employee_ID",
        not(isname(Name)),
        nl, write(Name," is not a legal name!").
```

In the Isname program, the rule *test_good_name* uses the *isname predicate to test whether employee_ID* is a Turbo Prolog name. Because it is a Turbo Prolog name, the rule succeeds and the output display is

```
employee_ID is a legal name.
```

The rule also tests *$employee_ID*. Because the prefixed "$" makes this a nonlegal Turbo Prolog name, the *isname* predicate fails; in the program the negative predicate

```
not(isname($employee_ID)).
```

succeeds and therefore the *test_bad_name* rule succeeds. The output display is

```
$employee_ID is not a legal name.
```

The *isname* predicate is useful when you write a Turbo Prolog program to convert one language's source file to another language source file. When a command is encountered, *isname* can tell whether it will convert to Turbo Prolog according to Turbo Prolog's definition for names. Another use of *isname* is to take keyboard input and generate source files (text files) that could be compiled by Turbo Prolog.

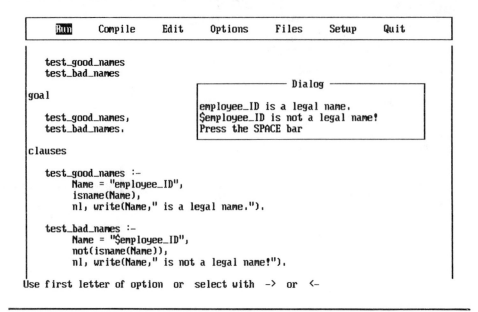

Fig. 6.12. *A dialogue with the program Isname.*

Exercise

6.11. Write a program that tests the following strings to see whether they are legal names:

1. %COPY
2. _town
3. address
4. Prescription
5. iodochlorhydroxyquin

Forming Tokens from Strings

A token is a sequence of characters. The grouping of the characters is a Turbo Prolog-specific string. A token may be a number. If the number has a preceding sign (+ or −), the sign is treated as a separate token. A token may be a character, but not a space character. *Variables* are used for passing parameters; variables are tokens, but not all tokens are variables.

Turbo Prolog provides a built-in predicate to extract a token from a string. It is the *front-token* predicate. The syntax is

```
fronttoken(String,Token,Rest_of_string).
```

Either *String* must be bound or both *Token* and *Rest_of_string* must be bound.

If the first character of the string is a symbol from groups one to four in figure 6.1, the symbol is bound to *Token* and the rest of the characters are bound to *Rest_of_string*. Or, if the string has a value, then *Token* is bound to the *string_value* and the *rest_of_the_string* is bound to a null string ("").

Here are some examples of the relationships established by this predicate:

1. The predicate *fronttoken(Str, "Default", "Directory")* binds *Str* to "Default Directory".

2. The predicate *fronttoken(Str, "$default", "$directory")* binds *Str* to "$default$directory".

3. The predicate *fronttoken("Pointer", Token, Rest)* binds *Token* to "Pointer" and *Rest* to "" (an empty string).

4. The predicate *fronttoken("$Command", Token, Trail)* binds *Token* to "$" and Trail to "Command".

5. The predicate *fronttoken("$$command", Token, Trail)* binds *Token* to "$" and *Trail* to "$command".

6. The predicate *fronttoken("!default", Token, Rest)* binds *Token* to "!" and *Rest* to "default".

7. The predicate *fronttoken("$RUN AI.BAS", Token, Rest)* binds *Token* to "$" and *Rest* to "RUN AI.BAS".

Program 6.15 illustrates the preceding examples; the output of the program is shown in figure 6.13. Notice that the results vary considerably according to the form of the arguments.

The *fronttoken* predicate can be used in a rule to convert a string to a list of tokens. The rule is similar to the rule that you used in converting a string to a list of characters:

```
convers(Str,[Head|Tail]) :-
    fronttoken(Str,Head,Str1),!,
    convers(Str1,Tail).
convers(_,[]).
```

```
/* Program: Token1    File: PROG06015.PRO */
/* Purpose: The use of the predicate      */
/*    fronttoken(String,Token,Reststring). */

predicates

    print_all

goal

    print_all.

clauses

    print_all :-
      fronttoken(Str1,"Default"," Directory"),
      nl, write(" Str1 = ",Str1),
      fronttoken(Str2,"$default","$directory"),
      nl, write(" Str2 = ",Str2),
      fronttoken("Pointer",Token1,Rest1),
      nl, write(" Token1 = ",Token1),
      nl, write(" Rest1 = ",Rest1),
      fronttoken("$Command",Token2,Trail1),
      nl, write(" Token2 = ",Token2),
      nl, write(" Trail1 = ",Trail1),
      fronttoken("$$command",Token3,Trail3),
      nl, write(" Token3 = ",Token3),
      nl, write(" Trail3 = ",Trail3),
      fronttoken(Str3,"!default","$default"),
      nl, write(" Str3 = ",Str3),
      fronttoken("$RUN AI.BAS",Token4,Rest2),
      nl, write(" Token4 = ",Token4),
      nl, write(" Rest2 = ",Rest2).
```

The variant convers(_,[]) succeeds when the list is a null list, as it must be at the point when the conversion begins. For example, the string "one two three" is converted to this list of tokens:

    [one, two, three]

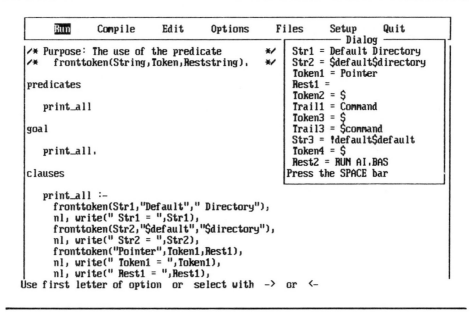

```
   Run      Compile     Edit     Options    Files    Setup    Quit
                                                     Dialog
/* Purpose: The use of the predicate      */   Str1 = Default Directory
/*    fronttoken(String,Token,Reststring).  */  Str2 = $default$directory
                                                Token1 = Pointer
predicates                                      Rest1 =
                                                Token2 = $
   print_all                                    Trail1 = Command
                                                Token3 = $
goal                                            Trail3 = $command
                                                Str3 = !default$default
   print_all.                                   Token4 = $
                                                Rest2 = RUN AI.BAS
clauses                                         Press the SPACE bar

   print_all :-
     fronttoken(Str1,"Default"," Directory"),
     nl, write(" Str1 = ",Str1),
     fronttoken(Str2,"$default","$directory"),
     nl, write(" Str2 = ",Str2),
     fronttoken("Pointer",Token1,Rest1),
     nl, write(" Token1 = ",Token1),
     nl, write(" Rest1 = ",Rest1),
Use first letter of option  or  select with  ->  or  <-
```

Fig. 6.13. *Output of the program Token1.*

The program Token2, in listing 6.16, shows the conversion of strings to lists of tokens. The output of the program is shown in figure 6.14. Notice that the string "STARS AND STRIPES" is converted to the token list

```
["STARS", "AND", "STRIPES"]
```

The spaces are discarded.

```
/* Program: Token2      File: PROG06016.PRO */
/* Purpose: To show conversion of a string  */
/*          into a string list, using the   */
/*          predicate "fronttoken".          */

domains

   str_list = symbol *
   str      = string
```

```
predicates

   convers(str,str_list)

clauses

   convers(Str,[Head|Tail]):-
              fronttoken(Str,Head,Str1),!,
              convers(Str1,Tail).
   convers(_,[]).
```

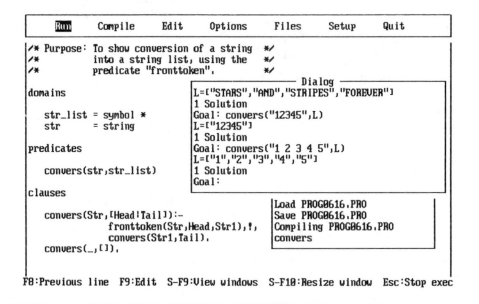

Fig. 6.14. *A dialogue with the program Token2.*

Exercise

6.12. Run the program Token2 and enter these external goals:

1. convers("from New_York to Los_Angeles"_).

2. convers("123 infinity").

3. convers("1 2 34 9 636").

4. convers("%% $ @ @ ##").

What are the outputs?

The program Token3, in listing 6.17, is a variation of Token2. This program uses an internal goal, which is the rule *do_convert_and_print*. This goal consists of two sub-goals. The sub-goal *convers* converts the string "STARS AND STRIPES FOREVER" to a list of tokens, and the sub-goal *print_list* prints the resulting list. The output of the program is shown in figure 6.15.

```
/* Program: Token3      File: PROG06017.PRO */
/* Purpose: To show conversion of a string  */
/*          into a string list, using the    */
/*          predicate "fronttoken".           */

domains

    str_list = symbol *
    str      = string

predicates

    convers(str,str_list)
    print_list(str_list)
    do_convert_and_print

goal

    do_convert_and_print.

clauses

    convers(Str,[Head|Tail]):-
            fronttoken(Str,Head,Str1),!,
            convers(Str1,Tail).
    convers(_,[]).

    print_list([]).
    print_list([Head|Tail]) :-
            write("    ",Head), nl,
            print_list(Tail).
```

```
do_convert_and_print :-
    nl, nl,
    write("STARS AND STRIPES FOREVER"),
    nl, nl,
    convers("STARS AND STRIPES FOREVER",
            List),
    print_list(List),
    nl, nl,
    write("          All done !"), nl.
```

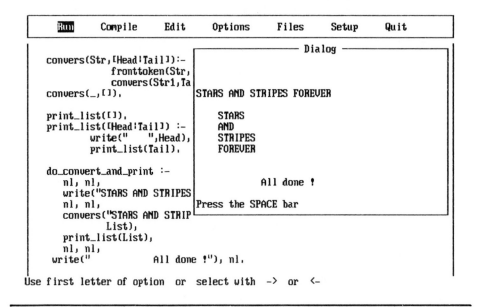

Fig. 6.15. Output of the program Token3.

Exercise

6.13. Modify Program 6.17 so that it converts these strings into lists:

"C> DIR C:\INVENT\AUTOPRT.FIL"

"A> TYPE ACCOUNTS.BAS"

Transforming Strings into Lists of Functored Tokens

Often it is convenient to transform data entered at the keyboard into a form that can be manipulated by Turbo Prolog. For example, you might like to have a set of variant clauses in a database in the form

```
fruit(apple).
fruit(peach).
fruit(orange).
fruit(pear).
```

These clauses can built from the input string *apple peach orange pear*. The method involves transforming the string into a list that incorporates a functor name. In this case the functor name is *fruit*. The result is the list

```
[fruit(apple),fruit(peach),fruit(orange),fruit(pear)]
```

This list can then be written into a database (or a file). A Turbo Prolog rule can be built to write the elements, one element per line. The rule will also append a period (.) to each functored element.

After building the rule to write the list, you build a transformation rule; the *fronttoken* predicate is a major component of this rule. For this example, we'll call the rule *transf*.

This rule must fulfill several requirements. First, it must allow a null string and a null list:

```
transf("",[]).
```

At the beginning of the transformation, this rule must succeed with a null list.

The purpose of the rule is to transform each string into a list. During this process, the rule also checks the data type of each element. If the element is an integer, the chosen functor name is *n*; if the element is a character, the functor name is *ch*; and if the element is a string, the functor name is *s*.

The complete recursive rule is

```
transf(Str,[Token_head|Token_tail])  :-
    fronttoken(Str,Symbol_type,Strx),
    choose_token(Symbol_type,Token_head),
    transf(StrX,Token_tail).
```

The sub-rule *choose_token* is

```
choose_token(S,n(N)) :- str_int(S,N).
choose_token(S,c(C)) :- str_char(S,C).
choose_token(S,s(S)) :- isname(S).
```

In this *transf* rule, the string *Str* can be composed of characters or numbers. When the rule is attempted, the value of *Symbol_type* can be a number, a character, or a name. If it is numeric, the *choose_token* rule determines it and the *Token_head* is of the form n(N), where N is a number. If it is a character, the *choose_token* rule gives the *Token_head* the form c(C), where C is a character. If it is a string, the Token_head is of the form s(S), where S is a string.

The program Token4, in listing 6.18, implements this transformation rule. The *domains* division includes declaration of the three types of tokens and it includes declaration of the type *token_list*, which is a list whose elements are of the type token.

```
/* Program: Token4      File: PROG06018.PRO */
/* Purpose: To show transformation of a      */
/* string into a list of functored tokens.  */

domains

    token_type  = n(integer);
                  c(char);
                  s(string)

    token_list = token_type *

predicates

    transf(string,token_list)
    choose_token(string,token_type)

clauses

    transf("",[]).
    transf(Str,[Token_head|Token_tail]):-
        fronttoken(Str,Symbol_type,StrX),
        choose_token(Symbol_type,Token_head),
        transf(StrX,Token_tail).

    choose_token(S,n(N)) :-
                    str_int(S,N).
    choose_token(S,c(C)) :-
                    str_char(S,C).
    choose_token(S,s(S)) :-
                    isname(S).
```

Two possible external goals are

transf("STARS AND STRIPES",FT).

and

transf("LOTUS 123"),FT).

The results of entering these goals are shown in figure 6.16. In the first list, all the elements are of the *string* type, whereas elements in the second list are of mixed types: a type *string* for the first element and a type *integer* for the second element.

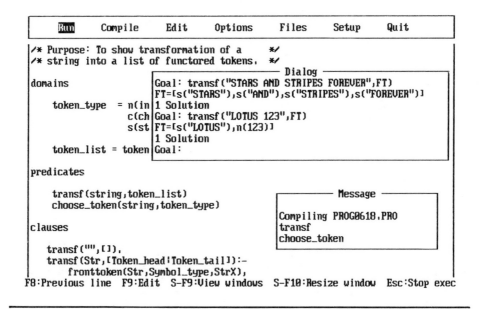

| Run | Compile | Edit | Options | Files | Setup | Quit |

```
/* Purpose: To show transformation of a   */
/* string into a list of functored tokens. */
                                    ┌─ Dialog ─────────────┐
domains                    Goal: transf("STARS AND STRIPES FOREVER",FT)
                           FT=[s("STARS"),s("AND"),s("STRIPES"),s("FOREVER")]
    token_type  = n(in   1 Solution
               c(ch   Goal: transf("LOTUS 123",FT)
               s(st   FT=[s("LOTUS"),n(123)]
                      1 Solution
    token_list = token  Goal:

predicates

    transf(string,token_list)              ┌──── Message ────┐
    choose_token(string,token_type)
                                  Compiling PROG0618.PRO
clauses                           transf
                                  choose_token
    transf("",[]).
    transf(Str,[Token_head!Token_tail]):-
        fronttoken(Str,Symbol_type,StrX),
F8:Previous line  F9:Edit  S-F9:View windows  S-F10:Resize window  Esc:Stop exec
```

Fig. 6.16. A dialogue with the program Token4.

Exercise

6.14. Run the program Token4 and enter these goals:

1. transf("beyond the year 2000",L)

2. transf("THREE SMALL HATS DO NOT MAKE ONE BIG HAT",L)

3. transf("Y = 27 * X + 6",L)

What is the output in each case?

Chapter Review

In this chapter, you learned the use of the Turbo Prolog character set, its representation by ASCII numbers, and how to write and use these. You also learned the uses of the built-in predicates for string manipulations: *str_len*, for finding the length of a string; *concat*, for concatenating two strings; *frontstr*, for splitting a string into two substrings; *frontchar* for prefixing a string with a character; and *fronttoken* for extracting a token from a string.

You also learned to convert data items into different types: uppercase string to lowercase strings, and vice versa; integers to a real numbers, or vice versa; characters to strings, and vice versa; and characters to ASCII numbers.

You applied these techniques in two Turbo Prolog situations: in using the predicate *frontchar* to build a rule to convert a string into a list of characters and in using the predicate *fronttoken* to build a rule to convert a string into a list of functored tokens. These two applications illustrate the uses of string manipulations in converting input data strings into forms that are understandable by Turbo Prolog. These applications are very useful in building rules for user-interface modules of Turbo Prolog programs. They are also useful in preparing data for easier manipulations and convenient storage.

7

Using Disk Files

Overview

In chapters 3 through 6 you worked with Turbo Prolog domain structures, domain types, lists, and strings. These structured objects are usually stored in the computer memory while you are manipulating them. Now you are ready to work with data items that are stored in files.

The manipulation of data stored in files is called *file processing*. Typical file operations include creating files, writing to files, reading from files, modifying data in existing files, and appending data to existing files.

Turbo Prolog provides excellent facilities for convenient and effective file processing, including built-in predicates for opening and closing files, reading from and writing to files, changing data in files, and appending data to existing files. Data in a file can be processed either as a continuous stream of characters or as structured objects similar to the records of a database file.

In this chapter, you will learn programming techniques for creating, accessing, and manipulating data files. You will also learn to use two helpful tools for designing programs, the structure chart and the data-flow diagram. Chapter 9 presents the related file-processing methods used for manipulation of Turbo Prolog's dynamic databases.

Device Configurations

Data files are usually maintained on disk storage devices. A short description of the device configuration on the IBM PC is included here so that you will understand better how the system handles the files you create.

When a Turbo Prolog program is running, it uses several input and output devices that are parts of the computer system. When you run a program with an external goal, for instance, you enter the goal at the keyboard. The program attempts to satisfy that goal and displays the results on the monitor screen. In other words, communication between you and the running program is performed by means of the keyboard, an input device, and the monitor, an output device.

The Turbo Prolog compiler and the running Turbo Prolog program both reside in random access memory (RAM). Memory is both the source of output information and the destination of input information.

Physical and Logical Device Assignments

Figure 7.1 shows the basic device configuration required by Turbo Prolog. The keyboard is an input device and the video monitor is an output device. Turbo Prolog designates the keyboard as the default input device (read-device) and the monitor as the default output device (write-device). In this default device configuration, input comes from the keyboard and output is sent to the monitor. The details of transferring data from these devices to memory, the processor, and other parts of the computer system are handled by routines in the operating system.

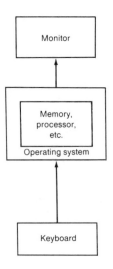

Fig. 7.1. *The basic device designations for input and output.*

The keyboard, monitor, and disk drive(s) are *physical devices*. To understand device configurations both in Turbo Prolog and in other languages, you need to understand a related concept, that of *logical devices*. Physical devices are part of the computer system hardware. Logical devices, on the other hand, are entities "created" by the operating system software.

Many PCs equipped with hard disks, for example, have only one floppy disk drive. But the operating system enables that single physical device to be treated as two logical devices, drive A: and drive B:. If you insert a disk in the floppy disk drive of such a machine and enter the command *DIR A:*, a directory of files on the disk is shown. If you then enter the command *DIR B:*, the operating system displays the message

```
Insert diskette for drive B: and strike
any key when ready
```

When you enter *DIR A:*, the *physical* disk drive is addressed as *logical* drive A:. When you then enter *DIR B:*, that same physical device is addressed as a different logical device. In simplified terms, the physical device is "equated" first with one logical device, then with another. Similar things happen when output is sent first to the screen, then to the printer, and finally to a disk file: a single logical device, which you could call the write-device, is equated first with the screen, then with the printer, and finally with the disk file. This process is known as *redirection*.

Most modern high-level computer languages handle the details of interfacing with the operating system so that data is moved to and from the physical devices. Turbo Prolog streamlines the use of physical devices by providing predicates to perform logical device designations.

The built-in Turbo Prolog predicate *readdevice* is provided to change the default input device. Similarly, the built-in predicate *writedevice* is provided to change the default output device. For example, the predicate

```
readdevice(myfile)
```

changes the default input device to *myfile*. The predicate

```
writedevice(yourfile)
```

changes the default output device to *yourfile*.

The Default Device Configuration

Default device configurations are a language's built-in facilities for using physical devices. Many programming situations call for the use of devices other than the keyboard and the screen. Examples are use of a printer for hardcopy output, of communication ports for telecommunication, and of disk drives for storage of data. Turbo Prolog provides a default device configuration that includes the keyboard, the screen, a printer, and a communications port.

Figure 7.2 shows Turbo Prolog's default device configuration. The printer is attached to the computer's parallel port. The device-designation predicate to send output to the printer is *writedevice(printer)*. The communications port is the primary serial port, or COM1:. (Some PCs have more than one serial port.) Two device-designation predicates are available for this device. The predicate used for writing data to the communications port is *writedevice(com1)*. For reading data from the device, the predicate is *read-device(com1)*. Two predicates are available because the communications device is used both for input (reading data from the incoming communications line) and for output (writing data to the outgoing communications line). The keyboard is a read-only device, and the screen and the printer port are write-only devices.

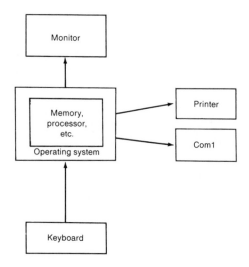

Fig. 7.2. *The default device configuration for input and output.*

In Turbo Prolog, some devices must be "opened" before they are used for input or output, and they must be closed after they are used. Opening a device signals the operating system that the device is about to be used; the operating system then prepares to use any internal resources that are needed to support the use of the device. Closing a device signals the operating system to finish any internal work it has been performing to support the device and to release any supportive resources for use by other parts of the system.

Because the keyboard, monitor, printer, and communications port are default devices, it is not necessary to open or close them. The Turbo Prolog system performs these operations automatically.

Turbo Prolog uses redirection to change input from one device to another. The same redirection can be used to change the output from one device to another device. Suppose, for example, that you want to write the string *Into the future* first to the screen, and then to the printer. These are the predicates you would use:

```
write("Into the future"),nl,
writedevice(printer),
write("Into the future"),nl,
writedevice(screen).
```

The first *write* predicate sends the string to the screen because the screen is the default output device when a program starts. The predicate *writedevice(printer)* redirects output to the printer, and the second *write* predicate writes the string to the printer. The last predicate redirects the output to the screen again.

Note that your computer must have a printer or a communications adapter to redirect input or output to the printer or to COM1. If you try to redirect input or output to a device that is not present, DOS will intervene and your program will be terminated.

The program Macbeth1, in listing 7.1, writes data strings to the screen and to the printer, illustrating the use of the predicates for input and output redirection.

```
/* Program: Macbeth1   File: PROG0701.PRO */
/* Purpose: To output data to the screen  */
/* and to a printer                        */

domains

    str = string

predicates

    data(str)
    write_lines

goal

    write_lines.

clauses

    data("A drum, a drum!").
    data("Macbeth doth come.").
    data("The weird sisters, hand in hand,").
    data("Posters of the sea and land,").
    data("Thus do go about, about:").
    data("Thrice to thine and thrice to mine").
    data("And thrice again, to make up nine.").
```

```
write_lines :-
   data(Line),
   write("   ",Line), nl,
   writedevice(printer),
   write("   ",Line), nl,
   flush(printer),
   writedevice(screen),
   fail.
write_lines.
```

The rule *write_lines* uses the *writedevice* predicate to direct output both to the screen and to the printer:

```
write_lines :-
    data(Line),
    write("   ",Line),nl,
    writedevice(printer),
    write("   ",Line),nl,
    writedevice(screen),
    fail.
write_lines.
```

Before this rule is attempted, the screen is the default write-device. The first subgoal, *data(Line)*, binds *Line* to the object of one of the database predicates. The second subgoal writes the data to the screen. Then the third line redirects the output to the printer, and the fourth line writes the data to the printer. The fifth line redirects output to the screen again. The screen output, an excerpt from Shakespeare's *Macbeth*, is shown in figure 7.3.

Notice the use of the *nl* predicate following each of the *write* predicates. You already know that when data is being written to the screen, *nl* moves the cursor to the next line of the video display. That predicate has a similar function when data is being written to the printer: it causes the print head to move to the beginning of the next line. Later in this chapter, when the program ShowFile is introduced, you'll learn the importance of using *nl* when data is being written to a file.

—————————————— **Exercises** ——————————————

7.1. Write a fragment of Turbo Prolog code to write the string *Thank Goodness, It's Friday* to the printer and then to the screen. (*Hint:* You can type in this code as a goal without having to enter it as a program.)

7.2. Write a fragment of Turbo Prolog code to write the string *Looks like we're going to the Rose Bowl!* to the screen, to the printer, and then to the communications port. Redirect the output to the screen. (You must use the MODE command to configure your communications port so that it will work with the device. See your DOS manual for details on using the MODE command.)

7.3. Modify the program Macbeth1 so that the data is your favorite poem. Briefly describe the data flow during program execution.

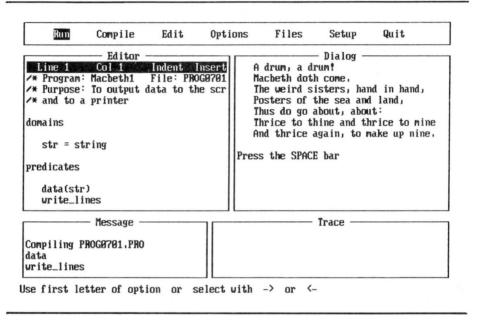

Fig. 7.3. Output of the program Macbeth1.

The Extended Device Configuration

Turbo Prolog's device configurations include disk files, which can be both input and output devices for your programs. Among other benefits, the use of files as (logical) input and output devices provides the means of storing databases, especially large ones, on disk. Figure 7.4 shows Turbo Prolog's extended device configuration, which includes the default configuration and files.

Each of the three files in figure 7.4 can be configured so that data can be written to it or read from it. Writing to a file can include creating a new file, appending data to an existing file, and modifying the data already in the file.

Reading an existing file can include reading all of the data in the file at once, or reading selective portions of the data. Turbo Prolog provides built-in predicates to accomplish these tasks.

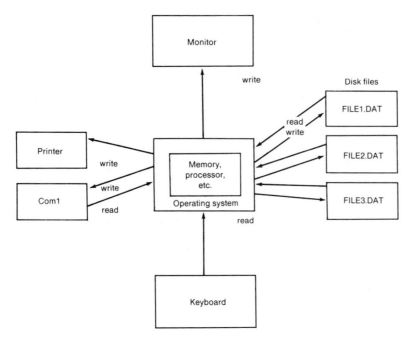

Fig. 7.4. *The extend device configuration for input and output.*

Turbo Prolog File Predicates

Turbo Prolog provides built-in "housekeeping" predicates for managing disk files:

deletefile	to delete a file
save	to save a file
renamefile	to give a file a different name
existfile	to test the existence of a file
flush	to flush data from the file buffers
disk	to select a disk drive and directory path
dir	to get a disk directory

These predicates take the following forms. In the examples, *file_domain* is a user-declared file domain (as explained in the following section) *DOS_filename* is the name of the file as shown in the disk directory. When the name is not self-explanatory, a brief explanation follows the example.

deletefile(DOS_filename)

save(DOS_filename) Saves to disk the clauses in the dynamic database (see Chapter 9).

renamefile(Old_DOS_filename,New_DOS_filename)

`existifile(DOS_filename)` This predicate succeeds if a file with *DOS_ filename* exists in the current directory.

`flush(file_domain)` This predicate flushes the internal buffers allocated to the current write-device.

`disk(Path)` If *Path* is bound to a valid path name (see Appendix C), then the current directory is changed to the directory specified in *Path*. If *Path* is not bound, then this predicate binds *Path* to the path name of the current directory.

`dir(Path,File_spec,File_name)` *Path* and *File_spec* must be bound to a valid DOS path name and file specification (see Appendix C). This predicate displays the names of files matching the file specification, and you can select a file by highlighting the file name and pressing Enter. The name of the selected file is bound to the variable *File_name*.

In addition to these housekeeping predicates, Turbo Prolog provides many others that are used for reading from files, writing to files, modifying files, etc. Those predicates are explained in the following sections.

Declaring the *file* Domain

To use files in a program, you need to declare the *file* domain. A declaration of one disk file named *datafile* is

```
file = datafile
```

This declaration may seem "backward" in comparison to those for other domain types. By now, you're probably accustomed to declarations such as

```
name = symbol
```

where *name* is the name you choose for the domain, and *symbol* is the standard Turbo Prolog domain type. In the declaration of the *file* domain, however, *file*—on the left side of the equal sign—is the standard domain type, and *datafile* is the name you assign to an object of that domain.

A symbolic file name, such as *datafile* in this example, is an identifier that can be logically equated in the program with a DOS file name (the name you see on the disk directory). The symbolic file name is also referred to as the *logical file name*.

More than one symbolic file name may be declared in the *file* declaration, but only one file declaration may appear in a program. If more than one symbolic file name is declared, the declared domains must be separated by semicolons (;), as in

```
file = datafile1; datafile2; datafile3
```

This declaration provides three symbolic file names for subsequent association with actual DOS files.

Writing to Data Files

A file must be created before data can be written to it. The *openwrite* predicate is provided for the purpose of creating a file. The steps for using *openwrite* and then writing to a file are given in this section.

1. Open the file. The Turbo Prolog predicate is

   ```
   openwrite(datafile,"FILE1.DAT").
   ```

   where *datafile* is a user-defined file domain and *FILE1.DAT* is the DOS file name. This predicate establishes a relationship between the objects *datafile1* and FILE1.DAT. This relationship can be translated: "References to *datafile1* mean FILE1.DAT for now." FILE1.DAT remains associated with the symbolic name *datafile* until the file is closed.

   Note that if a file named FILE1.DAT already exists in the current disk directory, that file will be deleted. To guard against this possibility, you can use the predicate

   ```
   existfile("FILE1.DAT")
   ```

   and have your program take appropriate action if *existfile* succeeds.

2. Designate the file as a write-device. The Turbo Prolog predicate is

   ```
   writedevice(datafile1).
   ```

   This predicate selects the opened device FILE1.DAT for the writing of data.

3. Write data to the file, using any appropriate predicate such as *write* or *writef*. Any *write* predicate now writes data to the file FILE1.DAT instead of to the screen.

4. Use any other predicates or rules that meet the requirements of the program. An example is a predicate to redirect the data flow from the screen to the printer.

5. Close the file. The predicate is

   ```
   closefile(datafile1).
   ```

   When the file has been closed, no more data can be written to or read from the file. This step also protects the integrity of the contents of the file from outside manipulation. Only the file as a whole can be processed.

Closing the file also resets the internal position indicator back to the beginning if the file is then reopened.

Here is an example of a Turbo Prolog code fragment that performs the preceding five steps:

```
openwrite(datafile1,"FILE1.DAT"),
writedevice(datafile1),
<any write predicate or rule>
<input/output redirection predicate, as needed>
closefile(datafile1).
```

Reading from Data Files

If FILE1.DAT already exists, several processes can be performed on it. You can read all the data from the file, read selected data from the file, modify data in the file, and append data to the existing file.

The steps for reading data from a file are

1. Open the file:

    ```
    openread(datafile1,"FILE1.DAT")
    ```

2. Designate the file for reading:

    ```
    readdevice(datafile1).
    ```

3. Read the file, using any appropriate predicate or rule.

4. Use any predicate or rule required by the program goal.

5. Close the file:

    ```
    closefile(datafile1).
    ```

A Turbo Prolog program fragment to perform the preceding five steps is

```
openread(datafile1,"FILE1.DAT"),
readdevice(datafile1),
<any appropriate read predicate or rule>,
<input/output redirection, if required>
closefile(datafile1).
```

Modifying an Existing File

The steps for modifying the data in an existing file differ from those for reading or writing a file. The file must be opened for modification (that is, for reading as well as writing). The Turbo Prolog predicate provided for that purpose is *openmodify*.

The predicate

```
openmodify(datafile1,"FILE1.DAT")
```

succeeds only if FILE1.DAT already exists. In other words, you must first create the file by means of the predicate *openwrite*. Remember that *openwrite* will create a new file even if a file with the same name already exists; the result is that the existing file is destroyed.

The contents of a file can be regarded as a stream of characters. Each character can be thought of as having a position within the file. A character's position is its distance (or "offset") from the first character in the file. The first character, then, is at position 0, the next character is at position 1, and so on. Now imagine an invisible "pointer" that can be directed to any position in the file. The position of this pointer is the position at which the next character will be read from or written to the file.

When a file is opened for modification, the file pointer is positioned at the beginning of the file. The Turbo Prolog predicate to change the position of this pointer is *filepos*. You'll learn more about *filepos* in this chapter's section on random access files. For now, you just need to remember where *openmodify* positions the file pointer.

The steps to modify a file are

1. Open the file:

```
openmodify(datafile1,"FILE1.DAT")
```

2. Redirect output to the file:

```
writedevice(datafile1)
```

3. Write the new data to the file.

4. Use any other predicates or rules required by the program goal.

5. Close the file.

An example of Turbo Prolog code to perform these tasks is

```
openmodify(datafile1,"FILE1.DAT"),
writedevice(datafile1),
<Rule to write the data selectively, using filepos.>
closefile(datafile1).
```

Appending Data to an Existing File

To append data to a file is to add new data at the end of an existing file. Turbo Prolog provides the predicate *openappend* for this purpose. When a data file is opened for appending, the file pointer (discussed in the preceding section) is automatically set to the end of the file.

The steps for appending data to a file are

1. Open the file:

   ```
   openappend(datafile1,"FILE.DAT")
   ```

2. Redirect output to the file:

   ```
   writedevice(datafile1).
   ```

3. Write (append) data to the file, using any appropriate predicate or rule.

4. Use any other predicates or rules required by the program goal.

5. Close the file.

Here is an example:

```
openappend(datafile1,"FILE1.DAT"),
    writedevice(datafile1),
    <any write predicate or rule to append data>
closefile(datafile1).
```

Tools for Program Design

Turbo Prolog programs illustrating use of the file-processing predicates are shown in the next section, "Using the File Predicates." Because of their structure and the use of input/output redirection, these programs are more sophisticated than those you've studied in previous chapters. This section introduces two design tools, the data-flow diagram and the structure chart, that you'll find useful in designing sophisticated programs of your own.

Writing a computer program begins with defining the objective of the program—that is, what the program is supposed to do. Defining the objective usually involves identifying input and output data and determining how to produce the desired output data. The input data can come from within the program and from several other sources (or devices): the keyboard, disk files, and communications ports. The output data can be displayed on the screen, printed on hardcopy, stored in a file, or transmitted through the communications port.

In Turbo Prolog, the task of producing output data from input data is performed by the program's goal. A goal usually consists of subgoals, which can be predicates or rules. These predicates and rules can be regarded as modules, each of which performs a distinct task. You may recall the domain-structure diagram and the predicate-structure diagram, which were introduced in Chapter 3. They can be used as guides in structuring domains and writing rules that meet the needs of your programs.

As your programs become more complex, you need additional design resources, particularly resources to assist in planning the structure of the program and the flow of data within it. The rule modules of a Turbo Prolog program form a hierarchical structure. A *structure chart* (SC) like the one shown in figure 7.5 can be used to describe the general function of the program. The SC is useful in planning a program.

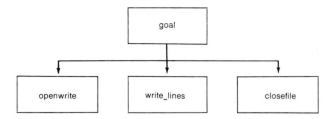

Fig. 7.5. *A structure chart.*

The goal, which is regarded as the main module, calls three other modules. Reading from left to right, you can see that the first module called is the *openwrite* predicate. The purpose of this module is to open a new file. The next module is *write_lines*, whose purpose is to write lines to the disk file as well as to the screen.

To complete the design of your program, you fill in your structure chart with additional details. You can start at the upper levels of the structure chart, where you describe the modules in general terms. The details at the lower levels describe the program more specifically. Within these modules you write Turbo Prolog predicates and rules to accomplish the subgoals of the program modules.

This approach is called *Top-Down Modular Design (TDMD)*. TDMD is generally considered an efficient and effective method of program design. The structure chart is both a tool for organizing program design and a scheme for creating program code. Together the TDMD and structure chart will provide you with sufficient direction to make good use of Turbo Prolog's many capabilities.

As you write the program, you need to keep track of where the input is coming from and where the output is going. A *data-flow diagram* (DFD), as shown in figure 7.6, illustrates the flow of data in the program. This diagram shows that the input data originates within the program; that is, the data is stored in the database. The data "flows" to the goal module for processing, and then to the screen for display and to a disk file for storage.

Of course, this is a simple example. However, for the design of complex programs that involve many rules and much input and output, the data-flow diagram and the structure chart are valuable tools for program organization and documentation. The DFD and the SC are especially useful when you are designing large or complex programs with other programmers. These tools are very helpful even if you work by yourself, because they can refresh your memory as to the details of a program if you need to modify it some time after it was written.

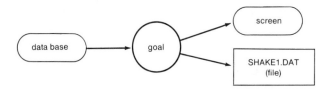

Fig. 7.6. *A data-flow diagram.*

Using the File Predicates

The preceding section introduced two tools, the data-flow diagram (DFD) and the structure chart (SC), that are useful in designing sophisticated programs with several modules and multiple input/output paths. The programs in this section will increase your familiarity with those tools and show you how to use the Turbo Prolog file-processing predicates.

Creating a New Disk File

The DFD in figure 7.6 illustrates the flow of data in the program Macbeth2, which is shown in listing 7.2. Macbeth2 takes data from the data clauses in the database and writes it both to the screen and to the disk file SHAKE1.DAT.

```
/* Program: Macbeth2    File: PROG0702.PRO */
/* Purpose: To output data from a database */
/* to the screen and to a disk file        */

domains

    str  = string
    file = datafile

predicates

    data(string)
    write_lines

goal

    openwrite(datafile,"SHAKE1.DAT"),
    write_lines,
    closefile(datafile).
```

```
clauses

    data("A drum, a drum!").
    data("Macbeth doth come.").
    data("The weird sisters, hand in hand,").
    data("Posters of the sea and land,").
    data("Thus do go about, about:").
    data("Thrice to thine and thrice to mine").
    data("And thrice again, to make up nine.").

    write_lines :-
      data(Line),
      write("   ",Line), nl,
      writedevice(datafile),
      write("   ",Line), nl,
      writedevice(screen),
      fail.
    write_lines.
```

The rule that does the writing uses the Backtrack After Fail (BAF) method:

```
    write_lines :-
        data(Line),
        write("   ",Line),nl,
        writedevice(datafile),
        write(Line),nl,
        writedevice(screen),
        fail.
    write_lines.
```

The first predicate in this rule (or program module) binds the object of a *data* clause to the variable *Line*. The value bound to *Line* then is written to the default output device, the screen. The next three predicates redirect output to the data file, write the data, and redirect output to the screen again. The *fail* predicate causes backtracking to other *data* predicates so that all the clauses in the database are accessed. The final *write_lines* predicate enables the goal to succeed when the first variant of that rule fails because it has accessed all clauses in the database.

The screen output is the same as that of the program Macbeth1. In addition, this program creates in the default directory a disk file named SHAKE1.DAT. To see the contents of the file, first save Macbeth2, then load SHAKE1.DAT into the Turbo Prolog editor. The contents of SHAKE1.DAT should be the same as the input data in the program database, except that each line is preceded by three spaces.

——————————————— **Exercise** ———————————————

7.4. Modify the *write _ lines* rule in the program Macbeth2 so that the data is written to the disk file first and then to the screen.

Reading an Existing File

Reading data from an existing file is the primary means of retrieving data from a storage device. The process requires opening the disk file for reading, outputting the read data to an output device such as the screen or the printer, and closing the file. (These steps were described in the section "Reading from Data Files.") The program Showfile, in listing 7.3, demonstrates this process.

```
/* Program: Showfile   File: PROG0703.PRO */
/* Purpose: To show the reading of a file */
/* and to display the file contents on    */
/* the screen                             */

domains

    str  = string
    file = datafile

predicates

    read_write_lines

goal

    openread(datafile,"SHAKE1.DAT"),
    read_write_lines,
    closefile(datafile).

clauses

    read_write_lines :-
        readdevice(datafile),
        not(eof(datafile)),
        readln(Line),
        writedevice(screen),
        write("   ",Line), nl,
        read_write_lines.
    read_write_lines.
```

Figures 7.7 and 7.8 show the data-flow diagram and the structure chart for this program. The DFD shows the data flow from the file SHAKE1.DAT (which was created by the program Macbeth2) to the program goal. From there, the data flows to the screen. The SC shows that the goal calls three submodules. The first one, on the left, opens the data file SHAKE1.DAT for reading. The next module performs the actual reading and writing of data to the screen. The last module closes the disk file.

Fig. 7.7. *A data-flow diagram for the program Showfile.*

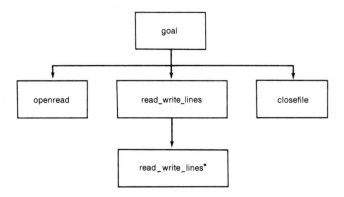

Fig. 7.8. *A structure chart for the program Showfile.*

The heart of the Showfile program is the middle module, a rule to read and write data:

```
read_write_lines :-
    readdevice(datafile),
    not(eof(datafile)),
    readln(Line),
    writedevice(screen),
    write("    ",Line),nl,
read_write_lines.
```

This module uses the built-in Turbo Prolog predicate *eof*, which succeeds when the end of the file is detected. If end-of-file is reached while the file is being read, no more reading can take place until the file pointer is moved to a position before the end-of-file marker. Any subgoal that attempts to read past the end of the file will fail.

The predicate *eof(datafile)* thus indicates the end of the logical file *datafile*. Notice that the negation of this file-ending predicate, *not(eof(datafile))*, is used here. In plain English, you are saying, "Keep reading and writing so long as you are not at the end of the file."

By using the *eof* predicate and having your programs take appropriate action when *eof* succeeds, you can ensure that your programs will behave properly when reading data files. Closing and then reopening the file will clear the end-of-file condition (so that the predicate *eof* no longer succeeds) and position the file pointer at the beginning of the file again.

The predicate *readln* is used in this program to read data strings from the file SHAKE1.DAT. You'll recall from the discussion of the program Macbeth1 that the *nl* predicate was used after the *write* predicate (see the rule *write_lines* in listings 7.1 and 7.2). When *nl* is used with output redirected to a file, an end-of-line indicator is written into the file. The end-of-line indicator consists of two characters, the carriage-return and linefeed characters (ASCII characters 13 and 10). This combination is sometimes called *CR-LF*.

Because *nl* follows *write(Line)* in the rule, a CR-LF combination is written to the file after each line of output. When the program Showfile reads these lines as input, the *readln* predicate reads characters from the file until a CR-LF combination is read. The effect is the same as when a return key is pressed to terminate an input string entered from the keyboard.

The last two predicates redirect output to the screen and then write data to the screen. If your program has not changed the read device from the default device (the screen), the output redirection predicate *writedevice(screen)* is not necessary. Including this predicate in the rule is not wrong, however; it is good programming practice to make sure you have selected the desired output device just prior to outputting the data. The screen output of this program is the same as the output of Macbeth2.

—————————————— **Exercise** ——————————————

7.5. For the program ShowFile:

A. Modify the rule *read_write_lines* so that the disk file data is displayed on the video screen and written to the printer.

B. Draw the data-flow diagram and the structure chart for this modified program.

Creating a Disk File from Keyboard Input

In file processing, a common practice is to input data at the keyboard and send the entries to a disk file. The data in the file can later be edited or manipulated in some other way. The Sendfile program, in listing 7.4, implements this method.

```
/* Program: Sendfile   File: PROG0704.PRO   */
/* Purpose: To show the reading of data     */
/* entered at the keyboard and to send the  */
/* data to a disk file                       */

domains

   file              = datafile
   dstring, cstring = string

predicates

   readin(dstring,cstring)
   create_a_file

goal

   create_a_file.

clauses

     create_a_file :-

     nl, nl,
     write("Please enter complete filename."),
     nl, nl,

     readln(Filename),
     openwrite(datafile,Filename),
         writedevice(datafile),
         readln(Dstring),
         concat(Dstring,"\13\10",Cstring),
         readin(Dstring,Cstring),
     closefile(datafile).

   readin("done",_) :- !.

   readin(_,Cstring) :-
         write(Cstring),
         readln(Dstring1),
         concat(Dstring1,"\13\10",Cstring1),
         writedevice(datafile),
         readin(Dstring1,Cstring1).
```

The data-flow diagram in figure 7.9 shows the flow of data from the keyboard to the goal module and finally to the disk file. The structure chart in figure 7.10 shows a simple diagram. The main module, *create_a_file*, calls the module *readin*, which reads and writes the data.

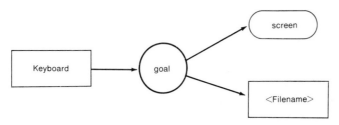

Fig. 7.9. *A data-flow diagram for the program Sendfile.*

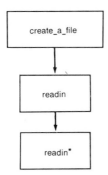

Fig. 7.10. *A structure chart for the program Sendfile.*

The module *create_a_file* writes a prompt to the screen, instructing the user to enter a name for the new file. When the user has entered the file name, Turbo Prolog creates a new disk file. Then each line of data the user enters from the keyboard is written to the file. To end the input process, the user enters the string "done" (note the lowercase spelling) and presses Enter. The file creation now is complete.

The most important new part of the *create_a_file* rule is

```
openwrite(datafile, Filename),
writedevice(datafile),
readln(Dstring),
concat(Dstring,"\13\10",Cstring),
readin(Dstring,Cstring),
closefile(datafile).
```

In these lines, the predicate *readln(Dstring)* reads the first string typed at the keyboard. The *concat* predicate appends to *Dstring* the character pair \ *13\10*, a carriage return-linefeed sequence. (Remember that the CR-LF sequence needs to be appended to *Dstring* so that the *readln* predicate can detect the end of the string, when *readln* is used later to access the data in the file.) The string resulting from the concatenation, *Cstring*, is written to the file.

The preceding rule calls a submodule to continue to write and then read. The first part,

```
readin("done",_) :- !.
```

lets the rule succeed if *Dstring* matches the string *done*. You will remember from Chapter 3 that the cut element (!) stops any backtracking to other solutions, thereby stopping the processing of the rule.

The second part is a recursive rule. The following method of reading data before the recursive writing and reading is often used. You will understand why this method is known as the *read-ahead technique* when you see how the rule works.

```
readin(_, Cstring) :-
    write(Cstring),
    readln(Dstring1),
    concat(Dstring1,"\13\10",Cstring1),
    writedevice(datafile),
    readin(Dstring1,Cstring1).
```

This rule writes the previously concatenated string first. Then it accepts *Dstring1* from the keyboard and concatenates that string with a CR-LF sequence to obtain *Cstring1*. (The concatenation of CR-LF to the string before writing it has the same effect as using the *nl* predicate after writing it. In both cases, the string is followed immediately by the CR-LF sequence.) Then output is redirected to the data file so that the data string is written to the file at the beginning of the next recursive call.

The predicate *writedevice(datafile)* in the preceding rule is not necessary, *writedevice(datafile)* has been declared so in the module that calls *readin*. However, in case you modify the rule so that some other input/output redirection predicate is specified in the rule body, you may need to redirect the input/output to the data file. Inclusion of *writedevice(datafile)* therefore is a good idea.

The program run takes the form of a "dialogue" between the program and the user, as shown in figure 7.11. The strings entered by the user, with the CR-LF sequence appended, make up the contents of the file FROGS.DAT.

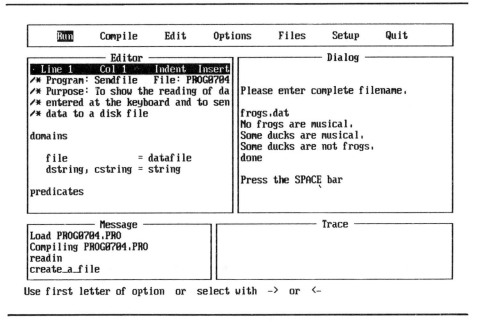

Fig. 7.11. *The dialogue with the program Sendfile.*

Reading a Disk File for Screen and Printer Output

If you've typed in and run the program Sendfile, you now have a new file on your disk. The file contains a number of strings, each terminated with a CR-LF sequence. These data strings can be read and output one line at a time because they end with CR-LF. The program Printfile, in listing 7.5, can be used to read your new file and send its contents to the printer.

```
/* Program: Printfile    File: PROG0705.PRO */
/* Purpose: To show the reading of a data   */
/* file and to send the file contents to    */
/* the screen and to the printer            */

domains

    file             = datafile
    cstring, gstring = string
```

```
predicates

    read_and_print
    read_and_display_file

goal

    read_and_display_file.

clauses

    read_and_display_file :-

        write("Please enter complete file name:"), nl,

        readln(Filename), nl,
        openread(datafile,Filename),
            readdevice(datafile),
            read_and_print,
        closefile(datafile),
        nl, write("Press the space bar."),
        readchar(_), exit.

    read_and_print :-
        not(eof(datafile)),
        readln(Cstring),
        concat(Cstring,"\13\10",Gstring),
        write(Gstring),
        writedevice(printer),
        write(Gstring),
        flush(printer),
        writedevice(screen),
        read_and_print.

    read_and_print :-
        eof(datafile), !.
```

Figures 7.12 and 7.13 show the data-flow diagram and the structure chart for Printfile. The DFD shows that data flows from the file to the *read _ and _ display _ file* module. Then the data is sent both to the screen and to the printer. The SC shows that the main module calls a submodule *read _ and _ print*, whose purpose is to read and write the data. This module is recursive.

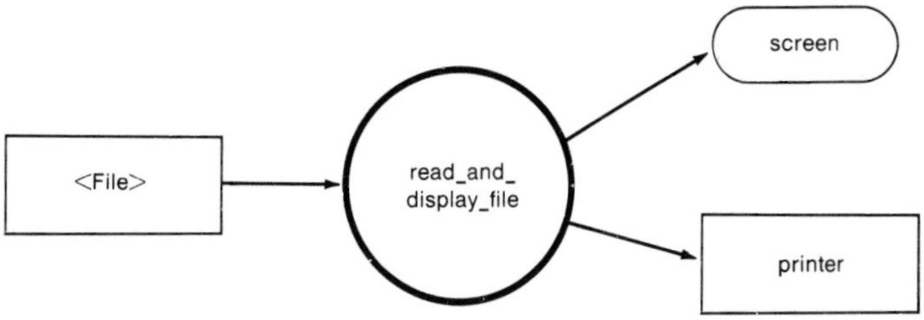

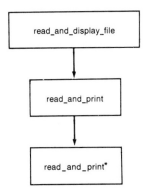

Fig. 7.12. *A data-flow diagram for the program Printfile.*

Fig. 7.13. *A structure chart for the program Printfile.*

The main module of the program is *read_and_display_file*, which calls the recursive rule *read_and_print*. Here is the most important part of the main module:

```
readln(Filename), nl,
openread(datafile, Filename),
      readdevice(datafile),
      read_and_print,
closefile(datafile).
```

These lines get the file name, open the file for reading, and call the rule *read_and_print*.

The rule **read_and_print** contains predicates that read the data file and write the data to the screen and the printer:

```
read_and_print :-
    not(eof(datafile)),
    readln(Cstring),
    concat(Cstring,"\13\10",Gstring),
    write(Gstring),
    writedevice(printer),
    flush(printer),
    writedevice(screen),
    read_and_print.
```

Notice that here, as in the program Sendfile, the CR-LF sequence is concatenated to the data string. This time, those characters are appended to the line so that each string is printed on a new line. In Sendfile, on the other hand, the CR-LF sequence was concatenated to the data strings so that the *readln* predicate in this program will work. The CR-LF indicates the end of the line for the *readln* predicate.

Also notice the use of the predicate *flush(printer)*. Many printers do not print data as soon as it is received; instead, the data is printed only when the printer's internal buffer is full. The *flush* predicate causes the data to be printed immediately.

A runtime dialogue with Printfile is shown in figure 7.14.

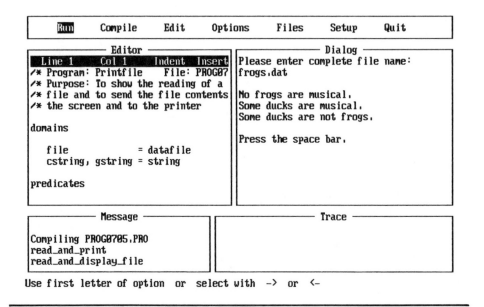

Fig. 7.14. *A dialogue with the program Printfile.*

―――――――――――――――――――― **Exercise** ――――――――――――――――――――

7.6. For the programs Sendfile and Printfile:

A. Run the programs, using data strings of your own choosing.

B. Modify Sendfile so that it does not concatenate a CR-LF sequence to the output string. Run the program again so you can check the result.

C. Modify Printfile so that the data strings output on the printer are double-spaced.

Creating Files with Character Data

The program Sendfile accepted string data from the keyboard and concatenated the CR-LF sequence to each string so that it could be read by the *readln* predicate in Printfile. The data, then, was entered as strings and processed a line at a time, both by Sendfile and by Printfile. Another method of receiving data from the keyboard is to treat the data as a stream of characters. In that method, the *readchar* predicate is used to read characters from the keyboard. One important difference between *readln* and *readchar* is that *readchar* does not echo the read characters to the screen during reading, so you must use the *write* predicate to display them as they are entered.

Figures 7.15 and 7.16 show the data-flow diagram and the structure chart for a program using this method. The DFD shows that the data originates at the keyboard and flows to the program module *process_file*. Then the data flows to the screen and to the file. In the SC, the main module *process_file* calls the recursive submodule *readin* to read and write the data.

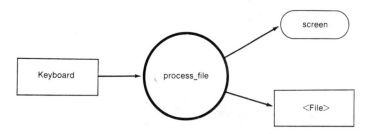

Fig. 7.15. *A data-flow diagram for the program Writechar.*

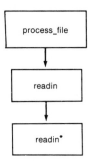

Fig. 7.16. *A structure chart for the program Writechar.*

The program Writechar, in listing 7.6, implements the design shown in figures 7.15 and 7.16. This program accepts character data from the keyboard and writes the characters to the disk file. It also echoes the characters to the screen as they are entered.

```
/* Program: Writechar  File: PROG0706.PRO  */
/* Purpose: To read data from the keyboard  */
/* and to write the data to a disk file      */

domains

    file = datafile

predicates

    process_file
    readin(char)

goal

    process_file.

clauses

    process_file :-
      write("Enter the complete file name:"), nl,
      readln(Filename),
      openwrite(datafile,Filename),
      writedevice(datafile),
      readchar(C),
      readin(C),
      closefile(datafile).
```

```
readin( '#' ) :- !.

readin('\13') :- !,
    write("\13\10"),
    writedevice(screen),
    write("\13\10"),
    readchar(C),
    writedevice(datafile),
    readin(C).

readin(  C  ) :-
    write(C),
    writedevice(screen),
    write(C),
    readchar(C1),
    writedevice(datafile),
    readin(C1).
```

As you can see from analyzing the program listing, both the *process_file* and *readin* modules have *readchar* predicates. In addition, the submodule *readin(C)* reads and writes multiple characters:

```
readin('#') :- !.

readin('\13') :- !,
    write("\13\10"),
    writedevice(screen),
    write("\13\10"),
    readchar(C),
    writedevice(datafile),
    readin(C).

readin(C) :-
    write(C),
    writedevice(screen),
    write(C),
    readchar(C1),
    writedevice(datafile),
    readin(C1).
```

The second form of the *readin* rule succeeds when a carriage return (ASCII character 13) has been entered; this rule writes the CR-LF sequence to the screen and the data file, accepts another character by means of *readchar*, and recursively calls *readin*. The third form of *readin* succeeds when any other character has been entered. This rule, like the second variant of *readin*, writes a character to the file and to the screen, accepts another character, and calls *readchar*.

When a pound sign has been entered, the rule *readin(#)* succeeds; because that variant of *readin* has no recursive call, the subgoal *readin(C)* succeeds, and the next part of the program goal is attempted. The data file is closed and the program terminates.

——————————————— **Exercise** ———————————————

7.7. Run the program Writechar. When prompted, enter the file name MYPOEM.DAT and then enter your favorite short poem. Check the contents of the data file using the Turbo Prolog editor.

Reading Characters from a File

Now you have seen two methods of reading data from the keyboard. The first method uses the *readln* predicate, and the second uses the *readchar* predicate. The *readchar* predicate can also be used to read characters from a data file. Figures 7.17 and 7.18 show the data-flow diagram and structure chart for a program that reads characters from a disk file, displays the data on-screen, and prints the data.

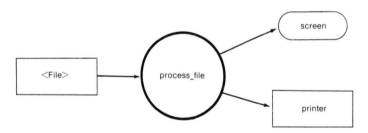

Fig. 7.17. *A data-flow diagram for the program Readchar.*

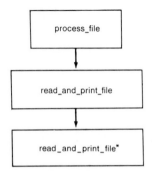

Fig. 7.18. *A structure chart for the program Readchar.*

The Readchar program, in listing 7.7, implements the design shown in figures 7.17 and 7.18.

```
/* Program: Readchar     File: PROG0707.PRO */
/* Purpose: To read a disk file and send     */
/* the output to the screen and to a         */
/* printer                                    */

domains

   file = datafile

predicates

   process_file
   read_and_print_file

goal

   process_file.

clauses

   process_file :-
     write("Enter complete file name:"), nl,
     readln(Filename),
     openread(datafile,Filename),
     readdevice(datafile),
     read_and_print_file,
     closefile(datafile).

   read_and_print_file :-
       not(eof(datafile)),
       readchar(Y),
       write(Y),
       writedevice(printer),
       write(Y),
       flush(printer),
       writedevice(screen),
       read_and_print_file.
```

```
read_and_print_file :-
    nl, nl,
    readdevice(keyboard),
    write("Please press the space bar"),
    readchar(_).
```

The module that does the reading and writing is the recursive rule *read_and_print_file*:

```
read_and_print_file :-
    not(eof(datafile)),
    readchar(Y),
    write(Y),
    writedevice(printer),
    write(Y),
    flush(printer),
    writedevice(screen),
    read_and_print_file.
```

The *readchar* predicate reads both printable characters (the data in the file) and control characters such as CR-LF.

—————————— **Exercise** ——————————

7.8. Run the program Readchar. When prompted for the file name, enter FROGS.DAT (or whatever name you assigned to the file created by the program Sendfile). The output on the screen should be the three lines of text you entered when running Sendfile. Draw the data-flow diagram and the structure chart for the program Readchar.

User-Friendly Programs for Processing Files

The programs presented so far have been written for a minimum of runtime interaction with the user. However, good design practice is to include modules that help the user in running the program. The help modules usually display menus and useful messages. They may include other helpful additions to the basic program functions, such as allowing time for the user to decide what data to enter.

User-Friendly File Writing

The Readdata program, shown in listing 7.8, is an example of a user-friendly program that writes the user's entries to a disk file.

```
/* Program: Readdata    File: PROG0708.PRO   */
/* Purpose: To read data from the keyboard  */
/* and write the data to a disk file        */

domains

    file            = datafile
    dstring, cstring = string

predicates

    write_message_1
    check_for_ready
    give_instruction
    process_input_output
    process_file
    write_message_2
    readin(dstring,cstring)
    create_a_file

goal

    create_a_file.

clauses

    create_a_file :-

        write_message_1,
        process_file,
        write_message_2,
        nl, nl, write("Press the space bar."),
        readchar(_), exit.

    process_file :-

        check_for_ready,
        give_instruction,
        process_input_output.
```

```
write_message_1 :-

    nl, write("Hello"),
    nl, write("This program accepts data from"),
    write(" keyboard and writes to a file."), nl.

check_for_ready :-

    write("PLEASE PRESS SPACE BAR WHEN"),
    write(" YOU ARE READY TO BEGIN."), nl,
    readdevice(keyboard),
    readchar(_).

give_instruction :-

    nl, write("You type in data from the keyboard."),
    nl, write("To terminate the input process,"),
    write(" enter 'done'.   Thank you."), nl.

process_input_output :-

    write("Please enter complete filename."),
    write(" Then press the return key."), nl,
    write("The format of the file name is"),
    write("    <file name>.<extension>."), nl, nl,
    readln(Filename),
    nl, write("Start typing in . . . "), nl,
    openwrite(datafile,Filename),
        writedevice(datafile),
        readln(Dstring),
        concat(Dstring,"\13\10",Cstring),
        readin(Dstring,Cstring),
    closefile(datafile).

write_message_2 :-

    writedevice(screen),
    nl, write("Your data has been written to the file."),
    write("   All done, bye!").

readin("done",_) :- !.
```

```
readin(_,Cstring) :-
      write(Cstring),
      readln(Dstring1),
      concat(Dstring1,"\13\10",Cstring1),
      writedevice(datafile),
      readin(Dstring1,Cstring1).
```

Figures 7.19 and 7.20 show the data-flow diagram and structure chart for the program Readdata. This program includes several help modules. The structure chart shows the main module, which is this rule:

```
create_a_file :-

      write_message_1,
      process_file,
      write_message_2.
```

The first and the last submodules are help modules.

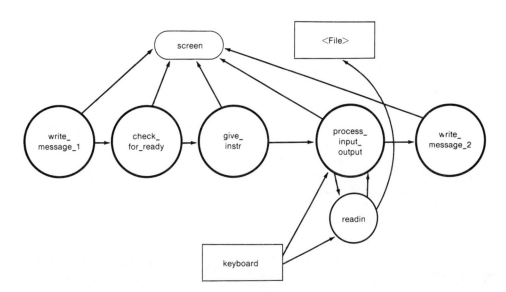

Fig. 7.19. *A data-flow diagram for the program Readdata.*

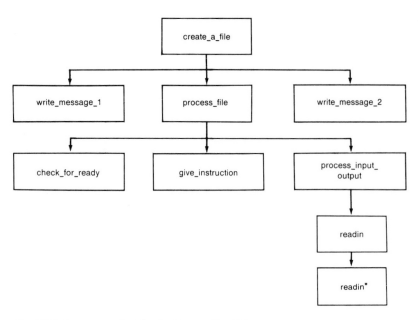

Fig. 7.20. *A structure chart for the program Readdata.*

The help modules write messages to the user:

```
write_message_1 :-
     nl,nl,write("Hello"),nl,nl,
     write("This program accepts data from"),nl,
     write("the keyboard and writes to a file."),nl,nl.

write_message_2 :-
     writedevice(screen),nl,nl,
     write("Your data has been written"),nl,
     write("to the file"),nl,nl,
     write("           All done, bye!").
```

As you can see, the first message explains how to use the program and tells what it does; the second tells what the program has done and indicates that the program is ending.

The second submodule, *process_file*, calls three other submodules:

```
process_file :-
     check_for_ready,
     give_instruction, nl, nl,
     process_input_output.
```

Each of these submodules performs a distinct task, and all three have helpful features.

The purpose of the submodule *check_for_ready* is to check whether the user is ready to proceed with the program:

```
check_for_ready
    write("PLEASE PRESS THE SPACE BAR WHEN"),nl,
    write("YOU ARE READY TO BEGIN."),nl,nl,
    readdevice(keyboard),
    readchar(_).
```

Notice that the predicate *readchar(_)* contains an underscore, signifying an anonymous variable. A "wait" module like this is useful in many programs.

The submodule *give_instruction* instructs the user in how to use the program:

```
give_instruction :-
    nl, nl,
    write("You type in data from the keyboard."),nl,nl,
    write("To terminate the input process"),nl,
    write("enter 'done'. Thank you."),nl,nl.
```

Notice that the last *write* predicate tells the user to type *done* when finished. Additions like this are very important to the user; they can mean the difference between success and failure in the use of the program.

The module *process_input_output* performs the central activity of the program. It accepts the file name and begins the reading and writing of data:

```
process_input_output :-
    nl,nl, write("Please enter complete file name."),nl,
    write("Then press the return key."),nl,
    write("The format of the file name is"),
    nl,nl,
    write("<filename>.<extension>"),nl,nl,
    readln(Filename),
    write(Start typing ... "),nl,nl,
    openwrite(datafile, Filename),
    writedevice(datafile),
    readln(Dstring),
    concat(Dstring,"\13\10",Gstring),
    readin(Dstring,Cstring),
    closefile(datafile).
```

This module calls the recursive module *readin* to continue the reading and writing of data. This *readin* module is the same one you saw in the program Sendfile. Notice the inclusion of the predicate *write("start typing . . . ")* to prompt the user for input. This is a nice addition to the program.

The DFD in figure 7.19 shows the data flow and the devices used in this program. It shows the six submodules and the input device (the keyboard), the output device (the screen), and the disk file with the variable name Filename. The diagram shows clearly where the data originates and where it is going.

The runtime dialogue with the program Readdata shows the help messages and useful instructions for the user. A portion of this dialogue is shown in figure 7.21. The dialogue also shows the importance of clear instructions and a pleasant format. These aesthetic considerations may seem to be of secondary importance to the programmer, but they are often extremely important to the user.

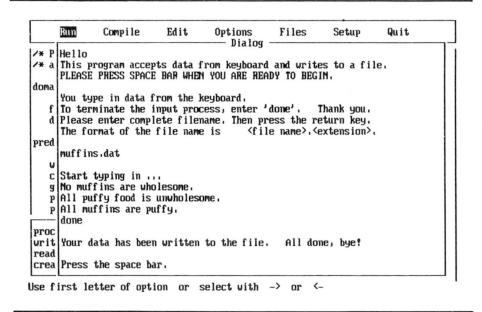

Fig. 7.21. *A dialogue with the program Readdata.*

Exercise

7.9. Modify the Readdata program by including your own help messages, then test-run the program.

User-Friendly File Reading

A user-friendly program should provide helpful messages about how to begin, show how to select a file, and provide time-delay prompts as needed. The Readfile program, in listing 7.9, is such a user-friendly program.

```
/* Program: Readfile    File: PROG0709.PRO    */
/* Purpose: To read data from a disk file     */
/* and print the data on the screen and on    */
/* a printer                                   */

domains

    file = datafile

predicates

    write_message_1
    check_for_ready
    process_file
    process_input_output
    write_message_2
    read_and_print
    create_output_from_a_file

goal

    create_output_from_a_file.

clauses

    create_output_from_a_file :-

                write_message_1,
                process_file,
                write_message_2.

    process_file :-

        check_for_ready,
        process_input_output.

    write_message_1 :-

      nl, nl, write("HELLO"), nl, nl,
      write("This program reads and writes "),
      nl,
      write("data from a data file."),
      nl, nl.
```

```
check_for_ready :-

    write("PLEASE PRESS SPACE BAR WHEN"),
    nl,
    write("YOU ARE READY TO BEGIN."),
    nl, nl,
    readdevice(keyboard),
    readchar(_).

process_input_output :-

    write("Please enter complete file name."),
    nl,
    write("Then press the Return key."), nl,
    write("The format of a file name is"),
    nl, nl,
    write("<filename>.<extension>"),
    nl, nl,

    readln(Filename), nl,
    openread(datafile,Filename),
        readdevice(datafile)
        read_and_print,
    closefile(datafile).

write_message_2 :-

    writedevice(screen), nl, nl,
    write("Printing of data from the file"),
    nl,
    write("has been completed."), nl, nl,
    write("             Good bye !"), nl.

read_and_print :-

        not(eof(datafile)),
        readchar(Y),
        write(Y),
        writedevice(printer),
        write(Y),
        flush(printer),
        writedevice(screen),
        read_and_print.
```

```
read_and_print :-

    nl, nl,
    write("Please press the space bar"),
    readdevice(keyboard),
    readchar(_).
```

The design of the Readfile program is similar to that of the Readdata program. Readfile has seven modules. The help modules contain messages relevant to file reading. The module *process_input_output* contains prompts for the file name and for processing the named file:

```
process_input_output:-
    write("Please enter complete file name."),nl,
    write("Then press the Return key."),nl,
    write("The format of the file name is"),nl,nl,
    write("<filename>.<extension>"),nl,nl,
    readln(Filename),
    openread(datafile, Filename),
    readdevice(datafile),
    read_and_print,
    closefile.
```

This module calls another module to read and write the data:

```
read_and_print :-

    not(eof(datafile)),
    readchar(Y),
    write(Y),
    writedevice(printer),
    write(Y),
    writedevice(Screen),
    read_and_print.
```

This module reads and writes data a character at a time; you might call this a "character reader." A module like this can read any text file, whether the data was written to the file as strings or as characters. You should note, however, that reading data character by character takes more time than does reading strings. Except for programming tasks that require inspecting and processing each character of the data, programs that read strings are more efficient.

—————————— **Exercises** ——————————

7.10. Run the program Readfile. When prompted for the file name, enter the name of a data file that already exists on your disk.

7.11. Draw a data-flow diagram and a structure chart for the Readfile program. Consult figures 7.19 and 7.20 for help.

Appending Data to a Disk File

Appending data to an existing disk file is an important activity. As more information becomes available, this information must be appended to existing files. The files of databases and expert systems are maintained in this way. The program Players, in listing 7.10, implements a typical file-appending method. This program accepts string data from the keyboard and appends it to a file chosen by the user.

```
/* Program: Players      File: PROG0710.PRO */
/* Purpose: To read data from the keyboard  */
/* and append the data to a disk file       */

domains

    file            = datafile
    dstring, cstring = string

predicates

    write_message_1
    check_for_ready
    give_instruction
    process_file
    process_input_output
    write_message_2
    readin(Dstring,Cstring)
    append_a_file

goal

    append_a_file.

clauses
```

```
append_a_file :-

    write_message_1,
    process_file,
    write_message_2,
    nl, write("Press the space bar."),
    readchar(_), exit.

process_file :-

    check_for_ready,
    give_instruction,
    process_input_output.

write_message_1 :-

    nl, write("Hello"), nl,
    write("This program accepts data from"),
    write(" keyboard and appends it to a file."), nl.

check_for_ready :-

    write("PLEASE PRESS SPACE BAR WHEN"),
    write(" YOU ARE READY TO BEGIN."), nl,
    readdevice(keyboard),
    readchar(_).

give_instruction :-

    nl, write("You type in data from the keyboard."),
    nl, write("To terminate the input process,"),
    write(" enter 'done'.    Thank you."), nl.

process_input_output :-

    write("Please enter complete filename."),
    write("Then press the return key."), nl,
    write("The format of the file name is"),
    write("      <file name>.<extension>."), nl, nl,
    readln(Filename),
    nl, write("Start typing in ... "), nl,
    openappend(datafile,Filename),
```

```
        writedevice(datafile),
        readln(Dstring),
        concat(Dstring,"\13\10",Cstring),
        readin(Dstring,Cstring),
    closefile(datafile).

write_message_2 :-

    writedevice(screen),
    nl, write("Your data has been appended"),
    write(" to the file."),
    write("        All done, bye!").

readin("done",_) :- !.

readin(_,Cstring) :-
        write(Cstring),
        readln(Dstring1),
        concat(Dstring1,"\13\10",Cstring1),
        writedevice(datafile),
        readin(Dstring1,Cstring1).
```

This program also has modules to make it user-friendly. The structure of the program is similar to that of the Writechar program, a program that accepts string data from the keyboard and writes it to a new disk file.

The essential part of the program Players is the module *process_input_output*:

```
process_input_output :-

    write("Please enter complete file name."),
    write("Then press the return key."), nl,
    write("The format of the file name is"),
    write("        <file name>.<extension>."), nl, nl,
    readln(Filename),
    nl, write("Start typing in ... "), nl,
    openappend(datafile,Filename),
        writedevice(datafile),
        readln(Dstring),
        concat(Dstring,"\13\10",Cstring),
        readin(Dstring,Cstring),
    closefile(datafile).
```

The *openappend* predicate is used to open an existing file for the purpose of appending more data to the end of the file. The called module *readin* is the same as in the program Readfile.

The help modules in this program display appropriate help messages. To illustrate the working of this program, imagine that you want to append data to a file named BROWNS.DAT, whose existing contents are

```
browns("Chip Banks",26,"6-4",233,"WR").
browns("Gary Danielson",34,"6-2",195,"QB").
browns("Bob Golic",29,"6-2",260,"NT").
```

To append more players' statistics to this file, you run the Players program. A runtime dialogue is shown in figure 7.22.

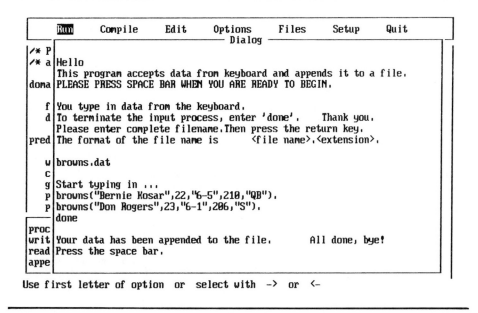

Fig. 7.22. *A dialogue with the program Players.*

The data file BROWNS.DAT now has the appended data. To view the contents of the file, use the Turbo Prolog editor. You should see all five lines in the order of entry.

——————————— Exercise ———————————

7.12. Draw the data-flow diagram and the structure chart for the Players program. Then run the program, and append data to a file created by another program in this chapter. View the data file before and after appending the new data.

Using Random Access Files

You'll recall from the section "Modifying an Existing File" that each character in a file has a position that can be expressed as its distance, or offset, from the first character. A file pointer can be placed at any position in the file; this pointer's position determines where the next character will be read or written. Files that are accessed in this way are known as *random access I/O files* or *random access files*. The process of accessing files in this way is *random access file I/O*.

Random access file I/O methods make it possible to read and write logical units such as file records at any position in a file. In files used for these purposes, the records are all of the same length. When the file pointer is moved in multiples of this record length, the pointer always "comes to rest" at the beginning of a record. Turbo Prolog provides two built-in predicates that are convenient for random access file I/O: *openmodify* and *filepos*. In this section, you'll learn how to use them.

Suppose, for example, that you want to modify a file named PLAYERS.DAT. The form of the *openmodify* predicate is

```
openmodify(players,"PLAYERS.DAT").
```

The symbol *players* is the logical file name used within the Turbo Prolog program. The *openmodify* predicate attaches the DOS file name to the logical file name; any subsequent references to *players* within a program containing this predicate will be interpreted as references to PLAYERS.DAT. (Of course, this file must have been created first.)

The *filepos* predicate has the form

```
filepos(Logical_filename,File_position,Mode).
```

The *File_ position* parameter must be bound to a real number that indicates the position of a first character to be read from or written to the file. (Any decimal part of this real number is discarded.)

Mode must be bound to an integer value of 0, 1, or 2. That value specifies how *Fileposition* is to be interpreted. Table 7.1 shows the meaning of the three permissible *Mode* values.

———————————— **Table 7.1** ————————————
Modes for the *filepos* Predicate

Mode	Remarks
0	File position relative to the beginning of the file
1	File position relative to the current position
2	File position relative to the end of the file

For example, consider the *filepos* predicate

```
filepos(players,100,0).
```

In this predicate expression, the logical file name is *players*. The *File_position* value is 100, indicating that the character to be read is at position 100 in the file. The *Mode* value of 0 indicates that the file position is defined relative to the beginning of the file.

If the mode position is changed to 1, then the expression is

```
filepos(players,100,1).
```

The *Mode* value of 1 indicates that the position is relative to the current position. When this predicate succeeds, it advances the file pointer to a position 100 characters past the current position.

In this section, two programs are developed. The first creates a random access file and writes some data to it. The second program, using the file-position values as input reference data, reads data from a random-access file.

Writing a Random Access File

The program design for creating a random access file begins with determination of the way in which the data is to be organized. Consider, for example, a file that contains information about some football players. Let us call the file PLAYERS.DAT. The file's contents—the players' names, numbers, and teams—are

```
John Elway, 7, Denver Broncos---------
Jim McMahon, 9, Chicago Bears---------
Bernie Kosar, 19  Cleveland Browns----
Phil Sims, 11, New York Giants--------
```

There are four lines of data, each with a total of 38 characters. You want to access a player's data selectively after the creation of the file. To do that, it is necessary to append linefeed (LF) and carriage-return (CR) characters to each line. At this point, then, each line is a string of 40 characters. The four lines are known as *fixed-length string data* because they all have the same length. Hyphens are inserted in the lines to show the "fill" characters that pad each string to the full 38 characters.

In the section "Writing to Data Files," you learned the basic steps for modifying the data in an existing file. A rule for creating a random access file uses some of the same steps. Such a rule is

```
create_a_random_access_file :-
    openwrite(datafile,Filename),
    closefile(datafile),
    openmodify(datafile,Filename),
    readln(Dstring),
    write_read_more(0,Dstring),
    closefile(datafile).
```

The first two predicates, *openwrite* and *closefile*, create a file that is initially empty. Then the predicate *openmodify* reopens the same file for the purpose of modification (writing data). The predicate *readln* reads a data string from the keyboard. Then the rule *write_read_more* writes strings to the file and reads additional strings from the keyboard.

The program CreateRandy, in listing 7.11, uses rules similar to these. The main module is *create_a_random_access_file*, and *write_read_more* is a submodule called by the main module. This submodule is a recursive rule that repeatedly writes and reads data. Recursion ends when the user enters *done*.

```
/* Program: CreateRandy    File: PROG0711.PRO */
/* Purpose: To read data from the keyboard    */
/* and write the data to a random-access I/O   */
/* file                                        */

domains

    file  = datafile

predicates

    create_a_random_access_file
    write_read_more(real,string)
    pad_string(string,string,integer)

goal

    create_a_random_access_file.

clauses

    create_a_random_access_file :-
        write("Please enter filename:"), nl,
        readln(Filename),
        openwrite(datafile,Filename),
        closefile(datafile),
        openmodify(datafile,Filename),
        write("Type in data string."), nl,
        readln(Dstring),
        write_read_more(0,Dstring),
        closefile(datafile).
```

```
write_read_more(_,"done") :-
    nl, write(" Press the space bar."),
    readchar(_), exit.

write_read_more(Index,Dstring) :-
    writedevice(datafile),
    filepos(datafile,Index,0),
    pad_string(Dstring,Padstring,38),
    concat(Padstring,"\10\13",Cstring),
    write(Cstring),
    writedevice(screen),
    write("Type in data string."), nl,
    readln(Dstring1),
    Index1 = Index + 40,
    write_read_more(Index1,Dstring1).

pad_string(Instring,Instring,Length) :-
    str_len(Instring,Testlength),
    Testlength >= Length,!.
pad_string(Instring,Padstring,Length) :-
    concat(Instring,"-",Newstring),
    pad_string(Newstring,Padstring,Length).
```

The recursive rule *write_read_more* pads the string to a length of 38 characters, concatenates a CR-LF combination to the string, and writes the concatenated string to the
file:

```
write_read_more(_,"done") :-
        nl, write(" Press the space bar."),
        readchar(_), exit.

write_read_more(Index,Dstring) :-
        writedevice(datafile),
        filepos(datafile,Index,0),
        pad_string(Dstring,Padstring,38),
        concat(Padstring,"\10\13",Cstring),
        write(Cstring),
        writedevice(screen),
        write("Type in data string."), nl,
        readln(Dstring1),
        Index1 = Index + 40,
        write_read_more(Index1,Dstring1).
```

Notice that the *Index* value (used by *filepos*) is increased by 40 before each recursive call. The index is increased so that on each call, the file pointer is positioned at the proper point for writing of the new record.

The rule *write_read_more* uses the rule *pad_string* to concatenate hyphens to the data strings. The recursive rule *pad_string* is

```
pad_string(Instring,Instring,Length) :-
    str_len(Instring,Length),!.
pad_string(Instring,Padstring,Length) :-
    concat(Instring,"-",Newstring),
    pad_string(Newstring,Padstring,Length).
```

Recursion ends when the length of *Padstring* is equal to the value bound to the integer variable *Length*.

String-padding techniques are useful in creating fixed-length string data. In *pad_string*, the string is padded with hyphens for purposes of clarity. If you use a rule like this one in programs of your own, you will probably want to pad with spaces, instead. Also, you will probably want to provide a variant of the rule to accommodate cases in which *Instring* is longer than the desired length.

Figure 7.23 shows a dialogue with the CreateRandy program. In this figure, the random access file name is PLAYERS.RAT. Notice that each data line is 38 characters long.

| Run | Compile | Edit | Options | Files | Setup | Quit |

```
                    ─────── Dialog ───────
/* Purpo │Please enter filename:
/* and w │players.dat
/* file  │Type in data string.
         │John Elway, 7, Denver Broncos
domains  │Type in data string.
         │Jim McMahon, 9, Chicago Bears
   file  │Type in data string.
         │Bernie Kosar, 19, Cleveland Browns
predicat │Type in data string.
         │Phil Simms, 11, New York Giants
  creat  │Type in data string.
  write  │done
  pad_s  │
         │  Press the space bar.
goal     │

Compilin
create_a
write_re
pad_stri

Use first
```

Fig. 7.23. A dialogue with the program CreateRandy.

—————————————— **Exercises** ——————————————

7.13. Design a random access I/O file structure for auto parts data. Each data string should include the following information:

Part number, Part name, Quantity on hand, Unit price.

7.14. Write a Turbo Prolog program to create a random access file, using the auto-parts inventory file designed in exercise 7.13.

Reading a Random Access File

Reading a random access file requires knowledge of the file's structure. You need to know, for example, the length of each data record stored at each position, the number of data records, and the starting position in the file of the first record. Remember that in the random access file PLAYERS.DAT, created by the program CreateRandy, each data string has a fixed length of 40 characters. Also recall that the first string was indexed at position zero in the file. Thus, the first characters of each of the four strings written to the file are at positions 0, 40, 80, and 120 in the file.

A rule for reading this file is

```
read_a_random_access_file :-
    openread(datafile,Filename),
    readreal(Index),
    readdevice(datafile),
    filepos(datafile,Index,0),
    readln(Cstring),
    write(Cstring), nl, nl,
    closefile(datafile).
```

In this rule, the *openread* predicate is used to open for reading the file attached to the logical file name *datafile*. The *readreal* predicate is used to read from the keyboard a real number indicating the user's choice of a record to read. Then the *readdevice* predicate redirects input to *datafile*. The *filepos* predicate is used to position the file pointer at the position entered by the user; the value zero in the *Mode* parameter indicates that the position is relative to the beginning of the file. The *readln* predicate then reads the string starting at that file position, and the variable *Cstring* is bound to the value of the string. Note that it is not necessary in this rule to use the *openmodify* predicate, because the file is only going to be read.

The ReadRandy program, in listing 7.12, uses an implementation of the basic rule for reading a random access I/O file.

```
/* Program: ReadRandy    File: PROG0712.PRO    */
/* Purpose: To read data from a random-access  */
/* file and write the data to the screen       */

domains

   file            = datafile

predicates

   read_a_random_access_file

goal

   read_a_random_access_file.

clauses

   read_a_random_access_file :-
      write("Please enter filename:"), nl,
      readln(Filename),
      openread(datafile,Filename),
      write("Type in record number: "), nl,
      readreal(Record),
      Index = (Record - 1) * 40,
      readdevice(datafile),
      filepos(datafile,Index,0),
      readln(Cstring),
      write(Cstring), nl, nl,
      write("Press the space bar."), nl,
      readdevice(keyboard),
      readchar(_),
      closefile(datafile),
      exit.
```

ReadRandy is a "single read" or "single query" program. The goal (a rule) is *read_a_random_access_file*:

```
read_a_random_access_file :-
   makewindow(1,7,7," Quarterbacks ",4,10,18,50),
   write("Please enter filename:"), nl,
   readln(Filename),
   openread(datafile,Filename),
   write("Type in record number: "), nl,
```

```
readreal(Record),
Index = (Record - 1) * 40,
readdevice(datafile),
filepos(datafile,Index,0),
readln(Cstring),
write(Cstring), nl, nl,
write("Press the space bar."), nl,
readdevice(keyboard),
readchar(_),
closefile(datafile),
exit.
```

Notice how the *Index* value is calculated. This rule subtracts 1 from the record number and multiplies the result by 40 to obtain the value for *Index*. If the resulting value is not beyond the end of the file, then the rule succeeds and the data string is displayed on-screen. The program then displays a prompt, closes the file, and terminates.

Figure 7.24 shows a dialogue with the program. Notice that the user's entry is 1, and the program displays the data for player John Elway.

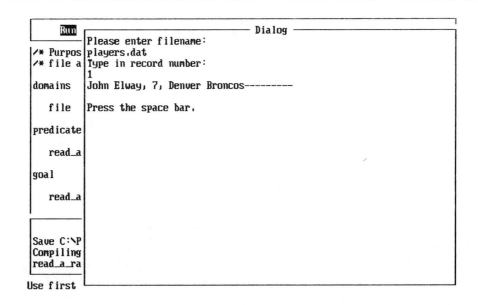

Fig. 7.24. *A dialogue with the program ReadRandy.*

——————————————— **Exercises** ———————————————

7.15. Modify the ReadRandy program so that it reads all the strings in the file.

7.16. Modify the ReadRandy program so that the output string is displayed in the following format:

```
Name:           <player's name>

Number:         <player's number>

Team:           <player's team>
```

Hint: Break up the output string using the *substring* predicate (refer to Chapter 6).

Chapter Review

In this chapter, you have learned to create and use data files with your Turbo Prolog programs. You have learned to use Turbo Prolog's file-handling predicates—*openwrite, openread, openappend, openmodify, closefile, readdevice, writedevice, eof,* and *filepos*—by studying and running programs that use those predicates. You have also been introduced to other related predicates such as *save, rename, delete, disk, dir, existfile,* and *flush.*

You have learned to process data either as character streams or as strings. Careful management of data files, you have learned, involves details such as using the carriage return-linefeed sequence to terminate strings of input or output data. In learning to use the output redirection predicate *writedevice* and the predicate *writechar* to echo input characters to the screen, you have learned much about data flow. The predicate *readchar* reads a character, but it does not echo the character to the screen. You have learned that when you use *readln* to read strings from the keyboard, the strings are automatically echoed to the screen.

You have also been introduced to modern structured program-design methods. The usefulness of the data-flow diagram to describe the flow of data in Turbo Prolog file-processing programs has been demonstrated. Structure charts have been utilized to describe program structures in terms of hierarchical module structures. You have seen the use of top-down modular design (TDMD) in building structure charts.

You have seen how the inclusion of messages in the program modules makes them "user-friendly." These help modules are highly desirable as they communicate with the user in affirmative ways, thus improving the effectiveness of your Turbo Prolog programs.

Finally, you have learned the fundamentals of writing and reading random access files. You have seen how the *filepos* predicate is used to access data at a specified position in the file, and have learned about managing fixed-length string data.

8

Using Windows, Graphics, and Sound

Overview

Continuing the tradition of software from Borland International, Turbo Prolog has first-class capabilities for windowing, graphics, and sound. With Turbo Prolog you can create multiple windows, set attributes such as foreground and background colors from color palettes, change window sizes, and switch input and output from window to window. The language offers a variety of graphics modes, supporting both the Color/Graphics Adapter and the Enhanced Graphics Adapter. The sound capabilities enable your programs to produce musical tones over a wide frequency range, with precise control of durations.

Until now, your programs have been "flat": that is, their input and output are based on lines printed in the Dialog window. This chapter, however, will show you how to give your programs some depth with Turbo Prolog's windowing, graphics, and sound facilities.

Turbo Prolog's graphics capabilities include the basic *dot* and *line* predicates. These two predicates are used to make graphic shapes on the video screen. This chapter discusses the use of the *line* and *dot* predicates to build both regular and complex shapes. The techniques described will be used to draw line graphs, bar graphs and pie graphs.

Turtle graphics are supported in the same graphics environment. Thus you have the option of mixing regular graphics and turtle graphics in your programs.

Turbo Prolog has two sound predicates, *sound* and *beep*. Along with these, you will be introduced to some basic musical concepts of pitch and duration that are used to build musical tags.

After learning the material in this chapter, you can make your Turbo Prolog programs come alive with multiple windows, informative graphs, and music.

Using the Window Predicates

Five Turbo Prolog predicates enable your programs to handle windows of variable sizes. These predicates are *makewindow*, *shiftwindow*, *removewindow*, *clearwindow*, and *gotowindow*. Using these predicates, you can create multiple windows, perform input and output in selected windows, and set window attributes.

Designing Windows with the *makewindow* Predicate

The *makewindow* predicate is fundamental to all Turbo Prolog windowing operations. The syntax is

```
makewindow(Window_number,
      Screen_attribute,
      Frame_attribute,
      Frame_string,
      Starting_row,
      Starting_column,
      Window_height,
      Window_width)
```

The values of the eight arguments specify a window.

The *Window_number* argument, an integer, identifies a window in the program. That number is used as a reference by *gotowindow* and other predicates.

The integer value bound to *Screen_attribute* determines the colors of the characters and the background. Of course, the attribute values you choose will depend on whether your computer has a monochrome monitor or a color monitor.

Calculating Monochrome Screen Attributes

For monochrome monitors, integer values are used to select the combination of foreground and background colors. These values are given in table 8.1.

—————— **Table 8.1** ——————
Monochrome Attribute Values

Foreground	Background	Screen attribute	Remark
Black	Black	0	Blank screen
White	Black	7	Normal video
Black	White	112	Reverse video

Although these colors are referred to as "black" and "white," "white" actually refers to the normal foreground (or character) color of the monitor, which is usually either green or amber. Note that a black foreground with black background is a blank screen. A white foreground on a black background is a normal-video display, and a black foreground with a white background is a reverse-video display.

Three optional attribute values can be used to produce underlined characters, create a high-intensity display, and make the characters blink. To underline characters, add 1 to the screen attribute value. To create a high-intensity display, add 8 to the basic screen attribute value. To make the characters blink, add 128 to the screen attribute value.

Suppose, for example, that you have a monochrome monitor and that you want to create a window with normal video display. The value of the *Screen_attribute* argument is 7. To produce underlined characters, you add 1 to the 7. For a high-intensity display, add 8 to the attribute value 7; the result is 15. If you wish to substitute blinking characters, add 128 to the attribute value 7, for a result of 135.

Calculating Color Screen Attributes

For the Color Graphics Adapter, the screen attribute values are as shown in tables 8.2 and 8.3.

—————————————————— **Table 8.2.** ——————————————————
Foreground Colors for Turbo Prolog Windows

Foreground color	*Attribute value*
Black	0
Blue	1
Green	2
Cyan	3
Red	4
Magenta	5
Brown	6
White	7
Gray	8
Light blue	9
Light green	10
Light cyan	11
Light red	12
Light magenta	13
Yellow	14
High-intensity white	15

—————————————— **Table 8.3.** ——————————————
Background Colors for Turbo Prolog Windows

Background color	Attribute value
Black	0
Blue	16
Green	32
Cyan	48
Red	64
Magenta	80
Brown	96
White	112

To calculate the screen attribute value for various color combinations, you first choose the desired foreground color and background color. Then you add the corresponding attribute values. If you want the characters to blink, add 128 to the resulting value. The result is presented as the second argument of the *makewindow* predicate.

For example, to create a window with white characters on a black background, you add 7 (for white foreground) and 0 (for the black background). The sum is 7, and that is the *Screen_attribute* argument of the *makewindow* predicate. To create a window with red characters on a yellow background, add 4 (red foreground) and 104 (yellow background), for a result of 108. To create a window with blue characters on a light red background, add 1 (for the blue foreground) and 0 (for the black background). The sum, 41, is used as the second argument of the predicate.

Selecting Frame Attributes

The *Frame_attribute* argument of the *makewindow* predicate is an integer whose value determines the attributes of the window border. If the attribute value is 0, the window has no visible border. Other values create borders with attributes as shown in table 8.4.

Some of the frame attribute values represent the same colors as the screen attribute values. If you select a blinking border, the border background is always white, and the blinking thin line (at the middle of the border) is of the specified color.

The *Frame_string* argument is a label for the window. Examples that come readily to mind are "Main Menu", "Bar Graph", "Sub-menu", and "Output Window". Any string you provide for the frame-string attribute will be centered on the top line of the window frame. The frame string value can also be null—that is, no string. In this case, the argument you enter is two adjacent quotation marks.

—————————————— **Table 8.4.** ——————————————
Frame Color Attributes for Turbo Prolog

Attribute value	Attribute
0	No border
1	Blue border
2	Green border
3	Light blue border
4	Red border
5	Magenta border
6	Yellow border
7	White border
8	Brown boarder
−1	Blinking white border
−2	Blinking yellow border
−3	Blinking magenta border
−4	Blinking red border
−5	Blinking light blue border
−6	Blinking light green border
−7	Blinking blue border
−8	Blinking gray border

Sizing and Positioning Windows

The *Starting_row* argument of the *makewindow* predicate is an integer that designates the top row (line) of the window. The maximum number of rows is 24. A value of 4 indicates that the window starts at the fourth row. Possible values are 0 to 24.

The *Starting_column* argument of the *makewindow* predicate is an integer that specifies the left column of the window. The maximum number of columns is 80. Because the columns are numbered starting with zero, a *Starting_column* value of 9 specifies a window starting at column 10. The possible values are 0 to 79.

The *Window_height* argument is an integer specifying the total number of rows occupied by the window. The maximum possible value is 25.

The *Window_width* argument is an integer specifying the total number of columns occupied by the window. The maximum possible value is 80.

If you accidentally enter starting row and window height arguments that place the bottom line below the bottom of the screen, Turbo Prolog will flag the error during the program run. An example would be choosing a starting-row value of 20 and a window height of 7. In this case, Turbo Prolog will display the error message

```
The parameters in makewindow are illegal.
```

Similarly, an error will result if your starting-column and window-width arguments place the right-hand column beyond right edge of the screen. Such an error would result if you were to specify a starting-column value of 5 and a window width of 79.

The following examples use the five window attributes just described. In the first example, the predicate for a window is specified as

```
makewindow(1,7,7,"FULL SCREEN",0,0,25,80)
```

This window is designated window number 1. It has white characters on black background, a white border, and the window label "FULL SCREEN". The top left corner is at row 0, column 0, and the window has 25 rows and 80 columns. This window is shown in figure 8.1.

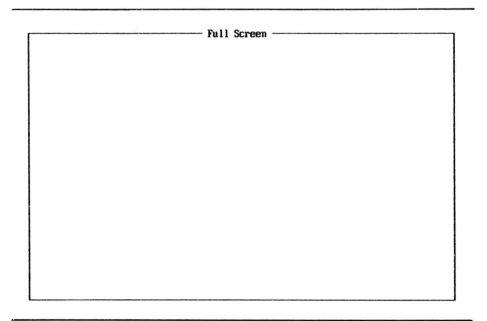

Fig. 8.1. *The largest Turbo Prolog window (25 rows × 80 columns).*

In the second example, the following window is specified in the predicate

```
makewindow(2,4,1,"MENU",4,20,16,40)
```

This is designated window number 2. It has red characters on a black background, with a blue border and the window label *MENU*. The window begins at row 4, column 20. The number of rows is 16 and the number of columns is 60. A black-and-white rendition of this window is shown in figure 8.2.

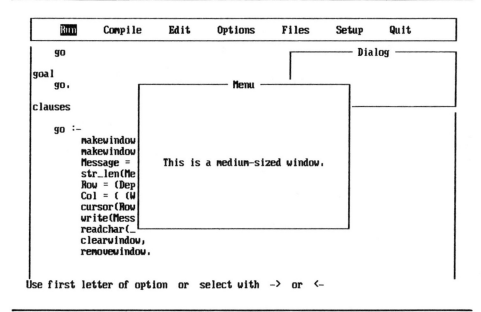

Fig. 8.2. *A medium-sized window (16 rows × 40 columns).*

If all arguments of the *makewindow* predicate are unbound variables, the variables are bound to the parameters of the current window. For example, if the predicate

```
makewindow(_,_,_,Title,_,_,_,_,_)
```

is attempted while the window in figure 8.2 is active, then the variable *Title* is bound to *Menu*.

Exercises

8.1. Write the *makewindow* predicate for a window with the following attributes:

Window number:	3
Foreground color:	blue
Background color:	light green
Frame attribute:	red border
Frame label:	"Database"
Starting row:	6
Starting column:	10
Window height:	12
Window width:	50

8.2. Write a complete *makewindow* predicate to create a window with black characters, a white background and a black border. Position the window in the top left quarter of the screen.

Using Other Window Predicates

Constructing a window requires that you specify each attribute; that process can be time-consuming. But once you have specified the attributes, you've done the most difficult part. The predicates discussed in the following sections, which are used to manipulate the windows in various ways, typically have one or zero arguments.

The *shiftwindow* predicate

The *shiftwindow* predicate is used to move (shift) from one window to another. The syntax is

```
shiftwindow(Window_number)
```

The parameter *Window_number* is the integer number that was assigned when the window was created. (This is the *Window_number* parameter of the *makewindow* predicate.) When you specify window 3 in the predicate *shiftwindow(3)*, all inputs and outputs are rerouted to that window.

At the same time, Turbo Prolog "remembers" the previous window and all its attributes. For example, if the arguments for window 3 indicate that it will overlap the current window (window 4), then *shiftwindow(3)* causes window 3 to appear in front of window 4. The information in window 4, now partially covered by window 3, is buffered so that it can be written to the screen again when window 4 again moves to the foreground.

The *gotowindow* Predicate

The *gotowindow* predicate allows a fast shift between two windows that do not overlap. The syntax is

```
gotowindow(Window_number)
```

Again, *Window_number* is the number assigned when the window was created. Suppose that windows 2 and 3 in your program do not overlap, and that window 2 is the active window. You would use the predicate *gotowindow(3)* to make 3 the active window. This predicate works faster than *shiftwindow*, and should be used when shifting between windows containing large amounts of text.

The *clearwindow* Predicate

This predicate clears any text or graphic display from the current window. The predicate has no arguments:

```
clearwindow
```

The window remains intact; so does the border, if the window has one. The window is filled with its background color.

The *removewindow* Predicate

The *removewindow* predicate removes the currently active window from the screen. No parameters are specified, so the syntax is simply

```
removewindow
```

Any text or graphic display within the window is removed. If another window is behind the removed window, that window and all its contents become visible. If the last window is removed, the screen again displays whatever was displayed before the window was created.

Using Windows for Input and Output

The standard input and output predicates—*read*, *readint*, *readchar*, *write*, and *nl*—also work with any active window. That is, the input and output predicates work in whatever window has been made active with *makewindow*, *gotowindow*, or *shiftwindow*.

The default cursor position is the upper left corner of the window. However, the *cursor* predicate can be used to place the cursor at any desired position within the current window. The syntax is

```
cursor(Row_number,Column_number).
```

The arguments *Row_number* and *Column_number* are integers that represent the row and column numbers with respect to the top row and left column. Rows and columns are numbered starting with zero: the predicate *cursor(0,0)* causes text to be written starting at the upper left corner. If you accidentally specify a cursor position outside the current window, Turbo Prolog will flag the error with an error message during the program run.

For example, these three predicates can be used to display a message in the center of a window:

```
makewindow(1,7,7,"",1,1,8,28),
cursor(4,12),
write("Have a Nice Day").
```

If the *cursor* predicate is omitted, the message will be displayed starting at the top left corner of the window. The arguments of the *cursor* predicate can also be variables which are bound to integer values. Alternative subgoals to center a message in this window are

```
makewindow(1,7,7,"",1,1,8,28),
Row = 4, Col = 12,
cursor(Row,Col),
write("Have a Nice Day").
```

If unbound variables are used with the *cursor* predicate, those variables are bound to the current row and column numbers. The subgoals

```
makewindow(1,7,7,"",1,1,8,28),
Row = 4, Col = 12,
cursor(Row,Col),
write("Have a Nice Day"),
cursor(What_row,What_column).
```

bind *What_row* to 4 and *What_column* to 27.

Programs with Windows

In the following sections, you will learn to work with window predicates and to write programs that fully utilize Turbo Prolog's windowing facilities. Four complete Turbo Prolog programs are provided for your hands-on experimentation.

Writing Text to a Window

Using the predicates presented in the preceding sections, you can write programs that use multiple windows on the video screen. Windows not only create pleasing displays but also help increase the clarity and orderliness of your programs.

As a simple example, let's create a window with white characters on a black background (normal video), and then manipulate a text display in the window. This is a five-step sequence:

1. Make the window.

2. Write text in the window.

3. Erase the text in the window.

4. Write new text in the window.

5. Remove the window.

The Window program, in listing 8.1, implements these steps.

```
/* Program-id. Window          PROG0801.PRO */
/* Purpose: To make a window at the center   */
/* of the screen with a border, use white/   */
/* black characters, write text materials.   */

predicates

    make_window_and_write

goal

    make_window_and_write.

clauses

    make_window_and_write :-

        makewindow(1,7,7,
                    " A Message Window ",
                    6,20,14,40),

        cursor(3,14),
        write("New House"),
        cursor(5,10),
        write("When an old house"),
        cursor(6,10),
        write("gets new paint,"),
        cursor(7,10),
        write("it is a new house."),
        cursor(9,16),
        write("anonymous poet"),

        nl, nl,
        write("To read another message,"), nl,
        write("press the space bar."),
        readchar(_),
        clearwindow,
```

```
cursor(2,5),
write("? ? ? ? ? ? ? ? ?"),
cursor(4,10),
write("The future of arts"),
cursor(5,10),
write("in the electronic age"),
cursor(6,10),
write("is highly debatable."),

cursor(9,7),
write("To exit, press the space bar."),
readchar(_),
removewindow,
exit.
```

The goal statement is the rule *make_window_and_write*. The first predicate in the rule makes a window with white characters on a black background and a white border. The window starts at row 6, column 20. It is 14 lines high and 40 columns wide.

The next 10 predicates write text material in the window at positions determined by the *cursor* predicate. The following six predicates instruct the user to press the space bar to read another message. When the user has pressed any key (including the space bar), the program clears the window. Figure 8.3 shows the display before the window is cleared.

The next eight predicates write new text to the window. The last three predicates again tell the user to press the space bar, and the last predicate removes the window. The display before removal of the window is shown in figure 8.4.

Notice the use of the *readchar(_)* predicate, which allows the user to observe the text display for as long as desired. The first time *readchar* is used in this program, the window is cleared of text; the second time, the whole window is removed.

When you print text in a window, the number of rows available for printing is two rows less than the height of the window. Similarly, the number of columns available for printing is two less than the width of the window. As an example, consider a window specified with the predicate

```
makewindow(1,7,7,"",7,55,8,16).
```

The height of the window is eight rows, so the available number of rows for printing is six. The width of this window is 16 columns, so the available number columns for printing is 14.

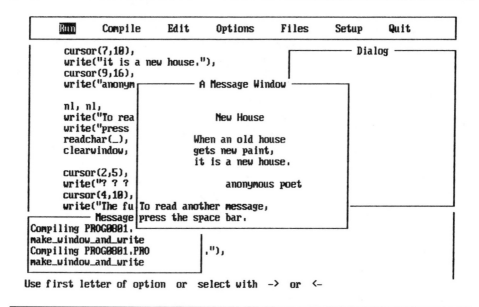

Fig. 8.3. *The first text display created by the Window program.*

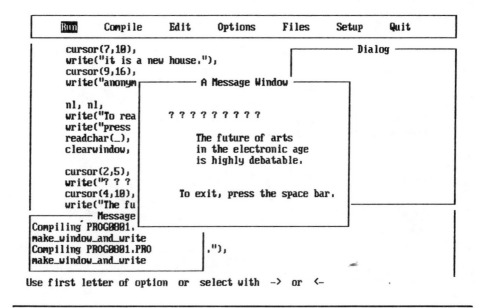

Fig. 8.4. *The second text window created by the Window program.*

——————————— **Exercise** ———————————

8.3. Modify the Window program, substituting a poem or prose selection of your choice. Change the window attributes until you feel comfortable with making windows. Change only one attribute at a time, so that you can be sure of the visual effect of each change you make.

Making Multiple Windows

Making multiple windows and writing text to those windows is easy in Turbo Prolog. Suppose that your program design includes four windows, each occupying about one fourth of the screen. Each window is used for accomplishing a particular program task. You want to write text in each of the windows to indicate the purpose of the area. Later, when the tasks are completed, you want to remove the windows one by one.

These four window predicates will create the desired windows with white characters on a black background:

```
makewindow(1,7,7,"Message Area #1",4,4,8,34)

makewindow(1,7,7,"Message Area #2",4,42,8,34)

makewindow(1,7,7,"Message Area #3",12,4,8,34)

makewindow(1,7,7,"Message Area #4",12,42,8,34).
```

The Message program, in listing 8.2, implements this program design. The program goal is the rule *make_windows_and; us write*. This rule consists of predicates that make windows and write text to them. Each window's text defines an artificial intelligence term. The windows are shown in figure 8.5.

```
/* Program: Message       File: PROG0802.PRO */
/* Purpose: To make four separate windows,    */
/*          with borders and white/black text.*/

predicates

    make_windows_and_write

goal

    make_windows_and_write.
```

```
clauses

   make_windows_and_write :-

   makewindow(1,7,7,
              " Message area #1 ",
              4,4,8,34),

   nl, write("Modus ponens"),
   nl, write("   A basic rule of logic that"),
   nl, write("asserts IF a condition is true,"),
   nl, write("THEN an action is true."), nl,

   makewindow(2,7,7,
              " Message area #2 ",
              4,42,8,34),

   nl, write("Himiko"),
   nl, write("   The name chosen by Japanese"),
   nl, write("scientists for their parallel"),
   nl, write("PROLOG programming language."), nl,

   makewindow(3,7,7,
              " Message area #3 ",
              12,4,8,34),

   nl, write("Unification"),
   nl, write("   A term used in Prolog to"),
   nl, write("indicate the matching of"),
   nl, write("patterns and assigning values."), nl,

   makewindow(4,7,7,
              " Message area #4 ",
              12,42,8,34),

   nl, write("Knowledgebase System"),
   nl, write("   A computer program to do"),
   nl, write("symbolic processing of"),
   nl, write("knowledgebase."), nl,

   write("To exit, press the space bar."),
   readchar(_),
   removewindow,
```

```
write("To exit, press the space bar."),
readchar(_),
removewindow,

write("To exit, press the space bar."),
readchar(_),
removewindow,

write("To exit, press the space bar."),
readchar(_),
removewindow,
exit.
```

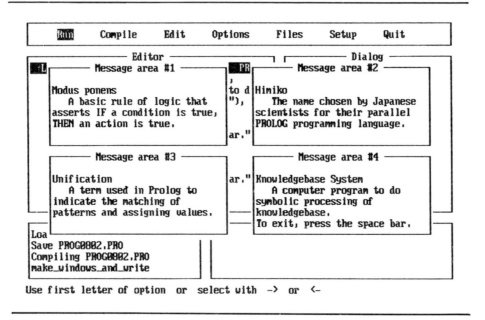

Fig. 8.5. *Four nonoverlapping windows created by the Message program.*

The last 12 predicates (grouped by threes in the listing) remove the windows one by one. Notice that it is not necessary to use the *clearwindow* predicate before exiting from a window; the *removewindow* predicate automatically clears the window before removing it. Figure 8.6 shows the screen after the two lower windows are removed. Notice that both the windows and their text are cleared from the screen.

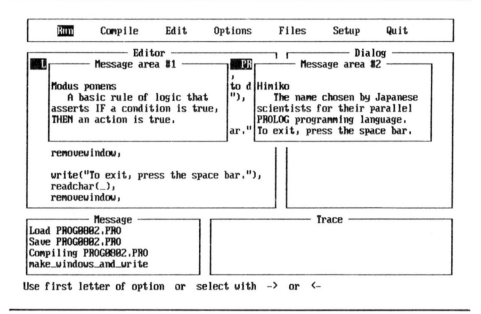

Fig. 8.6. *The screen display after removal of the two lower windows.*

In creating windows, Turbo Prolog "remembers" the window that was current when each new window was created. When any window is removed, the previous window becomes active.

Exercises

8.4. Modify the Message program so that you can remove the windows in the order 1, 2, 3, 4. Run the program to verify that your modifications are correct.

8.5. Modify the Message program again so that all text is written in red characters. If your computer has a monochrome screen, write black messages on a white background in windows 2 and 4.

8.6. Modify the Message program to add a fifth window that is centered on the screen. Write text of your choice to the window. Run the program to test your modifications.

8.7. Modify the Message program again so that your program writes seven lines of text in window 5. Then run the program. (Remember that a maximum of eight lines of text, including the exit prompt lines, can be displayed in windows of the height specified in this program.)

Creating Overlapping Windows

Overlapping windows can be individually designed to suit the needs of your program and to benefit the user of your program. The order in which the overlapping windows are created is part of the program design. The program Overlap, which is shown in listing 8.3, illustrates the creation of overlapping windows.

```
/* Program: Overlap      File: PROG0803.PRO */
/* Purpose: To make overlapping windows.    */

predicates

    make_windows_write_text

goal

    make_windows_write_text.

clauses

    make_windows_write_text :-

        makewindow(1,7,7,
                "Life of a star",3,12,10,40),
        cursor(3,8),
        write("A BLACK HOLE APPEARS."), nl,

        makewindow(2,7,7,
                "Life of a star",5,14,10,40),
        shiftwindow(2),
        cursor(3,12),
        write("THE STAR BURNS."), nl,

        makewindow(3,7,7,
                "Life of a star",7,16,10,40),
        shiftwindow(3),
        cursor(3,11),
        write("THE STAR SHINES."), nl,
```

```
makewindow(4,7,7,
          "Life of a star",9,18,10,40),
shiftwindow(4),
cursor(3,11),
write("A STAR IS BORN."), nl,

cursor(6,4),
write("Press the space bar"),
readchar(_),
removewindow,

cursor(6,2),
write("Press the space bar"),
readchar(_),
removewindow,

cursor(6,2),
write("Press the space bar"),
readchar(_),
removewindow,

cursor(7,2),
write("Press the space bar"),
readchar(_),
removewindow,
exit.
```

In this program, the goal is *make_windows_write_text*. The purpose of the rule is to make four overlapping windows and write text to each window. The text comprises four sentences that describe the history of a star:

A STAR IS BORN	*Window 4*
THE STAR SHINES	*Window 3*
THE STAR BURNS	*Window 2*
A BLACK HOLE APPEARS	*Window 1*

The windows are created in numerical order, and are removed one by one starting with the last window created, window 4. This removal sequence creates the effect of peeling off message labels. Notice that the windows in figure 8.7 are slightly offset to make the layers visible.

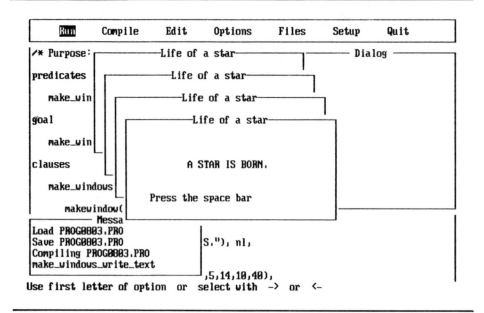

Fig. 8.7. *Four windows created by the program Overlap.*

—————————————— **Exercise** ——————————————

8.8. Design and write a program that creates four overlapping windows with the following texts:

Top window:

Who is the author of the book "Lake Woebegon Days"?

Second window:

Garrison Keillor

Third window:

What is the most popular main dish in the U.S.?

Fourth window:

Fried chicken.

Your program should pause for a keypress before it proceeds to the next stage.

Building Menus with Windows

User-friendly programs often are designed to let the user select one task from several or select the order in which tasks are performed. Such programs often offer the choices in the form of a menu. When a choice is made, the program can then either perform the chosen task or present a submenu from which subtasks are chosen. In both cases, using different windows to frame different menus or tasks is less confusing (and therefore more user-friendly) than many other methods. Figure 8.8 shows a structure chart for a file-utility menu system that uses submenus in this manner.

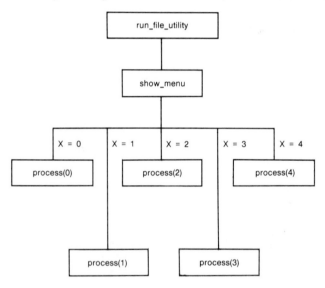

Fig. 8.8. *A structure chart for a menu system.*

The main module of this program creates the main menu. From this menu, the user can choose 0 to exit the menu (end the program), 1 to delete a file, 2 to rename a file, 3 to create a file, or 4 to exit to the operating system. The main menu is displayed in a window, and each sub-menu also is displayed in a separate window. From each sub-menu window, the intended task can be performed.

The program Menu, in listing 8.4, implements this menu system. The goal is the rule *run_file_utility*. The rule *show_menu* is the main module:

```
show_menu :-
    repeat,
    makewindow(1,7,7,
                "MainMenu",4,10,16,36),
    nl,
    write("           Menu Utilities"), nl, nl,
    write("        0  Exit"), nl,
    write("        1  Delete file"), nl,
    write("        2  Rename file"), nl,
    write("        3  Create file"), nl,
```

```
write("          4  Exit to PC DOS"), nl, nl,
write(" Please enter your choice:(0-4)  "),
readint(X),
X < 5,
process(X),
X = 0, !.
```

A *repeat* predicate is used so that the user is always returned to the main menu after execution of the sub-module ends; the exception is choice *0*, in which case program execution is terminated.

Notice that this rule uses a variation of the Backtrack After Fail method (refer to Chapter 3 if you need to review that method). The *readint(X)* predicate reads the integer value and instantiates the variable *X* to the integer value. The rule $X < 5$ ensures that the value is less than 5. If the integer value is equal to or greater than 5, then this rule fails and backtracking occurs. Otherwise the rule succeeds and the next rule, *process(X)*, is attempted.

Each *process* rule contains a *makewindow* predicate and *write* predicates to display a message identifying the task, as well as the sentence *This process will be implemented later*. In a fully-developed program, predicates to perform the chosen task would be written in place of the last *write* predicate. The purpose of this program is just to show the menu construction, not actually to perform the tasks. Notice that each process ends by removing the window.

After the *process* rule succeeds, the remaining subrules are attempted. If *X* is equal to zero, then the cut (!) prevents backtracking to the *repeat* rule, and the program terminates.

```
/* Program: Menu       File: PROG0804.PRO */
/* Purpose: To show menu construction      */
/*          with windows.                  */

predicates

   repeat
   process(integer)
   show_menu
   run_file_utility

goal

   run_file_utility.
```

```
clauses

    run_file_utility :-
        show_menu,
        nl, write(" Press the SPACE BAR."),
        readchar(_),
        exit.

    repeat.
    repeat :- repeat.

    show_menu :-
        repeat,
        makewindow(1,7,7,
                    "Main Menu",4,10,16,36),
        nl,
        write("        Menu Utilities"), nl, nl,
        write("     0  Exit"), nl,
        write("     1  Delete file"), nl,
        write("     2  Rename file"), nl,
        write("     3  Create file"), nl,
        write("     4  Exit to PC DOS"), nl, nl,
        write(" Please enter your choice:(0-4) "),
    readint(X),
    X < 5,
    process(X),
    X = 0, !.

process(0) :-
    nl, write(" You exit the menu. Bye !"), nl.

process(1) :-
    makewindow(2,7,7,
                "File Deletion",12,36,10,36),
    write("This is file deletion utility."),
    nl, nl,
    write("This process will be"), nl,
    wri  ("implemented later."), nl, nl,
    write("When ready, press the space bar."),
    readchar(_),
    removewindow.
```

```
process(2) :-
   makewindow(3,7,7,
              "File Renaming",10,40,10,36),
   write("This is file renaming utility."),
   nl, nl,
   write("This process will be"), nl,
   write("implemented later."), nl,
   write("When ready, press the space bar."),
   readchar(_),
   removewindow.

process(3) :-
   makewindow(4,7,7,
              "File Creation",5,10,15,60),
   write("This is file creation utility."), nl, nl,
   write("This process will be"), nl,
   write("implemented later."), nl, nl,
   write("When ready, press the space bar."),
   readchar(_),
   removewindow.

process(4) :-
   makewindow(5,7,7,
           "Temp Exit to PC DOS",10,40,10,35),
   write("You exit to PC DOS."), nl,
   write("See you later !"), nl, nl,
   write("When ready, press the space bar."),
   readchar(_),
   removewindow.
```

Figure 8.9 shows the main menu and a task window for the file-deletion utility. Notice that the user cannot be confused as to which task is active, because the label *File Deletion* is clearly shown in the window frame.

—————————————— **Exercises** ——————————————

8.9. Run Program 8.3. Make choices and observe that on completion of the task, you are always returned to the main menu.

8.10. Change the window sizes, background colors and foreground colors to determine which window color combinations you find pleasing.

8.11. Replace the dummy sentence in rule *process(2)* with a rule to rename a file (see Chapter 7 for information on Turbo Prolog file predicates).

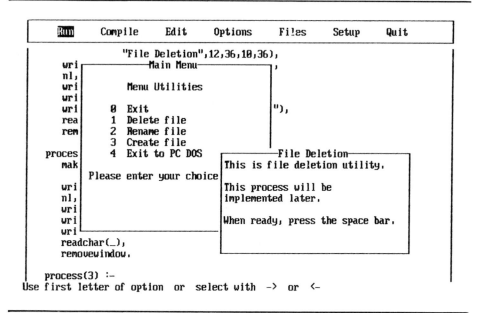

Fig. 8.9. *Windows created by the Menu program.*

Using Graphics in Your Programs

Graphics programming in Turbo Prolog is exciting, and Turbo Prolog's graphics capabilities are powerful. You can create graphics displays of considerable precision on the monitor screen, and this section will show you how.

Turbo Prolog's graphics predicates support both the IBM Color/Graphics Adapter (CGA) and the IBM Enhanced Graphics Adapter (EGA), as well as compatible "work-alikes." The discussions of graphics attributes refer to these adapters. Other graphics adapters are compatible to varying degrees with one of these types, and you can find information for using them in your graphics adapter manual. (Graphics are not available with the Monochrome Adapter.)

The programs in this book are written for the CGA, because that is the most commonly used graphics adapter. The EGA operates in modes that are not available on the CGA, but the EGA supports all CGA modes as well. The programs will therefore run on EGA-equipped machines, but they do not make use of the EGA's full capabilities. If your machine has an EGA, you may want to adapt the programs for that adapter after you have learned the material presented in this section.

Turbo Prolog's graphics modes and colors are controlled by the parameters of two predicates: *graphics* and *makewindow*. The *graphics* predicate is used to activate the graphics mode of the CGA or EGA. This chapter's section on windows has introduced you to the use of the *makewindow* predicate in text mode. You'll recall that two of its parameters, *Screen_attribute* and *Frame_attribute*, are used to control the color of the window text and border. Those parameters control the same things in graphics mode, but they work differently. You'll learn in this section how to select the proper values for graphics mode.

The *dot* and *line* predicates are used to draw objects in graphics mode. Later in this section, you'll learn how to use them. First, however, you need to understand a few things about graphics resolution and the various graphics modes that are available with the CGA and EGA.

The *graphics* predicate and the *Screen_attribute* and *Frame_attribute* parameters of *makewindow* interact in ways that you may find complicated. In fact, it's fair to say that Turbo Prolog's behavior is quirky in this regard. Later versions of Turbo Prolog may behave differently (the information in this book is based on Turbo Prolog version 1.1). Table 8.11 summarizes the effects of the parameters to help you make the right choices for the *graphics*, *makewindow*, *line*, and *dot* predicates.

The information in tables 8.9, 8.10, and 8.11 was gathered through experimentation with an IBM PC AT equipped with an EGA and an IBM Enhanced Color Display. The information on the EGA does not appear in Borland International's *Turbo Prolog Owner's Handbook*. You should feel free to experiment with the graphics predicates, but you should realize that other machines (or later versions of Turbo Prolog) may give different results.

Resolution and Graphics Adapter Modes

When the computer's monitor is in graphics mode, it can be thought of as a board composed of many minute light bulbs of various colors. These components are usually called *pixels* (for "picture elements"). A graphics image is in effect a collective image formed by turning pixels on or off.

The graphics image is specified in terms of the graphics screen resolution. Resolution is specified by the number of pixels into which the screen is divided horizontally and vertically. The higher the resolution, the higher the quality of the image. Again, think of the screen as a board covered with light bulbs: a board with 640 × 200 bulbs can show much finer detail than will a board with 320 × 200 bulbs.

The number of pixels is determined by the operating mode of the graphics adapter. Both the CGA and the EGA have what are called *medium-* and *high-resolution* modes. In medium resolution, the screen is divided horizontally into 320 pixels; in high resolution, it is divided horizontally into 640 pixels. Both modes divide the screen vertically into 200 pixels. (The EGA has another mode known as *enhanced resolution*, in which the screen is divided horizontally into 640 pixels and vertically into 350 pixels. Use of that mode is covered later in this chapter.)

The resolutions and available colors for CGA and EGA modes are summarized in table 8.5.

—— Table 8.5 ——
Graphics Modes

Resolution mode	Resolution (horizontal × vertical)	Colors	Text columns
Medium (CGA)	320 × 200	4	40
High (CGA)	640 × 200	2	80
Medium (EGA)	320 × 200	16	40
High (EGA)	640 × 200	16	80
Enhanced (EGA)	640 × 350	13	80

The *graphics* Predicate

To create graphic displays in Turbo Prolog, you begin by setting the screen to graphics mode. The *graphics* predicate is used for this purpose:

```
graphics(Mode,Palette,Color)
```

The three parameters of this predicate control various elements of the graphics display. The details of selecting parameter values are discussed in the following sections.

Note that use of the *graphics* predicate clears the screen; any display created in text mode disappears. Also note (as shown in table 8.6) that text characters in the medium-resolution graphics modes are twice as wide as characters in the high-resolution modes (and in text mode); medium resolution supports only 40 characters per line. The *Width* parameter of the *makewindow* predicate is specified in characters (not pixels) in both text and graphics modes. You'll need to ensure, then, that your windows fit the screen. If they do not, a run-time error will occur. Guidelines for choosing appropriate values are given in the section "The *makewindow* Predicate and Graphics Mode."

The predicate *text* changes the display to text mode.

The *Mode* Parameter

The *Mode* parameter is an integer value used to select the graphics mode. Possible values are 1 to 5. The resolution modes and the mode parameters are specified in table 8.6.

—————— **Table 8.6** ——————
Resolution Modes and Mode Parameters

Resolution mode	Mode parameter
Medium (CGA)	1
High (CGA)	2
Medium (EGA)	3
High (EGA)	4
Enhanced (EGA)	5

The Color Graphics Adapter (CGA) supports modes 1 and 2. The Enhanced Graphics Adapter (EGA) supports modes 3, 4, and 5. Thus, you need to select a *Mode* parameter in accordance with your machine's adapter. As was mentioned earlier, other graphics adapters are compatible to varying degrees with one of these types; read the adapter manual and select the appropriate mode for your machine. Careful reading of the manual is worthwhile because choosing a mode that conflicts with the hardware configuration will cause erratic behavior in your programs.

The *Palette* Parameter

The *Palette* parameter is an integer with possible values of 0 and 1. This parameter is used to select one of the two color palettes. Table 8.7 shows the colors available in each of the two palettes. The numbers 1, 2, and 3 are used to assign a number to a graphics object such as a line or a dot.

—————— **Table 8.7** ——————
Color Palettes and Colors

Palette number	Colors:		
	1	*2*	*3*
0	Green	Red	Yellow (CGA) Brown (EGA)
1	Cyan	Magenta	White

In modes 1, 3, 4, and 5, the value of the *Palette* parameter also determines the color of text appearing on the graphics screen when that text is not within a window. In those modes, the text appears in color 2 of the current palette. Thus the text is red in palette 0 and magenta in palette 1.

In mode 1, the *Palette* parameter also controls the choice of colors for window borders and for any text displayed within windows. For full instructions on assigning colors to these elements, see the section "The *makewindow* Predicate and Graphics Mode."

And in mode 5, the color of the window frame (if your program creates a window) is determined by the current palette. The window frame appears in color 1 of the current palette: green for palette 0 and cyan for palette 1. (As was mentioned previously, the interaction of graphics parameters is complex; you'll want to refer to table 8.11 when you begin writing your own programs with graphics.)

The *Color* Parameter

The *Color* parameter is an integer used to select colors on the graphics display. The available colors are determined by the current graphics mode. Modes 1, 2, 3, and 4 give a choice of 16 colors, as shown in table 8.8. In mode 2, the background is always black, regardless of the value to which the *Color* parameter is bound; in that mode, the *Color* parameter selects the color of foreground objects, including text, lines, dots, and window borders. In modes 1, 3, and 4, however, the *Color* parameter determines the color of the graphics display background. Mode 5 gives a choice of 13 background colors, as shown in table 8.9.

—————————————— **Table 8.8** ——————————————
Colors for Graphics Modes 1, 2, 3, and 4

Background color	*Color number*
Black	0
Blue	1
Green	2
Cyan	3
Red	4
Magenta	5
Brown	6
White	7
Gray	8
Light blue	9
Light green	10
Light cyan	11
Light red	12
Light magenta	13
Yellow	14
High intensity white	15

—————— **Table 8.9** ——————
Colors for Graphics Mode 5

Background color	Color parameter
Black	0
Blue	1
Green	2
Cyan	3
Red	4
Magenta	5
Medium green	6
White	7
Dark green	8
Light blue	9
Light green	10
Light cyan	11
Brown	12

The *makewindow* Predicate and Graphics Mode

Earlier in this chapter, you learned how to use the *makewindow* predicate in text mode. The use of that predicate in graphics mode is similar, but there are some important differences that are detailed in this section. Again, you may find the relationships between modes and parameters to be complicated; you'll want to consult table 8.11 when you begin writing your own graphics programs with windows.

The *makewindow* parameters *Screen_attribute*, *Frame_attribute*, *Column*, and *Width* are used differently in graphics mode than in text mode. The differences are summarized in the following sections

The *Column* and *Width* Parameters

Graphics modes 2 and 4 display text in 40-column mode; each line has only 40 character spaces (or columns). Consequently, you must ensure that the values used for the *Row* and *Width* parameters do not specify a window whose right edge is beyond column 40. If that happens, you will not discover the error when you compile the program. The error will not become apparent until you run the program.

To avoid this error, simply make sure that the sum of the *Column* and *Width* parameters does not exceed 39. (Remember that columns are numbered from 0.) If the *Column* parameter is bound to the value 4, for example, so that the rightmost column of the window is in the fifth column of the screen, then the maximum permissible value for *Width* is 35.

The *Screen_attribute* and *Frame_attribute* Parameters

You'll recall from the discussion of using *makewindow* in text mode that the *Screen_attribute* parameter is calculated by adding values corresponding to the desired foreground and background colors. In graphics mode, however, the background color is determined by the current mode and by the value of the *Color* parameter of the *graphics* predicate. Thus you cannot assign a different background color to a window created in graphics mode; the background color is always the same as that of the screen as a whole.

In graphics mode, then, you can control only the color of the window text, not the window background. Thus the *Screen_attribute* value controls only the text color in graphics mode. Again, the effect of this parameter varies according to the current graphics mode. In mode 1, the *Screen_attribute* parameter interacts with the *Palette* parameter of the *graphics* predicate to determine the color of the window text.

The *Frame_attribute* parameter also functions differently in graphics mode than in text mode. As in text mode, a window frame is created if *Frame_attribute* is bound to a nonzero value. In graphics mode, however, you cannot use negative values to create flashing window frames as you can in text mode. Like *Screen_attribute*, *Frame_attribute* interacts with the *Palette* parameter of the *graphics* predicate in mode 1 to determine the color of the window frame. (Color/Graphics "work-alikes" not made by IBM may give different results.)

In mode 1, usable values of *Screen_attribute* and *Frame_attribute* are 1, 2, and 3; the window text or window frame appears in the specified color of the palette currently in effect. In palette 0, for example, a *Screen_attribute* value of 1 specifies green text, and a *Frame_attribute* value of 2 specifies a red frame. In palette 1, a *Screen_attribute* value of 2 specifies magenta text, and a *Frame_attribute* value of 3 specifies a white frame. (Refer to table 8.7 for the colors available in each palette.)

In mode 5, the only function of the *Frame_attribute* value is to determine whether the window has a frame. A frame is created for any nonzero value of *Frame_attribute*. The frame is color 1 of the current palette: green for palette 0, and cyan for palette 1.

The values for *Screen_attribute* and their colors in mode 5 are given in table 8.10. Notice that the colors specified by numbers 1, 3, 9, and 11 are determined by the current palette.

—————————— **Table 8.10** ——————————
Screen Attribute Values for Graphics Mode 5

Number	Color
0	(No text)
1	Green (palette 0), Cyan (palette 1)
2	(No text)
3	Green (palette 0), Cyan (palette 1)
4	Red
5	White
6	Red
7	White
8	(No text)
9	Green (palette 0), Cyan (palette 1)
10	(No text)
11	Green (palette 0), Cyan (palette 1)
12	Red
13	White
14	White

The *line* and *dot* Predicates

Now you've learned the basics of using the *graphics* predicate and of using *makewindow* in graphics mode. This section introduces the predicates used to draw shapes on the graphics screen. The syntax for *line* is

```
line(Row_1,Column_1,Row_2,Column_2,Palette_color)
```

and the syntax for *dot* is

```
dot(Row,Column,Palette_color)
```

All parameters take integer values. The row and column parameters determine the end-point positions for *line* and the point position for *dot*. With some exceptions, the *Palette_color* parameter specifies the color of the line or dot.

In modes 1 and 3, the *Palette_color* parameter specifies the color in accordance with the current palette. (The *Palette* parameter of the *graphics* predicate determines which palette is in effect.) In these modes, the dot or line is colored in accordance with table 8.7.

In modes 2, 4, and 5, the *Palette_color* parameter does not really determine the color of the dot or line. Dots and lines specified with a *Palette_color* value of 2 are not drawn at all. In mode 2, dots and lines with *Palette_color* values of 1 and 3 are drawn in the color specified by the *Color* parameter of the *graphics* predicate. In modes 4 and 5, lines and dots are drawn in color 1 of the current palette, regardless of whether the *Palette_color* value of the *dot* or *line* predicate is 1 or 3.

Both of these predicates use a coordinate system that differs from the one with which you have become familiar in text mode. In graphics mode, the screen coordinates range from 0 to 31,999 horizontally and vertically. Point (0,0) is the upper left corner of the screen, point (0,31999) is the upper right corner, point (16999,0) is the lower left corner, and point (31999,31999) is the lower right corner.

Summary of Graphics Modes and Parameter Values

Table 8.11 summarizes the effects of the graphics-parameter values in all graphics modes.

To use this table, select the row corresponding to the mode you want to use. The remaining entries in the row indicate what parameter is used to specify the color of elements on the graphics screen. Match the parameter names in the table with these examples:

```
graphics(Mode,Palette,Color)
makewindow(Number,Screen_attribute,
           Frame_attribute,
           " Title ",
           Row, Column,
           Depth, Width)
```

To choose color options, refer as directed in table 8.11 to the tables given earlier in this chapter.

In table 8.11, *Screen background* refers to the background color of the graphics screen. *Screen text* refers to text that is not enclosed in a window. *Window text* refers to text that is enclosed in a window, and *Window frame* refers to the color of the window frame. (Remember that a *Frame_attribute* value of zero specifies a window with no frame.)

Drawing Objects with *line* and *dot*

With the graphic predicates *line* and *dot*, you can build graphic objects with regular or irregular shapes. Regular shapes include rectangles, triangles, circles and ellipses. These shapes can be used to build irregular shapes of trees, leaves, branches, houses, animals and landscapes.

Table 8.11

Summary of Graphics Parameters and Colors

Mode	Screen background	Screen text	Window text	Window frame	Graphics objects
1	Screen_attribute Table 8.8	Palette 0 for red 1 for magenta	Screen_attribute Table 8.8	Frame_attribute (1, 2, or 3 for color from current palette)	Palette_color According to current palette
2	Always black	Color Table 8.8	Color Table 8.8	Color Table 8.8	Color (Only objects with Palette_color 1 or 3 are drawn.)
3	Color Table 8.8	Palette 0 for red 1 for magenta	Screen_attribute Table 8.8	Frame_attribute Table 8.8	Palette_color According to current palette
4	Color Table 8.8	Palette 0 for red 1 for magenta	Screen_attribute Table 8.8*	Frame_attribute Table 8.8*	Color (Only objects with Palette_color 1 or 3 are drawn.)
5	Color Table 8.8	Palette 0 for red 1 for magenta	Screen_attribute Table 8.10	Palette 0 for green 1 for cyan	Palette 0 for green 1 for cyan (Only objects with Palette_color 1 or 3 are drawn.)

Note: For attribute numbers 1, 2, and 3, the color is chosen from the current palette.

*For attribute numbers 1, 2, and 3, the color is chosen from the current palette.

You can combine several *line* predicates, for example, to draw a rectangle. The rule

```
draw_a_rectangle :-
    line(2000,2000,2000,12000,1),
    line(2000,12000,8000,12000,1),
    line(8000,12000,8000,2000,1),
    line(8000,2000,2000,2000,1).
```

draws a rectangle with proportions of roughly 3 × 5 in the upper left corner of the screen.

The *Palette_color* argument 1 specifies a green line in palette 0 or a cyan line in palette 1 (subject to the exceptions given in table 8.11).

To paint a dot at the starting point of your rectangle, you would specify the coordinates and the color in the predicate

```
dot(2000,2000,1).
```

The predicates

```
dot(2000,2000,1),
dot(3000,3000,1),
dot(1000,3000,1).
```

can be used to set a triangle in the upper left quadrant of the screen.

Building a Circle

A circle is a regular shape. All points on the circumference are equidistant from the center of the circle. Simple trigonometry tells you that the coordinate values *Column* and *Row* of any point on the circumference can be calculated from radius R and the center coordinates *Center_column* and *Center_row* (see fig. 8.10). The relations are

$$Row = Center\_row - R \cos A \qquad (1)$$
$$Column = Center\_column + R \sin A \qquad (2)$$

The Turbo Prolog predicates *sin* and *cos* take arguments expressed in radians (360 degrees = 2π radians). For a complete circle, the values of A range from 0 to approximately 6.283 (2π) radians. If you increment the values of A by 0.02 radians for each dot, you get about 314 points on the circumference. That number of points is enough to draw a circle. Once you have the *Row* and *Column* values, you can plot the point in a chosen color by using the *dot* predicate.

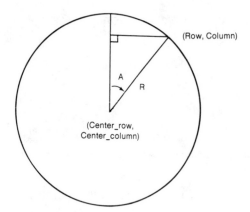

Fig. 8.10. *Mathematical relations between the radius, center, and circumference of a circle.*

Computer graphics programming is subject to a manufacturing "fact of life" that com-
plicates the programmer's task. The manufacturers of video graphic monitors and adapters do not use the same scale for the horizontal and vertical dimensions. These
dimensions are scaled by a factor called the *aspect ratio*. The aspect ratio is defined as
the ratio of the height to width of the screen in terms of video scan lines. The aspect
ratio is about 5/7 for most standard screens.

Consequently, you must modify your point-plotting equations to account for the aspect
ratio. Plotting a circle makes that fact readily apparent: if you plot the equations according
to the values derived by equations (1) and (2), you will see an ellipse. To account for
the aspect ratio, you need to modify equation (1) to give

$$\text{Row} = \text{Center\_row} - 1.40 \; R \cos A \qquad\qquad (3)$$

The aspect ratio differs among video monitors. You may therefore need to change the
number in equation (3).

Making Regular Shapes

For typical uses of the *line* and *dot* predicates, look at the program Shapes, in listing 8.5.
This program draws three regular shapes in different quadrants of the screen and writes
a caption in the fourth quadrant. A structure chart is shown in figure 8.11.

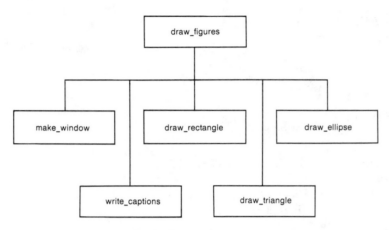

Fig. 8.11. *Structure chart for the Shapes program.*

```
/* Program: Shapes              PROG0805.PRO  */
/* Purpose: To draw regular figures, using a  */
/*   black-and-white window and graphics.     */

predicates

    draw_figures
    make_window
    write_captions
    draw_rectangle
    draw_triangle
    draw_ellipse(real)
    real_int(real,integer)

goal

    draw_figures.

clauses

    draw_figures :-
        make_window,
        write_captions,
        draw_rectangle,
        draw_triangle,
        draw_ellipse(0.02),
```

```
        write(" Press a key."),
        readchar(_),
        text.

    make_window :-
        graphics(2,0,7),
        makewindow(1,7,7,
                    "  REGULAR SHAPES   ",
                    1,10,23,60).

    write_captions :-
        cursor(4,10), write("RECTANGLE"),
        cursor(7,38), write("TRIANGLE"),
        cursor(15,9), write("ELLIPSE"),
        cursor(14,29),
          write("Use 'line' predicate"),
        cursor(16,29),
          write("and 'dot' predicate."),
        cursor(20,4).

    draw_rectangle :-
        line( 2000, 2000, 2000,10000,1),
        line( 2000,10000, 9000,10000,1),
        line( 9000,10000, 9000, 2000,1),
        line( 9000, 2000, 2000, 2000,1).

    draw_triangle :-
        line(12000,12000,12000,20000,1),
        line(12000,20000, 4000,18000,1),
        line( 4000,18000,12000,12000,1).

draw_ellipse(A) :-
        A >= 6.28, !.
draw_ellipse(A) :-
        Center_row = 20000, Center_col = 5000, R = 3600,
        Row_r = Center_row - R * cos(A),
        Column_r = Center_col + R * sin(A),
        real_int(Row_r,Row),real_int(Column_r,Column),
        dot(Row,Column,1),
        A1 = A + 0.02,
        draw_ellipse(A1).

    real_int(R,I) :- R = I.
```

The main module of the program is *draw_figures*. This module in turn calls other submodules—*make_window, write_captions, draw_rectangle, draw_triangle* and *draw_ellipse*. These rules are straightforward.

The submodule that draws the ellipse is the recursive rule *draw_ellipse(A)*. The parameter *A* is used to pass the value of the angle from the main rule to the sub-rule:

```
draw_ellipse(A) :-
     A >= 6.28, !.
draw_ellipse(A) :-
     Center_row = 18000, Center_col = 5000, R = 3600,
     Row_r = Center_row - R * cos(A),
     Column_r = Center_col + R * sin(A),
     real_int(Row_r,Row),real_int(Column_r,Column),
     dot(Row,Column,1),
     A1 = A + 0.02,
     draw_ellipse(A1).
```

The first variant of this rule succeeds if the value bound to *A* is greater than or equal to 6.28; thus the rule sets an upper limit on the value of *A*. The *dot* predicate paints a dot at the location specified by the values *Row* and *Column*, and the next subrule increments the value of angle A by 0.02 radians.

Figure 8.12 is the graphic display produced by the Shapes program. Notice that the rectangle is drawn first, then the triangle, and then the ellipse. Notice also that drawing the ellipse takes much longer than drawing the rectangle because a considerable amount of time is spent in computing the values of *Row* and *Column*. As you can see, the ellipse's major axis is along the horizontal line. This is because the aspect ratio is not included in the computation of the *Column* values. The absence of the aspect ratio causes the vertical axis of the ellipse to be shorter than the horizontal axis, even though the length of *R* is the same for both the horizontal and the vertical coordinates.

—————————————— **Exercises** ——————————————

8.12. Modify the Shapes program so that it uses different foreground and background colors (refer to the palette tables). Run the program and see the effects.

8.13. Modify the program by replacing the predicate

```
Row_r = Center_row - R * cos(A)
```

in *draw_ellipse* with the predicate

```
Row_r = Center_row - 1.40 * R * cos(A)
```

Now run the modified program. What happens to the ellipse?

8.14. Modify the Shapes program by replacing

```
A1 = A + 0.02
```

in the *draw_ellipse* rule with

```
A1 = A + 0.05
```

Run the program. What difference do you see in the appearance of the ellipse?

Making Presentation Graphics

Bar graphs and pie graphs are highly effective in business communications because they show pictorially the variations of quantities such as sales and production against time ranges or sales regions. These graphs are particularly useful for observing the trends of business activities without bringing unnecessary numerical details into the picture. The following sections present programs that illustrate fundamentals of presentation graphics. The complete Turbo Prolog programs in these sections show you how to create line graphs, bar graphs and pie graphs.

Drawing a Line Graph

Turbo Prolog's *line* predicate makes it easy to draw a simple line graph. For this example, imagine a hypothetical company, Mid-West Beer Distributors, Inc. The sales figures for the first half of 1986 are shown in table 8.12.

—————————— **Table 8.12** ——————————
Sales for Mid-West Beer Distributors, Inc.

Month (1986)	Sales amount ($1000s)
January	6000
February	9000
March	10000
April	6000
May	7000
June	9000

You want to draw a line graph with appropriate labels for these sales figures. The steps for achieving your goal are

1. Make a window.

2. Write the main title and sub-title.

3. Draw the *x*-axis and *y*-axis and write the axis labels.

4. Draw lines between the data points.

5. Write vertical scale labels.

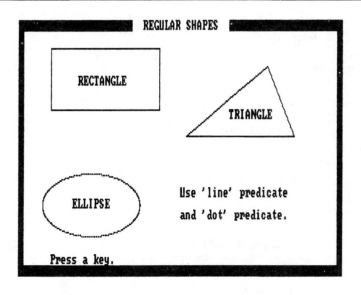

Fig. 8.12. *Simple shapes drawn with the* dot *and* line *predicates.*

The program LineGraph, in listing 8.6, shows that a single rule can be designed to carry out these steps.

```
/* Program: LineGraph      File: PROG0806.PRO */
/* Purpose: To draw a simple line graph.      */

domains

predicates

   draw_line_graph
   prompt_exit

goal

   draw_line_graph,
   prompt_exit.
```

```
clauses

    draw_line_graph :-

        graphics(2,0,7),

        makewindow(1,7,7,
                   " Line Graph ",
                   2,10,23,60),

        cursor(1,13),
        write("MID-WEST BEER DISTRIBUTORS, INC."),
        cursor(2,15),
        write("Sales: January - June, 1986"),

        line(16000,3000,16000,20000,1),
        line(16000,3000, 4000, 3000,1),

        cursor(13,11), write("Jan"),
        cursor(13,16), write("Feb"),
        cursor(13,21), write("Mar"),
        cursor(13,26), write("Apr"),
        cursor(13,31), write("May"),
        cursor(13,36), write("Jun"),
        cursor(15,20),
        write("M  O  N  T  H  S"),
        cursor(17,15),
        write("Sales: in units of $1000K"),

        line(10000, 5000, 7000, 7000,1),
        line( 7000, 7000, 6000, 9000,1),
        line( 6000, 9000,10000,11000,1),
        line(10000,11000, 9000,13000,1),
        line( 9000,13000, 7000,15000,1),

        cursor( 4,3), write("10 -"),
        cursor( 6,3), write(" 8 -"),
        cursor( 8,3), write(" 6 -"),
        cursor(10,3), write(" 4 -"),
        cursor(12,3), write(" 2 -").
```

```
prompt_exit :-
    cursor(19,35),
    write("Press the SPACE BAR."),
    readchar(_),
    removewindow,
    exit.
```

The rule *draw_line_ graph* performs all five steps involved in creating the graph. A second rule, *prompt_exit*, prompts the user to press the space bar and then removes the window.

The predicate *graphics(2,1,7)* selects the high-resolution black-and-white graphics screen. The predicate *makewindow* specifies a black and white window with the label *Line Graph*, a depth of 20 lines, and a width of 60 columns. The window's upper left corner is at row 2, column 10.

The next step performed by *draw_line_ graph* is to place the axes and label the points on the *x*-axis. The graph's *y*-axis line starts at the point (4000,3000) and ends at the point (16000,3000). The endpoints of the axes and the coordinates of the first data point are shown in figure 8.13. (Remember that the endpoints are described by row-and-column coordinates, not *x* and *y* values.)

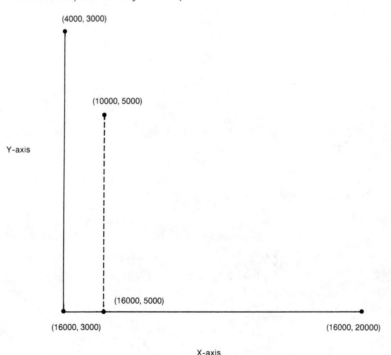

Fig. 8.13. *Coordinates for the axes and one data point of a line graph.*

The *x*-axis labels are the names of the months. These are spaced 2000 points apart. The *y*-axis labels are sales-volume amounts in increments of $200K. They are also spaced 2000 points apart. Guidelines for positioning text are given in the next section of this chapter.

The locations of the data points are given in terms of the row values and column values. The January data point, for example, is at (10000,5000). The row value 10000 is calculated by subtracting the data value 6000 (the sales amount) from the *x*-axis row value of 16000. The value is subtracted, not added, because points that are higher on the screen have lower (not higher) row coordinates.

A simple formula can be used in calculating the row values of points on a graph:

Row = Axis – (Quantity × Scale)

For this graph, the scaling factor is 1. When you plot your own graphs, you will need to determine the scaling factor either by experimentation or calculation. One way to calculate the scaling factor is to subtract the row coordinate of the highest data point on the graph (10000, in this case) from the row coordinate of the lowest point (the *y*-axis, in this case) and then to divide the difference by the largest quantity. The result is the scaling factor. For example, if the largest quantity to be graphed were 12000, then the scaling factor would be

(16000 – 10000) / 12000

or 1/2.

The column values for the data points are derived by adding an increment, 2000 in this case, to the column value of the *y*-axis. The column value for January, 5000, is obtained by adding 2000 to the column value of the origin of the line graph coordinate system, which is at column 3000.

Table 8.13 shows the month, the sales amount, the row values, and the column values for the six-month period of the graph.

—————— **Table 8.13** ——————
Row and Column Values for the Sales Graph

Month	Sales Amount	Row value (Axis – quantity)	Column value (Axis + 2000 increment)
Jan	6000	10000	5000
Feb	9000	7000	7000
Mar	10000	6000	9000
Apr	6000	10000	11000
May	7000	9000	13000
Jun	9000	6000	15000

The line graph is then constructed by drawing 5 straight lines joining these 6 points. The vertical scale labels show a scale from 0 to $100K (an arbitrary scale).

Figure 8.14 shows the line graph created by this program. Notice that the segments of the graph have the jagged slopes typical of diagonal lines in graphic displays.

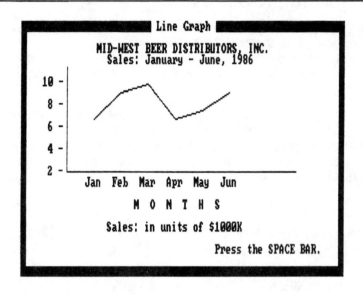

Fig. 8.14. *A simple line graph.*

Exercises

8.15. Modify The LineGraph program by varying the color parameters. Run the modified program and note the differences.

8.16. E-Z Office Supplies had these revenues for the last 6 months of 1986:

Month	Sales (in $10K)
July	6000
August	7500
September	11000
October	10250
November	9500
December	12325

Using the LineGraph program as an example, write a Turbo Prolog program to draw a line graph for this data.

8.17. What modification would you make to the LineGraph program to include all 12 months of the year? Describe the procedures briefly.

Drawing a Simple Bar Graph

Turbo Prolog makes drawing a simple bar graph as easy as drawing a line graph. The company sales statistics used as data for the line graph will be used for an example. In fact, only one change must be made to the steps for creating the line graph. Instead of drawing lines connecting the data points, we will draw bars from each data point to the *x*-axis.

The BarGraph program, in listing 8.7, is the same as the LineGraph program except that this program has predicates to draw the six vertical bars. Each bar requires three *line* predicates—two for drawing vertical lines from the *x*-axis to the data point, and one for drawing a horizontal line to close the top of the bar. For example, the predicates to draw the bar for the January data are

```
line(16000,5000,10000,5000,1),
line(16000,5500,10000,5500,1),
line(10000,5000,10000,5500,1).
```

```
/* Program: BarGraph     File: PROG0807.PRO */
/* Purpose: To draw a simple bar graph.     */

predicates

    draw_bar_graph
    prompt_exit

goal

    draw_bar_graph,
    prompt_exit.

clauses

    draw_bar_graph :-

        graphics(2,1,7),
```

```
makewindow(1,7,7,
          " Bar Graph ",2,10,23,60),

/* write title and subtitle */

cursor(1,13),
write("MID-WEST BEER DISTRIBUTORS, INC."),
cursor(2,15),
write("Sales: January - June, 1986"),

/* draw axes and put labels */

line(16000,3000,16000,20000,1),
line(16000,3000, 4000, 3000,1),

cursor(13,12), write("Jan"),
cursor(13,17), write("Feb"),
cursor(13,22), write("Mar"),
cursor(13,27), write("Apr"),
cursor(13,32), write("May"),
cursor(13,37), write("Jun"),
cursor(15,20),
write("M  O  N  T  H  S"),
cursor(17,15),
write("Sales: in units of $1000K"),

/* draw bars from data */

line(16000, 5000,10000, 5000,1),
line(16000, 5500,10000, 5500,1),
line(10000, 5000,10000, 5500,1),

line(16000, 7000, 7000, 7000,1),
line(16000, 7500, 7000, 7500,1),
line( 7000, 7000, 7000, 7500,1),

line(16000, 9000, 6000, 9000,1),
line(16000, 9500, 6000, 9500,1),
line( 6000, 9000, 6000, 9500,1),

line(16000,11000,10000,11000,1),
line(16000,11500,10000,11500,1),
line(10000,11000,10000,11500,1),
```

```
    line(16000,13000, 9000,13000,1),
    line(16000,13500, 9000,13500,1),
    line( 9000,13000, 9000,13500,1),

    line(16000,15000, 7000,15000,1),
    line(16000,15500, 7000,15500,1),
    line( 7000,15000, 7000,15500,1),

    /* write vertical scale labels */

    cursor( 4,2), write("10 -"),
    cursor( 6,2), write(" 8 -"),
    cursor( 8,2), write(" 6 -"),
    cursor(10,2), write(" 4 -"),
    cursor(12,2), write(" 2 -").

/* rule for prompting exit */

prompt_exit :-
    cursor(19,38),
    write("Press the SPACE BAR."),
    readchar(_),
    removewindow,
    exit.
```

Figure 8.15 shows the bar graph created by the BarGraph program. Notice that each bar has a width of 500 pixels.

────────────────────────── **Exercises** ──────────────────────────

8.18. Modify the BarGraph program so that the bars are twice as wide.

8.19. Write a Turbo Prolog program to draw a bar graph for the data given in exercise 8.17. Choose your color combinations to make a pleasing screen presentation.

Drawing a Pie Graph

A Turbo Prolog program to draw a pie graph requires the use of both of the graphics predicates, *line* and *dot*, that were discussed earlier in this chapter. As you read these steps for drawing a pie graph, refer to figure 8.16:

1. Draw the pie-cut lines, with the angles between them proportional to the data values.

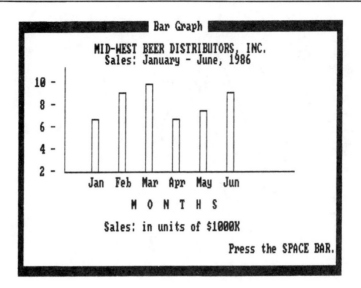

Fig. 8.15. *A simple bar graph.*

2. Calculate the positions for the labels, and write the labels.

3. Draw a circle representing the circumference of the pie.

Each of these steps involves several sub-steps, which are described in the following paragraphs. This example also uses the data for Mid-West Beer Distributors, Inc., so that you can easily compare the resulting graphs.

The central angles of the pie pieces are determined from the sales data given in table 8.12. From these angles, the positions of the cutting lines are calculated.

For example, consider the calculation of the angle of the pie piece for January. First you calculate the fractional size of the pie piece by adding all the quantities for the six-month period and dividing the January quantity by that sum. The fractional size is 6000/47000, which equals approximately 0.1277. Now you convert this fractional size to a pie-piece angle in radians. There are 6.283184 radians in a complete circle, so the angle in radians of the January pie piece is 0.1277 × 6.283184, or approximately 0.802 radians. The sides of that angle are the radial lines 0 and 1 in figure 8.16.

Notice that the rotation of the angle is clockwise, even though conventional practice is to express angles in counterclockwise rotation. The graph is set up in this way because clockwise "reading" is more natural for the users of the graph.

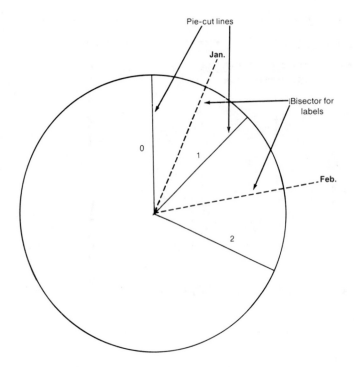

Fig. 8.16. Methods used in drawing a pie graph.

The initial side of each pie piece is the terminal side of the preceding piece. For simplicity in programming, the angle of each pie piece's terminal side is expressed as the sum of the angle for that pie piece and for the preceding pieces, so that the angle of all terminal sides can be calculated relative to a single initial side (line 0 in figure 8.16). For example, the February pie piece has the central angle 1.203 radians; the angle between line 2 and line 0 is .802 radians + 1.203 radians, or 2.005 radians.

The relative sizes and the angles of the other pie pieces are calculated in the same way. The sizes of the pie pieces, the corresponding angles in radians, and the terminal angle for each pie piece are shown in table 8.14. You'll notice that the terminal side for the June pie piece is 6.283 radians, or 360 degrees. That value indicates that we've gone full-circle; the terminal side for the June pie piece does not need to be plotted.

——— **Table 8.14** ———
Angles for the Pie Pieces

| Month | Pie-piece size | | Pie-piece angle | Terminal-side angle |
	Relative	Fractional		
Jan	6000	0.1277	0.802	0.802
Feb	9000	0.1915	1.203	2.005
Mar	10000	0.2128	1.337	3.342
Apr	6000	0.1277	0.802	4.144
May	7000	0.1489	0.936	5.080
Jun	9000	0.1915	1.203	6.283

Once the angles of the cut lines have been calculated, determining their endpoints is simple. The formula is the same one that is used to calculate points on a circle (refer to the section "Building a Circle").

The labels are positioned by determining the coordinates of a point just outside of the pie circle, so that lines joining these points and the center of the circle bisect the pie pieces. The angle between each bisector line and the initial line (line 0 in figure 8.16) is equal to the angle of the previous terminal side plus half the angle of the current pie piece. The angle of the February pie piece, for example, is 1.203 radians; the previous terminal-side angle is 0.802 (refer to table 8.14). The angle of the bisector for the February pie piece is

0.802 + 1.203 / 2

or 1.404. Table 8.15 shows the values for the bisectors of the pie pieces.

——— **Table 8.15** ———
Angles for the Pie Graph Labels

Month	Angle
Jan	0.401
Feb	1.404
Mar	2.674
Apr	3.743
May	4.612
Jun	5.681

The *Row* and *Column* coordinates of these external points are then used to compute the line and column numbers. The *cursor* predicate takes character-space arguments in graphics mode, just as it does in text mode. Thus the 32000 × 32000 coordinates of the graphics screen must be converted to the 25 × 80 coordinates used for positioning the cursor. The conversion factors are derived by dividing 32000 by 25 for rows and by 80 for columns, yielding 1280 and 400, respectively. The conversion formulas, then, are

Char_row = Row / 1280

and

Char_col = Column / 400

where *Char_row* and *Char_col* are cursor row and column coordinates, and *Row* and *Column* are the graphics-screen coordinates. (These values must be rounded to integers.)

The method used earlier in this chapter to draw a circle is used to draw the edge of the pie.

Figure 8.17 shows the structure for the pie-graph program. Remember that a convenient design method is to write a rule for each program module. The main module is the rule *draw_ pie_ graph*, which has this structure:

```
draw_pie_graph :-
    make_window,
    write_titles,
    cut_pie( [ 0.0, 0.802, 2.01, 3.345, 4.147, 5.083] ),
    put_pie_labels( [ 0.401, 1.404, 2.674, 3.743, 4.612, 5.681],
                    ["Jan","Feb","Mar","Apr","May","Jun"] ),
    draw_circle(0.0).
```

Notice that each component of the *draw_ pie_ graph* rule is also a rule or a sub-module. This kind of modular design is solid and efficient.

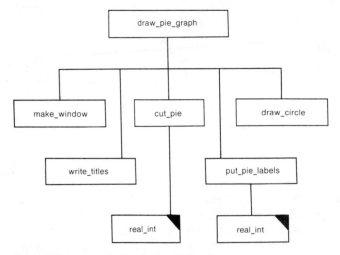

Fig. 8.17. *A structure chart for the PieGraph program.*

The PieGraph program, in listing 8.8, implements this program structure. The rule *make_window* is simple. It is the same rule that was used in the program LineGraph. The rule *write_titles* is also the same as the rule in the LineGraph program.

```
/* Program: PieGraph    File: PROG0808.PRO  */
/* Purpose: To draw a pie graph, using      */
/*          window and graphics predicates. */

domains

    real_list = real*
    string_list = string*

predicates

    draw_pie_graph
    make_window
    write_titles
    cut_pie(real_list)
    put_pie_labels(real_list,string_list)
    draw_circle(real)
    real_int(real,integer)

goal

    draw_pie_graph,
    cursor(20,2),
    write(" Press the SPACE BAR."),
    readchar(_),
    text.

clauses

    draw_pie_graph :-
      make_window,
      write_titles,
      cut_pie( [ 0.0, 0.802, 2.01, 3.345, 4.147, 5.083] ),
      put_pie_labels( [ 0.401, 1.404, 2.674, 3.743, 4.612, 5.681],
                      ["Jan","Feb","Mar","Apr","May","Jun"] ),
      draw_circle(0.0).
```

```
make_window :-
   graphics(2,0,7),
   makewindow(1,7,7," Pie Graph ",1,10,23,60).

write_titles :-
   cursor(1,13),
   write("MID-WEST BEER DISTRIBUTORS, INC."),
   cursor(2,16),
   write("Sales: First Quarter, 1986").

cut_pie([]).
cut_pie([ Angle | Other_angles ]) :-
   Center_row = 15000, Center_col = 11500,
   Radius = 5000,
   End_row_real = Center_row - Radius * 1.40 * cos(Angle),
   End_col_real = Center_col + Radius * sin(Angle),
   real_int(End_row_real,End_row_int),
   real_int(End_col_real,End_col_int),
   line(Center_row,Center_col,End_row_int,End_col_int,1),
   cut_pie(Other_angles).

put_pie_labels( [], [] ).
put_pie_labels( [Angle | Other_angles ],
                [Label | Other_labels]    ) :-
   Center_row = 14500, Center_col = 11000,
   Radius = 6500,
   Label_row = Center_row - Radius * 1.40 * cos(Angle),
   Label_col = Center_col + Radius * sin(Angle),
   Row_real = Label_row / 1280, Col_real = Label_col / 400,
   real_int(Row_real,Row), real_int(Col_real,Col),
   cursor(Row,Col),
   write(Label),
   put_pie_labels(Other_angles,Other_labels).

draw_circle(Angle) :-  Angle >= 6.28, !.
draw_circle(Angle) :-
    Center_row = 15000, Center_col = 11500, Radius = 5000,
    Dot_row_real = Center_row - Radius * 1.40 * cos(Angle),
    Dot_col_real = Center_col + Radius * sin(Angle),
    real_int(Dot_row_real,Dot_row),
    real_int(Dot_col_real,Dot_col),
```

```
        dot(Dot_row,Dot_col,1),
        Angle1 = Angle + 0.02,
        draw_circle(Angle1).

    real_int(Re,In) :-  Re = In.
```

Note that the rule *cut_ pie* uses the trigonometric functions discussed earlier to calculate the endpoints of the cut lines:

```
cut_pie([]).
cut_pie([ Angle | Other_angles ]) :-
   Center_row = 15000, Center_col = 11500,
   Radius = 5000,
   End_row_real = Center_row - Radius * 1.40 * cos(Angle),
   End_col_real = Center_col + Radius * sin(Angle),
   real_int(End_row_real,End_row_int),
   real_int(End_col_real,End_col_int),
   line(Center_row,Center_col,End_row_int,End_col_int,1),
   cut_pie(Other_angles).
```

The row values are multiplied by the factor 1.40 to compensate for the aspect ratio of the monitor screen. You may need to change this factor to create a "true" circle on your computer, because different screens have different aspect ratios. The resulting real-number values are converted (and truncated) to integers by means of the rule *real_int*, and the resulting integers are used to draw the pie-piece lines.

The rule *cut_ pie* uses the Head-Tail Method to access individual elements in a list of angles. Review Chapter 5 if that concept is not clear to you.

The rule *put_ pie_labels* is similar to the rule *cut_ pie*. Note, however, that the *Center_row* and *Center_col* values differ from those used in *cut_ pie*. The center point for the labels is offset slightly from the center of the pie so that the month labels are placed evenly around the circumference. The 32000 × 32000 graphics coordinates are converted to 25 × 80 character-space coordinates for positioning of the labels.

Like *cut_ pie*, *put_ pie_labels* also uses the Head/Tail Method to access list elements. This predicate, however, uses two lists of values, a list of angles and a list of labels.

The sub-rule *draw_circle(A)* draws a circle as the boundary of the pie. This rule works like the rule *draw_ellipse*, in the Shapes program. The factor 1.40 is used to compensate for the screen aspect ratio. Figure 8.18 shows the pie graph displayed by the program.

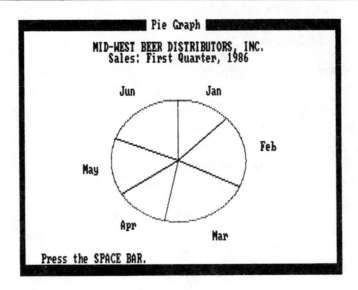

Fig. 8.18. *Output of the PieGraph program.*

Exercises

8.20. Modify the PieGraph program by enlarging the pie so that the pie piece labels are enclosed within the pie circle. *Hint:* You will need to modify the rules for both the radial lines and the circumference of the circle.

8.21. Modify the PieGraph program so that it draws a pie graph for the hypothetical company given in Exercise 8.16.

Using Turtle Graphics

Turbo Prolog includes turtle graphics among its graphics resources, thereby offering a wide range of graphics commands. In this section, you'll soon learn about a notable difference between the row-and-column graphics of the previous section and the turtle graphics of this section. The row-and-column graphics coordinates are absolute with relation to the screen corners. Turtle-graphics coordinates, however, are relative to the current position of the graphics cursor. Because this coordinate system is easier to understand for beginning programmers and math students, turtle graphics is often used as a teaching tool.

As the phrase *turtle graphics* suggests, you can think of the graphics cursor as a turtle with a pen tied to its tail. This turtle crawls about on a sheet of "paper" (the screen). By lowering and raising its tail, the turtle can lower and raise the pen. If the pen is down, it draws a line as the turtle moves; if the pen is up, no line is drawn. The turtle's direction of travel can be changed by rotating the turtle, and the distance the turtle travels can be specified. The predicates for controlling the turtle are discussed in this section.

Turtle Graphics Predicates

Turbo Prolog's built-in predicates give full support of turtle graphics. These predicates are *penup*, *pendown*, *pencolor*, *forward*, *back*, *right*, *left*, and *penpos*. To use these predicates the screen must be set for graphics mode by means of the *graphics* predicate.

The *penup* predicate is used when you want the turtle to move without drawing. This predicate has no arguments. The *pendown* predicate is used to lower the pen for drawing.

The *pencolor* predicate is used to select the color of the turtle's "trail." The syntax is

```
pencolor(Color_number)
```

where *Color_number* is an integer chosen from the color-palette values shown in table 8.7. For example, the predicate expression *pencolor(1)* selects green from color palette 0. Similarly, the predicate expression *pencolor(2)* selects magenta from color palette 1.

The *forward* predicate is used to move the turtle forward by a specified amount. The syntax is

```
forward(Step_size)
```

where *Step_size* is a number between 1 and 31999. The *back* predicate functions similarly, but moves the turtle backwards. For example, the predicate expression *back(500)* moves the turtle 500 units backwards. No error results if the turtle moves beyond the edge of the screen; however, anything drawn outside the screen border will not be visible.

The *right* and *left* predicates are used to turn the turtle. Each of these predicates takes as its argument an angle in degrees. The syntax is

```
left(Angle)
```

The predicate expression *left(45)* turns the turtle 45 degrees to the left.

Notice that the argument of the *left* and *right* predicates indicates a rotation away from the current heading. In other words, the argument indicates the angle between the new heading and the path the turtle would have traversed had *left* or *right* not been used, not the angle between the path before and the path after the turn. For example, the predicates

```
pendown,
forward(2000),
left(45),
forward(2000)
```

causes the turtle to draw two line segments with an angle of 135 degrees (or 180 degrees – 45 degrees).

The *penpos* predicated is used to position the turtle cursor at specified coordinates and "aim" it in a specified direction. The syntax is

```
penpos(Row,Column,Angle)
```

For example, the predicate expression *penpos(1000,2000,0)* positions the turtle at row 1000, column 2000, and heading 0.

The default heading angle for the turtle, corresponding to A = 0, is straight down—that is, in the direction of the increasing *Row* values. The predicate expression

```
penpos(3000,15000,180)
```

positions the turtle at the point (3000,15000), and orients the turtle so that the "head" points straight up.

The *penpos* predicate can also be used to examine the location of the turtle. If the objects of *penpos* are unbound variables, *penpos* binds them to values that specify the turtle's current position and heading.

A couple of illustrative examples will show the use of the turtle-graphics predicates.

For the first example, suppose that you want to draw a vertical line that is 8000 units long and that starts at the point (1000,16000). The turtle's direction is 0 degrees (straight down) and the step size is 8000. The complete rule therefore is

```
draw_straight line :-
    penpos(1000,16000,0),
    pendown,
    pencolor(1),
    forward(8000).
```

As another example, suppose that you want to draw a closed figure starting at the point (20000,16000). The figure is made up of straight line segments, each with a length of

1000 units. You can draw this figure by turning the turtle 2 degrees to the right at each step, starting from the default direction. The simple rules to achieve this goal are

```
draw_figure :-
     graphics(2,0,7),
     penpos(12000,20000,0),
     pendown,
     closed_figure(500).

closed_figure(A) :- A >= 30000, !.
closed_figure(Ao) :-
     forward(100),
     right(2),
     A = Ao + 50,
     circle (A).
```

Notice how the variant clause

```
closed_figure(A) :- A >= 30000, !.
```

is used to provide a boundary condition for the recursive call. This rule succeeds when the value bound to *A* is greater than 30,000. Without this variant clause, the program would loop indefinitely through the recursive calls to *closed_ figure*. Review Chapter 4 if this concept is not clear.

Making a Graphic Picture

Turtle graphics predicates can be used to draw pictures. You might, for example, want to draw a picture containing a simple house and tree. A simple program design would suggest this goal as a rule:

```
make_picture :-
     setup_graphics,
     draw_house,
     draw_tree.
```

The three sub-rules can be implemented in as much detail as you desire. The Picture program, in listing 8.9, is an implementation of this rule.

```
/* Program-id. House        File: PROG0809.PRO */
/* Purpose: To show the use of turtle          */
/*          graphics predicates.                */
```

```
predicates

    make_picture
    setup_graphics
    draw_house
    draw_tree
    draw_hemisphere(integer)

goal

    make_picture.

clauses

    make_picture :-
        setup_graphics,
        draw_house,
        draw_tree,
        cursor(16,40),
        write(" Press the SPACE BAR."),
        readchar(_),
        exit.

    setup_graphics :-

        graphics(2,0,7),
        makewindow(1,1,7,
                    " A Little House ",
                    1,5,22,75).

    draw_house :-

        pendown,
        left(90),forward(7000),right(90),
        forward(5000),right(90),forward(7000),
        right(90),forward(5000),

        penup,
        right(180),forward(5000),

        pendown,
        left(45),forward(5000),left(90),
        forward(5000),right(135),
```

```
        penup,
        back(5000),right(90),forward(3000),
        left(90),

        pendown,
        forward(3000),right(90),
        forward(1000),right(90),forward(3000),
        right(90).

    draw_tree :-

        penup,
        forward(9020),right(90),

        pendown,
        forward(9020),right(90),forward(2750),
        back(5580),left(90),
        draw_hemisphere(0).

    draw_hemisphere(Count) :- Count >= 360.
    draw_hemisphere(Count) :-
                forward(50), right(1),
                Count1 = Count + 2,
                draw_hemisphere(Count1).
```

In this program, the *setup_ graphics* rule sets up a white-on-black screen and a bordered window with 18 rows and 50 columns.

The rule *draw_house* draws a house composed of straight lines. The first four lines of predicates draw the house frame (a rectangle). The next two lines position the cursor at the upper left corner of the frame. The next three lines draw the roof (two straight lines inclined at 45 degrees to the horizontal).

Another set of three predicates positions the turtle at the lower left corner of the door frame (another rectangle). The next four lines then draw the door frame.

The *draw_tree* rule draws a simple tree. The rule is composed of predicates to position the cursor at the base of the tree (the first two lines), predicates to draw the straight-line portion of the tree (the next three lines), and a rule called *draw_circle*. This rule draws half a circle as part of the tree. The graphics output of this program is shown in figure 8.19.

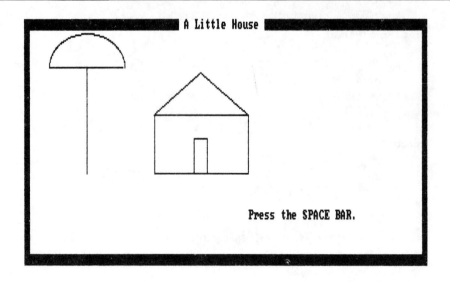

Fig. 8.19. *Output of the Picture program.*

<hr>

Exercise

8.22. Run the Picture program. Notice the amount of time it takes to draw the circle portion of the tree compared to the line portions of the picture. Now modify the program so that the *tree* is more realistic. Use graph paper to design your tree.

Making a Moving Spiral

Turbo Prolog's turtle graphics predicates provide you with effective ways to create artistic and interesting abstract drawings. The program Spiral, in listing 8.10, is just one example of what you can do with only a few predicates.

```
/* Program: Spiral    File: PROG0810.PRO */
/* Purpose: To draw a moving spiral.      */

predicates

    do_graphics
    do_penpos(integer,integer,integer)
```

```
goal

    do_graphics.

clauses

    do_graphics :-
        graphics(2,0,7),
        do_penpos(1400,1600,0),
        cursor(20,60),
        write("MOVING SPIRAL"),
        cursor(23,1),
        write(" Press the SPACE BAR."),
        readchar(_).

    do_penpos(R0,_,_) :- R0 >= 14000.
    do_penpos(R0,C0,A0) :-
                penpos(R0,C0,A0),
                pendown,
                R = R0 + 100,
                C = C0 + 100,
                A = A0 + 10,
                forward(R), left(A),
                penpos(R,C,A),
                do_penpos(R,C,A).
```

The Spiral program's graphics output consists of a series of straight lines with increasing lengths. Each line is oriented 10 degrees away from the previous one. The spiral starts near the upper left corner of the screen, at the point (1400,1600). After each line is drawn the center of the spiral is moved 100 points horizontally and vertically.

The *do_graphics* rule sets the graphic screen to white-on-black and writes the text *Moving Spiral*. The *do_penpos* rule draws the spiral.

The sub-goal *do_penpos(1400,1600,0)* passes the values of *R0*, *C0*, and *A0* to the rule in the *clauses* division of the program. The predicate *R0<1400* imposes a limit on the length of the line. The next two predicates select the pen position at the starting point (1400,1600), with the turtle head pointing down. The *pendown* predicate lowers the pen for drawing.

The next three predicates increment the coordinate values by 100 points and the angle value by 10 degrees. The *forward* and *left* predicates then draw a line segment. The next *penpos* predicate positions the turtle at the new point and direction. This sequence of predicates is repeated recursively until the condition on the maximum line length (1400) is met.

Figure 8.20 shows the spiral produced by the Spiral program. Many different abstract drawings can be produced through manipulation of the turtle graphics predicates; they are limited only by your imagination. The exercises that follow will help you to become more familiar with the Turtle Graphics manipulations.

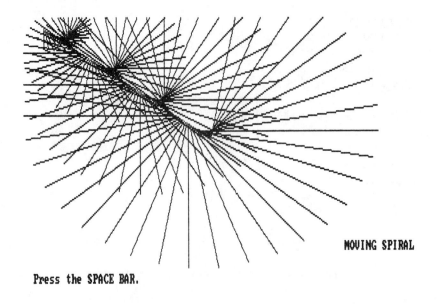

MOVING SPIRAL

Press the SPACE BAR.

Fig. 8.20. Output of the Spiral program.

Exercises

8.23. Run the Spiral program. Then modify it so that the length of the lines remains the same. Run the new program. *Hint*: Change the *forward(R)* predicate expression.

8.24. Modify the Spiral program so that the spiral starts at the lower right corner and moves towards the upper left corner.

Making Sound and Music

In addition to supporting multiple windows and color graphics facilities, Turbo Prolog also supports sound. When a programmer incorporates any of the enhancements discussed in this chapter into a program, the program execution is predictably more lively, better organized, and more user-friendly. In this section you will learn the elements of Turbo Prolog sound production and how to use them in your programs.

Sound Predicates

Turbo Prolog supports two sound predicates: *beep* and *sound*. The *beep* predicate produces a high-pitched sound. The syntax is simple, because this predicate has no parameters. A Turbo Prolog rule to beep the speaker three times is

```
do_beep :-
    beep,
    beep,
    beep.
```

The *beep* rule is useful in many computer applications. A program can beep to get the user's attention when input is required, for example. A sequence of beeps can be used to provide an audible signal, or to alert the user to an error condition.

These functions and others can be even more effective if the sound capabilities of Turbo Prolog are used. Turbo Prolog can produce notes through the entire range of sounds audible to the human ear. The syntax of the *sound* predicate is

```
sound(Duration,Frequency)
```

The parameter *Duration* is a number that represents time in hundredths of a second. The parameter *Frequency* is an integer that represents the frequency of a given note (the pitch). With some effort, you could use the *sound* predicate to reproduce any of the great melodies of classical or modern music.

Even simple musical tags can add interest to your programs and provide informative and attention-getting responses to various inputs. By varying the duration and frequency, you can make different notes to signal different points in program execution. The following rule provides an example of this technique.

```
make_a_note :-
    sound(5,165),
    sound(10,247).
```

This rule plays an E note for .05 second, followed by a B note for .10 second.

The notes used in these examples are chosen from concert-pitch frequencies. Table 8.16 gives the notes for the octave starting with middle C; this range is pleasing to the ear. The first column is the musical note and the second column is the frequency in cycles per second.

—————— **Table 8.16** ——————
Musical Notes and Frequencies

Note	Frequency
C	262
C sharp	278
D	294
D sharp	302
E	330
F	350
F sharp	370
G	392
G sharp	416
A	440
A sharp	466
B	494
C	524

Musical Tags

Using the information in table 8.16, you can build musical tags for your programs. A musical tag is a short, snappy, and easily recognizable sequence of notes. You have heard many of these before, and may want to create others to give your programs a personalized touch.

The following rule shows how easily musical tags can be constructed. The music-making rule is

```
do_yea_team :-
     sound(4,392),
     sound(4,440),
     sound(4,494),
     sound(8,440),
     sound(4,494),
     sound(12,392).
```

The next section will show how another musical tag can be easily incorporated in a Turbo Prolog program.

A Simple CAI Program with Musical Tags

Now that you have seen how musical tags are built, you can include them in your Turbo Prolog programs. As an example, consider a simple CAI (Computer Assisted Instruction)

program to drill students in addition of integer numbers. The design of the program is based on the following procedures:

1. Generate two integer numbers, using Turbo Prolog's random number generator. Compute their sum.

2. Display the two numbers. Prompt the user to enter the sum. Compare the user's sum with the computed sum. If they are the same, go to step 3. Otherwise, go to step 4.

3. Write a message telling the user his or her response is correct. Then go back to Step 1.

4. Write a message that tells the user the response is incorrect. Then go back to Step 2.

Figure 8.21 is a structure chart for a CAI program designed along these lines. The main module, *do_cai*, is the goal. It calls a sub-module *make_exercise_set*. This submodule in turn calls two other modules: *gen_rand_num*, to generate two random integer numbers, and *test_and_reward*, to accept an answer from the user and test it for correctness. If the answer is correct, *test_and_reward* calls the module *say_good_work*. If the answer is incorrect, it calls the module *say_more_work*.

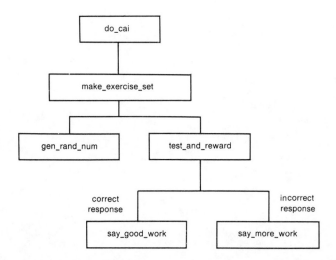

Fig. 8.21. *A structure chart for a simple computer assisted instruction program.*

The rule *say_good_work* writes a message to the user about the correct answer and plays a musical tag to indicate the user's success. Similarly, the *say_more_work* rule writes a message for the user about the incorrect answer and sounds three beeps.

The GoodWork program, in listing 8.11, implements this CAI program design. The goal is simply *do_cai*:

```
do_cai :-
    makewindow(1,7,7,"CAI SIMPLE ADDITIONS",
                2,20,20,34),
    nl, write("Here are the exercises!"),
    make_exercise_set(3),
    nl, write("    Have fun, bye!"),
    nl, write("Press the space bar"),
    readchar(_),
    removewindow.
```

This rule makes a bordered black-and-white window 20 rows deep and 34 columns wide. The rule *do_cai* calls the module *make_exercise_set* to give the exercise problems. On return from this sub-module, the main module prompts the user to press the space bar. Then the program ends.

```
/* Program: GoodWork      File: PROG0811.PRO */
/* Purpose: To drill students in            */
/*          simple addition.                 */

predicates

    gen_rand_num(integer)
    say_good_work
    say_more_work
    test_and_reward(integer,integer)
    make_exercise_set(integer)
    do_cai

goal

    do_cai.

clauses

    gen_rand_num(X) :-
            random(Y),
            X = Y * 5 + 1.
```

```
say_good_work :-
   makewindow(2,7,7,
              "Good Work",12,40,8,30),
   nl, write("You are right."), nl, nl,
   write("   LISTEN TO THE MUSIC !"),
      sound(4,262), sound(4,350),
      sound(4,440), sound(8,516),
      sound(4,440), sound(12,516),
   nl, nl, write("Press space bar"),
   readchar(_),
   removewindow.


say_more_work :-
   makewindow(3,7,7,
              "More Work",14,6,7,28),
   write("You need improvement."), nl, nl,
   write("   BEEP, BEEP, BEEP !"), nl, nl,
   beep, beep, beep,
   write("Press space bar"),
   readchar(_),
   removewindow.


test_and_reward(C,U) :-
              C = U,
              say_good_work.
test_and_reward(C,U) :-
              C <> U,
              say_more_work.


make_exercise_set(0) :- !.
make_exercise_set(Count) :-
   gen_rand_num(A),
   nl, write("1st. number is ",A), nl,
   gen_rand_num(B),
   write("2nd. number is ",B), nl,
   C = A + B,
   write("What is the sum ?"), nl,
   readint(U),
   test_and_reward(C,U),
   Newcount = Count - 1,
   make_exercise_set(NewCount).
```

```
do_cai :-
  makewindow(1,7,7,"CAI SIMPLE ADDITIONS",
             2,20,20,34),
  nl, write("Here are the exercises !"),
  make_exercise_set(3),
  nl, write("     Have fun, bye !"),
  nl, write("Press space bar"),
  readchar(_),
  removewindow.
```

The rule *make_exercise-set* makes three exercise questions. For each question, two random numbers are generated by the sub-rule *gen_rand_num*. The built-in Turbo Prolog predicate to generate a random number is *random(Y)*, where Y is a real variable. This predicate binds its variable argument to a random number greater than or equal to 0 and less than 1. The expression

$$Y * 5 + 1$$

yields a random real number between 1 and 6, depending on the random value bound to Y. To bind X to a random integer number between 1 and 5, you can use the rule

$$X = Y * 5 + 1$$

Because the argument of *gen_rand_num* is declared as an integer in the *predicates* division of the program, X is bound to a random integer number between 1 and 5. Turbo Prolog rounds the real-number value to the nearest integer.

The two random numbers generated in this way are then displayed on the screen. The module *make_exercise_set* also uses the subrule $C = A + B$ to compute the sum (S) of the two numbers. Then the user is prompted to input the sum of the random numbers; the user's entry is bound to the variable U. This answer is evaluated by the rule *test_and_reward*. If $C = U$, then the user's answer is correct. Otherwise, the user's answer is incorrect.

Figure 8.22 shows the screen display for a correct answer. The message displayed in the *Good Work* window is certainly encouraging to the user, and the pleasant sound produced adds further reinforcement. Figure 8.23 shows the screen display for an incorrect answer. The message suggests that the user needs to improve, but it is not flippant or discouraging in tone. The *beeps* are intended to stimulate the user to do better work.

The use of multiple windows simplifies the user's interaction with the program. This simplicity is highly desirable. The use of musical tags as a reward is exciting, especially for a young user. By indicating musically that more work is needed and by reinforcing good work, the musical tags encourage the student.

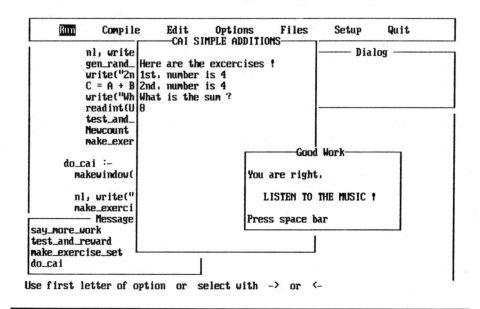

Fig. 8.22. *The CAI program's display for a correct answer.*

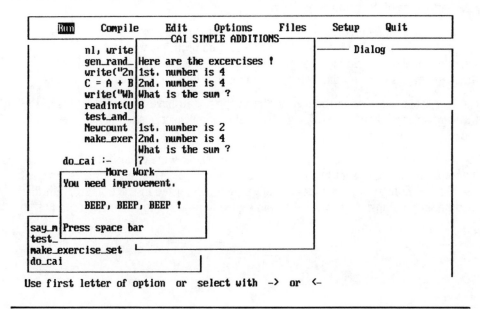

Fig. 8.23. *The CAI program's display for an incorrect answer.*

—————————————— **Exercises** ——————————————

8.25. Run the GoodWork program, and try out the simple addition problems. Respond to the prompts by giving incorrect as well as correct answers.

8.26. Modify the program so that it displays the correct answer in addition to the message *You need improvement*. Of course, seeing the correct answer helps the user to learn.

8.27. Modify the program so that the range of numbers to be added is from 20 to 80. *Hint*: Modify the predicate *(X = Y * 5 + 1)*.

Chapter Review

In this chapter you have learned to use Turbo Prolog's windowing predicates, and have seen that the built-in input and output predicates can be used with windows. You have also learned to use the *cursor* predicate to write text at any desired position within a window. You have seen that together these predicates allow you to write programs with pleasing and well-organized screen displays. Multiple and overlapping windows and windowed menus are now part of your programming toolkit.

This chapter has also introduced you to the elements of computer graphics, and to the graphic features supported by Turbo Prolog. You have learned how the agruments of the predicates *graphics*, *makewindow*, *dot*, and *line* interact to control the colors and other attributes of the graphics screen display.

With the *line* and *dot* predicates, you have learned to create graphic shapes in your programs. Possessing these skills, you have now gained proficiency in making simple presentation graphics, including line, bar and pie graphs. You have also been introduced to the mathematics used in transforming the input data into forms suitable for graphics.

Turtle graphics was also introduced in this chapter. You have learned the uses of the turtle graphics predicates in programs that make graphic pictures of regular objects and more artistic, abstract pictures.

Finally, the Turbo Prolog sound predicates and their uses were discussed. You can now incorporate musical tags into your programs. Further, you have seen some techniques useful in the construction of a user-friendly computer assisted instruction program that incorporates multiple windows and sound signals for a very professional appearance.

9

Building Dynamic Databases

Overview

In previous chapters, you have learned how to use many of Turbo Prolog's programming tools. When you have learned to build dynamic databases, you will be even more
able to use Turbo Prolog to its full potential. This chapter introduces some basic database
concepts, and introduces design tools that are useful in building databases. You'll learn
to use these design techniques in developing Turbo Prolog programs for database
manipulation.

The programs in this chapter use information about football teams, their players, and
their coaches. But you will learn to use Turbo Prolog's dynamic database capabilities to
manipulate your own data, including personnel rosters, sales figures, or information
about stock items, each with its own inventory number, size, manufacturer, code and
price.

Virtually everything you have learned in the first part of this book will be used in one
way or another in this applications chapter and the ones that follow. The short examples
demonstrating new techniques, the exercises, and the major program examples in these
chapters will lead up to one unifying applications program in each chapter.

The first section in this chapter introduces enough database concepts to get you started
in Turbo Prolog database programming. You can skim this part, or skip over it altogether
if you are already familiar with database fundamentals.

The second section presents the design of a Turbo Prolog database maintained in RAM.
A program is developed to implement the database design, and you will be able to run
the complete program to see how all the pieces fit together.

The third section presents the design of a Turbo Prolog database maintained on disk.
The Turbo Prolog tools needed to implement this design are discussed, and again, the
complete program can be run.

Database Fundamentals

The Turbo Prolog databases you will build and work with in this chapter are particular cases of database management systems. A database management system is basically a computerized information-keeping system. The data is a collection of facts and figures stored in forms that are "readable" to the computer. This organized collection of pieces of information constitutes a database.

Database management systems must support the addition, deletion, and retrieval of data. Computer programs are written to perform these database maintenance functions. The combination of a database and of all the functional programs constitutes a database management system.

There are three well-known database models. These are the *hierarchical model*, the *network model*, and the *relational model*. In the hierarchical model, the data is stored in a hierarchy of data clusters. In the network model, the data is stored in interconnected data aggregates, forming a network of data values. And in the relational model, the data is stored in the form of tables. The current trend in database management is toward more and more utilization of relational databases. Turbo Prolog performs powerfully with databases built on that model.

Database Files

A database file is a collection of related database records. The database file (or simply a database) has the appearance of an ordinary file, but the data values have an internal organization of relationships. The data in the records is arranged in the same way within each record. Often, one record contains a table representing the organization of the data. This table (or *schema*) serves as a "map" that the database management program uses to access the data.

In Chapter 7, you learned several file-processing techniques, including creating files, writing to files, reading from files, and modifying the data in existing files. These file-processing techniques are also useful in dealing with database files.

A file is a collection of records. A record is an assembly of fields. And each field holds a piece of data. The data used in a payroll program in Chapter 3 can be used to illustrate these concepts. The data can be organized as records in a file, as shown in figure 9.1.

Each record in this file has three fields, which could be labeled *Name*, *Department*, and *Rate*. The values contained in each field constitute the data, and the field values are given for as many records as the file contains. The data entries for the first record are *John Walker*, *ACCT*, and *$3.5*. This is the essential file structure for a relational database.

The fundamental operations performed on any database include adding new records, modifying existing records, and querying the database. Turbo Prolog's rule-based inferencing capabilities enable the results of queries to be used in the production of new data, which can then be added to the database file as new records.

	Name Field	Department field	Rate field
Record 1	John Walker	ACCT	3.5
Record 2	Tom Sellack	OPER	4.5
Record 3	Jack Hunter	ADVE	4.5
Record 4	Sam Ray	DATA	6.5

Fig. 9.1. *The structure of a database file.*

In a conventional database file, all records have the same length so that records can be located by calculating their distance, or *offset*, from the beginning of the file. In a Turbo Prolog database, on the other hand, records need not be all of the same length because Turbo Prolog locates the records by pattern matching.

Relational Databases

As was mentioned earlier, data values in a relational database can be regarded as elements of a table. Such a table is made up of rows and columns, as in figure 9.2.

Relation: *player*

	Attribute 1 (name)	Attribute 2 (team)	Attribute 3 (position)
Tuple 1	Dan Marino	Miami Dophins	QB
Tuple 2	Richard Dent	Chicago Bears	DE
Tuple 3	Bernie Kosar	Cleveland Browns	QB
Tuple 4	Doug Cosbie	Dallas Cowboys	TE
Tuple 5	Mark Malone	Pittsburgh Steelers	QB

Number of tuples (cardinality) = 5
Number of attributes (arity) = 3

Fig. 9.2. *A database relation.*

This data table has three columns and five rows. The top label, *Player*, is the name of the table and its organization. *Player* is the *relation*. The name of a column represents an *attribute*, which is related to the other attributes in the table. There are three attributes for the *player* relation. The set of attributes—*Name, Team,* and *Position*—is called the *relational scheme*. The number of columns (attributes) is known as the *arity* of the relation. The arity of the *player* relation is 3.

In a conventional relational database, a row in the table is known as a *tuple*. The first tuple in the *player* database is

```
Dan Marino, Miami Dolphins, QB
```

The number of tuples in a table is known as the *cardinality* of the relation. The cardinality of the *Player* relation is 5.

These terms provide a useful set of concepts for understanding relational database management systems. You will find this framework of ideas useful in the following discussions of dynamic databases.

Turbo Prolog Databases

Turbo Prolog has its own facilities for manipulating databases. These facilities offer excellent support for relational database systems. Turbo Prolog is particularly suited for writing a query system for a relational database: the language's internal unification routines automatically select facts with the correct values for the known parameters, and bind values to unknown parameters. In addition, Turbo Prolog's backtracking mechanism can be used to find all the solutions to a given query. The following sections will show you how to use Turbo Prolog in the design and construction of two database programs.

By comparing figure 9.2 and figure 9.3, you can see the similarities between a conventional relational database and a Turbo Prolog database.

Clause: *dplayer*

Variant clause	object 1 (name)	object 2 (team)	object 3 (position)
Clause 1	Dan Marino	Miami Dolphins	QB
Clause 2	Richard Dent	Chicago Bears	DE
Clause 3	Bernie Kosar	Cleveland Browns	QB
Clause 4	Doug Cosbie	Dallas Cowboys	TE
Clause 5	Mark Malone	Pittsburgh Steelers	QB

Number of variant clauses = 5
Number of objects (arity) = 3

Fig. 9.3. *Turbo Prolog's equivalents of database relations.*

To illustrate Turbo Prolog's handling of conventional relational databases, consider the query

```
dplayer("Bernie Kosar",Team,Pos).
```

In this query, *Team* and *Pos* are variables whose possible values are being sought. When the query (or goal) is attempted, Turbo Prolog's pattern-matching routines search the database for a match with *Bernie Kosar*. Because the database contains a matching clause, *Team* is bound to *Cleveland Browns* and *Pos* is bound to *QB*.

If you treat *dplayer* as a Turbo Prolog database predicate, you immediately have the following Turbo Prolog program segment, which declares the database:

```
database
     dplayer(name,team,position)
```

Turbo Prolog provides a *database* division for the declaration of database predicates such as *dplayer*. All the variant clauses of the *dplayer* predicate constitute a Turbo Prolog *dynamic database*. The database is called *dynamic* because variant clauses of the database predicate can be removed or new clauses can be added during execution of the program. With a normal "static" database, on the other hand, database clauses are written into the program code; new clauses cannot be added during execution of the program. Another important feature of the dynamic database is that the database can be written to a disk file, or a disk database file can be read into memory.

Sometimes it is desirable to store part of the database in the program as a static database, and to assert the database information during the run of the program. (This process is called "asserting" the database because the *asserta* and *assertz* predicates are used. Those predicates are discussed later in this chapter.) Generally, the static database predicates have a different name but the same form as the dynamic database predicates. Static database predicates corresponding to the dynamic database predicate *dplayer* are

```
predicates
     player(name,team,position)

clauses
     player("Dan Marino","Miami Dolphins","QB").
     player("Richard Dent","Chicago Bears","DE").
     player("Bernie Kosar","Cleveland Browns","QB").
     player("Doug Cosbie","Dallas Cowboys","TE").
     player("Mark Malone","Pittsburgh Steelers","QB").
```

Notice that this predicate differs from the *dplayer* predicate only in the predicate term, *player*. The *d* is a convenient way to distinguish dynamic database predicates from the corresponding static predicates.

A rule to assert the information in the *player* predicates is

```
assert_database :-
    player(Name,Team,Number),
    assertz( dplayer(Name,Team,Number) ),
    fail.
assert_database :- !.
```

By now, you should be familiar with the Backtrack After Fail method, which causes this rule to access all the clauses of the *player* predicate. The BAF method is discussed in Chapter 4.

Comparing this example with the database relation shown in table 9.1, you can see the following correspondences:

Turbo Prolog database	*Relational database*
Database predicate	Relation
Object	Attribute
Arity	Arity
Variant clause	Tuple
Number of variant clauses	Cardinality

This comparison suggests that the Turbo Prolog terminology with which you are already familiar will now take on new importance as you apply it to relational databases. Concepts such as predicates, objects, clauses, and arity, which have been discussed in previous chapters, should be reviewed as needed so that you feel comfortable with these new applications of the concepts.

From this point forward, we will use Turbo Prolog terminology to describe databases. The traditional terms such as *relations* and *attributes* are useful to know, but the Prolog terms such as *predicates* and *objects* are more appropriate for this context.

Turbo Prolog Database Predicates

Many of the things you have learned already are applicable in creating Turbo Prolog databases. For example, most of what you learned in chapters 2 and 3 about Turbo Prolog predicates and clauses can be applied here. You can build rules to manipulate the database for your specific purposes. You can also use the file-processing predicates presented in Chapter 7 for manipulating database files that are stored on disk.

Turbo Prolog provides built-in predicates specifically for use in manipulating dynamic databases. These predicates are *asserta*, *assertz*, *retract*, *save*, *consult*, *readterm*, and *findall*. The following section describes those predicates and shows how they are used.

Predicates for Manipulating Database Clauses

The predicates *asserta*, *assertz*, and *retract* enable you to insert facts at specified locations in the dynamic database and to remove facts from the database.

The predicate *asserta* inserts a new fact in a memory-resident database. The new fact is inserted before all existing clauses of the same predicate. The syntax is

```
asserta(Clause).
```

Thus, to assert the clause

```
dplayer("Bernie Kosar","Cleveland Browns","QB")
```

before the existing clause

```
dplayer("Doug Cosbie","Dallas Cowboys","TE")
```

(which is the first clause in the existing database), the predicate expression is

```
asserta(dplayer("Bernie Kosar","Cleveland Browns","QB")).
```

Now the database contains the two clauses, with Kosar's clause first and then Cosbie's:

```
dplayer("Bernie Kosar","Cleveland Browns","QB).
dplayer("Doug Cosbie","Dallas Cowboys","TE").
```

It is important to realize that only facts, not rules, can be asserted to the dynamic database. This is one way in which Turbo Prolog differs from some other implementations of the Prolog language.

Like *asserta*, the predicate *assertz* inserts a new clause in the database. But *assertz* inserts the new clause after the existing clauses for the same predicate. The syntax is equally simple:

```
assertz(Clause).
```

To insert another clause such as

```
dplayer("Mark Malone","Pittsburgh Steelers","QB")
```

after the previous two, you would use the predicate expression

```
assertz(dplayer("Mark Malone","Pittsburgh Steelers","QB")).
```

Now the database has three clauses:

```
dplayer("Bernie Kosar","Cleveland Browns","QB").
dplayer("Doug Cosbie","Dallas Cowboys","TE").
dplayer("Mark Malone","Pittsburgh Steelers","QB").
```

Notice that the new clause follows the first two.

The *retract* predicate removes a clause from a dynamic database. (Remember that a dynamic database can contain only facts, and not rules.) The syntax is

```
retract(Existing_clause).
```

For an example, suppose that you want to remove the middle clause of the football database. The predicate expression is

```
retract(dplayer("Doug Cosbie","Dallas Cowboys","TE") ).
```

Now the dynamic database has only two clauses:

```
dplayer("Bernie Kosar","Cleveland Browns","QB").
dplayer("Mark Malone","Pittsburgh Steelers","QB").
```

As with the *asserta* and *assertz* predicates, *retract* is only to be used with facts, not rules.

You can use *retract* along with *asserta* or *assertz* to edit the database clauses. For example, to edit a clause in the database, your program should accept new data from the user, construct a new clause, retract the old clause, and then assert the new clause.

Predicates for Manipulating the Entire Database

This section describes the predicates that manipulate the database itself, rather than specific clauses within the database. The predicates *save* and *consult* are used to store the dynamic database in a disk file and to load the contents of a disk file into the dynamic database.

The *save* predicate saves the whole memory-resident database in a text file. The syntax is

```
save(DOS_file_name).
```

where *DOS_file_name* is any file name that is valid for MS-DOS or PC DOS. (If you are uncertain as to the requirements for a valid file name, see the appendix "DOS Fundamentals.") To save the contents of your football database under the file name *football.dba*, for example, use the predicate

```
save("football.dba").
```

The result of this predicate is that all the clauses in the memory-resident database are stored in a disk file named *football.dba*. If an existing file has the same name, the file will be overwritten. You should therefore be cautious in using the *save* predicate.

A database file can be read (or "loaded") into memory by means of the *consult* predicate. The syntax is

```
consult("DOS_file_name").
```

To load the football database file, the predicate expression is

```
consult("football.dba").
```

The *consult* predicate will fail if the database file is not found; if the database file has errors, such as predicates that do not match the *database* predicate declaration; or if there is not enough room in memory for all the clauses in the database file.

The *readterm* predicate is used to read from a disk file objects that are included in data domains. The syntax is

```
readterm(Domain,Term).
```

where *Domain* is the name of a domain and *Term* is a variant clause in the domain. For example, consider the predicate expression

```
readterm(auto_record,auto(Name,Year,Price)).
```

The *Domain* object is *auto_record*, and the *Term* is *auto(Name,Year,Price)*. The term *auto* specifies the variant clauses that belong to the *auto_record* domain.

The necessary domain declarations are

```
domains

    name            = string
    year            = integer
    price           = real
    auto_record     = auto(name,year,price)
    file            = auto_file
```

The *readterm* predicate is commonly used to read data stored in clausal form in a disk file. For example, the file might contain these clauses:

```
auto("Pontiac",1984,8550)
auto("Chevrolet",1982,2300)
auto("Chevette",1982,1500)
auto("Toyota",1986,11000)
```

To access the file, first you use the *openread* and *readdevice* predicates, and then the *readterm* predicate.

In this example, the *readterm* predicate attempts to bind the variable *auto* to the matching clauses in the file. When this predicate succeeds, the variables *Name*, *Year* and *Price* are instantiated to the values in the matching clauses. Those values can then be written to the video screen or another output device.

—————————————— **Exercise** ——————————————

9.1. Write a program to display the automobile data in the preceding example. Use the Turbo Prolog editor to create the data file.

The *findall* predicate collects data from the database and puts it into a list. The data can then be utilized in various ways. (You probably recall the use of the *findall* predicate in Chapter 4.) The *findall* predicate can be used to make a list of the players' names. After the predicate expression

```
findall(Name,dplayer(Name,_,_),Name_list)
```

succeeds, the variable Name_list contains the players' names.

Building a Memory-Resident Database

The process of building a Turbo Prolog database begins with program-design considerations. The things you must assess in designing the database include

1. The size of the database
2. The organization of the data elements
3. The methods used in manipulating and maintaining the database.

Use of a memory-resident database is entirely appropriate if the database is of a limited size.

First you will organize the initial data and create the database. Then you will design the user-oriented features of the program. The features you will want to have in any Turbo Prolog database program include capabilities to

1. Add data to the database
2. Delete data from the database
3. Retrieve and output data from the database

In addition, you will want to organize these features in a logical and user-friendly way, with a menu system so that the user can easily select database management functions, and a window system so that the user can have a clear view of the system commands and features.

Design Considerations

The best way to start designing your program is to create a data-flow diagram (DFD), as shown in figure 9.4. The arrows in the DFD show the flow of control as well as the flow of data. A data-flow line indicates the path of the data manipulated by the program. A control-flow line indicates the flow of commands to initiate a task.

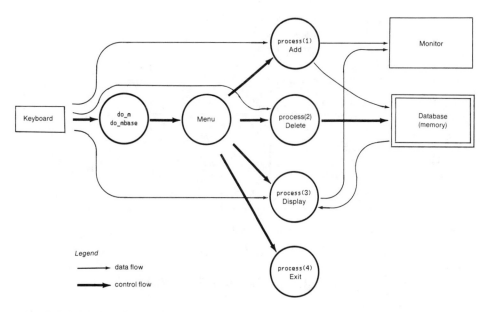

Fig. 9.4. *A data-flow diagram for a memory-resident database program.*

Consider the task of adding data to the database. You, the user, sit at the keyboard and take charge of running the program. You select the *Add* module to add data. Thus control flows from the keyboard to the main module *do_mbase*, then to the *menu* module and then to the module *process(1)*. You enter data at the keyboard, initiating the flow of data from the keyboard to the *process(1)* module and finally to the database and the monitor.

The DFD in figure 9.4 suggests a hierarchical structure of program modules. Control of the data flow to each of these modules is dependent on the user's choice. A structure chart (SC) resulting from the DFD is shown in figure 9.5. The SC shows that the *menu* module lets the user choose any one of the four modules—*process(1)* for adding data to the database, *process(2)* for deleting, *process(3)* for displaying data, and *process(4)* for exiting from the program.

Building the Database

The designs outlined in the DFD and the SC can serve as guides for writing a Turbo Prolog database program. The data consists of information on five pro football players. It includes their names, teams, numbers, positions, height, weight, years of NFL experience, and the college for which each one played before turning pro. The information is given in table 9.1.

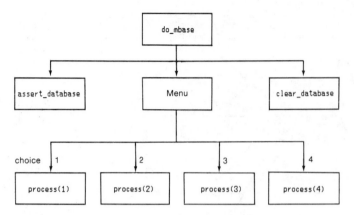

Fig. 9.5. *A structure chart for a memory-resident database program.*

—————————————————————— Table 9.1 ——————————————————————
Information for the Pro Football Database

Name	Team	No.	Pos.	Ht.	Wt.	Yrs.	College
Dan Marino	Miami Dolphins	13	QB	6'3"	215	4	Pittsburgh
Richard Dent	Chicago Bears	95	DE	6'5"	263	4	Tenn. State
Bernie Kosar	Cleveland Browns	19	QB	6'5"	210	2	Miami
Doug Cosbie	Dallas Cowbows	84	TE	6'6"	235	8	Santa Clara
Mark Malone	Pittsburgh Steelers	16	QB	6'4"	223	7	Arizona State

To work with this information, you need to design a predicate to encode the information. A suitable predicate is

```
player(p_name,   /* player's full name (string) */
       t_name,   /* team name (string)     */
       p_number, /* player's number  (integer) */
       pos,      /* player's position (string) */
       height,   /* player's height (string)   */
       weight,   /* player's weight (integer)  */
       nfl_exp,  /* NFL experience, years  (integer)  */
       college). /* player's college (string) */
```

The objects of the predicate are given names that are designed to be easily remembered. The object *p_name* encodes the information "player's name," *t_name* is "team name," and so on. This clause is the basis of the database.

Turbo Prolog requires that all the variant clauses of a predicate be grouped together. When you implement the clauses in accordance with this requirement, the result is this group of predicates:

```
clauses
        player("Dan Marino","Miami Dolphins",13,"QB",
                "6-3",215,4,"Pittsburgh").
        player("Richard Dent","Chicago Bears",95,"DE",
                "6-5",263,4,"Tennessee State").
        player("Bernie Kosar","Cleveland Browns",19,"QB",
                "6-5",210,2,"Miami").
        player("Doug Cosbie","Dallas Cowboys",84,"TE",
                "6-6",235,8,"Santa Clara").
        player("Mark Malone","Pittsburgh Steelers",16,"QB",
                "6-4",223,7,"Arizona State").
```

Notice that when the objects are strings and the first characters of the string values are uppercase letters, the string values are enclosed in quotation marks. Also notice that the players' height is given as a string: even though it symbolizes a numerical quantity, it is not intended to be used as a numerical value in this database.

The next phase in the design of your database is to decide on the proper data-type declarations. The *domains* declaration for your program is as follows:

```
domains
        p_name, t_name, pos, height, college   =  string
        p_number, weight, nfl_exp              =  integer
```

Of course, in a database of your own design you may want or need to include objects of type *symbol* and *real*. Those, too, would be declared in the *domains* section.

The database predicate is declared in the *database* division of the program. In this program, there is only one entry:

```
database
        dplayer(p_name, t_name, p_number, pos,
                height, weight, nfl_exp, college)
```

When the program is run, the database clauses are placed in a part of the internal memory that is separate from the memory used to store "ordinary" clauses. (That is why dynamic database predicates are declared in a section separate from the one in which the other predicates in the program are declared.) At this point in the design, the database is ready for manipulation.

The *predicates* division is where you declare the other predicates that are to be used in the program. The declarations are

```
predicates
     repeat
     do_mbase
     assert_database
     menu
     process(integer)
     clear_database
     player(p_name, t_name, p_number, pos,
              height, weight, nfl_exp,college)
     error
```

As was mentioned earlier, in the section "Turbo Prolog's Dynamic Databases," database information stored in static database predicates must be asserted to the dynamic database when the program begins. The predicate *assert_database* performs this task. The predicate *clear_database* performs a related task: clearing the dynamic database just before the program ends. Such a step is not really necessary for this program; the programming technique is useful for some applications, however, so the *clear_database* predicate is included in this program.

The purpose and function of the *repeat* predicate are explained in Chapter 4. The *error* predicate performs another useful function: processing invalid entries.

The *player* predicate stores initial database entries, which contain the information shown in table 9.1. This information is stored in variant clauses of the *dplayer* predicate when the program begins.

The predicate *do_mbase* is the main rule (or module). This predicate is also the goal of the program. The predicate *menu* declares a rule that creates a menu interface. The predicate *process(integer)* specifies various rules whose purposes are to manipulate the database in various ways.

The *goal* division of the program includes the rule *do_mbase*:

```
goal
     do_mbase.
```

Now you can put these all together to form the structural core of your Turbo Prolog database program. The code for the rules and the goal will be placed in the *clauses* division.

Implementing the Program Modules

After completion of the design phase, you move on to the implementation phase. The next task is to attend to details such as the writing of the predicate expressions and sub-rules that are to be included in the modules.

The Main Module

The module **do_mbase** is designed to serve as both the main module and the goal of the program:

```
do_mbase :-
    assert_database,
    makewindow(1,7,7," PRO FOOTBALL DATABASE ",0,0,25,80),
    menu,
    clear_database.
```

This module asserts the *player* information to the database, creates a window, displays a menu, and clears the database when the program ends.

This program stores initial database entries in static predicate clauses. A rule to assert information in these clauses to the dynamic database is

```
assert_database :-
    player(P_name,T_name,P_number,Pos,Ht,Wt,Exp,College),
    assertz( dplayer(P_name,T_name,P_number,
                     Pos,Ht,Wt,Exp,College) ),
    fail.
assert_database :- !.
```

This predicate uses the Backtrack After Fail method, as described in Chapter 4, to access variant *player* clauses.

The predicate for clearing the database is similar:

```
clear_database :-
    retract( dplayer(_,_,_,_,_,_,_,_) ),
    fail.
clear_database :- !.
```

Because the objects of the *dplayer* clauses are of no concern for this rule, anonymous variables are used.

The menu is designed for the user's convenience in choosing program functions. To provide adequate screen space, a full-screen window (25 rows by 80 columns) is created. You may want to refer to Chapter 7 to review details on windows and color palettes. The *menu* module displays four options. As described in the design section of this chapter, the options are

1. Adding player information to the database
2. Deleting player information from the database
3. Viewing player information
4. Exiting the program

The *menu* module mainly consists of a series of *write* predicates to display the four options. A border of asterisks is used to clearly delineate the menu space. The module contains *write* predicates to create such a border, and others that prompt the user to enter an integer from 1 to 4.

This *menu* module meets the design specifications we've been considering:

```
menu :-
    repeat,
    clearwindow,
    write("  * * * * * * * * * * * * * * * * * * "), nl,
    write("  *                                  * "), nl,
    write("  * 1.  Add a player to database     * "), nl,
    write("  * 2.  Delete a player from database * "), nl,
    write("  * 3.  View a player from database   * "), nl,
    write("  * 4.  Quit from this program        * "), nl,
    write("  *                                  * "), nl,
    write("  * * * * * * * * * * * * * * * * * * "), nl, nl,
    write("  Please enter your choice, 1, 2, 3 or 4 : "),
    readint(Choice), nl,
    process(Choice),
    Choice = 4,
    !.
```

The menu screen is shown in figure 9.6.

Notice the technique used to cause repeated execution of the *menu* module. If the user's entry is not equal to 4—the choice for exiting the program—the subgoal *Choice = 4* fails, causing backtracking to the *repeat* predicate.

The *process* rules are discussed in the following sections.

The Data-Entry Module

The submodule rule *process(1)* for adding data to the database. This module creates a window for the text, prompts the user for the individual entries, accepts data from the keyboard, and asserts the data into the database in a new *dplayer* clause. Then the new window is removed, and control returns to the main menu.

A separate, smaller window can be easily made to accommodate the "dialogue" between the user and the program. A *makewindow* predicate to create this window is

```
┌─────────────────────── PRO FOOTBALL DATABASE ───────────────────────┐
│ * * * * * * * * * * * * * * * * * * *                                │
│ *                                   *                                │
│ * 1.  Add a player to database      *                                │
│ * 2.  Delete a player from database *                                │
│ * 3.  View a player from database   *                                │
│ * 4.  Quit from this program        *                                │
│ *                                   *                                │
│ * * * * * * * * * * * * * * * * * * *                                │
│                                                                      │
│ Please enter your choice, 1, 2, 3 or 4 :                             │
│                                                                      │
│                                                                      │
│                                                                      │
│                                                                      │
│                                                                      │
└──────────────────────────────────────────────────────────────────────┘
```

Fig. 9.6. *The menu of the Pro Football Database program.*

followed by a series of *write*, *readln*, and *readint* predicates that prompt the user for each data item and accept the data from the keyboard:

```
process(1) :-
     makewindow(2,7,7,"Add Player to DATABASE ",
               2,20,18,58),
     shiftwindow(2),
     write("Enter player name:  "),
     readln(P_name),
     write("Enter team: "),
     readln(T_name),
```

Similar *write*, *readln*, and *readint* predicates prompt the user to enter data for the player number, position, height, weight, experience, and college. An example of the user's interaction with the program during data entry is shown in figure 9.7.

The *write*, *readln*, and *readint* predicates are followed by the *assertz* predicate. This predicate inserts a new *player* clause in the database after all the existing *player* clauses.

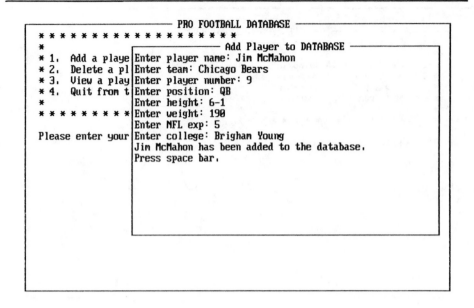

Fig. 9.7. *The data-entry window of the Pro Football Database program.*

The objects of this new clause are the values bound to the variables *P_name*, *T_name*, *P_number*, etc., by the preceding "read" predicates.

```
assertz(dplayer(P_name,T_name,P_number,Pos,Ht,Wt,Exp,College)),
write(P_name," has been added to the database."),
nl, !,
write("Press space bar. "),
readchar(_),
removewindow.
```

The last lines report the completion of the process and remove the window.

The Player-Deletion Module

The purpose of the submodule *process(2)* is to delete player information from the database. This rule, like the rule *process(2)*, creates its own window, then prompts the user for a player's name, and finally removes the database clause for that player. After erasing the window, control again is returned to the main menu.

Predicates to create the window and shift to that window are followed by predicates to prompt the user for the player's name. The user's entry is bound to the variable *P_name*:

```
process(2) :-
    makewindow(3,7,7," Delete Player from DATABASE ",
            10,30,7,40),
    shiftwindow(3),
    write("Enter name to DELETE: "),
    readln(P_name),
```

The next few subrules perform the deletion, write a short message to the user, pause until the user presses a key, and remove the window:

```
retract(dplayer(P_name,_,_,_,_,_,_,_,_)),
write(P_name," has been deleted from the database."),
nl, !,
write("Press space bar."),
readchar(_),
removewindow.
```

Notice the use of the *retract* predicate to remove the indicated clause from the database. In this predicate, all information other than the player's name is of no interest, so anonymous variables are used for the rest of the objects of the *dplayer* predicate.

The Data-Retrieval Module

The purpose of the submodule *process(3)* is to retrieve data from the database; this module, too, has its own window. After creating the window, the module prompts the user to enter the player's name. Then it finds the matching clause associated with the name, retrieves the data, and displays it in a suitable format.

The following code performs those functions:

```
process(3) :-
    makewindow(4,7,7,"View Window ",7,30,16,47),
    shiftwindow(4),
    write("Enter name to view:  "),
    readln(P_name),
    dplayer(P_name,T_name,P_number,Pos,
            Ht,Wt,Exp,College),
```

The *dplayer* predicate searches the database for the appropriate clause and retrieves the string and integer values for each item requested.

A series of *write* predicates then displays the retrieved data:

```
nl, write("        NFL League Player"), nl,
nl, write(" Player Name :       ",P_name),
nl, write(" Team Name :         ",T_name),
nl, write(" Position :          ",Pos),
nl, write(" Player Number :     ",P_number),
nl, write(" Player's Height :   ",Ht," ft-in"),
nl, write(" Player's Weight :   ",Wt," lb "),
nl, write(" Player's NFL-exp : ",Exp," year(s)"),
nl, write(" Player's College : ",College),
nl, nl, !,
nl, write("Press space bar. "),
readchar(_),
removewindow.
```

Figure 9.8 shows the screen display of this module.

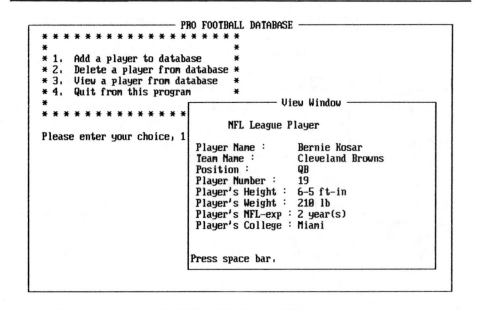

Fig. 9.8. *Data retrieved from the pro football database.*

The program should display an error message if the database does not contain a clause for the player whose name the user has entered. The window for this message should be in a prominent location, such as the center of the screen. A variant of the *process(3)* rule displays the error message:

```
process(3) :-
    makewindow(5,7,7," No Luck ",14,7,5,60),
    shiftwindow(5),
    write("Can't find that player in the database."), nl,
    write("Sorry, bye!"),
    nl, !,
    write(Press space bar."),
    readchar(_),
    removewindow,
    shiftwindow(1).
```

The Exit Module

The submodule *process(4)* provides an orderly exit from the program. This module does not have a window of its own. Creation of a new window is not necessary, because not much room is needed for displaying information. However, this module should prompt the user to indicate clearly that he or she wants to exit the program:

```
process(4) :-
    write("Are you sure you want to quit (y/n)"),
    readln(Answer),
    frontchar(Answer,'y',_), !.
```

Notice the use of the *frontchar* predicate. It only succeeds if the first character of the user's response is *y*. If this predicate fails because the user enters *y*, backtracking to the *repeat* predicate in *menu* occurs.

An Error-Trapping Module

A well-designed program should take appropriate action when the user makes an invalid entry. One of these rules succeeds if the user enters a number less than 1 or more than 4:

```
process(Choice) :-
    Choice < 1,
    error.
process(Choice) :-
    Choice > 4,
    error.
```

These rules both call the subrule *error*:

```
error :-
    write("Please enter a number from 1 to 4."),nl,
    write("Press the SPACE bar to continue"),
    readchar(_).
```

The Pro Football Database Program

The complete implementation of the design presented in the previous section is the Pro Football Database program, in listing 9.1.

```
/* Program: Pro Football Database        File: PROG0901.PRO */
/*                                                          */
/* Purpose: To show the working of an example database. It is */
/*          a pro football database shell. You can do the    */
/*          following operations : add data, delete data and */
/*          retrieve data. Retrieval includes viewing data.  */
/*                                                          */
/* Remark: This program creates a database and maintains it  */
/*         in memory.                                        */

domains

    p_name, t_name, pos, height, college   =  string
    p_number, weight, nfl_exp              = integer

database

    dplayer(p_name, t_name, p_number, pos,
            height, weight, nfl_exp,college)

predicates

    repeat
    do_mbase
    assert_database
    menu
    process(integer)
    clear_database
    player(p_name, t_name, p_number, pos,
            height, weight, nfl_exp,college)
    error
```

```
goal
   do_mbase.

clauses

   repeat.
   repeat :- repeat.

   /* Pro Football Database */

   player("Dan Marino","Miami Dolphins",13,"QB",
         "6-3",215,4,"Pittsburgh").
   player("Richart Dent","Chicago Bears",95,"DE",
         "6-5",263,4,"Tennessee State").
   player("Bernie Kosar","Cleveland Browns",19,"QB",
         "6-5",210,2,"Miami").
   player("Doug Cosbie","Dallas Cowboys",84,"TE",
         "6-6",235,8,"Santa Clara").
   player("Mark Malone","Pittsburgh Steelers",16,"QB",
         "6-4",223,7,"Arizona State").

   /*  end of initial database entry */

   assert_database :-
      player(P_name,T_name,P_number,Pos,Ht,Wt,Exp,College),
      assertz( dplayer(P_name,T_name,P_number,Pos,Ht,Wt,Exp,College) ),
      fail.
   assert_database :- !.

   clear_database :-
      retract( dplayer(_,_,_,_,_,_,_,_) ),
      fail.
   clear_database :- !.




   /* This database management system is a menu driven system.
   It uses Turbo Prolog's window facilities. Based on the
   user's query, it calls appropriate processes to serve the
   need. You may expend the menu to include more functions.*/

   /* goal as a rule */
```

```
do_mbase :-
   assert_database,
   makewindow(1,7,7," PRO FOOTBALL DATABASE ",0,0,25,80),
   menu,
   clear_database.

menu :-
   repeat,
   clearwindow,
   write("  * * * * * * * * * * * * * * * * * * "), nl,
   write("  *                                 * "), nl,
   write("  * 1.  Add a player to database    * "), nl,
   write("  * 2.  Delete a player from database * "), nl,
   write("  * 3.  View a player from database  * "), nl,
   write("  * 4.  Quit from this program       * "), nl,
   write("  *                                 * "), nl,
   write("  * * * * * * * * * * * * * * * * * * "), nl, nl,
   write("  Please enter your choice, 1, 2, 3 or 4 : "),
   readint(Choice), nl,
   process(Choice),
   Choice = 4,
   !.

/* Add a player to the database */

process(1) :-
   makewindow(2,7,7," Add Player to DATABASE ",
             2,20,18,58),
   shiftwindow(2),
   write("Enter player name: "),
   readln(P_name),
   write("Enter team: "),
   readln(T_name),
   write("Enter player number: "),
   readint(P_number),
   write("Enter position: "),
   readln(Pos),
   write("Enter height: "),
   readln(Ht),
   write("Enter weight: "),
   readint(Wt),
   write("Enter NFL exp: "),
```

```
    readint(Exp),
    write("Enter college: "),
    readln(College),

    assertz(dplayer(P_name,T_name,P_number,Pos,Ht,Wt,Exp,College)),
    write(P_name," has been added to the database."),
    nl, !,
    write("Press space bar. "),
    readchar(_),
    removewindow.

/* Delete a player from the database */

process(2) :-
    makewindow(3,7,7," Delete Player from DATABASE ",
              10,30,7,40),
    shiftwindow(3),
    write("Enter name to DELETE: "),
    readln(P_name),
    retract(dplayer(P_name,_,_,_,_,_,_,_)),
    write(P_name," has been deleted from the database."),
    nl, !,
    write("Press space bar."),
    readchar(_),
    removewindow.

/*  View a player in the database */

process(3) :-
    makewindow(4,7,7," View Window ",7,30,16,47),
    shiftwindow(4),
    write("Enter name to view:  "),
    readln(P_name),
    dplayer(P_name,T_name,P_number,Pos,
           Ht,Wt,Exp,College),
    nl, write("       NFL League Player"), nl,
    nl, write(" Player Name :      ",P_name),
    nl, Write(" Team Name :        ",T_name),
    nl, write(" Position :         ",Pos),
    nl, write(" Player Number :    ",P_number),
    nl, write(" Player's Height :  ",Ht," ft-in"),
```

```
    nl, write(" Player's Weight :   ",Wt," lb "),
    nl, write(" Player's NFL-exp : ",Exp," year(s)"),
    nl, write(" Player's College : ",College),
    nl, nl, !,
    nl, write("Press space bar. "),
    readchar(_),
    removewindow.

process(3) :-
    makewindow(5,7,7," No Luck ",14,7,5,60),
    shiftwindow(5),
    write("Can't find that player in the database."), nl,
    write("Sorry, bye!"),
    nl, !,
    write("Press space bar."),
    readchar(_),
    removewindow,
    shiftwindow(1).

/* Quit from the program */

  process(4) :-
      write("Are you sure you want to quit (y/n)"),
      readln(Answer),
      frontchar(Answer,'y',_), !.

/* Invalid entry */

process(Choice) :-
    Choice < 1,
    error.
process(Choice) :-
    Choice > 4,
    error.

error :-
    write("Please enter a number from 1 to 4."),nl,
    write("(Press the SPACE bar to continue)"),
    readchar(_).

/*    end of program    */
```

Each of the sections designed and discussed in the preceding sections is given in its logical place in the program. Notice that the program has comments that are useful to the programmer.

The initial database entries are placed at the beginning of the *clauses* division. When the program is run, the subgoal *assert_database* creates *dplayer* clauses containing the contents of the *players* database predicates and asserts those clauses to the dynamic database. You can now add, delete or display data as you choose by selecting the appropriate menu option.

The deft handling of a variety of queries, the visual handling of menus and output display, and the capacity to deal with large quantities of data make Turbo Prolog's dynamic database capabilities a true example of its strengths. In the second half of this chapter, you can expand your ability to use Turbo Prolog's database power by learning to create and use a disk-resident database.

—————————————— **Exercises** ——————————————

9.2. Run the Pro Football Database program. Choose option 1 from the menu and add a player's data (check the Sunday paper for a good prospect). Then choose option 3; at the prompt, enter the name of the player you just added. Observe that the displayed data is correct. Now, choose option 2 and delete the data that you have just added. And finally, choose 3 again to verify the deletion. (You should get the error message *Can't find that player in the database.*)

9.3. Modify the Pro Football Database program so that it offers one more choice on the main menu:

5. List players in database

Design a submodule whose purpose is to display the names of all the players. Run your modified program and verify that it does find and display all the players' names. *Hint:* You need to use the database predicate in the form

player(Name,_,_,_,_,_,_).

and apply the Backtrack After Fail (BAF) method to get the names of all the players.

9.4. Modify the Pro Football Database program so that the database is saved to a disk file. The *save* predicate syntax is

save("player.dba").

Insert this predicate into your program at the appropriate point so that the database is saved at the end of the program run. Run your modified program to test the changes you have made.

9.5. Modify the Pro Football Database program so that you can retrieve selected information about the players. Change the visual display of the information until you are satisfied with the display and with your command of the various program sections and their output.

Building a Disk-Based Database

In the previous section of this chapter, you learned to design and create a database system that maintains its data in memory. Such a database management system has a major weakness: as more data is added, memory space may become a limiting factor. This limitation will likely be a problem in any practical database application.

A more practical database management system is one that stores the database on disk. Because disk space is much larger than memory space, disk-based databases are used for almost all large database applications.

Turbo Prolog provides all the necessary facilities to maintain and manipulate such large databases. You will be able to appreciate Turbo Prolog's capacity for database system operation as your databases become larger and your programs become more complex.

Design Considerations

Building any Turbo Prolog database program begins with design considerations. You have been introduced to these considerations in the preceding discussion of memory-resident database design.

Similar considerations apply here. In designing a disk-based database system, you need also to consider rules to perform disk input and output, typically known as *disk I/O*. Your program will need rules for reading and writing disk database files. You may want to review the section "Turbo Prolog File Predicates" in Chapter 7 before proceeding further with the database design.

A particularly important feature of your program is fast and efficient access to the database. This consideration implies that the database file must be indexed, and that an index file must be created and manipulated along with the database file.

The development of a disk-based database management system follows design principles similar to those used for the memory-resident dynamic database management system. You begin with the data flow diagram (DFD). Figure 9.9 shows the DFD for the disk-based database management system.

Structurally, this DFD is an extension of the DFD for the memory-resident database management system (refer to fig. 9.4). If you compare the two DFDs, however, you will notice that the one for the disk-based system has several modules between the *process* modules and the database. These modules are called by the *process* modules. For ex-

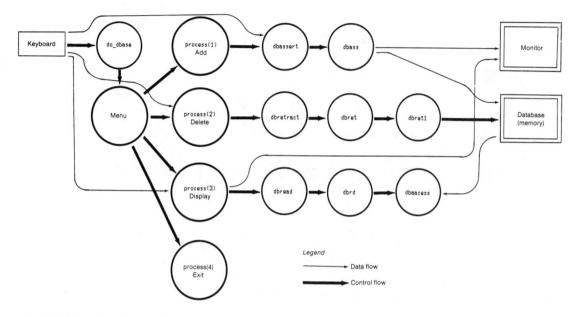

Fig. 9.9. A data-flow diagram for a disk-based database program.

ample, *process(1)* calls the module *dbassert*, and this module in turn calls the module *dbass*. The thin arrows in the DFD show data flow, and the thick arrows show control flow.

A structure chart (SC) for the disk-based database program in figure 9.10 is likewise similar to the SC for the memory resident database system (refer to fig. 9.5).

The *process(1)* module uses the submodules *dbassert* and *dbass* to add data to the database. Similar structures of modules and submodules are used to delete, retrieve, and display data.

Building the Database

The College Football database contains information on college football teams. The information and the associated Turbo Prolog objects are shown in table 9.2. After studying the table, you'll be able to write a predicate for those objects.

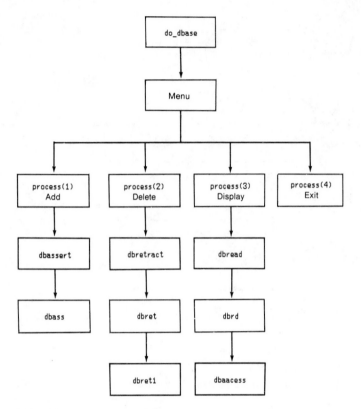

Fig. 9.10. *A structure chart for a disk-based database program.*

—————————— **Table 9.2** ——————————
Information in the College Football Database

Information	Object	Data type
Name of team	*name*	string
Name of school	*school*	string
City in which school is located	*city*	string
State in which school is located	*state*	string
School colors	*color*	string
Home stadium	*stadium*	string
Coach's name	*coach*	string
Year for which statistics were gathered	*year*	integer

Power-rating value	*team_power*	integer
Offensive power rating	*offensive_power*	integer
Defensive power rating	*defensive_power*	integer
Winning chance rating	*winning_power*	integer
Home-base booster rating	*home_power*	integer

Notice that each of the 13 different data values adds a new dimension to the overall team picture. When designing a database, you want to avoid using redundant values in the relation. Another way to state this principle is to say that if one value is true for all attributes in a database, you probably don't need to include it in the database. For example, you would not want to include the object *sport* because this is a football database; every clause in the database would have the value *football* for that object. This feature of a relation is known as *normalization*. Normalization saves storage space and makes the application of rules for accessing the database smoother.

The data items call for a database predicate with this structure:

```
team(name,school,city,state,color,stadium,coach,year,
     team_power,offensive_power,defensive_power,
     winning_power,home_power)
```

This predicate is declared in the *database* division of the program.

You also need to specify (in the *domains* division of your program) the objects of the database predicate and their data types. In addition, you need to declare the two variables to be used for the database file and the ancillary index file that were discussed earlier in this section. These design considerations lead to the following domain declarations:

```
file                                           = datafile ;
                                                 indexfile
name, school, city, state, color, stadium, coach = string
year, team_power, offensive_power,
defensive_power, winning_power, home_power        = integer
```

The next stage in the design is to specify the database manipulation predicates in the *predicates* division. As in the implementation of the memory-resident database system program, you can adopt these predicate names:

```
do_dbase          /* goal          */
menu              /* menu interface */
process(integer).  /* processes      */
```

In addition, you now declare the submodules that perform disk I/O operations such as adding, deleting and displaying data. The following predicate declaration completes the implementation of this part of the Turbo Prolog disk database program. The complete *predicates* division is given below.

```
predicates

    do_base
    menu
    process(integer)

    dbassert(dbasedom)
        dbass(dbasedom,string,string)

    dbretract(dbasedom)
        dbret(dbasedom,string,string)
            dbret1(dbasedom,real)

    dbread(dbasedom)
        dbrd(dbasedom,string,string)
            dbaaccess(dbasedom,real)
```

The module *do_dbase* is also the goal of the program. You will need to write the rule expressions in the *clauses* division.

As in the previous program, *do_dbase* calls the *menu* module. The *menu* module calls a *process* module; the module called is determined by the user's input at the menu. The structures of the *do_dbase* and *menu* modules are the same as in the Pro Football Database program. The *process* modules are similar to those of the other program, with the following exceptions:

1. **process(1)** calls the submodule *dbassert*, to insert the data in the disk database

2. **process(2)** calls the submodule *dbretract* to delete data from the disk database

3. **process(3)** calls the sub-module *dbread* to retrieve data from the disk database for viewing

The rules, or queries, to manipulate the database are

```
dbassert(Term) :-
    dbass(Term,"cfootbal.ind","cfootbal.dba").

dbretract(Term) :-
    bret(Term,"cfootbal.ind","cfootbal.dba").

dbread(Term) :-
    dbrd(Term,"cfootbal.ind","cfootbal.dba").
```

Each of these rules calls a related submodule to perform the work indicated. Notice that these rules contain references to the index and database database files *cfootbal.ind* and *cfootbal.dba*.

The disk I/O tasks are performed by the file manipulation predicates you learned about in Chapter 7. The *openwrite* predicate is used to open a new database file. Other predicates used include *writedevice*, *filepos*, and *closefile*.

The Data-Entry Module

The complete module for entering data in a disk file is

```
dbass(Term,IndexFile,DataFile) :-
    existfile(DataFile),
    existfile(IndexFile), !,
    openappend(datafile, Datafile),
    writedevice(datafile),
    filepos(datafile,Pos,0),
    write(Term), nl,
    closefile(datafile),
    openappend(indexfile, Indexfile),
    writedevice(indexfile),
    writef("%7.0\n",Pos),
    closefile(indexfile).

dbass(Term, IndexFile, Datafile) :-
    openwrite(datafile, DataFile),
    writedevice(datafile),
    filepos(datafile, Pos, 0),
    write(Term), nl,
    closefile(datafile),
    openwrite(indexfile, Indexfile),
    writedevice(indexfile),
    writef("%7.0\n",Pos),
    closefile(indexfile).
```

Notice the use in this rule of the predicate

```
writef("%7.0\n",Pos)
```

This predicate is used to write the index number, whose variable name is *Pos*. The integer is to be written in a field seven characters wide. The value bound to *Pos* expresses the position of the data in the database file.

A first variant form of *dbass* is used to add data to an existing file. The two variants are identical in most respects. The first begins, however, with the *existfile* predicate, and uses *openappend* instead of *openwrite* to add data to the database.

Figure 9.11 shows the screen display after a user has entered data for a college football team.

```
┌─────────────────── COLLEGE FOOTBALL DATABASE ──────────────────┐
│                                                                │
│  * * * * * * * * *┌──────────── Add a Team to DATABASE ──────┐ │
│  *                │Enter team's nickname: Boilermakers       │ │
│  * 1.  Add a team │Enter school: Purdue University           │ │
│  * 2.  Delete a te│Enter city: West Lafayette                │ │
│  * 3.  View a team│Enter state: Indiana                      │ │
│  * 4.  Quit from t│Enter color: Black and Gold               │ │
│  *                │Enter stadium: Ross-Ade Stadium           │ │
│  * * * * * * * * *│Enter coach's name: Leon Burtnett         │ │
│                   │Enter year: 1986                          │ │
│  Please enter your│Enter team power: 99                      │ │
│                   │Enter offensive power: 26                 │ │
│                   │Enter defensive power: 19                 │ │
│                   │Enter winning power: 3                    │ │
│                   │Enter home power: 4                       │ │
│                   │                                          │ │
│                   │Boilermakers has been added to the database.│
│                   │Press space bar.                          │ │
│                   └──────────────────────────────────────────┘ │
│                                                                │
│                                                                │
└────────────────────────────────────────────────────────────────┘
  Use first letter of option  or  select with  ->  or  <-
```

Fig. 9.11. *Data for a college team.*

The Data-Deletion Module

The submodule *dbretract* deletes data from the database. It calls the submodule *dbret*, which performs the deletion after opening the database file and the index file:

```
dbret(Term, Indexfile, Datafile) :-
    openread(datafile,DataFile),
    openmodify(indexfile, IndexFile),
    dbret1(Term, -1),
    closefile(datafile),
    closefile(indexfile).
```

This rule uses the submodule *dbret1* to locate the data in the database file and delete it. The rule expression to delete the data is

```
dbret1(Term, Datpos) :-
    Datpos >= 0,
    filepos(datafile, Datpos, 0),
    readdevice(datafile),
```

```
readterm(Dbasedom, Term), !,
filepos(indexfile, -9, 1),
flush(indexfile),
writedevice(indexfile),
writef("%7.0\n", -1),
readdevice(keyboard),
writedevice(screen).
```

Notice the predicate *flush*, included above. This predicate forces the contents of the internal file buffers to be written to the indexfile. Thus the *dbret1* module essentially prevents the flushed data from being accessed again.

A variant of *dbret1* is needed to read index numbers from the index file. This rule has the form

```
dbret1(Term, _) :-
    readdevice(indexfile),
    readreal(Datpos1),
    dbret1(Term,Datpos1).
```

The Data-Retrieval Module

The submodule *dbread* is used to locate and read data in the database. The submodule *dbrd*, which follows, shows how this process is implemented:

```
dbrd(Term, IndexFile, DataFile) :-
    openread(datafile, DataFile),
    openread(indexfile, IndexFile),
    dbaccess(Term, -1),
    closefile(datafile),
    closefile(indexfile).
```

This submodule uses the submodule *dbaccess* to locate and retrieve the data. An expression for dealing with the database file is

```
dbaccess(Term, Datpos) :-
    Datpos >= 0,
    filepos(datafile, Datpos,0),
    readdevice(datafile),
    readterm(dbasedom, Term).
```

The predicate *readterm* reads the data value associated with the index number *Datapos*. To get the corresponding index value, you need another form of *dbaaccess* to access the index file:

```
dbaaccess(term,_) :-
    readdevice(indexfile),
    readreal(Datpos1),
    dbaaccess(Term, Datpos1).
```

This rule attempts to search for and match the index value of the record with those values in the database. If a matching value is not found this rule fails; otherwise it succeeds. On success of this rule, the variable *Term* is instantiated to the data value desired for retrieval.

A screen display that would result from a user's request to view the data for a college football team is shown in figure 9.12. Notice that the display is designed to be pleasing and easy to read.

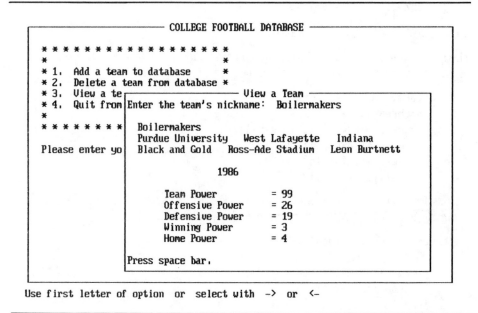

Fig. 9.12. *Data retrieved from the College Football database.*

The College Football Database Program

The College Football program, shown in listing 9.2, implements the design discussed in the preceding sections.

```
/* Program: College Football Database      File: PROG0902.PRO */
/*                                                             */
/* Purpose: To show the working of an example database. It is */
/*          a college football database shell. You can do the */
/*          following operations : add data, delete data and  */
/*          retrieve data. Retrieval includes viewing data.   */
/*                                                             */
/* Remark: This program creates a database and maintains an   */
/*          index file on the disk. The name of the file is   */
/*          CFOOTBAL.DBA and the name of the related index    */
/*          file is CFOOTBAL.IND. These files are placed in   */
/*          the default directory.                            */

domains

    file                                        = datafile ;
                                                  indexfile
    name, school, city, state, color, stadium, coach = string
    year, team_power, offensive_power,
    defensive_power, winning_power, home_power   = integer

database

    team(name, school, city, state, color, stadium, coach,
        year, team_power, offensive_power, defensive_power,
        winning_power, home_power)

predicates

    do_dbase
    menu
    process(integer)
    repeat

    dbassert(dbasedom)
        dbass(dbasedom,string,string)
```

```
    dbretract(dbasedom)
       dbret(dbasedom,string,string)
          dbret1(dbasedom,real)

    dbread(dbasedom)
       dbrd(dbasedom,string,string)
          dbaaccess(dbasedom,real)

goal

    do_dbase.

clauses

    /* This database management system is a menu driven
       system. It uses Turbo Prolog's window facilities.
       Based on the user's query, it calls appropriate
       routine to handle the desired task.                */

    /* goal as a rule */

    do_dbase :-
       makewindow(1,7,7," COLLEGE FOOTBALL DATABASE ",
                0,0,24,80),
       menu.

    menu :-
       repeat,
       clearwindow,
       nl,
       write(" * * * * * * * * * * * * * * * * * * "), nl,
       write(" *                                 * "), nl,
       write(" * 1.  Add a team to database      * "), nl,
       write(" * 2.  Delete a team from database * "), nl,
       write(" * 3.  View a team from database   * "), nl,
       write(" * 4.  Quit from this program      * "), nl,
       write(" *                                 * "), nl,
       write(" * * * * * * * * * * * * * * * * * * "), nl, nl,
       write(" Please enter your choice: 1, 2, 3 or 4 : "),
       readint(Choice), nl,
       Choice > 0, Choice < 5,
       process(Choice),
       Choice = 4,!.
```

```
/* Add a team to the database */

process(1) :-
   makewindow(2,7,7," Add a Team to DATABASE ",2,20,18,58),
   shiftwindow(2),
   write("Enter team's nickname: "),
   readln(Name),
   write("Enter school: "),
   readln(School),
   write("Enter city: "),
   readln(City),
   write("Enter state: "),
   readln(State),
   write("Enter color: "),
   readln(Color),
   write("Enter stadium: "),
   readln(Stadium),
   write("Enter coach's name: "),
   readln(Coach),
   write("Enter year: "),
   readint(Year),
   write("Enter team power: "),
   readint(TMP),
   write("Enter offensive power: "),
   readint(OFP),
   write("Enter defensive power: "),
   readint(DEP),
   write("Enter winning power: "),
   readint(WNP),
   write("Enter home power: "),
   readint(HMP), nl,
   dbassert(team(Name,School,City,State,Color,Stadium,Coach,
                 Year,TMP,OFP,DEP,WNP,HMP)),
   write(Name," has been added to the database."),
   nl, !,
   write("Press space bar. "),
   readchar(_),
   removewindow,
   shiftwindow(1).

/* Delete a team from the database */
```

```
process(2) :-
   makewindow(3,7,7," Delete a Team from DATABASE ",
              10,30,7,40),
   shiftwindow(3),
   write("Enter name to DELETE: "),
   readln(Name),
   dbretract(team(Name,_,_,_,_,_,_,_,_,_,_,_,_)),
   write(Name," has been deleted from the database."),
   nl, !,
   write("Press space bar."),
   readchar(_),
   removewindow,
   shiftwindow(1).


/*  View a team in the database */

process(3) :-
   makewindow(4,7,7," View a Team ",6,18,17,58),
   shiftwindow(4),
   write("Enter the team's nickname:  "),
   readln(Name),
   dbread(team(Name,School,City,State,Color,Stadium,Coach,
            Year,TMP,OFP,DEP,WNP,HMP)), nl,
   write("   ",Name), nl,
   write("   ",School,"    ",City,"    ",State), nl,
   write("   ",Color,"    ",Stadium,"    ",Coach), nl, nl,
   write("                    ",Year), nl, nl,
   write("      Team Power        = ",TMP), nl,
   write("      Offensive Power   = ",OFP), nl,
   write("      Defensive Power   = ",DEP), nl,
   write("      Winning Power     = ",WNP), nl,
   write("      Home Power        = ",HMP), nl, !,
   nl, write("Press space bar. "),
   readchar(_),
   removewindow,
   shiftwindow(1).

process(3) :-
   makewindow(5,7,7," Message Window ",14,7,5,50),
   shiftwindow(5),
   write("Can't find that team in the database."), nl,
   write("Sorry, bye!"),
   closefile(datafile),
```

```
      closefile(indexfile), nl, !,
      write("Press space bar."),
      readchar(_),
      removewindow,
      shiftwindow(1).

/* Quit from the program */

process(4) :-
   write("You are now exiting the 'College"),
   write(" Football Database' program."), nl,
   write("Please press the SPACE bar."),
   readchar(_),
   exit.

repeat. repeat :- repeat.

/* Queries (rules) to manipulate the database */

   dbassert(Term) :-
        dbass(Term,"cfootbal.ind","cfootbal.dba").

   dbretract(Term) :-
        dbret(Term,"cfootbal.ind","cfootbal.dba").

   dbread(Term) :-
        dbrd(Term,"cfootbal.ind","cfootbal.dba").

/* The rule "dbass" appends a term to the datafile and
   updates the indexfile. */

   dbass(Term,IndexFile,DataFile) :-
        existfile(DataFile),
        existfile(IndexFile), !,
        openappend(datafile, Datafile),
        writedevice(datafile),
        filepos(datafile,Pos,0),
        write(Term), nl,
        closefile(datafile),
        openappend(indexfile, Indexfile),
        writedevice(indexfile),
        writef("%7.0\n",Pos),
        closefile(indexfile).
```

```
    dbass(Term, IndexFile, Datafile) :-
        openwrite(datafile, DataFile),
        writedevice(datafile),
        filepos(datafile, Pos, 0),
        write(Term), nl,
        closefile(datafile),
        openwrite(indexfile, Indexfile),
        writedevice(indexfile),
        writef("%7.0\n",Pos),
        closefile(indexfile).
```

/* The rule "dbret" removes terms from the datafile. */

```
    dbret( Term, Indexfile, Datafile ) :-
        openread(datafile, DataFile),
        openmodify(indexfile, IndexFile),
        dbret1(Term, -1),
        closefile(datafile),
        closefile(indexfile).

    dbret1(Term, Datpos) :-
        Datpos >= 0,
        filepos(datafile, Datpos, 0),
        readdevice(datafile),
        readterm(Dbasedom, Term), !,
        filepos(indexfile, -9, 1),
        flush(indexfile),
        writedevice(indexfile),
        writef("%7.0\n", -1),
        readdevice(keyboard),
        writedevice(screen).

    dbret1(Term, _) :-
        readdevice(indexfile),
        readreal(Datpos1),
        dbret1(Term,Datpos1).
```

```
/* The rule "dbrd" returns terms from the datafile. */

   dbrd(Term, IndexFile, DataFile) :-
        openread(datafile, DataFile),
        openread(indexfile, IndexFile),
        dbaaccess(Term, -1),
        closefile(datafile),
        closefile(indexfile).

   dbaaccess(Term, Datpos) :-
        Datpos >= 0,
        filepos(datafile, Datpos,0),
        readdevice(datafile),
        readterm(dbasedom, Term).

   dbaaccess(Term,_) :-
        readdevice(indexfile),
        readreal(Datpos1),
        dbaaccess(Term, Datpos1).



/*                      end of program                      */
```

Notice the comments in this program, which tell what the program is to accomplish. The comments also explain the purposes of the program modules.

Also notice that this program, unlike the Pro Football Database program, contains no database. To create a database, you need to run the program and choose the menu option *Add a team to database* to add team data to the disk database file. After entering the data, you can choose the menu option *View a team from the database* to see the screen display. You can add as much data to the database file as disk space permits. If you wish, you can type in data for your favorite teams. You may wish to enter your own ratings for the teams. It should be an enjoyable experience for you, as you truly make the database come alive as you enter the data and then manipulate it.

—————————————————— **Exercises** ——————————————————

9.6. Run the College Football program. Choose the menu option *Add a team to database*, and enter data for several of your favorite college football teams. Then choose the option *View a team from database* and select several teams for display.

9.7. Choose the menu option *Delete a team from database* and delete a few teams. Then choose the menu option *View a team from database* and select the teams that you have already deleted. You should see the error message indicating that those teame are not in the database.

9.8. Modify the program by adding the menu option *Display names of teams*, and insert appropriate rules to implement this option. Then run your modified program to verify that it works properly. *Hint:* You need to create a *process(5)* module and install it in the menu module. You also need to create rules similar to those of the *dbread* module. Instead of accessing data for one selected team, you need to select all the teams. Use the Backtrack After Fail (BAF) method.

9.9. Modify the College Football program so that you can retrieve selected information about the teams. Change the display of the information until you feel comfortable with your ability to manipulate the database program.

Enhancements to the Database Management System

Now you have seen the working of the two Turbo Prolog database management systems presented in this chapter: one for a memory-resident database and one for a disk-resident database. The menus for both systems present options for adding, deleting and viewing the data. You may want to add other options to your system, however. They are listed here for your further experimentation after you have become familiar with how the database management systems work.

- *Verifying data entry:* When data is entered, it should be verified before it is added to the database. In other words, your program should display the entered data and let the user verify that the data is correct. If not, the program should give the user a chance to reenter the data.

- *Editing data:* You may want to enable the user to edit existing data. Implementing this change would entail adding a program module to display the data, accept the user's changes, and rewrite the data to the file.

- *Performing numerical computations:* An example of this capability would be a module that adds all the power points for a selected team from the *College Football* database to determine a team ranking.

- *Additional database predicates:* You can add more database predicates to the program and provide modules to manipulate those predicates. For example, you may want to add the database predicate

      coach(name, team, personal statistics)

  to the Pro Football database.

- *Providing hardcopy output:* Add a menu option so that selected data can be either displayed on the screen or sent to the printer for hardcopy output.

- *Using natural-language queries:* Replace the menu with a natural-language query system. You will learn the techniques for natural-language processing in Chapter 10.

The enhancements described here will make the example programs described in this chapter even more flexible and better adapted to your needs. You are encouraged to continue with experiments of your own; you'll see more of Turbo Prolog's flexibility as you use the language in different applications. As you can see, Turbo Prolog provides all these facilities to manage dynamic databases. You can now truly appreciate the power and ease of program development in Turbo Prolog.

Chapter Review

In this chapter you have learned the fundamental concepts of databases. You have seen what relational databases are and how they are related to Turbo Prolog databases. You then learned how to design and implement simple yet practical Turbo Prolog dynamic databases, both memory-resident and disk-resident. In doing so, you learned to use various file-processing predicates and rules that were discussed in previous chapters.

Your involvement in the design of these programs has given you opportunities to use data-flow diagrams and structure charts, two design tools that were introduced earlier. You have seen how these tools are put to practical use as you have followed the steps of structured design methodology.

Writing database management programs in Turbo Prolog has introduced you to the details of data selection and organization. In fact, you have been introduced to the fundamental ideas of *knowledge engineering*, namely the practice of *knowledge representation*. You will continue to learn this aspect of database technology in the next chapter, which deals with expert system design and development.

Finally, you saw the development of the two database programs, the Pro Football Database program and the College Football Database program. The exercises have encouraged you to run the programs, modify them, and expand them. The technical database knowledge you have gained will be a good foundation for writing your own Turbo Prolog database programs.

10

Creating Expert Systems

Overview

In this chapter you will learn about Turbo Prolog expert systems, a fast-developing field and one of Turbo Prolog's strongest areas. As expert systems have the potential to be used in virtually every field, understanding how expert systems work is important. The expert systems you build can then take full advantage of Turbo Prolog's capabilities.

The first section of this chapter describes fundamentals of expert systems and the organization of expert systems in terms of their components: the knowledge base, the inference engine, and the user-interface system. This section also discusses the basic features and workings of the Turbo Prolog rule-based system and the Turbo Prolog logic-based system.

The second section shows you how to design and implement rule-based and logic-based expert systems for dog selection. The third section describes a logic-based expert system extended so that the knowledge base can be stored on disk as a database file. This last system is a Turbo Prolog Medical Diagnosis expert system.

Expert System Fundamentals

An expert system is a computer program that exhibits a degree of intelligence similar to that of a human expert in some field, usually a field that is narrowly defined. Expert systems can be used for a great variety of applications, including speech understanding and image analysis, weather forecasting and crop-yield estimation, medical diagnosis, integrated circuit layout, financial budgeting, air-traffic control, and battle management.

A number of expert systems are already regarded as "classics." For example, DENDRAL, developed at Stanford University, is capable of using data obtained from mass spectometry to determine the molecular structure of an unknown chemical compound. MYCIN, also developed at Stanford University, can determine whether a patient has a significant infection, identify the organisms possibly involved, select drugs that are likely to be appropriate, and choose an effective drug regimen for the patient. The expert system XCON, developed at Carnegie-Mellon University, configures Digital Equipment Corporation's VAX computer systems, checking that all parts are correctly specified and that the parts can be put together to form the desired computer system.

The Structure of Expert Systems

To exhibit "expertise," a computer program must be able to solve problems through reasoning and to arrive at results that are reliable to a good extent. The program must have access to an organization of facts, known as a *knowledge base*. The program must also be able to *infer* conclusions from the available information in the knowledge base during a *consultation* session. Some expert systems can also use new information added during a consultation session.

An expert system can thus be seen as consisting of three units:

1. A knowledge base (KBS)
2. An inference engine (INE)
3. A user-interface system (UIS)

The organization of these units in the expert system is shown in figure 10.1.

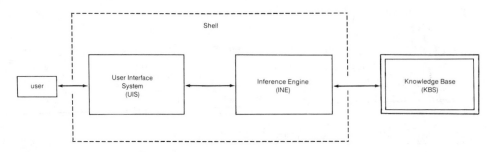

Fig. 10.1. *General structure of an expert system.*

The *knowledge base* is the central part of the expert system. It contains rules describing relations or phenomena, methods, and knowledge for solving problems in the system's area of expertise. The knowledge base can be thought of as consisting of factual knowledge and inferential knowledge. The statement "John F. Kennedy was the 35th President of the United States" is an example of factual knowledge. "If you have a headache, take two acetaminophen tablets" is an example of inferential knowledge. The knowledge base itself is usually maintained on disk or other storage devices.

The *inference engine* consists of operating rules and principles. The inference engine "knows" how to use the knowledge base so that reasonably consistent conclusions (inferences) can be drawn from the information in the knowledge base.

When the expert system is queried, the inference engine decides which techniques are used to determine how the rules in the knowledge base are to be applied to the problem posed in the query. In effect, the inference engine runs the expert system by determining which rules are to be invoked and accessing the appropriate rules in the knowledge base. The inference engine executes the rules, determines when an acceptable solution has been found, and passes the results to the user interface.

When a user query is to be processed, the knowledge base is accessed through the *user interface*. The user interface is the part of the expert system that communicates with the user.

Many users will have little knowledge of the organization of the knowledge base, so the user-interface system can help them work with the expert system even when they do not know how it is organized. It can also tell the user how the expert system infers its results.

The user-interface system both accepts information from the user and communicates information to the user. In simple terms, the user interface makes sure that all needed information is received as the user describes a problem. Based on the type and nature of the user's input, the interface passes the pertinent information to the inference engine. When the inference engine returns the available knowledge inferred from the knowledge base, the user interface passes the received knowledge back to the user in a suitable form.

The user interface and the inference engine can be viewed as components that are "fitted" to the knowledge base. The user interface and inference engine together constitute the *expert system shell*, as shown in figure 10.1. For a knowledge base that contains extensive and varied information, several different expert-system shells can be developed and implemented. An advanced expert system shell usually includes mechanisms for adding to and updating the information in the knowledge base.

You have seen that an expert system consists of three basic units. The relationship among the units can be complex, depending on the nature and organization of knowledge and the methods and goals of inference. The following sections present these aspects of expert systems. First, knowledge representation is described, along with some simple examples. This discussion is applicable to both rule-based systems and logic-based systems. Then the methods of inference are described. Next you will be given descriptions of user-interface systems along with examples of handling input and output. Then you will be ready for the discussion of two specific expert system designs: a rule-based system and a logic-based system.

Knowledge Representation

A knowledge representation is a set of syntactic and semantic conventions used to describe objects of knowledge. A rule of thumb in designing knowledge representations is that the knowledge should be rendered in forms that are reasonably easy to access by natural and simple mechanisms. "Keep It Simple, Scholar" (KISS) is a good rule to bear in mind when working with knowledge representation.

Expert systems are often built by "knowledge engineers" (or expert-system designers), who work with a human expert to encode the expert's knowledge in the knowledge base. An expert-system designer must be able to manipulate the knowledge presented and to work with the human expert. These activities constitute the developing area of *knowledge engineering*.

In the Turbo Prolog expert systems presented in this chapter, knowledge will always be represented in one of two ways. One way is to classify and place facts and figures (bits of factual knowledge) in Turbo Prolog rules. Such representations are appropriate for use in rule-based expert systems. The other way is to organize facts and figures in clauses that form a clausal knowledge base. These clausal representations are appropriate for use in logic-based expert systems.

There are other systems of knowledge representation. They include the *frame-based system* and the recently developed *model-based system*. A frame-based system uses a representation of knowledge based on logical groups of object attributes. The logical groups are described in frames for storage and retrieval. In the model-based system, the design and structure of the system are based on knowledge of the structure and behavior of the device that is the subject of investigation. An example is an expert system that studies a model of an automobile. Detailed discussions of those systems is beyond the scope of this book.

Rule-based expert systems are today's most popular systems. They have been developed and used in a wide range of applications from science and engineering to business. For this reason, the rule-based expert system has been chosen for inclusion in this chapter. Logic-based expert systems fit naturally in the structures of the Turbo Prolog language and are included for that reason.

To construct an expert system, you might begin with a table of two columns, one with names of countries and the other with the names of corresponding capitals. This table constitutes a small knowledge base:

Country	Capital
USA	Washington, D.C.
England	London
Spain	Madrid

Of course, a table like this one is used only for planning a knowledge base; in an expert system, knowledge is represented in ways that are more appropriate to the programming language used for developing the system.

Turbo Prolog clauses representing this knowledge can be written as follows:

```
capital("Washington DC","USA").
capital("London","England").
capital("Madrid","Spain").
```

Clauses like these can form the basis of a logic-based expert system.

The same knowledge can be put in the form of *if-then* rules. Rules for the preceding three clauses can be written as follows:

```
capital_is("Washington DC") :-
    country(is,"USA"), !.

capital_is("London") :-
    country(is,"England"), !.

capital_is(Madrid") :-
    country(is,"Spain"), !.
```

These rules could be the basis of a rule-based expert system. You can see that the representation of knowledge in an expert system is the same as the representation of facts and rules that you've been using throughout this book.

These are, of course, simple examples. They are useful, however, in demonstrating the principles of the Turbo Prolog expert system. The next section will show you how these knowledge representations are used.

Methods of Inference

A method of inference is a systematic way of showing that a set of assumptions implies a conclusion. This systematic method is encoded in inference rules, which specify the logic taken to arrive at a conclusion. The inference is performed by means of searching and pattern-matching. Other languages require you to write your own rules for searching and pattern-matching. In Turbo Prolog, however, these tasks are carried out by the internal unification routines. You need only to describe the needed specifications to Turbo Prolog so that it can carry out the task.

In both rule-based and logic-based systems, the user's questions are answered in accordance with the logic appropriate to the system. In rule-based system, user queries are transformed into forms matching those in the rules of the knowledge base. The inference engine initiates the matching processes starting with the "dptop" rule. This act of starting a rule is known as "firing." The matching process continues, firing appropriate rules, until a match is found or until the whole knowledge base is exhausted and no match has been found. In the logic-based system, the transformed queries are values, which are matched with those in the knowledge-base clauses.

When the inference engine finds that more than one rule can fire, a decision must be made. Priority is usually given either to rules that are more specific or to rules that take into account more of the current data. This process is known as *conflict resolution*.

For an example of the inferencing process, suppose that the task is to find out whether Madrid is the capital of Spain. The query (Q) is "Is Madrid the capital of Spain?" In a logic-based expert system, the inference engine forms the goal

```
capital("Madrid","Spain").
```

If a matching fact is found in the database, then the answer (A) is "True."

A rule-based system uses a rule-form to find an answer (A) to a question (Q): "If there is a rule in the knowledge base of the form 'If <condition> then Q,' (look for) <condition> in order to find answer A." The representation of the query has the form

```
capital_is("Madrid") :-
    country(is,"Spain"), !.
```

This is an example of *backward chaining*. The outcome of the rule application is specified, and the inference engine searches the knowledge base for all the conditions that give rise to the outcome.

The Turbo Prolog expert systems developed in this chapter incorporate both the rule-based and the logic-based methods of inferencing.

The User–Interface System

The user-interface system is designed to provide communication between the expert system and the user. This communication normally includes several functions:

1. Handling keyboard and screen input and output
2. Supporting dialogue between the user and the system
3. Recognizing cognitive mismatches between the user and the system
4. Providing user-friendly features

The user-interface system should effectively handle input and output. This specification calls for handling input/output data quickly and in clear and concise forms. It also includes handling alternative storage devices such as printers, storage disks and auxiliary data files.

In addition, the user-interface system needs to support smooth dialogue between the user and the expert system. Dialogues are common forms of consultation with an expert system. The end of a consultation session should result in clear statements of the goals prescribed by the system, as well as explanations concerning the reasoning used to arrive at those such goals.

The user-interface system also needs to be able to recognize any error or cognitive mismatch between the user and the system. The UIS must be able to handle these mismatches and errors smoothly. For example, the system should not crash if the user enters *1* when a response of *y* or *n* is requested, or if the user asks an "irrelevant" question.

The ability of an expert system to emulate a human expert varies from emulation of simple cognitive processes to the incorporation of new knowledge or new problem-solving skills. The user-interface system should be able to inform the user of the system's method of operation and of its growth, if growth is a system feature.

Finally, the user-interface system should be user-friendly. For example, a menu system showing tasks that the user can select is a desirable feature of an expert system. The user should also be able to interact with the expert system in a natural manner. Ideally, the user should be able to use a natural language. Typing *What is the prescription for an allergy headache?* is easier than entering

```
medication(Prescription,"allergy headache").
```

Although natural-language processing capabilities are highly desirable in expert systems, such capabilities are difficult to design and implement. The Turbo Prolog expert systems presented in this chapter will use menus. Natural-language processing will be discussed in Chapter 11. You may later wish to incorporate natural-language interfaces in your expert systems.

The Rule-Based Expert System

All expert systems have a strong association between the input data stream and the data in the knowledge base. In a consultation session, the input data is matched with data in the knowledge base. The result of the matching process should give affirmative or negative results consistently. In the rule-based system, the affirmative result is the act of one of the production rules. These production rules are "fired" by the input data.

The Turbo Prolog rule-based expert system thus has a collection of rules, the *rule set*, which are capable of being fired by input data when a match occurs. The expert system also has an "interpreter" in the INE that selects and activates the various modules of the system. The working of the interpreter can be described in three steps:

1. It matches the patterns of rules with data elements in the knowledge base.
2. If more than one rule can be fired, the interpreter uses conflict resolution to select a rule.
3. The interpreter applies the chosen rule to find a result for the query.

This three-step process of the interpreter is a cyclic (repeating) process known as the *recognize-act* cycle.

In the rule-based system, the number of production rules determines the extent of the knowledge base. Some larger systems have knowledge bases with more than 5,000 production rules. You can start with a small number of rules and add more to the knowledge base as the expert system expands.

Perhaps more important than the size of the knowledge base is the structure of the production rules themselves. The knowledge-base designer is responsible for building consistent rules. Currently, no proven principles govern the structure of the rules, but there are ongoing discussions concerning production-rule formation. Some guidelines have become apparent over the past several years, however, and should be adhered to as much as possible:

1. Use a minimally sufficient set of conditions to define a production rule.
2. Avoid having any two production rules in conflict.
3. Construct rules that take advantage of the data-domain structure.

The first Turbo Prolog expert system you will see in this chapter is a dog-identification system. It is designed to assist a potential pet owner in selecting a breed of dog according to certain criteria.

Assume that the user has provided a set of preferred dog characteristics in response to prompts from the expert system. The interpreter proceeds with the recognize-act cycle. If the characteristics match those of a breed of dog whose characteristics form part of the knowledge base, then the appropriate production rule fires, and the inferred result of the identity of the dog is determined. This result is then communicated to the user. Likewise, if no dog can be identified, that result is communicated to the user.

Now consider two breeds of dog whose characteristics are in the knowledge base. A Beagle has short hair, height less than 22 inches, long ears, and a good-natured personality. A Great Dane has short hair, a low-set tail, long ears, a good-natured personality, and weight above 100 pounds.

You can see from these descriptions that both dogs have short hair, long ears, and good-natured personalities. The Beagle's height is less than 22 inches, whereas no information is given concerning the height of the Great Dane. The Great Dane's low-set tail and weight of more than 100 pounds are likewise characteristics that are not given for the Beagle. The description of the two dogs in terms of these characteristics is sufficient to make a distinction between the two breeds, and indeed, between these and any other breed in the knowledge base.

The following production rules can be built from these characteristics:

```
dog_is("Beagle") :-
   it_is("short-haired dog"),
   positive(has,"height under 22 inches"),
   positive(has,"long ears"),
   positive(has,"good natured personality"), !.

dog_is("Great Dane") :-
   it_is("short-haired dog"),
   positive(has,"low-set tail"),
   positive(has,"longer ears"),
   positive(has,"good natured personality"),
   positive(has,"weight over 100 lb"), !.
```

In the preceding rule, the length of hair could be encoded using the predicate *positive*, giving

```
positive(has,"short-hair").
```

But the use of the predicate *it_is* makes it possible to limit the "search space" (the amount of data examined for solutions to queries) to one subtree of the tree structure containing the information on different breeds of dog (refer to fig. 10.2).

A rule-based expert system allows the designer/programmer to build rules that represent naturally associated pieces of knowledge in groups or "chunks." Each production rule can be independent of the others. This independence keeps the production rule base semantically modular—that is, the chunks of information are inherently not interrelated. Furthermore, the modularity of the rule base allows for incremental development of the knowledge base; this feature is highly desirable in many applications. Turbo Prolog makes this feature particularly easy to implement in an expert system.

The Logic-Based Expert System

In a logic-based expert system, the knowledge base consists of statements of facts in terms of predicate-logic clauses. Such clauses can be grouped to form a Turbo Prolog database. The rules can either describe the data or control the operation of Turbo Prolog's internal unification processes.

As in the rule-based system, the logic-based system has a collection of rules that are capable of being fired by the input data stream. The system also has an interpreter that is capable of selecting and activating the modules involved in the operation of the system.

The interpreter performs various functions within the system, based on this scheme:

1. The system has knowledge-base clauses that trigger searching and pattern matching. The interpreter matches these clauses with data elements in the database.

2. If more than one rule can fire, then the system uses Turbo Prolog's conflict-resolution capability. Consequently, the user/programmer need not be concerned with this potential conflict.

3. The system gets the results of the unification process automatically so that the results can be directed to the desired output device.

As with the rule-based system, this is a cyclical recognize-act process. The beauty and power of the logic-based system is that it mirrors the structure of Turbo Prolog itself. Thus it is very efficient and effective in its operation.

The most important aspect of the knowledge base in any logic-based system is the design of the knowledge base, its clauses, and their structure. The knowledge base must have an unambiguous logical organization, and it should include a minimum of redundant data. As in the rule-based system, the least sufficient amount of data will produce the most effective system.

Constructed in clauses, the knowledge base for the Beagle and the Great Dane looks like this:

```
rule(1,"dog","Beagle",[1,2,3,4]).
rule(2,"dog","Great Dane",[1,5,3,4,6]).

cond(1,"short-haired").
cond(2,"height under 22 inches").
cond(3,"longer ears").
cond(4,"good natured personality").
cond(5,"low-set tail").
cond(6,"weight over 100 lb").
```

Notice that in each *rule* clause, the first object stands for the rule number, the second object stands for the object type "dog", and the next object is the breed of dog—in this case, either "Beagle" or "Great Dane". The list of integers gives the condition numbers from the *cond* ("condition") clauses. These *cond-clauses* give all the characteristics pertaining to any breed represented in the knowledge base.

The lists of condition numbers are programmer's artifacts used to keep track of the selection of the rule clauses. The interpreter in the logic-based expert system uses these condition numbers to make appropriate selections.

Adding and updating knowledge-base clauses is easy. You may want to review the discussion of the *assert* and *retract* predicates in Chapter 9 to review these techniques. A logic-based expert system is easy to design, develop and maintain in Turbo Prolog because as the knowledge base expands, the program need not be modified; expansion primarily requires only the addition of new clauses. This addition can be done incrementally.

Basic Expert System Development

Building an expert system requires considerable organization and attention to detail. These requirements vary, naturally, with the size and sophistication of the desired expert system.

If the expert system you want to build may eventually contain hundreds of production rules, determining the effect of adding more rules is difficult. In Turbo Prolog, production rules are placed in the program, and therefore the program size will grow as you add more rules to it. The size of available memory eventually puts a limit on the number of rules. Under these circumstances, the rule-based system would become problematic. On the other hand, a logic-based system with the knowledge base stored in a disk file does not impose a limit on the size of the knowledge base. The appropriate choice would be the logic-based system.

If your expert system will contain not more than a few hundred rules, using the rule-based system is preferable. Because production rules are implemented almost independently of one another, the building and testing of the expert system is easier. Changing rules to see different effects is easy. In the logic-based system, changing parameters within the knowledge base has to be done with more care as the the changes are less visible, while the effects can be damaging and difficult to repair.

If speed is a requirement for the expert system you wish to build, your choice may be either a RAM-resident logic-based system or a rule-based system; both will work well. If the expert system is to contain a large knowledge base, however, you have only one choice: the disk-resident logic-based system.

When you have decided whether you will build a rule-based or a logic-based expert system, and have carefully examined the data that will form your knowledge base, you can begin designing the knowledge base with the features and functions that are desired or specified.

The next step is to develop the data-flow diagram and structure chart for your expert system. From these design tools, you can construct the modules that make up your system. Then you can begin writing the code, based on the data-flow diagram and the structure chart. After you have the program working, you should always include validation of the results by the human experts involved in the project.

The dog-selection program that is designed and developed in the next sections will be used to illustrate the construction of a rule-based expert system and a logic-based expert system. You will thus be able to compare these different treatments of the same data. The last section of this chapter will then discuss an extended logic-based expert system for medical diagnosis.

The Knowledge Base for a Dog-Selection System

For the dog-selection expert systems, the basic data will be the same. The dogs chosen are all common pets, so the data will be familiar. The classification-system knowledge base can be based on a tree structure, as shown in figure 10.2. According to the tree structure, breeds of dog are classified either as short-haired or long-haired. As shown on the tree, the English Bulldog, Beagle, Great Dane and American Foxhound are short-haired; the Cocker Spaniel, Irish Setter, Collie and Saint Bernard are long-haired.

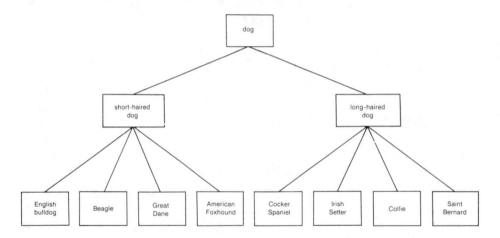

Fig. 10.2. *The tree structure of the knowledge base for the Dog Expert System.*

A list of attributes can be used to identify a breed within each classification. The numbers of characteristics will determine the extent of the classification. These distinguishing characteristics are not necessarily unique, but are convenient for the purposes of building expert system rules.

The eight attributes listed are useful precisely because they do not describe all the dogs. You will recall from Chapter 9 that an attribute that applies to all the objects probably is not useful in a data set. The characteristics that are used in these expert systems are

1. Short hair
2. Long hair
3. Height under 22 inches

4. Height under 30 inches
5. Low-set tail
6. Longer ears
7. Good-natured personality
8. Weight over 100 pounds

Each characteristic applies in either a positive or negative way; that is, each breed of dog either possesses or does not possess a certain characteristic. The characteristics for each breed are as follows:

Breed	Characteristics				
English Bulldog	1,	3,	5,	7	
Beagle	1,	3,	6,	7	
Great Dane	1,	5,	6,	7,	8
American Foxhound	1,	4,	6,	7	
Cocker Spaniel	2,	3,	5,	6,	7
Irish Setter	2,	4,	6		
Collie	2,	4,	5,	7	
St. Bernard	2,	5,	7,	8	

The way this information is used depends on the implementation of the expert system.

In this knowledge-base design, the tree structure, the set of identifying characteristics, and the association of these numbers constitute the working model of the dog knowledge base. Notice again that the set of characteristic numbers are only designer's artifacts; they are introduced for the purpose of identifying and manipulating by the expert system functional modules.

Designing and Implementing a Rule-Based System

Once you have designed the knowledge base, you can write your Turbo Prolog program to manipulate it. For simplicity and clarity, the program discussed in this section concentrates on the processes involved in consultation with the expert system. These processes include managing the user's data stream, inferring information from the knowledge base, and displaying the results of the consultation. The data-flow diagram that illustrates these tasks is shown in figure 10.3.

Figure 10.3 shows the data-flow lines emanating from the keyboard. These lines represent the user's input stream. Data-flow lines also emanate from the knowledge base. These lines indicate data that is retrieved from the knowledge base. The data-flow lines running to the video monitor represent data to be displayed.

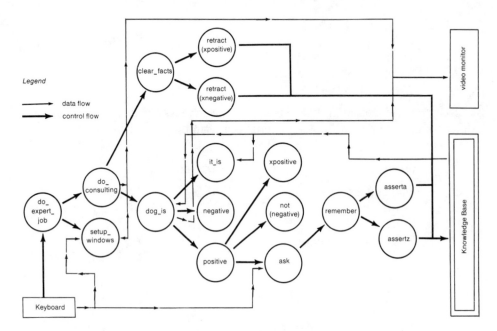

Fig. 10.3. *The data-flow diagram for the rule-based Dog Expert System.*

Based on the data-flow diagram, you can now develop a structure chart to fix the organization of program modules and rules. Figure 10.4 shows the resulting structure chart.

You can see in figure 10.4 that the main module (or goal) is *do_expert_job*. The sub_modules *dog_is* and *it_is* access data from the knowledge base. The sub_modules *ask(X,Y)* and *remember(X,Y,Reply)* manage the user's input data stream. The other modules update the working data and display the results of the consultation.

Using these design tools, you can now develop your Turbo Prolog rule-based expert system. First, you need to make the database declarations. The database will store the user's responses to questions from the UIS; this data will consist of *yes* or *no* answers. Then you need to declare predicates to perform the inferencing (the inference machine) and to communicate with the user (the user-interface system). These declarations are as follows:

```
database

    xpositive(symbol,symbol)
    xnegative(symbol,symbol)
```

```
predicates

    do_expert_job
    do_consulting
    ask(symbol,symbol)
    dog_is(symbol)
    it_is(symbol)
    positive(symbol,symbol)
    negative(symbol,symbol)
    remember(symbol,symbol,symbol)
    clear_facts
```

The database predicates *xpositive* and *xnegative* are for storing *yes* and *no* responses from the user. The first four predicates are for interacting with the user, and the last six predicates are for the inference engine.

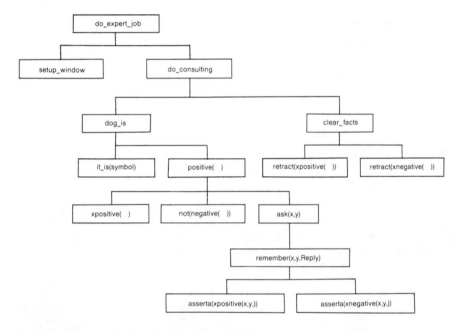

Fig. 10.4. *The structure chart for the rule-based Dog Expert System.*

Eight production rules are to be written—one rule for each breed of dog. Each rule should identify the breed as belonging to the long-haired or short-haired category. These are the major subcategories as determined from the data and as shown in the tree chart (refer to fig. 10.2). The subrule *it-is* makes this identification. Then the subrule *positive* identifies the characteristics of the dog in each case. Both *it_is* and *positive* are used by the inference engine. Here is the complete production rule for the Cocker Spaniel:

```
dog_is("Cocker Spaniel") :-
    it_is("long-haired dog"),
    positive(has,"height under 22 inches"),
    positive(has,"low set tail"),
    positive(has,"longer ears"),
    positive(has,"good natured personality"), !.
```

The inference engine must have rules to manage user input, to match it with the production rules, and keep track of (or "remember") the *yes* and *no* responses. The rules *positive* and *negative* are used to match the user-input data with those in the production rules. The rule *remember* makes assertions with *yes* and *no* responses to be used for pattern matching. And finally, the *clear_facts* rule removes the knowledge-base entries at the end of the recognize-act cycle.

The complete inference engine is constructed as follows:

```
positive(X,Y) :-
    xpositive(X,Y), !.
    positive(X,Y) :-
    not(negative(X,Y)), !.
    ask(X,Y).

negative(X,Y) :-
    xnegative(X,Y), !.

remember(X,Y,yes) :-
    asserta(xpositive(X,Y)).
remember(X,Y,no) :-
    asserta(xnegative(X,Y)),
    fail.

clear_facts :-
    retract(xpositive(_,_)),
    fail.
    clear_facts :-retract(xnegative(_,_)),
    fail.
```

The purpose of the UIS is to link the user input and the inference system. The main module *do_expert_job* and the submodule *do_consulting* perform this linking. The module *ask(X, Y)* requests data from the user and stores the responses in the knowledge base. In addition, a window provides user convenience during consultation sessions.

The complete user-interface system is as follows:

```
do_expert_job :-
    setup_window,
    do_consulting,
    write("Press space bar."), nl,
    readchar(_),
    removewindow,
    exit.

setup_window :-
    makewindow(1,7,7,"AN EXPERT SYSTEM",1,16,22,58),
    nl, write(" * * * * * * * * * * * * * * * * *"),
    nl, write("            A Dog Expert          "),
    nl, write("                                  "),
    nl, write(" This is a dog identification system."),
    nl, write(" Please answer the questions about   "),
    nl, write(" the dog you would like by typing in "),
    nl, write(" 'yes' or 'no' .                     "),
    nl, write(" * * * * * * * * * * * * * * * * *"),
    nl, nl.

do_consulting :-
    dog_is(X), !, nl,
    write("The dog you have indicated is a(n)",
        X,"."),nl,
    clear_facts.

do_consulting :-
    nl, write("Sorry I can't help you !").
    clear_facts.

ask(X,Y) :-
    write("  Question :- ",X," it, ",Y," ?  "),
    readln(Reply),
    remember(X,Y,Reply).
```

Notice that the main module *do_expert_job* calls the modules *setup_window* and *do_consulting*. The consulting module has two variant forms. The first communicates with the inference engine; if the result of the recognize-act cycle is positive, that result is communicated to the user. The second form reports a negative result.

Now you can put the individual components together to form the complete rule-based Dog Selection Expert System. Program 10.1 is the implementation of this design.

```
/* Program: Dog Expert                    File: PROG1001.PRO */
/* Purpose: To show the working of an expert system. It is  */
/*          a production rule-based system.                 */
/*                                                          */
/* Remark:  This is a dog classification expert system.     */
/*          It uses a set of production rules for the        */
/*          purpose of inferring.                            */


domains

database

    xpositive(symbol,symbol)
    xnegative(symbol,symbol)

predicates

    do_expert_job
    do_consulting
    ask(symbol,symbol)
    dog_is(symbol)
    it_is(symbol)
    positive(symbol,symbol)
    negative(symbol,symbol)
    remember(symbol,symbol,symbol)
    clear_facts

goal

    do_expert_job.

clauses

    /*  USER INTERFACE SYSTEM (UIS)  */
```

```
do_expert_job :-
   makewindow(1,7,7," AN EXPERT SYSTEM",1,16,22,58),
   nl, write("  * * * * * * * * * * * * * * * * * * *"),
   nl, write("    WELCOME TO A DOG EXPERT SYSTEM       "),
   nl, write("                                        "),
   nl, write("    This is a dog identification system. "),
   nl, write("    Please respond by typing in          "),
   nl, write("    'yes' or 'no'.            Thank you. "),
   nl, write("                                        "),
   nl, write("  * * * * * * * * * * * * * * * * * * *"),
   nl, nl,
   do_consulting,
   write(" Press space bar. "), nl,
   readchar(_),
   clearwindow,
   exit.

do_consulting :-
   dog_is(X), !,
   nl, write(" Your dog may be a(n) ",X,"."), nl,
   clear_facts.

do_consulting :-
   nl, write(" Sorry, unable to determine the dog."), nl,
   clear_facts.

ask(X,Y) :-
   write("  Question :- ",X," it, ",Y," ? "),
   readln(Reply),
   remember(X,Y,Reply).

/*   INFERENCE ENGINE (INE)   */

positive(X,Y) :-
       xpositive(X,Y), !.
positive(X,Y) :-
       not(negative(X,Y)), !,
       ask(X,Y).

negative(X,Y) :-
       xnegative(X,Y), !.
```

```
remember(X,Y,yes) :-
    asserta(xpositive(X,Y)).
remember(X,Y,no) :-
    asserta(xnegative(X,Y)),
    fail.

clear_facts :-
    retract(xpositive(_,_)),
    fail.
clear_facts :-
    retract(xnegative(_,_)),
    fail.

/* Production rules */

dog_is("English Bulldog") :-
    it_is("short-haired dog"),
    positive(has,"height under 22 inches"),
    positive(has,"low-set tail"),
    positive(has,"good natured personality"), !.

dog_is("Beagle") :-
    it_is("short-haired dog"),
    positive(has,"height under 22 inches"),
    positive(has,"long ears"),
    positive(has,"good natured personality"), !.

dog_is("Great Dane") :-
    it_is("short-haired dog"),
    positive(has,"low-set tail"),
    positive(has,"longer ears"),
    positive(has,"good natured personality"),
    positive(has,"weight over 100 lb"), !.

dog_is("American Foxhound") :-
    it_is("short-haired dog"),
    positive(has,"height under 30 inches"),
    positive(has,"longer ears"),
    positive(has,"good natured personality"), !.
```

```
dog_is("Cocker Spaniel") :-
    it_is("long-haired dog"),
    positive(has,"height under 22 inches"),
    positive(has,"low-set tail"),
    positive(has,"longer ears"),
    positive(has,"good natured personality"), !.

dog_is("Irish Setter") :-
    it_is("long-haired dog"),
    positive(has,"height under 30 inches"),
    positive(has,"longer ears"), !.

dog_is("Collie") :-
    it_is("long-haired dog"),
    positive(has,"height under 30 inches"),
    positive(has,"low-set tail"),
    positive(has,"good natured personality"), !.

dog_is("St. Bernard") :-
    it_is("long-haired dog"),
    positive(has,"low-set tail"),
    positive(has,"good natured personality"),
    positive(has,"weight over 100 lb"), !.

it_is("short-haired dog") :-
    positive(has,"short-haired"), !.

it_is("long-haired dog") :-
    positive(has,"long-haired"), !.


/*                    end of program                    */
```

This program prompts the user to choose either *consultation* or *exiting from the program*. The expert system then selects a breed of dog based on the user's responses to questions, or displays the statement *Sorry I can't help you* at the end of a negative search. Figure 10.5 shows a screen display during a consultation session.

The program inference rules designed through the process described ensure that the program moves smoothly through the user dialogue and the search, providing convenience and user-friendly language throughout the process. Turbo Prolog's internal unification routines and its searching and pattern-matching capabilities ensure that the process is efficient and thorough.

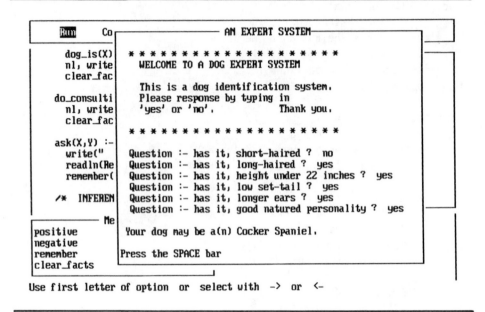

Fig. 10.5. *A consultation with the rule-based Dog Expert System.*

Exercises

10.1 Run the rule-based Dog Selection Expert System. Enter several different sequences of "yes" and "no" answers while observing how the program works.

10.2. Observe what happens when your responses are purposely not matched to dogs whose characteristics are stored in the knowledge base. You will see that Turbo Prolog's internal unification routines attempt exhaustive pattern-matching. Only when no match is possible will the system display the **Sorry** statement.

10.3. Modify the rule-based Dog Selection Expert System by adding a hypothetical dog to it. Write a production rule for this breed of dog, and incorporate the rule into the program. Test the program to see whether it will identify the dog you have "designed." Note that your dog's characteristics should be a combination of those already in the program, but the combination of characteristics should differ from that of another breed. A short table may help you design your dog's data characteristics.

Designing and Implementing a Logic-Based System

The structure of the logic-based expert system is similar to that of the rule-based expert system. Again, for simplicity and clarity, the program developed in this section concentrates on consultation with the expert system. The program needs to manage the user's data stream, infer conclusions from the knowledge base, and display the results of the consultation. The data-flow diagram illustrating these tasks is as shown in figure 10.6.

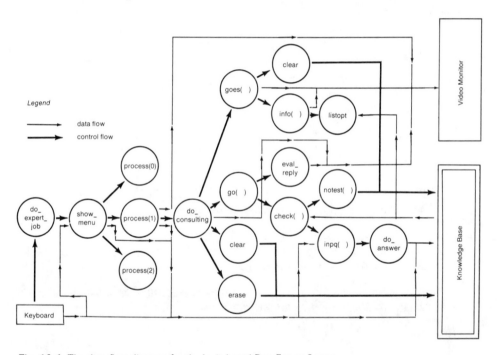

Fig. 10.6. The data-flow diagram for the logic-based Dog Expert System.

The data-flow lines originating at the keyboard in figure 10.6 represent the user's input stream. Data-flow lines also originate at the knowledge base; these indicate the flow of the retrieved data. The data-flow lines also go to the video screen. From this data-flow diagram, you can construct the structure chart in figure 10.7.

The structure chart shows that the main module, *do_expert_job*, calls the submodule *show_menu*. This submodule offers the user a choice of program functions. The user's response is read into the integer variable *Choice*, and a call to *process(Choice)* causes the appropriate program function to be performed. The modules *process(0)* and *process (2)* are for exiting the program. The module *process(1)* calls the submodule *do_consulting*.

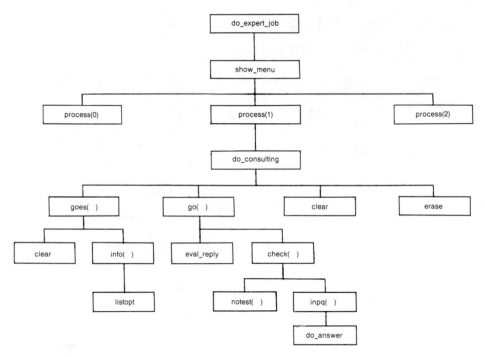

Fig. 10.7. *The structure chart for the logic-based Dog Expert System.*

The various submodules called by *do_consulting* display the dog types, carry out the inferencing tasks, and update the working data. The *eval_reply* submodule provides a user-friendly ending to the consultation dialogues.

You are now ready to begin developing your Turbo Prolog logic-based expert system. The first sections you need to write are the *domains* section

```
domains

    CONDITIONS      = BNO *
    HISTORY         = RNO *
    RNO, BNO, FNO   = INTEGER
    CATEGORY        = SYMBOL
```

and the *database* declarations for the knowledge base:

```
database
    rule(RNO, CATEGORY, CATEGORY, CONDITIONS)
    cond(BNO, STRING)
    yes(BNO)
    no(BNO)
    topic(string)
```

The database predicate *rule* stores the dog data, and the predicate *cond* stores the conditions (or attributes) that characterize the different breeds. The *yes* and *no* predicates store the user's responses. The predicate *topic* stores the data for the dog types (long- or short-haired).

The *predicates* division has eight predicates for the user interface:

```
do_expert_job
show_menu
do_consulting
process(integer)
info(CATEGORY)
goes(CATEGORY)
listopt
erase
clear
eval_reply(char)
```

The predicate *do_expert_job* is the goal of the program. The *erase* rule removes knowledge base entries after the recognize-act cycle is completed. The *clear* rule clears all *yes* and *no* responses from the database.

Seven predicates for the inference engine also are declared:

```
go(HISTORY, CATEGORY)
check(RNO, HISTORY, CONDITIONS)
notest(BNO)
inpq(HISTORY, RNO, BNO, STRING)
do_answer(HISTORY, RNO, STRING, BNO, INTEGER)
```

These predicates and rules search through the knowledge base and keep track of the values of knowledge base objects and user inputs for the purpose of inferencing. The *check* rules look for data patterns matching the user's input data. Variants of the *notest* rule keep track of *yes* and *no* responses. The *do_answer* predicates assert the user's entries into the dynamic database.

The logic-based expert system consists of a knowledge base of predicate-logic clauses. These clauses are of the two predicate forms *rule* and *cond*. The knowledge base is as follows:

```
topic("dog").
topic("short-haired dog").
topic("long-haired dog").

rule(1,  "dog",                "short-haired dog",  [1]      ).
rule(2,  "dog",                "long-haired dog",   [2]      ).
rule(3,  "short-haired dog",  "English Bulldog",   [3,5,7]  ).
```

```
rule(4,  "short-haired dog",  "Beagle",             [3,6,7]   ).
rule(5,  "short-haired dog",  "Great Dane",         [5,6,7,8] ).
rule(6,  "short-haired dog",  "American Foxhound",  [4,6,7]   ).
rule(7,  "long-haired dog",   "Cocker Spaniel",     [3,5,6,7] ).
rule(8,  "long-haired dog",   "Irish Setter",       [4,6]     ).
rule(9,  "long-haired dog",   "Collie",             [4,5,7]   ).
rule(10, "long-haired dog",   "St. Bernard",        [5,7,8]   ).

cond(1,  "short-haired"            ).
cond(2,  "long-haired"             ).
cond(3,  "height under 22 inches"  ).
cond(4,  "height under 30 inches"  ).
cond(5,  "low-set tail"            ).
cond(6,  "longer ears"             ).
cond(7,  "good natured personality" ).
cond(8,  "weight over 100 lb."     ).
```

You will recall from the section "Building the Knowledge Base" that the last object of the *rule* clause is a list of integers. This list contains condition numbers, which characterize each breed of dog in the knowledge base. The *cond* clauses contain lists of all possible characteristics for the dogs in this database.

Now you need to construct the predicates and rules for the inference engine. In practice, the inference engine must have a top rule, such as *go*, to accept the user's goal and initiate the recognize-act cycle. The engine looks through the knowledge base clauses *rule* and *cond* to identify the existence or absence of the pertinent data values.

The top rule calls subrules, such as *check*, to process detail tasks as needed. This subrule keeps track of rule numbers, condition numbers, and the classified objects in the knowledge base. It attempts to match the classified objects in terms of the condition numbers.

If matching occurs, this module of the program must assert these matching values and continue the process with the user's new inputs. If matching does not occur, the engine stops the current process and takes another track for matching. The searching and matching continue until all possibilities for matching are exhausted.

On completion of the inferencing, the top rule passes the results to the user by means of the user interface.

This is the complete inference engine for the logic-based expert system:

```
go ( HISTORY, Mygoal ) :-
            rule(RNO,Mygoal,NY,COND),
            check(RNO,HISTORY, COND),
            go([RNO|HISTORY],NO).
```

```
check( RNO, HISTORY, [BNO|REST] ) :-
                    yes(BNO), !,
                    check(RNO, HISTORY, REST).
check( _, _, [BNO| ] ) :- no(BNO), !, fail.
check( RNO, HISTORY, [BNO|REST] ) :-
                    cond(BNO,NCOND),
                    fronttoken(NCOND,"not",_COND),
                    frontchar(_COND,_COND),
                    cond(BNO1,COND),
                    notest(BNO1, !,
                    check(RNO, HISTORY, REST).
check(_,_, [BNO|_] ) :-
                    cond(BNO,NCOND),
                    fronttoken(NCOND,"not",_COND),
                    frontchar(_COND,_,COND),
                    cond(BNO1,COND),
                    yes(BNO1),
                    !, fail.
check( RNO, HISTORY, [BNO|REST] ) :-
                    cond(BNO,TEXT),
                    inpg(HISTORY,RNO,BNO,TEXT),
                    check(RNO, HISTORY, REST).


check(_,_,[]).

notest(BNO) :- no(BNO), !.
notest(BNO) :- not(yes(BNO)), !.

do_answer(_,_,_,_,0) :- exit.
do_answer(_,_,_,BNO,1) :-
                assert(yes(BNO)),
                shiftwindow(1),
                write(yes), nl.
do_answer(_,_,<_,BNO,2) :-
                assert(no(BNO)),
                write(no), nl,
                fail.

erase :- retract(_), fail.
erase.

clear :- retract(yes(_)), retract(no(_)), fail, !.
clear.
```

To describe the working of the inference engine, a "walk-through" is presented here. Suppose the inference engine's task is to identify a dog whose characteristics will turn out to be those of a Cocker Spaniel, specified in the knowledge base by the conditions 3, 5, 6, and 7.

When the program is run, the goal of the program provides a display of useful information by means of the user interface. After this, the module *do_consulting* is called, which in turn calls the rule *go*. This rule is the top rule of the inference engine:

```
go ( HISTORY, Mygoal ) :-
                rule(RNO,Mygoal,NY,COND),
                check(RNO,HISTORY, COND),
                go([RNO|HISTORY],NO).
```

At the beginning, the user's input, *dog*, causes the instantiation of the variable Mygoal to "dog". The knowledge-base clause *rule(1, "dog", "short-haired dog",[1])* is accessed, and the list variable COND is instantiated to [1].

Now the *rule* rule passes this parameter of COND to the *check* rule. The *check* rule in turn accesses the knowledge base *cond* rule with the parameter BNO instantiated to 1. The *check* rule passes this value to the *fronttoken* predicate to build the value of _COND. This rule fails.

The *check* rule returns to the *cond* rule and the COND retains its parameter value. Then the *check* rule accesses the value "short-haired" and passes it under the variable name TEXT to the *inpq* rule. The *inpq* rule displays this text string:

```
Question:- short-haired?
```

The user is prompted to press 1 for yes or 2 for no. The *inpq* rule accepts the user's response, which is 2 in this example, and interprets it as a negative response.

The process continues with the next knowledge-base *rule* clause, with RNO instantiated to 2. Now, the *check* rule uses the COND value 2 for the current *rule*, repeats the cyclic form of building the *COND* list values, and prompts the user for more input.

Based on the user's input responses as shown in figure 10.12, the *rule* clauses and *cond* clauses are accessed in the following order:

```
rule(1), cond(1),
rule(2), cond(2),
rule(7), cond(3),
rule(7), cond(5),
rule(7), cond(6),
rule(7), cond(7).
```

At the end of this process, the list variable COND is bound to *[3,5,6,7]*. This list matches the list of conditions in rule 7. This match is now associated with the classified object

"Cocker Spaniel" in the *rule* clause, and the inference engine has found the desired result.

The user-interface system contains three parts. The largest portion consists essentially of rules for providing a menu and removing the window when it is not needed. The second part of the UIS is governed by the user's choice of program functions. The subrule *process (1)* calls the rule *do_consulting*, which in turn calls *goes(Mygoal)*. This subrule offers the display of dog types available and calls the rule *go(Mygoal)*, which initiates the searching and pattern-matching process.

The third part of the UIS requests and receives the user's *yes* and *no* responses. It is implemented as follows:

```
inpq(HISTORY,RNO,BNO,TEXT) :-
    write("Question :-",TEXT," ? "),
    makewindow(2,7,7,"Response",10,54,7,20),
    write("Type 1 for 'yes',"), nl,
    write("Type 2 for 'no': "), nl,
    readint(RESPONSE),
    clearwindow,
    shiftwindow(1),
    do_answer(HISTORY,RNO,TEXT,BNO,RESPONSE).
```

Notice that this rule communicates with both the user and the inference engine. The *write* and *readint* predicates are used for communicating with the user, and the rule *do_answer* communicates with the INE.

Now you are ready to put the individual components together to form the complete logic-based Dog Selection Expert System. Program 10.2 is the implementation of this design.

```
/* Program: A Dog Expert              File: PROG1002.PRO */
/* Purpose. To show the working of an expert system. It is a  */
/*          logic-based system.                           */
/*                                                        */
/* Remark: This is a dog identification expert system. The   */
/*         system is made up of a knowledge base (KBS), an   */
/*         inference engine (INE) and a user interface      */
/*         system (UIS). The knowledge base is maintained    */
/*         in the internal memory.                        */
```

```
domains

    CONDITIONS      = BNO *
    HISTORY         = RNO *
    RNO, BNO, FNO   = INTEGER
    CATEGORY        = SYMBOL

database

    /* Database Predicates */

    rule(RNO, CATEGORY, CATEGORY, CONDITIONS)
    cond(BNO, STRING)
    yes(BNO)
    no(BNO)
    topic(string)

predicates

    /* User Interface Predicates */

    do_expert_job
    show_menu
    do_consulting
    process(integer)
    info(CATEGORY)
    goes(CATEGORY)
    listopt
    erase
    clear
    eval_reply(char)

    /* Inference Engine Predicates */

    go(HISTORY, CATEGORY)
    check(RNO, HISTORY, CONDITIONS)
    notest(BNO)
    inpg(HISTORY, RNO, BNO, STRING)
    do_answer(HISTORY, RNO, STRING, BNO, INTEGER)

goal

    do_expert_job.
```

```
clauses

    /* The Knowledge Base (KBS) */

        topic("dog").
        topic("short-haired dog").
        topic("long-haired dog").

        rule(1,  "dog",                "short-haired dog",   [1]        ).
        rule(2,  "dog",                "long-haired dog",    [2]        ).
        rule(3,  "short-haired dog",  "English Bulldog",    [3,5,7]    ).
        rule(4,  "short-haired dog",  "Beagle",             [3,6,7]    ).
        rule(5,  "short-haired dog",  "Great Dane",         [5,6,7,8]  ).
        rule(6,  "short-haired dog",  "American Foxhound",  [4,6,7]    ).
        rule(7,  "long-haired dog",   "Cocker Spaniel",     [3,5,6,7]  ).
        rule(8,  "long-haired dog",   "Irish Setter",       [4,6]      ).
        rule(9,  "long-haired dog",   "Collie",             [4,5,7]    ).
        rule(10, "long-haired dog",   "St. Bernard",        [5,7,8]    ).

        cond(1,  "short-haired"              ).
        cond(2,  "long-haired"               ).
        cond(3,  "height under 22 inches"    ).
        cond(4,  "height under 30 inches"    ).
        cond(5,  "low-set tail"              ).
        cond(6,  "longer ears"               ).
        cond(7,  "good natured personality"  ).
        cond(8,  "weight over 100 lb."       ).

    /* User Interface System (UIS) */

do_expert_job :-
    makewindow(1,7,7," DOG EXPERT SYSTEM ",0,0,25,80),
    show_menu,
    nl, write(" Press space bar. "),
    readchar(_),
    exit.
```

```
show_menu :-
    write("                                    "), nl,
    write("  * * * * * * * * * * * * *"), nl,
    write("  *                       *"), nl,
    write("  *        Dog Expert      *"), nl,
    write("  *                       *"), nl,
    write("  *    1. Consultation     *"), nl,
    write("  *                       *"), nl,
    write("  *    2. Exit the system  *"), nl,
    write("  *                       *"), nl,
    write("  * * * * * * * * * * * * *"), nl,
    write("                                    "), nl,
    write("Please enter your choice: 1 or 2 : "),
    readint(Choice),
    process(Choice).

process(1):-
        do_consulting.

process(2) :-
        removewindow,
        exit.

do_consulting :-
    goes(Mygoal),
    go([],Mygoal),
    !.
do_consulting :-
    nl, write(" Sorry I can't help you."),
    clear.
do_consulting.

goes(Mygoal) :-
    clear,
    clearwindow,
    nl, nl,
    write("                                                    "), nl,
    write("              WELCOME TO THE DOG EXPERT SYSTEM      "), nl,
    write("                                                    "), nl,
    write("              This is a dog identification system.  "), nl,
    write("              To begin the process of choosing a    "), nl,
    write("              dog, please type in 'dog'. If you     "), nl,
    write("              wish to see the dog types, please     "), nl,
```

```
        write("                type in a question mark (?).           "), nl,
        write("                                                       "),
        readln(Mygoal),
        info(Mygoal), !.

info("?") :-
        clearwindow,
        write(" Reply from the KBS."), nl,
        listopt,
        nl, write(" Press any key. "),
        readchar(_),
        clearwindow,
        exit.

info(X) :-
        X >< "?".

listopt :-
        write(" The dog types are : "), nl, nl,
        topic(Dog),
        write("      ",Dog), nl,
        fail.
listopt.

inpg(HISTORY,RNO,BNO,TEXT) :-
        write(" Question :- ",TEXT," ? "),
        makewindow(2,7,7," Response",10,54,7,20),
        write("Type 1 for 'yes',"), nl,
        write("Type 2 for 'no': "), nl,
        readint(RESPONSE),
        clearwindow,
        shiftwindow(1),
        do_answer(HISTORY,RNO,TEXT,BNO,RESPONSE).

eval_reply('y') :-
        write(" I hope you have found this helpful !").
eval_reply('n') :-
        write(" I am sorry I can't help you !").
```

```
go( _,MYGOAL) :-
    not(rule(_,Mygoal,_,_)), !,
    nl, write(" The dog you have indicated is a(n) ",Mygoal,"."),
    nl, write(" Is this a dog you would like to have (y/n) ?"), nl,
    readchar(R),
    eval_reply(R).

/* The Inference Engine (INE) */

go( HISTORY, Mygoal ) :-
    rule(RNO,Mygoal,NY,COND),
    check(RNO,HISTORY, COND),
    go([RNO|HISTORY],NY).

check( RNO, HISTORY, [BNO|REST] ) :-
    yes(BNO), !,
    check(RNO, HISTORY, REST).
check( _, _, [BNO|_] ) :-
    no(BNO),
    !, fail.
check( RNO, HISTORY, [BNO|REST] ) :-
    cond(BNO,NCOND),
    fronttoken(NCOND,"not",_COND),
    frontchar(_COND,_,COND),
    cond(BNO1,COND),
    notest(BNO1), !,
    check(RNO, HISTORY, REST).
check(_,_, [BNO|_] ) :-
    cond(BNO,NCOND),
    fronttoken(NCOND,"not",_COND),
    frontchar(_COND,_,COND),
    cond(BNO1,COND),
    yes(BNO1),
    !, fail.
check( RNO, HISTORY, [BNO|REST] ) :-
    cond(BNO,TEXT),
    inpq(HISTORY,RNO,BNO,TEXT),
    check(RNO, HISTORY, REST).
check(_,_,[]).
```

```
notest(BNO) :-
        no(BNO), !.
notest(BNO) :-
        not(yes(BNO)), !.

do_answer(_,_,_,_,0) :- exit.
do_answer(_,_,_,BNO,1) :-
        assert(yes(BNO)),
        shiftwindow(1),
        write(yes), nl.
do_answer(_,_,_,BNO,2) :-
        assert(no(BNO)),
        write(no), nl,
        fail.

erase :-
   retract(_),
   fail.
erase.

clear :-
   retract(yes(_)),
   retract(no(_)),
   fail, !.
clear.

/*              end of program              */
```

This program displays the opening menu, asking the user to choose either **consulta-tion** or **exit from the system**. If the user chooses consultation, a dialogue takes place between the user. Then the result is communicated to the user; the result is either a suggested choice of a dog or the message **Sorry I can' t help you**.

Figure 10.8 shows a dialogue during a consultation session. Notice that this dialogue leads to an affirmative result. That is, the knowledge base contains information about a breed of dog that fits the user's specifications.

——————————— Exercises ———————————

10.4. Run the logic-based Dog Selection Expert System program. Engage in several consultation sessions, and observe how the system works.

10.5. Modify the program to include information about other breeds of dog. Write the appropriate predicate logic clauses incorporating characteristics as integer lists. Make sure each list is unique.

10.6. Substitute an entirely new category of knowledge, such as fish or politicians, for the dog information. Begin by organizing the attributes of your subject in a systematic way. Then determine which attributes will distinguish each from the others. Test all the categories when you are done to make sure each one is properly constructed.

```
┌────────────────── DOG EXPERT SYSTEM ──────────────────┐
│                                                        │
│                                                        │
│             WELCOME TO THE DOG EXPERT SYSTEM           │
│                                                        │
│             This is a dog identification system.       │
│             To begin the process of choosing a         │
│             dog, please type in 'dog'. If you          │
│             wish to see the dog types, please          │
│             type in a question mark (?).               │
│                                                   dog  │
│  Question :- short-haired ? no                         │
│  Question :- long-haired ? yes                         │
│  Question :- height under 22 inches ? yes              │
│  Question :- low-set tail ? yes                        │
│  Question :- longer ears ? yes                         │
│  Question :- good natured personality ? yes            │
│                                                        │
│  The dog you have indicated is a(n) Cocker Spaniel.    │
│  Is this a dog you would like to have (y/n) ?          │
│                                                        │
│                                                        │
└────────────────────────────────────────────────────────┘
```

Fig. 10.8. *A consultation with the logic-based Dog Expert System.*

An Extended Logic-Based Expert System

The two expert systems developed in the preceding sections are simple in structure and easy to implement. One important feature of both systems, however, is that they can be expanded to support larger knowledge bases. The inference engines in these expert systems are structured to allow easy expansion to include more specific clauses of knowledge; these clauses can form larger and more heterogeneous knowledge bases.

A medical diagnosis expert system can illustrate an extension along these lines. The purpose of this logic-based system is to identify a probable illness. The user gives information concerning symptoms in response to questions from the expert system.

Design Considerations

The design of the Medical Diagnosis expert system is similar to that of the logic-based dog selection expert system. The added features are the inclusion of modules to load and save the knowledge base.

The data-flow diagram for this system is shown in figure 10.9. You'll notice that the data-flow diagram resembles the one shown in figure 10.6. Consequently, the details of the data flow are not specified in figure 10.9. The added modules are *process(1)*, for loading the knowledge base file into memory; and *process(3)*, for saving the knowledge base to disk. (Notice the data-flow lines between the knowledge base in memory and the knowledge-base disk file.)

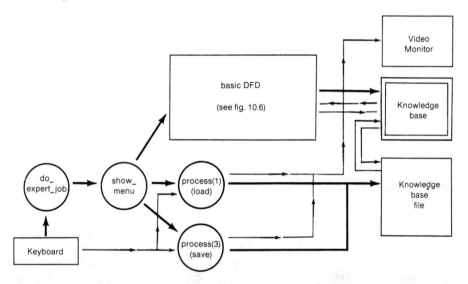

Fig. 10.9. *The data-flow diagram for the Medical Diagnosis Expert System.*

The structure chart obtained from the data-flow diagram is shown in figure 10.10. This structure chart is again similar to the one shown in figure 10.7 for the logic-based dog selection system. Notice, however, the two added modules *process (1)* and *process (3)*, which load and save the knowledge base.

The contents of the knowledge base for the Medical Diagnosis system are shown in figure 10.11. This knowledge base has information on 15 illnesses; this information is stored in 15 *rule* database clauses. The knowledge base also contains 18 symptom descriptions, which are stored in the *cond* database clauses. The list of integers associated with each *rule* clause characterizes the illness. Thus the two are related by the lists at the end of each medical problem rule. For example, the rule

```
rule(11,"illness","social anxiety",[12,15,16,17,18,13])
```

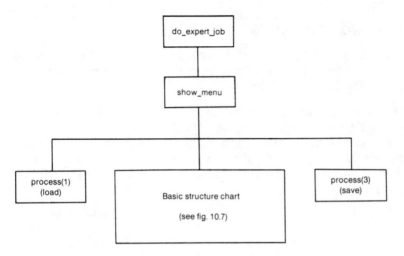

Fig. 10.10. *The structure chart for the Medical Diagnosis Expert System.*

is related to the following symptoms (conditions):

```
cond(12,"feel anxious most of the time")
cond(15,"anxious since giving up tobacco, alcohol, drugs")
cond(16,"recently had a major upset in life")
cond(17,"loss weight or eyes bulging")
cond(18,"have sex life problem")
cond(13,"feel anxious in meetings, parties, interviews")
```

The clause *topic("illness")* provides the choice of knowledge base to the user. In this case, the topic is "illness." If you wish to create a knowledge base for infectious diseases, for example, you would add the topic clause *topic("infectious diseases")*. Then you would design and implement *rule* and *cond* clauses to build the infectious diseases knowledge base.

Building the Medical Diagnosis Expert System

The listing for the rule-based dog selection program can be used as a "starter" for this program; the designs of the two programs are similar. If you wish, you can simply edit program 10.2 to create the Medical Diagnosis expert system. The complete program, shown in listing 10.3, is the implementation of this modified design.

Notice that the knowledge base is not contained in the listing. Instead, it is contained in a disk file. This file can be created by means of the Turbo Prolog editor. The file-handling predicates *consult* and *save* are used to load the knowledge-base file and to write it to disk. The user menu in the program provides convenient modules to do saving and loading of the knowledge base.

```
topic("illness")
rule(1,"illness","drugs - side effects",[1,2,3,4,5])
rule(2,"illness","jet lag",[1,2,3,4,6,7,8,9,10,11])
rule(3,"illness","general depression",[1,2,3,4,6,7,8,9,10])
rule(4,"illness","regular alcoholic",[1,2,3,4,6,7,8,9])
rule(5,"illness","anemia",[1,2,3,4,6,7,8])
rule(6,"illness","hypothyroidism",[1,2,3,4,6,7])
rule(7,"illness","insufficient sleep",[1,2,3,4,6])
rule(8,"illness","fever",[1,2,3])
rule(9,"illness","weight loss",[1,2])
rule(10,"illness","phobia",[12,15,16,17,18,13,14])
rule(11,"illness","social anxiety",[12,15,16,17,18,13])
rule(12,"illness","sex anxiety",[12,15,16,17])
rule(13,"illness","thyrotoxcosis",[12,15,16])
rule(14,"illness","stress",[12,15])
rule(15,"illness","sudden withdrawal",[12])
cond(1,"continually on edge")
cond(2,"lost more than 10 lb.")
cond(3,"temperature over 100 deg F")
cond(4,"tired, lacking in energy")
cond(5,"taking any medication")
cond(6,"suffering from sleeplessness")
cond(7,"feel cold, thin or brittle hair, dry skin, wt. gain")
cond(8,"symptoms - pale, faint,breathless, palpitations")
cond(9,"drinks more than 3 beers, 3 shots most days")
cond(10,"hard to concentrate, headaches, feeling blue")
cond(11,"recently on long air travel")
cond(12,"feel anxious most of the time")
cond(13,"feel anxious in meetings, parties, interviews")
cond(14,"feel anxious only when faced with objects of fear")
cond(15,"anxious since giving up tobacco, alcohol, drugs")
cond(16,"recently had a major upset in life")
cond(17,"loss weight or eyes bulging")
cond(18,"have sex life problem")
```

Fig. 10.11. *The knowledge base for the Medical Diagnosis Expert System.*

```
/* Program: Medical Expert System          File: PROG1003.PRO */
/*                                                            */
/* Purpose. To show the working of a disk-based expert system. */
/*                                                            */
/* Remark. This is a medical expert system. The system is made */
/*         up of the knowledge base (KBS), an inference engine */
/*         (INE) and a user interface system (UIS).           */
/*         The knowledge base is loaded from disk.            */

domains

    CONDITIONS    = BNO *
    HISTORY       = RNO *
    RNO, BNO, FNO = INTEGER
    CATEGORY      = SYMBOL
```

```
database

   /* Database Predicates */

   rule(RNO,CATEGORY,CATEGORY,CONDITIONS)
   cond(BNO,STRING)
   yes(BNO)
   no(BNO)
   topic(string)

predicates

   /* User Interface Predicates */

   do_expert_job
   show_menu
   do_consulting
   process(integer)
   listopt
   evalans(char)
   info(CATEGORY)
   goes(CATEGORY)

   /* Inference Engine Predicates */

   go(HISTORY,CATEGORY)
   check(RNO,HISTORY,CONDITIONS)
   notest(BNO)
   inpg(HISTORY,RNO,BNO,STRING)
   do_answer(HISTORY,RNO,STRING,BNO,INTEGER)
   erase
   clear

goal
   do_expert_job.

clauses

   /* User Interface System (part 1) */
```

```
do_expert_job :-
    makewindow(1,7,7," MEDICAL EXPERT SYSTEM ",0,0,25,80),
    show_menu,
    write(" Press space bar. "),
    readchar(_),
    exit.

show_menu :-
  clearwindow,
  write("* * * * * * * * * * * * *"), nl,
  write("*                       *"), nl,
  write("*     Medical Expert    *"), nl,
  write("*                       *"), nl,
  write("*    1. Load KBS        *"), nl,
  write("*    2. Consultation    *"), nl,
  write("*    3. Save KBS        *"), nl,
  write("*    4. Exit the system *"), nl,
  write("*                       *"), nl,
  write("* * * * * * * * * * * * *"), nl, nl,
  write("Please enter your choice: 1, 2, 3 or 4 : "),
  readint(Choice),
  process(Choice),
  show_menu.

process(0).

process(1) :-
    consult("illness.dba").

process(2) :-
    do_consulting.

process(3) :-
    save("ILLNESS.DBA").

process(4) :-
    exit.
```

```
do_consulting :-
    goes(Mygoal), nl, nl,
    go([],Mygoal), !.
do_consulting :-
    nl, write("     Sorry, I cannot determine that one."),
    nl, write("     Please see a PHYSICIAN."), nl,
    clear.

goes(Mygoal) :-
    clear,
    clearwindow,
    nl, nl,
    write("     WELCOME TO THE MEDICAL EXPERT SYSTEM     "), nl, nl,
    write("   This is an illness identification system."), nl,
    write("   To start the consultation process,         "), nl,
    write("   please type in 'illness'.                   "), nl,
    readln(Mygoal),
    info(Mygoal), !.

go( _, Mygoal ) :-
  not(rule(_,Mygoal,_,_)), !, nl,
  write("   I think it is ",Mygoal,"."), nl, nl,
  write("   Is my diagnosis right (y/n) ?"), nl,
  readchar(Answer),
  evalans(Answer).

/* Inference Engine */

go( HISTORY, Mygoal ) :-
      rule(RNO,Mygoal,NY,COND),
      check(RNO,HISTORY, COND),
      go([RNO|HISTORY],NY).

check( RNO, HISTORY, [BNO|REST] ) :-
    yes(BNO), !,
    check(RNO, HISTORY, REST).
check( _, _, [BNO|_] ) :-
    no(BNO),
    !, fail.
```

```
check( RNO, HISTORY, [BNO|REST] ) :-
    cond(BNO,NCOND),
    fronttoken(NCOND,"not",_COND),
    frontchar(_COND,_,COND),
    cond(BNO1,COND),
    notest(BNO1), !,
    check(RNO, HISTORY, REST).
check(_,_, [BNO|_] ) :-
    cond(BNO,NCOND),
    fronttoken(NCOND,"not",_COND),
    frontchar(_COND,_,COND),
    cond(BNO1,COND),
    yes(BNO1),
    !, fail.
check( RNO, HISTORY, [BNO|REST] ) :-
    cond(BNO,TEXT),
    inpg(HISTORY,RNO,BNO,TEXT),
    check(RNO, HISTORY, REST).
check(_,_,[]).

notest(BNO) :-
        no(BNO), !.
notest(BNO) :-
        not(yes(BNO)), !.

do_answer(_,_,_,_,0) :-
                exit.
do_answer(_,_,_,BNO,1) :-
                assert(yes(BNO)),
                shiftwindow(1),
                write(yes), nl.
do_answer(_,_,_,BNO,2) :-
                assert(no(BNO)),
                write(no),
                nl, fail.

erase :-
    retract(_),
    fail.
erase.
```

```
clear :-
   retract(yes(_)),
   retract(no(_)),
   fail, !.
clear.

/* User Interface System (part 2) */

inpq(HISTORY,RNO,BNO,TEXT) :-
          write(" Question :- ",TEXT," ? "),
          makewindow(2,7,7," Response Window ",19,42,4,32),
          write("Type 1 for 'yes', 2 for 'no' : "),
          readint(RESPONSE),
          clearwindow,
          shiftwindow(1),
          do_answer(HISTORY,RNO,TEXT,BNO,RESPONSE).

info("?") :-
     clearwindow,
     write(" The knowledge base has these illnesses. "),
     nl, nl,
     listopt,
     nl, nl, write(" Press any key."),
     readchar(_),
     clearwindow,
     show_menu.

info(X) :-
     X >< "?".

listopt :-
     write(" The illnesses are:"), nl, nl,
     topic(Ins),
     write("     ",Ins,"  "), nl,
     fail.
listopt.

evalans('y') :-
     write(" I am glad I can help you !"), nl, nl,
     write(" Press the space bar."),
     readchar(_),
     clearwindow,
     show_menu.
```

```
evalans('n') :-
      write(" I am sorry I can't help you !"), nl, nl,
      write(" Please press space bar."),
      readchar(_),
      clearwindow,
      show_menu.
```

```
/*                          end of program                          */
```

When the program is run, a menu prompts the user to choose a program function. The consultation then proceeds on the basis of questions and the user's responses. The responses inform the expert system in its pattern-matching process. The user-interface interlink submodules in the program provide appropriate graphics and user-friendly, natural language throughout the dialogue. When the expert system's recognize-act cycle is finished, the system will display an ending message, either the identification of a probable illness or a message that the user may want to consult a physician. A typical dialogue during a consulting session is shown in figure 10.12. In this session, the dialogue leads to the identification of an illness.

```
┌──────────────────── MEDICAL EXPERT SYSTEM ────────────────────┐
│   WELCOME TO THE MEDICAL EXPERT SYSTEM                         │
│                                                               │
│   This is an illness identification system.                   │
│   To start the consultation process,                         │
│   please type in 'illness'.                                  │
│ illness                                                       │
│                                                               │
│                                                               │
│   Question :- continually on edge ? yes                       │
│   Question :- lost more than 10 lb. ? yes                     │
│   Question :- temperature over 100 deg F ? yes                │
│   Question :- tired, lacking in energy ? yes                  │
│   Question :- taking any medication ? no                      │
│   Question :- suffering from sleeplessness ? yes              │
│   Question :- feel cold, thin or brittle hair, dry skin, wt. gain ? yes │
│   Question :- symptoms - pale, faint,breathless, palpitations ? no │
│                                                               │
│   I think it is hypothyroidism.                               │
│                                                               │
│   Is my diagnosis right (y/n) ?                               │
│ I am glad I can help you !                                    │
│                                                               │
│ Press the space bar.                                          │
└───────────────────────────────────────────────────────────────┘
```

Fig. 10.12. A consultation with the Medical Diagnosis Expert System.

The heart of the Medical Diagnosis logic-based expert system is the inference engine. The working of this inference engine is the same as that discussed in the logic-based Dog Classification expert system.

The starting point for the inference engine is the acceptance of the user's input, *illness*. The first question communicated to the user comes from the first *cond* clause. The display is

```
Question:- continually on edge?
```

The remaining questions are based on *cond* clauses 2 through 8. The responses to conditions 5 and 8 are negative; thus the list variable COND is bound to *[1,2,3,4,6,7]*. This list matches the list of conditions in rule (6). This match is now associated with the classified object "hypothyroidism" in the *rule* clause, and the inference engine has found the desired result—hypothyroidism.

——————————————————— **Exercises** ———————————————————

10.7. Run the Medical Diagnosis expert system. Remember that the knowledge base does not exist until you "create" it, that is, until you load the knowledge base file just discussed. Conduct several consulting sessions so you see how both the positive and negative matches result.

10.8. Add information on a few more illnesses to the knowledge base (terminal fever, T.G.I.F., or Monday morning blues, for example). Use the Turbo Prolog editor to add these to the knowledge base file. Run the program and ensure that the system properly diagnoses the illness.

Chapter Review

In this chapter you have learned the principles of operation of two widely used types of expert systems: the rule-based system and the logic-based system. You have also become familiar with the component parts of these systems: the knowledge base, the inference engine, and the user-interface system.

You have also learned to design knowledge bases according to the quantity and category of the knowledge. You have learned how to build production rules for rule-based systems and clausal knowledge bases for logic-based systems.

Finally, in the discussion of the Medical Diagnosis expert system, you saw how to create a disk-based knowledge base. Use of a disk-based KBS necessitates additional processing modules for loading and saving the KBS.

You have seen, throughout this chapter, how Turbo Prolog's graphics and editing facilities, its powerful internal unification routines, and its searching and pattern-matching capabilities all contribute to the effectiveness of the programs. As expert-system development seems likely to become one of the most promising and practical applications for artificial intelligence programming, Turbo Prolog's potential for growth in this area appears to be unlimited.

11

Processing Natural Language

Overview

This chapter introduces natural-language processing (NLP), which is regarded as one of the most important fields in artificial intelligence research. The chapter begins with a definition of NLP and a brief outline of how it has been approached over the years.

Several methods of analysis of natural language will be briefly discussed. Two approaches, *keyword analysis* (KA) and the context-free grammar (CFG) approach, are discussed in some detail and presented in Turbo Prolog programs. Keyword analysis is adaptable for use in natural-language interfaces to databases and expert systems. The context-free grammar approach offers additional insight into NLP. Turbo Prolog's built-in predicates to handle lists and strings are powerful assets in analyzing natural-language structures.

Approaches to Natural-Language Processing

A natural language is a human language such as English, Japanese, or French. Such languages have structures and rules according to which the people who speak them combine words into phrases, sentence fragments, and complete sentences. You could say that a person who speaks a natural language knows how to "process" the language, both for understanding sentences and for generating them.

The science of natural-language processing is as old as artificial intelligence itself. LISP, the first AI language, was invented to process symbols, words, lists, and higher-order aggregates of list structures. LISP is often used in NLP research. The Prolog language grew out of research on natural languages, computer languages, and language translation.

Several important NLP systems have been developed. INTELLECT, a product of AI Corporation, was developed by Larry Harris in 1979 as a user interface to databases and information retrieval systems in finance, marketing, manufacturing, and personnel management. SCRIPTS, an intelligent retrieval system from Cognitive Systems, Inc., is another example of this kind of system. NaturalLink, developed by Harry Tennant and others at Texas Instruments, serves as a user interface to microcomputers. ELIZA, a natural-language program that simulates a Rogerian psychological counselor, works by excerpting keywords from the user's input sentences and giving programmed responses based on those keywords. For some time, ELIZA was regarded as one of the most significant computer programs. Serious suggestions that ELIZA could take the place of a human counselor dismayed its developer, Joseph Weizenbaum.

The various approaches to NLP are concerned with developing computer systems that can process natural language in ways that are comparable to the human processing of language. These approaches generally work with text material that is keyed in or scanned rather than spoken. Voice recognition and synthesis, however, will play an increasing role as the field develops.

Keyword analysis is a method of analyzing the content of a sentence for keywords that the computer has been programmed to recognize. The keywords become values of objects in predicates. In this context, then, the grammatical structure is not important because the program does not analyze the relationships between words. The computer can handle variations in the input sentences because only the keywords are used to select processing tasks.

Context-free grammar analysis has been shown to yield useful results. The words of every natural language are organized in accordance with a collection of rules called a *grammar*. The rules of the grammar dictate which symbols or strings of words constitute valid sentences in the language. In context-free grammars, specific phrases are categorized in accordance with their internal structures. In context-sensitive grammars, on the other hand, the analysis of structures is dependent upon the context in which they appear in the natural-language sentence.

For example, the sentence

　　Mary reads books

is a valid sentence. It exhibits the familiar subject-verb-object structure. The meaning of this sentence is understood without the need to refer to other sentences. This sentence can therefore be analyzed as a solitary unit.

Natural languages offer many instances of sentences that are *context-sensitive*. Consider, for example, the sentence

　　John talked to Joe before he went to lunch.

Here, the word *he* is ambiguous. Whether it stands for *John* or *Joe* is not clear. Although human languages thrive despite such ambiguities, a language can be constructed in which all sentences can be understood without reference to context. Such sentences are necessary for successful use of the CFG approach.

Prolog is a convenient tool for use in the CFG approach to natural-language processing. Context-free rules can be expressed as Prolog clauses. The problem of recognizing a sentence then is reduced to the problem of proving a set of clauses that form the grammatical structure of the language.

In *syntactic analysis*, the elements of a sentence are analyzed according to the rules of the grammar. The analysis requires that the sentence be separated into its component parts; this is done by *parsing* the sentence. Parsing takes advantage of the grammatical regularities and common patterns of sentences.

Parsing techniques include augmented transition network parsing, bottom-up parsing, and top-down parsing. Augmented transition network parsing is a method of breaking down a sentence into smaller and smaller units until the sentence is completely parsed. In bottom-up parsing, the analysis proceeds word by word from left to right until all words are analyzed. In the process, all possible syntactical structures are determined. In top-down parsing, the sentence is analyzed according to its anticipated (presumed) structure. The technique of top-down parsing is used in one of the programs presented in this chapter.

Pragmatic analysis deals with the study of what people really mean, as opposed to what the words alone indicate. As an example, the answer to the question "Why is John so quiet today?" is probably not "John has not spoken today." Behind the "why" of the question is another question, which might be verbalized in the form "What is bothering John today?" Answering the real question, rather than the literal question, requires a great deal of information about our (human) perceptions, relationships, and feelings. This approach to natural-language processing is certainly among the most complex. Achieving meaningful results therefore is difficult.

A Simple Keyword-Identifier Interface

Keyword analysis allows a program's user-interface system to accommodate considerable variations in input. Consider the following three queries:

Tell me about George Washington.

Show me the information on George Washington.

Who is George Washington?

Each of these sentences could be a query command to a database, requesting information on George Washington. Although they are structured differently, all three sentences can be treated as operationally equivalent. For example, all three have in common the name *George Washington*. The program can pick out this key phrase and use it as a value for an object in a database clause. Using this method, you can construct a simple natural-language interface to a database.

In structuring the program's responses, you might consider the words at the beginning of each sentence: *Tell*, *Show*, and *Who*. The first two words can be regarded as key-words indicating that the user wants *all* the information available on George Washington. The third sentence, however, might indicate that the user wants only a limited amount of information. You see, then, that you need to consider all three keywords to determine appropriate degrees and kinds of information retrieval.

In developing a simple natural-language interface, you can use the following assumptions about the command sentences:

1. The structure of the command sentences does not affect the keyword selection.

2. Only a few keywords need to be examined to determine the degree and kind of access desired by the user.

Both of these assumptions can be illustrated in a comparison of these two command sentences:

Describe George Washington.

Tell me everything you have stored related to the life and history of George Washington.

Many of the words in the second sentence are "noise words." They can be ignored, and the information retrieved can be the same in each case.

The major task in developing a keyword-analysis interface program is to analyze the command sentence and extract the keywords. Identification of keywords is easily accomplished in Turbo Prolog. The procedures are

1. Accept a command sentence as a string.
2. Convert the sentence to a list of words.
3. Identify the keyword(s).

Step 1 is easy to implement, as the string is a basic data type in Turbo Prolog. Step 2 requires writing a rule to convert a string into a list of words. This step can be performed by means of the built-in Turbo Prolog predicate *fronttoken*. (Refer to the section "Transforming Strings into Lists of Tokens" in Chapter 6 to review the use of this predicate.)

Step 3 is normally performed in one of two ways. In the first method, you determine whether the keywords (and their variants, if any) are stored in Prolog database clauses. Then Turbo Prolog's internal unification routines can match the elements in the sentences to the database values. If the matching is successful, the program will proceed to the next stage. In the second method, keywords are determined according to the position they occupy in the sentence. This method relies heavily on the fact that certain grammatical patterns occur frequently. For example, the first and last words of the list can be used as keywords. This is the case, for example, with questions such as "Where is Boston?" The identification routine then entails looking into a database for the specified words or phrases. As with the first method, successful matching allows the program to proceed.

This kind of keyword analysis is a simple example of parsing a command. As the analysis identifies and utilizes more keywords, it can produce more specific and detailed information from the database.

A List-Maker Program

Having learned the fundamentals of the keyword-analysis method, now you can design and write a simple Turbo Prolog KA program. This program will accept a command sentence, convert the sentence to a list of words, and display the list on the screen. The program will also identify the last word in the list and print that on the screen.

The user's input sentence is instantiated to the variable *Sentence*. Then this string is converted into a list of words with the *convers* rule, which was introduced in Chapter 6. The form of this rule is

```
convers(Sentence,List)
```

The rule is

```
convers(Str,[Head|Tail]) :-
      fronttoken(Str,Head,Str1), !,
      convers(Str1,Tail).
convers(_,[]).
```

After *convers* succeeds, *List* contains a list of words from the sentence. Each element is a word from the sentence.

The next step is to identify the last element in the list by means of a rule like this:

```
last_element([Head],Last_element)  :-
    Last_element = Head, !.
last_element([_|Tail],Last_element) :-
    last_element(Tail,Last_element).
```

The first variant of this recursive rule instantiates the last element of the list to the variable *Last_element*. The second form of the rule walks through the list.

The List Maker program, shown in listing 11.1, implements the keyword method of analysis. The method used in this program can be the basis for the development of other, more elaborate programs. You will notice that the program uses Turbo Prolog's window facilities. It also uses a list-printing rule *print_list*, which was introduced in Chapter 6.

```
/* Program: List Maker                  PROG1101.PRO   */
/* Purpose: To convert an input sentence into a list of */
/*          words and extract the last word.            */

domains

    str_list = symbol *
    str      = string

predicates

    convers(str,str_list)
    print_list(str_list)
    do_convert_and_print
    find_last_word(str_list)
    last_element(str_list,symbol)

goal

    do_convert_and_print.

clauses

    /* rule to convert a sentence into a list of words */

    convers(Str,[Head|Tail]):-
              fronttoken(Str,Head,Str1),!,
              convers(Str1,Tail).
    convers(_,[]).

    /* rule to print a list */

    print_list([]).
    print_list([Head|Tail]) :-
              write("       ",Head), nl,
              print_list(Tail).

    /* rule to find last element in a list */
```

```
last_element([Head],Last_element) :-
                 Last_element = Head.
last_element([_|Tail],Last_element) :-
                 last_element(Tail,Last_element).

/* rule to find and print last word in the target list */

find_last_word(List) :-
    last_element(List,Lname),
    nl, write(" Here is the last word : ",Lname), nl.

/* rule as a goal */

do_convert_and_print :-
    makewindow(1,7,7,"",0,0,25,80),
    makewindow(2,7,7," A List Maker ",1,10,23,40),
    nl, write(" PLEASE TYPE IN A SENTENCE."),
    cursor(3,6), readln(Sentence),
    nl, write(" THE INPUT SENTENCE IS "), nl, nl,
    write("        ",Sentence), nl, nl,
    write(" THE OUTPUT LIST OF WORDS IS "), nl, nl,
    convers(Sentence,List),
    print_list(List),
    find_last_word(List),
    nl, write(" PRESS THE SPACE BAR."),
    readchar(_),
    clearwindow,
    exit.

/*            end of program            */
```

Figure 11.1 shows a dialogue with the List Maker Program. The input sentence is

a man loves a woman

Notice that no period (.) appears at the end of this sentence. If the sentence ends with a period, the period is treated as a token; the *last_element* predicate will bind the period to the variable *Last_element*. The period must therefore be omitted because it cannot be used for identification purposes in your database.

```
┌──────────────── A List Maker ─────────────────┐
│ PLEASE TYPE IN A SENTENCE.                     │
│                                                │
│       a man loves a woman                      │
│ THE INPUT SENTENCE IS                          │
│                                                │
│       a man loves a woman                      │
│ THE OUTPUT LIST OF WORDS IS                    │
│                                                │
│       a                                        │
│       man                                      │
│       loves                                    │
│       a                                        │
│       woman                                    │
│                                                │
│ Here is the last word : woman                  │
│                                                │
│ PRESS THE SPACE BAR.                           │
│                                                │
└────────────────────────────────────────────────┘
```

Fig. 11.1. A dialogue with the List Maker program.

──────────────────── **Exercises** ────────────────────

11.1. Run the List Maker Program. At the *Goal:* prompt, enter the following sentences and check the outputs (remember to omit the period):

When it rains it pours

Who is Joe Montana

Tell me about your spit_fire_87

11.2. Experiment with the List Maker Program by trying your own sentences. Then modify the program so that the last element in the sentence is displayed in uppercase letters. (*Hint:* Use the built-in Turbo Prolog predicate *upper_lower.*) Run the modified program and check the results.

11.3. Modify the List Maker program so that it selects the first element of the list instead of the last. Run the modified program and check the results.

A Database Keyword-Identifier Program

As was stated in the preceding section, a user-interface system may need to access a database in order to identify keywords. This section shows how to design a Turbo Prolog program that accesses a database and attempts to match the user's input with the data contained in the database clauses.

A database query in the form of a command line consists of words, some of which are to be identified as keywords. To achieve this, the command line (a string) is decomposed into a list of its constituent words. Each word in the list is used in an attempt to match it with specified data values contained in database clauses. In the case of a successful match, the values are then bound to variables in rules that are used to access the database. The Database Keyword Program presented in this section illustrates that technique.

Assume that you want to access the Pro Football database developed in Chapter 9. You want to identify the players' last names so that queries about them can be answered. Your program will need rules to extract data from the *dplayer* clauses, to identify the players' names, and then extract the players' last names from the full names, which are stored as a single data item.

To perform the last step, your program needs to convert each player's full name into a list containing the first and last names, and then find the last element of the list. The essential part of the goal has the form

```
do_trick :-
    dplayer(P_name,T_name,_,_,_,_,_,_),
    D_name = P_name,
    write("  ",D_name," ",T_name), nl,
    convers(D_name,D_list),
    last_element(D_list,L_name),
    write("  Last name =  ",L_name),nl, nl,
    fail.
```

The variable *D_name* is bound to the player's full name. This value is processed by the *convers* rule, which creates a list whose elements are the first and last names. The rule *last_element* binds the last element in the list *L_name*.

The complete Database Keyword Program is shown in listing 11.2. This program uses Turbo Prolog's window facilities to frame the program functions and responses. Figure 11.2 shows the output of the program. Notice that all the players' names, last names, and team names are displayed in windows.

```
┌─────────── Foot Ball Database Query ───────────┐
│                                                │
│     Dan Marino  Miami Dolphins                 │
│     Last name = Marino                         │
│                                                │
│     Richart Dent  Chicago Bears                │
│     Last name = Dent                           │
│                                                │
│     Bernie Kosar  Cleveland Browns             │
│     Last name = Kosar                          │
│                                                │
│     Doug Cosbie  Dallas Cowboys                │
│     Last name = Cosbie                         │
│                                                │
│     Mark Malone  Pittsburgh Steelers           │
│     Last name = Malone                         │
│                                                │
│ no more names                                  │
│ Finished                                       │
└────────────────────────────────────────────────┘
```

Fig. 11.2. *The output of the Database Keyword program.*

```
/* Program: Database Keyword      File: PROG1102.PRO */
/* Purpose: To make a list out of a database object.  */

domains
     str_list                         = string *
     p_name, t_name, pos, height, college = string
     p_number, weight, nfl_exp         = integer

database
     dplayer(p_name,t_name,p_number,pos,
          height,weight,nfl_exp,college)

predicates
     do_trick
     convers(string,str_list)
     last_element(str_list,string)
     assert_database
     clear_database
     player(p_name,t_name,p_number,pos,
          height,weight,nfl_exp,college)
```

```
goal
    assert_database,
    makewindow(1,7,7,"",0,0,25,80),
    makewindow(2,7,7," Foot Ball Database Query ",
        2,10,22,50),
    nl, nl,
    do_trick,
    write("Finished"),nl,
    readchar(_),
    clear_database.

clauses
    assert_database :-
        player(P_name,T_name,P_number,Pos,Ht,Wt,Exp,College),
        assertz( dplayer(P_name,T_name,P_number,
                Pos,Ht,Wt,Exp,College) ),
        fail.
    assert_database :- !.

    clear_database :-
        retract( dplayer(_,_,_,_,_,_,_,_) ),
        fail.
    clear_database :- !.

    do_trick :-
        dplayer(P_name,T_name,_,_,_,_,_,_),
        D_name = P_name,
        write("  ",D_name,"  ",T_name), nl,
        convers(D_name,D_list),
        last_element(D_list,L_name),
        write("  Last name = ",L_name), nl, nl,
        fail.
    do_trick:- write("no more names"),nl.

    /* rule to convert a string into a list */

    convers(Str,[Head|Tail]) :-
        fronttoken(Str,Head,Str1), !,
        convers(Str1,Tail).
    convers(_,[]).

    /* rule to select the last word */
```

```
last_element([Head],Last_element) :-
    Last_element = Head.
last_element([_|Tail],Last_element) :-
    last_element(Tail,Last_element).


/* database */

player("Dan Marino","Miami Dolphins",13,"QB",
    "6-3",215,4,"Pittsburgh").
player("Richart Dent","Chicago Bears",95,"DE",
    "6-5",263,4,"Tennessee State").
player("Bernie Kosar","Cleveland Browns",19,"QB",
    "6-5",210,2,"Miami").
player("Doug Cosbie","Dallas Cowboys",84,"TE",
    "6-6",235,8,"Santa Clara").
player("Mark Malone","Pittsburgh Steelers",16,"QB",
    "6-4",223,7,"Arizona State").
```

—————————————————— **Exercises** ——————————————————

11.4. Run the Database Keyword Program. Verify that the results you obtain match those shown in figure 11.2. Add several of your favorite players to the database.

11.5. Modify the *do_trick* rule so that the *nfl_experience* data item is displayed, in addition to the other data. Then modify the program so that only the *nfl_experience* data is displayed in addition to the last name of each player.

11.6. Modify the Database Keyword Program so that it uses a disk-resident database that is read into memory when the program is run. (Examine the College Football Database Program in Chapter 9 if you need to review the methods.)

The Football NLP Interface Program

The List Maker program has demonstrated the use of keyword analysis in processing user queries, and the Database Keyword program has showed you how to select keywords from the database clauses. Now you can combine the techniques from those two programs to build a Turbo Prolog program with a natural-language user interface to a database.

The main purpose of the program is to find the matching last name of a player based on the user's input. If the first word of the input sentence is *Tell*, *Show*, or *Who* and the last word of the sentence is the last name of a player, Turbo Prolog's internal unification

routines quickly search for a matching last name in the database. The desired information then is displayed. Variant forms of the action predicates inform the user if no match
is found.

Figure 11.3 shows the structure chart for the Football NLP Interface Program. The main
module, *do_query*, calls six submodules. The first and last submodules assert and retract
the dynamic database. The second submodule, *convers*, converts the input string to a
list. The next two submodules, *first_element* and *last_element*, extract the first and last
keywords from the input sentence. The first keyword is checked to verify that it is contained in the program's set of valid keywords; the second keyword (the last word of the
sentence) is the last name of a football player.

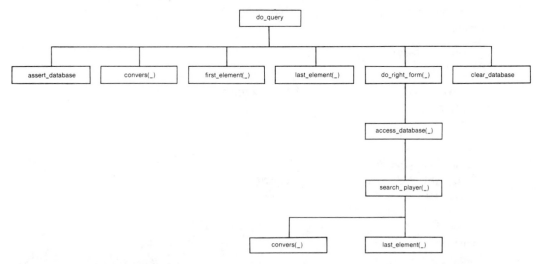

Fig. 11.3. *The structure chart for the Football NLP Interface program.*

The fifth submodule called by *do_query* is *do_right_form*. This submodule calls *keyword* to verify that the first word of the input sentence is a valid keyword—*SHOW*,
WHO, or *TELL*. The *do_right_form* module passes the last keyword to the submodule
(or "sub-submodule") *access_database*. This submodule, in turn, calls the submodule
search_player to search for the player's last name in the database. This module calls
two other modules, *convers* and *last_element*, to identify the player's last name.

The main module is implemented as follows:

```
do_query :-
     assert_database,
     makewindow(1,7,7,"",0,0,25,80),
     makewindow(2,7,7,"",1,3,4,71),
```

```
cursor(1,22), write("PRO FOOTBALL DATABASE"),
makewindow(3,7,7," Input Info ",6,3,6,37),
repeat, nl, write(" Please type in your question."),
cursor(3,2), readln(Sentence),
makewindow(4,7,7," List Maker ",6,42,6,32),
convers(Sentence,List),
first_element(List,Kname),
last_element(List,Lname),
do_right_form(Kname,Lname),
clear_database.
```

In this module, the rules *convers* and *last_element* are the same as in the preceding programs. The rule *first_element* finds the first element in the list obtained from the input sentence:

```
first_element([Head|_],Fname) :-
    Fname = Head.
```

The submodule *do_right_form* checks the first keyword and extracts the last name of the player from the database:

```
do_right_form(Kname,Lname) :-
    keyword(Kname),
    nl, write(" THE KEY WORDS ARE "), nl,
    nl, write("      ",Kname,"    ",Lname),
    makewindow(5,7,7," Player Info ",12,3,12,71),
    access_database(Lname),
    nl, write(" ANY KEY CONTINUES."),
    readchar(_),
    removewindow,
    gotowindow(4),
    removewindow,
    gotowindow(3),
    clearwindow,!,
    fail.
```

The first keyword is checked with a call to the rule *keyword*:

```
keyword(Key) :-
    upper_lower(Upkey,Key),
    Upkey = "SHOW",!.
```

This predicate succeeds if the uppercase equivalent of the first word of the input sentence is *SHOW*. Variant clauses check for the keywords *WHO* and *TELL*. Additional clauses can be easily added to increase the number of keywords.

If *keyword* does not succeed, variants of *do_right_form* are attempted:

```
do_right_form(Kname,_) :-
    Kname="Done",!,
    exit.


do_right_form(Kname,_) :-
    nl, write(" This keyword is unknown:"), nl,
    nl, write("        ",Kname),
    nl, write(" Press any key to try again."),
    readchar(_),
    removewindow,
    clearwindow,!,
    fail.
```

The first variant ends the program; the second informs the reader that an unknown keyword has been entered.

The first variant of *do_right_form* module calls the submodule *access_database*, which in turn calls the submodule *search_player* to search for the player by his last name.

The module *search_player* is implemented as follows:

```
search_player(Lname) :-
    dplayer(Name,Team,Number,Position,
        Height,Weight,NFL_Exp,College),
    Temp_name = Name,
    convers(Temp_name,Dlist),
    last_element(Dlist,Dname),
    Lname = Dname,
    nl, write(" Available information:"),
    nl, nl, write(" ",Name," is a player "),
        write("on the ",Team," team."),
    nl, write(" His number is ",Number),
        write(" and his position is ",Position,"."),
    nl, write(" His weight and height are ",Weight),
        write(" lb. and ",Height," ft-inch."),
    nl, write(" He has ",NFL_Exp," years of NFL experience."),
    nl, write(" He is a graduate of ",College,"."), nl,
    !.

search_player(_) :-
    nl, nl,
    write("That player is not in the database."),
    nl.
```

In this *search_player* rule, the *dplayer* database clause includes eight object variables. Among these objects is the *Name* variable, which represents the name of each player. *Temp_name* is the temporary data variable which is used to refer to the *Name* data copied from the player clause. The *convers* rule converts the name string into a list of words, *Dlist*. The rule *last_element* extracts the last name of the player.

The Football NLP Interface Program, in listing 11.3, implements this design. The program uses multiple windows, as Turbo Prolog's graphics capabilities make this sophisticated presentation easy and effective. Notice that the football player database is in the *clauses* division of the program.

```
/* Program: Football NLP Interface  File: PROG1103.PRO */
/* Purpose: To create a NLP interface to a database    */
/*          and retrieve information.                  */

domains

    str_list = symbol *
    str      = string

    p_name,t_name,pos,height,college = string
    p_number,weight,nfl_exp          = integer

database

    dplayer(p_name,t_name,p_number,pos,
            height,weight,nfl_exp,college)

predicates

    repeat
    assert_database
    clear_database
    do_query
    convers(string,str_list)
    first_element(str_list,string)
    last_element(str_list,string)

    access_database(string)
    search_player(string)
    do_right_form(string,string)
    keyword(string)
    player(p_name,t_name,p_number,pos,
            height,weight,nfl_exp,college)
```

```
goal

    do_query.

clauses

    repeat. repeat:- repeat.

    assert_database :-
        player(P_name,T_name,P_number,Pos,Ht,Wt,Exp,College),
        assertz( dplayer(P_name,T_name,P_number,
                Pos,Ht,Wt,Exp,College) ),
        fail.
    assert_database :- !.

    clear_database :-
        retract( dplayer(_,_,_,_,_,_,_,_) ),
        fail.
    clear_database :- !.

    /* rule to convert an input string */
    /* into a list of words           */

    convers(Str,[Head|Tail]):-
                fronttoken(Str,Head,Str1), !,
                convers(Str1,Tail).
    convers(_,[]).

    /* rule to find the first element in a list */

    first_element([Head|_],Fname) :-
        Fname = Head.

    /* rule to find last element in a list */

    last_element([Head],Last_element) :-
        Last_element = Head.
    last_element([_|Tail],Last_element) :-
        last_element(Tail,Last_element).

    /* access database and print information */
```

```
access_database(Lname) :-
    search_player(Lname).

/* search for the player */

search_player(Lname) :-
    dplayer(Name,Team,Number,Position,
        Height,Weight,NFL_Exp,College),
    Temp_name = Name,
    convers(Temp_name,Dlist),
    last_element(Dlist,Dname),
    Lname = Dname,
    nl, write(" Available information:"),
    nl, nl, write(" ",Name," is a player "),
        write("on the ",Team," team."),
    nl, write(" His number is ",Number),
        write(" and his position is ",Position,"."),
    nl, write(" His weight and height are ",Weight),
        write(" lb. and ",Height," ft-inch."),
    nl, write(" He has ",NFL_Exp," years of NFL experience."),
    nl, write(" He is a graduate of ",College,"."), nl,
    !.

search_player(_) :-
    nl, nl,
    write("That player is not in the database."),
    nl.

/* rule as a goal */

do_query :-
    assert_database,
    makewindow(1,7,7,"",0,0,25,80),
    makewindow(2,7,7,"",1,3,4,71),
    cursor(1,22), write("PRO FOOTBALL DATABASE"),
    makewindow(3,7,7," Input Info ",6,3,6,37),
    repeat, nl, write(" Please type in your question."),
    cursor(3,2), readln(Sentence),
    makewindow(4,7,7," List Maker ",6,42,6,32),
    convers(Sentence,List),
    first_element(List,Kname),
    last_element(List,Lname),
    do_right_form(Kname,Lname),
    clear_database.
```

```
/* rule to choose and do the right form */

do_right_form(Kname,Lname) :-
    keyword(Kname),
    nl, write(" THE KEY WORDS ARE "), nl,
    nl, write("      ",Kname,"    ",Lname),
    makewindow(5,7,7," Player Info ",12,3,12,71),
    access_database(Lname),
    nl, write(" ANY KEY CONTINUES."),
    readchar(_),
    removewindow,
    gotowindow(4),
    removewindow,
    gotowindow(3),
    clearwindow,!,
    fail.

do_right_form(Kname,_) :-
    Kname="Done",!,
    exit.

/* Inform user of unknown keyword */

do_right_form(Kname,_) :-
    nl, write(" This keyword is unknown:"), nl,
    nl, write("       ",Kname),
    nl, write(" Press any key to try again."),
    readchar(_),
    removewindow,
    clearwindow,!,
    fail.

/* Check for valid keyword */

keyword(Key) :-
    upper_lower(Upkey,Key),
    Upkey = "SHOW",!.

keyword(Key) :-
    upper_lower(Upkey,Key),
    Upkey = "WHO",!.
```

```
keyword(Key) :-
    upper_lower(Upkey,Key),
    Upkey = "TELL",!.

/*  football player database */

player("Dan Marino","Miami Dolphins",13,"QB",
    "6-3",215,4,"Pittsburgh").
player("Richard Dent","Chicago Bears",95,"DE",
    "6-5",263,4,"Tennessee State").
player("Bernie Kosar","Cleveland Browns",19,"QB",
    "6-5",210,2,"Miami").
player("Doug Cosbie","Dallas Cowboys",84,"TE",
    "6-6",235,8,"Santa Clara").
player("Mark Malone","Pittsburgh Steelers",16,"QB",
    "6-4",223,7,"Arizona State").

/*      end of program          */
```

Figure 11.4 shows a dialogue with the Football NLP Interface Program. The topmost window identifies the database. The **Input Info** window displays the user input, and the **List Maker** window shows the values of the two keywords. The **Player Info** window displays the output values selected from the database. Notice that the retrieved information is displayed in complete sentences, adding to the "friendliness" of the program.

As you work with this program, you will find that neither the size of the database nor the seeming complexities of additional keywords in the interface significantly affect the time Turbo Prolog's internal unification routines take. Turbo Prolog performs effortlessly to give you the information you need. The display of data takes much longer than other processes.

—————————————————— **Exercises** ——————————————————

11.7. Enter and run the Football NLP Interface Program. At the prompt, enter these sentences and check the results. (Each sentence should produce the database information you have stored.)

Tell me about Dan Marino

Who is Mark Malone

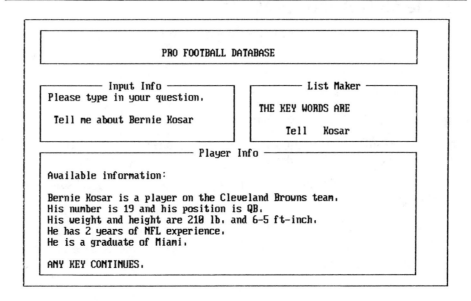

Fig. 11.4. *A dialogue with the Football NLP Interface program.*

Now enter the following sentences and observe the responses. (Both sentences should produce the response *That player is not in the database*.)

Tell me about Joe Montana

How tall is Chip Banks

11.8. Incorporate the Football NLP Interface Program into the Pro Football Database Program in Chapter 9 so that the natural-language interface is an option in the main menu of the final program. (*Hint:* Refer to the structure chart for the Pro Football Database program. Use that chart to determine where you will add the module.) Now run the expanded Pro Football Database Program, select the Natural Language Interface option, and observe the results.

Context-Free Grammar Analysis

Context-free grammar (CFG) analysis begins with a model of a sentence. Because many types of sentences exist, many models are required to represent them. This section will utilize simple models which are common to many basic sentences.

456 — USING TURBO PROLOG

Simple CFG Analysis Models

For CFG analysis, a sentence can be treated as a list of words:

sentence body = [dogs, bark]

sentence body = [Tom, loves, Lana]

sentence body = [Some, boys, love, furry, dogs]

Each sentence also must conform to a model. These models allow you to implement analyses in Turbo Prolog. The models can be fairly simple, as in the following structures.

The words in a basic declarative sentence, placed from left to right, are consistent with the following syntax model:

sentence = noun phrase, verb phrase

This model can be further elaborated, so that each of these elements is seen as having component parts, as follows:

noun phrase = [determiner,] [adjective,] noun | pronoun |

verb phrase = [adverb,] intransitive verb | [adverb,] transitive verb, noun phrase

Square brackets enclose optional items and commas separate constituents of *noun phrase* and *verb phrase*. The vertical bars indicate necessary alternatives. For example, a noun phrase consists of either a noun (optionally preceded by an adjective and/or an adjective or a pronoun.

While you may not choose to include all the optional items in your own programs, they are presented here so you have a more complete concept of the possibilities.

Many of the most common sentences follow this model. Some examples of sentences that illustrate this are

Sue loves color_tv

Tom hates herbal_tea

Sam eats fries

Given a collection of nouns and verbs, you can both generate and analyze sentences of this form. Analysis of the sentence involves determining that the first word is a noun, the second word a verb, and the third word a noun. When the sentence structure has been determined to be "legal," the "meanings" of the individual words can be used to trigger desired actions in a program. This method is useful in applications such as user-interface and robot-control systems. In the following section, you will see how you can design a Turbo Prolog program to perform a simple lexical analysis.

A Lexical Sentence-Analyzer Program

Consider the small hypothetical world of Sam, Sue, and Tom. They live very simply; only five verbs can be used to describe all possible actions in their world. Sam and Sue subsist on hamburgers, fries, herbal tea and water; they help Tom, their neighbor; they have allergies and headaches; and they love each other and Tom. Table 11.1 shows the nouns and verbs in this small world.

Table 11.1

Words for a Lexical-Analyzer Program

Nouns:

People	*Food*	*Ailments*	*Possessions*
sam	hamburger	head_ache	color_tv
sue	fries	allergy	
	water		
	herbal_tea		

Verbs

	Actions
	eats
	loves
	gives
	hates
	helps

The words shown in table 11.1 are placed in database clauses and are labeled as nouns and verbs. Sentences make statements about Sam and Sue's world. The program checks the sentences for syntax and for use of legal words. If both checks give affirmative results, the sentence is "legal"; otherwise the sentence is "illegal."

Figure 11.5 shows the structure chart for the Lexical Sentence Analyzer program. The program's main module is *show_the_work*. It calls the submodule *do_windows* to create three windows and the submodule *print_vocabulary* to display the words in the program vocabulary.

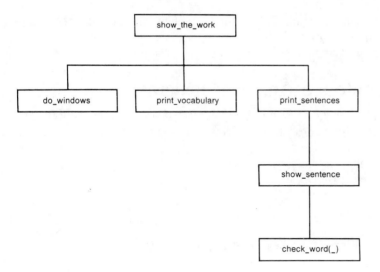

Fig. 11.5. *The structure chart for the Lexical Sentence Analyzer program.*

The submodule *print_sentences* analyzes the sentences stored in the *sentence* database clauses. The sentences are stored in the form of lists. This submodule calls another sub-module, *show_sentence*, to access the sentences in the database. Another submodule, *check_word*, is called to verify that the words are legal. If so, the sentence is accepted; otherwise the program displays the message

```
??? Not legal sentence ???
```

The main module is implemented like this:

```
show_the_work :-
      do_windows,
      print_vocabulary,
      print_sentences.
```

The module *print_vocabulary* performs a straightforward printing of the lists of nouns and verbs. In real-life applications, these collections of words for the various grammatical elements tend to be quite large.

The module *print_sentences* is

```
print_sentences :-
    gotowindow(3),
    nl, write("        Sentence Analysis"),
    nl, nl,
    write("  sentence = <subject, verb, object>"),
    nl, nl,
    write("  Here are the sentences."),
    nl, nl, nl,
    show_sentence.
```

The module *show_sentence* accesses the *sentence* clauses:

```
show_sentence :-
    sentence([W1,W2,W3]),
    write(W1," ",W2," ",W3),
    check_word(W1,W2,W3),
    nl, fail.

show_sentence :-
    cursor(19,5),
    write(" Press the space bar."),
    readchar(_),
    exit.
```

This module determines whether the input sentence structure is legal.

To check the validity of the words, *show_sentence* calls the submodule *check_word*, which is implemented as follows:

```
check_word(W1,W2,W3) :-
    noun(W1), verb(W2), noun(W3), !.

check_word(_,_,_) :-
    nl, write(" ??? Not legal sentence ???"), nl.
```

This submodule attempts to match the first word in the sentence with the objects of the *noun* clauses. If a match is found, the rule succeeds. Similar attempts are made to match the second and third words with verbs and nouns. If one of the three matches fails, the first variant of *check_word* fails. Then backtracking causes the second variant to be attempted; this variant rule displays the message

??? Not legal sentence ???

to indicate that the sentence is not recognized.

Now the complete Lexical Sentence Analyzer Program can be assembled, as in listing 11.4.

```
/* Program-id. Lexical Sentence Analyser  PROG1104.PRO */
/* Book.                          Using Turbo PROLOG */
/* Purpose. To demonstrate sentence analysis using a   */
/*          simple lexical analysis.                   */
/* Direction. Run the program. A goal is provided.     */

domains
   str_seq  = string *

database

   noun(string)
   verb(string)

predicates

   show_the_work
   do_windows
   print_vocabulary
   print_sentences
   show_sentence
   check_word(string,string,string)
   sentence(str_seq)

goal

   show_the_work.

clauses

   /* goal as a rule */

   show_the_work :-
        do_windows,
        print_vocabulary,
        print_sentences.

   /* rule to make windows */
```

```
do_windows :-
    makewindow(1,7,7,"",0,0,25,80),
    makewindow(2,7,7," Vocabulary ",2,40,22,34),
    makewindow(3,7,7," Sentences ",2,2,22,36).


/* rule to print the vocabulary */

print_vocabulary :-
    gotowindow(2),
    nl,
    write(" Legal Nouns"), nl, nl,
    write("        sam"), nl,
    write("        sue"), nl,
    write("        tom"), nl,
    write("        hamburger"), nl,
    write("        fries"), nl,
    write("        water"), nl,
    write("        herbal_tea"), nl,
    write("        color_tv"), nl,
    write("        head_ache"), nl,
    write("        allergy"), nl, nl,
    write(" Legal Verbs"), nl, nl,
    write("        eats"),  nl,
    write("        loves"), nl,
    write("        gives"), nl,
    write("        hates"), nl,
    write("        helps").

/* rule to print sentences */

print_sentences :-
    gotowindow(3),
    nl, write("      Sentence Analysis"),
    nl, nl,
    write(" sentence = <subject,verb,object>"),
    nl, nl,
    write(" Here are the sentences."),
    nl, nl, nl,
    show_sentence.

/* rule to test sentences */
```

```
show_sentence :-
    sentence([W1,W2,W3]),
    write(W1," ",W2," ",W3),
    check_word(W1,W2,W3),
    nl, fail.

show_sentence :-
    cursor(19,5),
    write(" Press the space bar."),
    readchar(_),
    exit.

/* rule to match words in the sentence */
/* against the words in the database */

check_word(W1,W2,W3) :-
                noun(W1), verb(W2), noun(W3), !.

check_word(_,_,_) :-
    nl, write(" ??? Not legal sentence ???"), nl.

/* database (vocabulary) */

    /* nouns */

    noun(sam).
    noun(sue).
    noun(tom).
    noun(hamburger).
    noun(fries).
    noun(water).
    noun(herbal_tea).
    noun(color_tv).
    noun(head_ache).
    noun(allergy).

    /* verbs */

    verb(eats).
    verb(loves).
    verb(gives).
    verb(hates).
    verb(helps).
```

```
/* input sentences */

sentence([sam,eats,french_fries]).
sentence([tom,hates,herbal_tea]).
sentence([sue,loves,color_tv]).
sentence([herbal_tea,helps,head_ache]).
sentence([hamburger,gives,allergy]).


/*                   end of program                   */
```

This Lexical Sentence Analyzer program demonstrates the techniques described and implemented in the preceding sections. Notice that the program creates two windows for the display of the results of the analysis.

Figure 11.6 shows a dialogue with the Lexical Sentence Analyzer program. The right window displays legal nouns and verbs. The left window shows the results of analysis. Notice that the first sentence, *sam eats french_fries*, is not a legal sentence. The word *fries* is legal in Sam's world, but *french_fries* is not. In other words, *french_fries* is not a noun in the vocabulary. The other four sentences are legal.

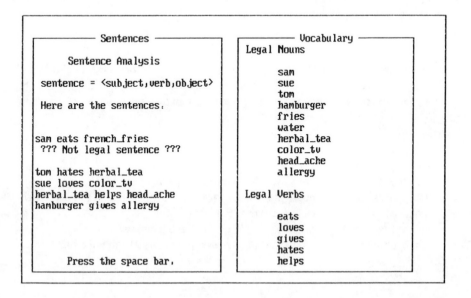

Fig. 11.6. *The output of the Lexical Sentence Analyzer program.*

This program makes good use of Turbo Prolog's facilities for parsing and pattern matching. It runs smoothly and can be very effective with a large vocabulary or grammar.

—————————————— **Exercises** ——————————————

11.9. Run the Lexical Sentence Analyzer Program. Using the Turbo Prolog editor, modify one sentence in the program to substitute an illegal word for a legal word. Run the modified program and observe the results.

11.10. Modify the program so that a sentence can be entered from the keyboard. Enter several sentences, both legal and illegal, to verify that the program works properly. The sentence you enter will be a natural sentence instead of a list. Run the program. Try these legal sentences first so you know you have the correct structures in place:

sue helps tom

color_tv gives head_ache

A Context-Free Grammar (CFG) Sentence Analyzer Program

Earlier in this chapter, sentence parsing was described briefly. The Sentence Parser program, in listing 11.5, implements the top-down parsing technique for sentences that conform to CFG syntax.

```
/* Program: Sentence Parser              File: PROG1105.PRO */
/* Purpose: To show the working of a sentence parser.       */
/* Directions: Run the program. A goal is provided.         */

domains

    Tklist          = String *
    Sentence        = sentence(Noun_phrase,Verb_phrase )
    Noun_phrase     = noun_phrase(Determiner,String,Relative_clause)
    Determiner      = nil ; determ(String)
    Relative_clause = nil ; relcl(String,Verb_phrase)
    Verb_phrase     = verb(String) ; verbp(String,Noun_phrase)

database

    noun(string)  dete(string)  rela(string)    verb(string)
```

```
predicates

   toklist(String,Tklist)
   match(String)

   nphrase(Tklist,Tklist,Noun_phrase)
   determiner(Tklist,Tklist,Determiner)
   sentex(Tklist,Tklist,Sentence)
   relclause(Tklist,Tklist,Relative_clause)
   vphrase(Tklist,Tklist,Verb_phrase)

   do_dcg
   analyse_it
   request_a_sentence
   analyse_sentence(string)
   print_list(Tklist)
   process(integer)

goal

   do_dcg.

clauses

   do_dcg :-
      makewindow(1,7,7,"",0,0,25,80),
      makewindow(2,7,7," Main Window ",1,0,22,39),
      nl, nl, write("      SENTENCE ANALYZER"),
      nl, nl, write("   1. Analyze a sentence"),
      nl, nl, write("   2. Exit the program"),
      nl, nl, write("      Please enter: 1 or 2. "),
      readint(Choice),
      process(Choice),
      do_dcg.

   process(1) :- analyse_it.
   process(2) :- exit.

   /* user interface */
```

```
analyse_it :-
   makewindow(3,7,7," Sentence Analyzer ",2,4,23,72),
   nl, write("          This program analyzes"),
       write(" a sentence in a CFG Model."), nl,
   nl, write("                   "),
   write("sentence = noun-phrase + verb-phrase"),
   request_a_sentence.
analyse_it :- removewindow.

request_a_sentence :-
   makewindow(4,7,7," Dialogue Window ",8,2,4,38),
   nl, write("Type in a sentence."),
   nl, readln(Line),
   analyse_sentence(Line), !,
   request_a_sentence.

analyse_sentence(Line):-
   makewindow(5,7,7," Result Window ",8,41,16,38),
   toklist(Line,Tklist),
   sentex(Tklist, _,Sent_model),
   nl, write("Input Sentence : ",Line), nl,
   nl, write("List of words : "), nl, nl,
   print_list(Tklist),
   nl, write("The sentence model is:"), nl,
   nl, write(Sent_model).
analyse_sentence(_).

print_list([]).
print_list([Head|Tail]) :-
     write("   ",Head), nl,
     print_list(Tail).

/* analysis rules */

toklist(Str,[Token|Tklist]) :-
             fronttoken(Str,Token,Str1),
             match(Token),!,
             toklist(Str1,Tklist).
toklist(_,[]).
```

```
match(W) :- noun(W),!.        match(W) :- dete(W),!.
match(W) :- rela(W),!.        match(W) :- verb(W),!.
match(W) :- write( W," - is not recognized."),
            nl, write(" Press the SPACE bar."),
            readchar(_).

sentex(Tklist,Tklist2,sentence(Noun_phrase,Verb_phrase)):-
     nphrase(Tklist,Tklist1,Noun_phrase),
     vphrase(Tklist1,Tklist2,Verb_phrase), !.

sentex(_,_,_) :-
   write(" That sentence is not recognized."), nl, fail.

nphrase(Tklist,Tklist2,
        noun_phrase(Determiner,Noun,Relative_clause) ) :-
          determiner(Tklist,[Noun|Tklist1],Determiner),
          noun(Noun),
          relclause(Tklist1,Tklist2,Relative_clause).

determiner([Determiner|Tklist],Tklist,determ(Determiner)) :-
                   dete(Determiner).
determiner(Tklist,Tklist,nil).

relclause([Relative|Tklist],Tklist1,
        relcl(Relative,Verb_phrase)):-
                rela(Relative),
                vphrase(Tklist,Tklist1,Verb_phrase).
relclause(Tklist,Tklist,nil).

vphrase([Verb|Tklist],Tklist1,verbp(Verb,Noun_phrase)):-
                verb(Verb),
                nphrase(Tklist,Tklist1,Noun_phrase).
vphrase([Verb|Tklist],Tklist,verb(Verb)) :-
                verb(Verb).

/* database */

noun("Lana"). noun("Tom"). noun("cat").  noun("dog").
dete("a").    dete("an"). rela("that"). rela("who").
verb("loves").    verb("hates").     verb("likes").
verb("sleeps").   verb("dislikes").  verb("scares").

/*                  end of program                    */
```

The CFG syntax structure is declared in the *domains* division:

```
Sentence = sentence(Noun_phrase,Verb_phrase)
Noun_phrase = noun_phrase(Determiner,String,Relative_clause)
Determiner  = nil ; determ(String)
Relative_clause = nil; relcl(String,Verb_phrase)
Verb_phrase = verb(String) ; verbp(String,Noun_phrase)
```

The database division contains clauses to store the values of nouns, verbs, determiners, and relative clauses. The declarations are simple:

noun(string)
verb(string)
dete(string)
rela(string)

The essential tasks of the Sentence Parser program are summarized as follows:

1. The program requests that the user input a sentence from the keyboard. This is accomplished by the rule *request_a_sentence*:

```
request_a_sentence
    makewindow(4,7,7," Dialogue Window  ",8,2,4,38) ,
    nl, write(Type in a sentence."),
    nl, readln(Line),
    analyze_sentence(Line), !,
    request_a_sentence.
```

2. The subrule *analyze_sentence* calls the rule *toklist* to make a list of words (tokens) from the input string. The rule then calls the *sentex* rule to build the model of the sentence. The complete *analyze_sentence* rule is

```
analyze_sentence(Line):-
    makewindow(5,7,7," Result Window ",8,41,16,38),
    toklist(Line,Tklist),
    sentex(Tklist, _,Sent_model),
    nl, write("input Sentence : ",Line), nl,
    nl, write("List of words : "), nl, nl,
    print_list(Tklist),
    nl, write("The sentence model is:"), nl,
    nl, write(Sent_model).
analyze_sentence(_).
```

3. The *toklist* rule builds the lists while it performs the matching of the words with those in the database. The first word in the input sentence is bound to *Token* by the *fronttoken* predicate. Then the *match* rule searches the database and attempts to match the *Token* word, thus identifying the word's part of speech. If the *Token* word does not match any of the words in the database clauses, the user receives the message *<word> – is not recognized.* At this point, however, the sentence can no longer be analyzed, so the *toklist* rule fails. Thus, in order for the *toklist* rule to be successful, all words in the sentence must be found in the database.

```
toklist(Str,[Token|Tklist]) :-
    fronttoken(Str,Token,Str1),
    match(Token),!,
    toklist(Str1,Tklist).
toklist(_,[]).

match(W) :- noun(W),!.    match(W) :- dete(W),!.
match(W) :- rela(W),!.    match(W) :- verb(W),!.
match(W) :- write( W," - is not recognized."),
            nl, write("Press the SPACE bar."),
            readchar(_).
```

4. The *sentex* rule builds the sentence model. In doing so, it calls the *hphrase* rule to build the noun phrase, and the *vphrase* rule to build the verb phrase:

```
sentex(Tklist,Tklist2,sentence(Noun_phrase,Verb_phrase)):-
    nphrase(Tklist,Tklist1,Noun_phrase),
    vphrase(Tklist1,Tklist2,Verb_phrase), !.

sentex(_,_,_) :-
    write(" That sentence is not recognized."), nl, fail.
```

5. The *nphrase* rule calls two rules. One is the *determiner* rule to match the determiners. If there is no match in the database, it fails; otherwise it succeeds. The other is the *relclause* rule, which matches the relative clause. If there is a match in the database, it succeeds; otherwise it fails.

```
nphrase(Tklist,Tklist2,
        noun_phrase(Determiner,Noun,Relative_clause) ):-
            determiner(Tklist,[Noun|Tklist],Determiner),
            noun(Noun),
            relclause(Tklist1,Tklist2,Relative_clause).
```

```
determiner([Determiner|Tklist],Tklist,determ(Determiner)) :-
                    dete(Determiner).
determiner(Tklist,Tklist,nil).

relclause([Relative|Tklist],Tklist1,
          relcl(Relative,Verb_phrase)):-
                    rela(Relative),
                    vphrase(Tklist,Tklist1,Verb_phrase).
relclause(Tklist,Tklist,nil).
```

6. The *vphrase* rule calls the *nphrase* rule for matching possible verb phrases. Notice the the *nphrase* rule also calls the *vphrase* rule, as shown in (4) above. The two variants of the *vphrase* rules are

```
vphrase([Verb|Tklist],Tklist1,verbp(Verb,Noun_phrase)):-
                    verb(Verb),
                    nphrase(Tklist,Tklist1,Noun_phrase).
vphrase([Verb|Tklist],Tklist,verb(Verb)) :-
                    verb(Verb).
```

The program has user interface modules (rules) and makes use of Turbo Prolog's window facilities.

Figure 11.7 shows a dialogue with the Sentence Parser program. Notice that the program creates a Dialog Window to accept the user's input sentence. The Results window is created to display the results of the analysis. In the case of a "legal" sentence, the display includes the input sentence, the list of words and the sentence model built from the input sentence.

—————————————————— **Exercise** ——————————————————

11.11. Modify the Sentence Parser program so that the words in the database are displayed in a suitable window before the program prompts for an input sentence.

Chapter Review

In this chapter you learned several different approaches to natural-language processing. Each approach offers limited application within this complex field. The beauty of human language and its nuances and subtle variations make natural-language processing an area of continuing investigation and development.

The keyword analysis approach lends itself to the creation of simple natural-language interfaces to databases. Three Turbo Prolog programs demonstrated the programming techniques for creating keyword-oriented natural-language interfaces. You also saw that the context-free grammar model of sentence analysis offers interesting and useful fea-

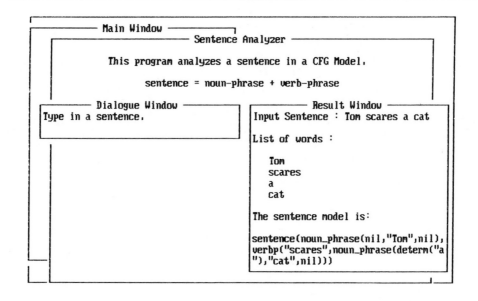

Fig. 11.7. *A dialogue with the CFG Sentence Parser program.*

tures. The simple and effective lexical sentence analyzer and the CFG sentence analyzer programs can be extended to analyze fairly complex structures, so long as the grammar structures are understood by the program designer.

The programs in this chapter have presented the basic steps in natural-language processing, which enable programs to understand and generate information in ways that are comparable to human language processing. These programs put several of Turbo Prolog's features to good use. Turbo Prolog's inherent capabilities make the implementation of language analyzers straightforward and effective.

12

Games and Puzzles

Overview

In the first eleven chapters, you used Turbo Prolog to solve many kinds of problems, ranging from simple database manipulations to expert systems. This chapter introduces you to the creation of games and puzzles with Turbo Prolog. You will probably learn to appreciate the methods and techniques used in programming games and puzzles. Games and puzzles with varying complexities offer a challenge to the programmer. There is no doubt that creating games and puzzles improves the programmer's ability to manipulate many kinds of data in various ways.

In this chapter you will be guided through the development of five Turbo Prolog programs. The first one solves a number-guessing puzzle, and the second and third play two-person games. The fourth solves a classic AI problem, and the fifth solves a logic problem. This last program shows the use of user-interface facilities in making the running of the program more user-oriented and more interesting.

In each of these programs, Turbo Prolog's techniques are employed to solve the particular goals of the program. The richness of Turbo Prolog's internal routines, its graphics, and its fast processing all come together in this chapter to demonstrate programming techniques that can be used in a wide variety of applications.

Problem-Solving in Games and Puzzles

Your everyday activities involve many repeated actions, such as cooking, eating, sleeping, and driving to work. For the normal adult, these activities may require considerable energy, but little application of new thought processes.

Games and puzzles, however, require thought; that is one reason they are popular. Because the problems posed by games and puzzles are well defined, some of the first efforts in artificial-intelligence research were oriented toward game-playing and puzzle-solving.

Computer programs have been written to play games against human players. Board-game programs, such as those that play checkers and chess, can handle the logic of the games. Programs that solve puzzles such as tic-tac-toe and the Towers of Hanoi are classics of artificial-intelligence literature.

You can design and develop complete programs to solve puzzles and games using Turbo Prolog. Turbo Prolog's internal unification routines are capable of performing many levels of searching and pattern-matching that enable your problem-solving methods to work quickly and effectively.

You may already know what the results (or goals) of your work will be in solving some problems. Your method in these cases may therefore involve reasoning backward from the desired result to the necessary preconditions. In AI, this approach is known as *backward chaining*. Turbo Prolog provides backward chaining as its fundamental feature.

In Prolog in general, and in Turbo Prolog in particular, often a rule-head (goal) contains parameters whose values are known. The subgoals in the rule-body attempt to match the parameters in the goal. This is a fundamental feature of rule making in Prolog, and thus, backward chaining is "natural" in Prolog.

In solving other problems, you may have all the necessary steps and conditions to lead to a possible solution or answer. In these cases, your solution may begin with known facts and conditions and work forward to the possible solutions. This approach is known as *forward chaining*.

Number-Guessing Games

Number-guessing games are a particular case of games based on symbol-matching. In computer programs for guessing games, symbols may be numbers, characters, words or sentences, and graphic objects that are represented and stored in memory. Number-guessing games are interesting in that they can be constructed to offer different levels of challenge to the player.

Design Considerations

In designing a number-guessing game program, you need to set a limit on the domain of numbers. As an example, consider a game whose object is to guess an integer number from 1 to 100 inclusive. If you were to guess the number "blindly," it would take you as many as 99 guesses to find the right number. If, on the other hand, you have a plan to head you towards the right guess, then the total number of guesses required can be considerably reduced.

If you use the computer to generate a random number and also use the computer to give you some guidance during your game, the computer is participating in the play passively; you are the "real" player. This in an example of a one-player game. You can also write a game program in which the computer plays an active role as your opponent. In this case, both you and the computer are real players. The game is then a two-player game.

A Game Plan

For an example of a one-player game, consider a game in which the computer selects an integer from 1 to 100. You try to guess the number and communicate your guess to the computer. The computer then lets you know whether your guess is correct or not.

If your guess is not correct, the computer will let you know whether your guess is too high or too low. In this way you can respond with increasing accuracy on each guess. Eventually your guess will be correct. The pleasure of playing this type of game is in being able to guess the correct number with a minimum number of trial guesses.

This game provides a simple illustration of a heuristic approach. In contrast to "blind" methods, the heuristic approach allows you to proceed toward a solution to your problem by correcting your search path according to certain rules. As you proceed in the analysis of this game, you hope to find a *rule of thumb* (or a heuristic) to guide your actions.

For example, let X, the number to be guessed, equal 36. Table 12.1 shows a progression of logical guesses to find the number.

Table 12.1
Logical Progression To Guess a Number

Turn	Your guess	Computer's guidance for next guess
1	50	Enter a smaller number
2	25	Enter a bigger number
3	37	Enter a smaller number
4	31	Enter a bigger number
5	34	Enter a bigger number
6	35	Enter a bigger number
7	36	Right guess

The guesses are obtained by halving the interval of the active part of the domain of X (0 $< X <= 100$). Guessing any number would take seven turns at the most. Notice that after the fourth guess, the active interval is 32 through 36. That is, there are five candidate numbers. You might choose randomly any one of them as the fifth guess. Your chance of selecting the correct number is 20 percent at this point.

Such a game program implements the following steps:

1. Generate a random integer number from 1 to 100, both numbers inclusive.

2. Prompt the player to enter an integer number guess.

   a. If the guess is correct, display a message to that effect and exit.

   b. If the guess is too small, display a message to that effect and accept another guess.

   c. If the guess is too large, display a message to that effect and accept another guess.

Notice that step 1 is carried out only once, whereas step 2 is carried out repeatedly until the guess is correct.

A Number-Guessing Game Program

A Turbo Prolog program to implement a number-guessing game is interesting to write and the game is interesting to play. The integer number between 1 and 100 will be determined by using Turbo Prolog's random-number generator. And the information to guide you toward the correct guess is not difficult to display. You can implement this game in Turbo Prolog by following these procedures:

A rule to generate a random number is

```
generate_rand(X) :-
    random(R),
    X = 1 + R * 100
    nl, write(" I have thought of a number."),
    nl, write(" Now, it is your turn !"), nl.
```

This rule instantiates the variable X to the integer value of the random number. The built-in Turbo Prolog predicate *random(R)* generates a random real number X where $0 <= X < 1$. The equational predicate

```
X = 1 + R * 100
```

converts the random number into the domain of X, that is, from 1 to 100. It also accomplishes the conversion of the real number into an integer number.

To request the player's input (guess) and test it repeatedly, you write the following rule:

```
play_it_sam(X) :-
    nl, write(" Type in your guess. "),
    nl, readint(G),
    test_and_tell(X,G),
    play_it_sam(X).
```

The predicate *readint(G)* reads the user's guess *(G)*. The rule *test_and_tell(X,G)* tests whether the user's guess is correct or not. As described earlier, three possibilities exist for each guess: the guess will be too large, too small, or correct. Each condition calls a separate rule to advise the player of the next move to make. The Turbo Prolog rules for these test conditions are

```
test_and_tell(X,G) :-
            X = G,
            say_you_got_it_right(X).
test_and_tell(X,G) :-
            G > X,
            say_too_big.
test_and_tell(X,G) :-
            G < X,
            say_too_small.

say_too_big :-
    nl, write(" Your guess is too big."),
    nl, write(" Try a smaller number.").
say_too_small :-
    nl, write( "Your guess is too small."),
    nl, write( "Try a bigger number.").
say_you_got_it_right(X) :-
    nl, write( "You got it right."),
    nl, write(" It is ",X,"."),
    nl, write("              Good bye !"),
    nl, write(" Press the space bar."),
    nl, readchar(_),
    exit.
```

You can now construct the program goal, *play_the_game*, as a rule that includes the preceding two rules as subgoals:

```
play_the_game :-
        give_info,
        play_it.
```

The rule *give_info* tells the reader how the game works. The rule *play_it* plays the game. This rule calls *generate_rand(A)* to generate a random integer number, and then calls *play_it_sam(A)* to play the game:

```
play_it:-
        generate_rand(A),
        play_it_sam(A).
```

The Number Guess program, in listing 12.1, implements this program design. Notice that G and X are declared as integers and R is declared as a real number. In addition to Turbo Prolog's built-in random number predicate, the program also utilizes Turbo Prolog's window facilities.

```
/* Program: Number Guessing Game    File: PROG1201.PRO */
/* Purpose: To show a simple number guessing game.     */
/* Direction: Run the program. A goal is included.     */

predicates

    play_the_game
    give_info
    play_it
    generate_rand(integer)
    play_it_sam(integer)
    test_and_tell(integer,integer)
    say_you_got_it_right(integer)
    say_too_big
    say_too_small

goal

    play_the_game.

clauses

    /* goal as a rule */

    play_the_game :-
            give_info,
            play_it.

    /* give information */

    give_info :-
        makewindow(1,7,7,"",0,0,25,80),
        makewindow(2,7,7," A NUMBER Guessing Game ",
                2,20,22,45),
        nl, write(" This is a number guessing game."),
        nl, write(" I shall think of an integer number"),
        nl, write(" between 1 and 100. You make a guess"),
        nl, write(" and type in your guess. If your guess"),
```

```
         nl, write(" is correct, I shall say so. If not, "),
         nl, write(" I shall say your guess is too big or"),
         nl, write(" too small."), nl,
         nl, write(" When you are ready, press the space bar."),
         nl, readchar(_),
         clearwindow.

/* play the game */

play_it :-
   generate_rand(A),
   play_it_sam(A).

/* generate a random number */

generate_rand(X) :-
   random(R),
   X = 1 + R * 100,
   nl, write(" I have thought of a number."),
   nl, write(" Now, it is your turn !"), nl.

/* request user's guess */

play_it_sam(X) :-
     nl, write(" Type in your guess. "),
     nl, readint(G),
     test_and_tell(X,G),
     play_it_sam(X).

/* test and tell the result */

test_and_tell(X,G) :-
            X = G,
            say_you_got_it_right(X).

test_and_tell(X,G) :-
            G > X,
            say_too_big.

test_and_tell(X,G) :-
            G < X,
            say_too_small.
```

```
/* write messages */

say_too_big :-
    nl, write(" Your guess is too big."),
    nl, write(" Try a smaller number.").

say_too_small :-
    nl, write(" Your guess is too small."),
    nl, write(" Try a bigger number.").

say_you_got_it_right(X) :-
    nl, write(" Now you've got it right."),
    nl, write(" It is ",X,"."),
    nl, write("            Good bye !"),
    nl, write(" Press the space bar."),
    nl, readchar(_),
    exit.



/*                    end of program            */
```

Figure 12.1 shows a dialogue with the Number Guess program. Notice that the player takes the computer's advice and uses the interval-halving method as a heuristic.

———————————— Exercises ————————————

12.1. Run the Number Guess program several times. Use the interval-halving strategy to achieve the best results.

12.2. Modify the Number Guess program so that the random number X is between 1 and 10. What is the maximum number of guesses for this domain of X?

12.3. Run the modified Number Guess program several times. Use the interval-halving guessing strategy. What is your maximum number of "best guesses"?

12.4. Modify the program so that it keeps track of the number of the player's guesses. If this count is less than the maximum possible number of trial guesses, display the text "WELL DONE!" in a separate window. (*Hint:* To implement a counter, see Chapter 3 on recursion.)

```
┌─────────────────────────────────────────────────────┐
│      ┌──────── A NUMBER Guessing Game ────────┐      │
│      │ I have thought of a number,            │      │
│      │ Now, it is your turn !                 │      │
│      │                                        │      │
│      │ Type in your guess,                    │      │
│      │ 50                                     │      │
│      │                                        │      │
│      │ Your guess is too big,                 │      │
│      │ Try a smaller number,                  │      │
│      │ Type in your guess,                    │      │
│      │ 25                                     │      │
│      │                                        │      │
│      │ Your guess is too small,               │      │
│      │ Try a bigger number,                   │      │
│      │ Type in your guess,                    │      │
│      │ 37                                     │      │
│      │                                        │      │
│      │ Your guess is too small,               │      │
│      │ Try a bigger number,                   │      │
│      │ Type in your guess,                    │      │
│      └────────────────────────────────────────┘      │
└─────────────────────────────────────────────────────┘
```

Fig. 12.1. *A session with the Number Guess game.*

The Game of 23 Matches

One of many two-player games, 23 Matches is interesting because it can be implemented as a simple game or as a sophisticated one, with many variations. You will learn how to develop a Turbo Prolog program for both simple and sophisticated versions of the game.

The 23 Matches game proceeds as follows: The players begin with 23 matches (or sticks). Each player, in turn, removes 1, 2, or 3 matches. The one who takes the last match is the loser. The object of the game, then, is to force the other player to take the last match.

The first Turbo Prolog program will be developed in the following section.

Design Considerations

There are two versions of the 23 Matches game:

A Single-Pile Version

Pile No.	Configuration	No. of Matches
1	1,2,3, . . . 22,23	23

A Four-Pile Version

Pile No.	Configuration						No. of Matches
1	1	2	3	4	5		5
2	6	7	8	9	10	11	6
3	12	13	14	15	16	17	6
4	18	19	20	21	22	23	6

In the single-pile version, each player in turn takes 1, 2, or 3 matches from each pile. In either case, the total number of matches after each player's turn is important in eventually determining who is the loser.

For simplicity, begin with the single-pile version. To implement this game in Turbo Prolog, you will designate the computer as one player and the user as the other player.

The basic procedure includes several steps:

1. Select the starting number of matches as 23 and place them in a single pile.

2. Ask the user to remove 1, 2, or 3 matches. Update the number of matches remaining in the pile.

    a. If there is only one match left, the computer must remove this last match. In that case, the computer loses.

    b. If there is more than 1 match, go on to step 3.

3. The computer removes 1, 2 or 3 matches. Update the number of matches in the pile.

    a. If only one match is left, the user must remove this last match. In that case, the user loses.

    b. If more than 1 match is left, repeat step 2.

As you can see, the procedure is simple. However, the number of matches removed by a player cumulatively decides the winner of the game. Thus strategy is an important part of the game structure.

The Simple 23 Matches Game Program

To implement a simple game, you may leave the user's game-playing strategy to him or her. Your concern at this point is with the computer as player. The computer must generate a random number 1, 2, or 3 and use the number in the program play module.

To write a Turbo Prolog program for the 23 Matches Game, you need to implement the three steps outlined in the preceding section. The first step is to set the initial number of matches to 23. You can then pass this number to the submodules from the main module in the structure chart of your Turbo Prolog program (see fig. 12. 2).

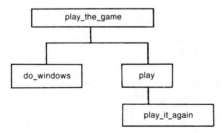

Fig. 12.2. *A structure chart for the Simple 23 Matches Game program .*

The main module is

```
play_the_game :-
          do_windows,
          play(23,0,0).
```

In this module, the rule *do_windows* makes windows and displays helpful information. The rule *play (23,0,0)* actually plays the game. This rule calls other submodules and passes to them the first number, 23.

The rule *play(23,0,0)* is built from the following sub-rule that plays the game sequence repeatedly until a winner is determined:

```
play(M,H,C) :-
          play_it_again(M,H,C).
```

The variables *M, H, C* refer to *matches, human,* and *computer.*

The rule *play_it_again(M,H,C)* is recursive. It has three versions implemented for three possible endings: if the human wins, if the computer wins, and if the play is repeated.

If the human wins, the rule is written in this form:

```
play_it_again(M,H,C) :-
     M <= 0,
     nl, write(" You, the human, won !"), nl,
     nl, write(" Press the SPACE bar."),
     readchar(_),
     clearwindow, !
```

The equational predicate $M \leq 0$ indicates that the computer has made the last move. In doing so, it has taken all the matches (so M=0), or it has taken more matches than there actually are (M<0). In either case, the computer is the loser, and the human is the winner.

If the computer wins, the rule is

```
play_it_again(M,H,C) :-
    M = 1,
    nl, write(" I, the computer, won !"), nl,
    readchar(_),
    clearwindow, !
```

In this version of the rule, the equational predicate $M = 1$ indicates that the current value of the number of matches is 1 and that this last match must be removed by the human on the next turn. Thus the computer is the winner. Both the first and second versions of the *play_it_again* rule exit from the program when they succeed.

The third version of the rule is the heart of the game-playing sequence. It is

```
play_it_again(M,H,C) :-
    nl, write(" Your turn."),
    nl, write(" How many would you remove ? "),
    readint(Hn),
    M2 = M - Hn,
    H2 = Hn,
    write(" Now there is (are) ",M2," match(es)."),
    nl, nl, write(" My turn."),
    nl, write(" I am deciding !"),
    random(F),
    Rea = 1 + 3 * F,
    real_int(Rea,Rint),
    M3 = M2 - Rint,
    nl, write(" I remove ",Rint,"."),
    nl, write(" Now there is(are) ",M3," match(es)."),nl,
    M7 = M3,
    H7 = H2,
    C7 = Rint,
    play_it_again(M7,H7,C7).
```

This version of the rule accepts the user's input, updates the number of matches, and displays the updated value. The rule then continues to accept the computer's input (a random integer number, 1, 2, or 3), updates the number of matches, and displays the updated value. This third version is a recursive rule, as required by the need to *play_it_again*.

These rules are used in the Simple 23 Matches Game program shown in listing 12.2. The program uses Turbo Prolog's window facilities and to display helpful text and prompts.

```
/* Program: Simple 23 Matches Game    File: PROG1202.PRO */
/* Purpose. To demonstrate a game of 23-match.         */
/* Direction. Run the program. A goal is given.        */

predicates

    play_the_game
    do_windows
    play(integer,integer,integer)
    play_it_again(integer,integer,integer)
    real_int(real,integer)

goal

    play_the_game.

clauses

    /* goal as rule */

    play_the_game :-
            do_windows,
            play(23,0,0).

    do_windows :-
        makewindow(1,7,7,"",0,0,25,80),
        makewindow(2,7,7," Game of 23 Matches ",1,5,22,40),
        nl, write(" Welcome to the game of 23 Matches."),
        M = 23,
        H = 0,
        C = 0,
        nl, write(" There are ",M," matches to begin."),
        nl, write(" We will take turns removing matches."),nl,
        nl, write(" Each time you may remove 1, 2, or 3"),
        nl, write(" matches and then I'll do the same."),nl,
        nl, write(" The player who has to remove"),
        nl, write(" the last match will lose."),
        nl, write(" To begin, there are 23 matches."),
        nl, write(" The human has removed ",H," match."),
        nl, write(" The computer has removed ",C," match."), nl.
```

```
play(M,H,C) :-
    play_it_again(M,H,C).

/* rule to test for winner */

play_it_again(M,_,_) :-
    M <= 0,
    nl, write(" You've won !"), nl,
    nl, write(" Press the SPACE bar."),
    readchar(_),
    clearwindow, !,
    exit.

play_it_again(M,_,_) :-
    M = 1,
    nl, write(" I, the computer, won !"), nl,
    readchar(_),
    clearwindow, !,
    exit.

play_it_again(M,_,_) :-
    nl, write(" Your turn."),
    nl, write(" How many do you want to remove ?"),
    readint(Hn),
    M2 = M - Hn,
    H2 = Hn,
    write(" Now there are ",M2," match(es)."),
    nl, nl, write(" My turn."),
    nl, write(" I am deciding !"),
    random(F),
    Rea = 0.5 + 3 * F,
    real_int(Rea,Rint),
    M3 = M2 - Rint,
    nl, write(" I removed ",Rint,"."),
    nl, write(" Now there is(are) ",M3," match(es)."), nl,
    M7 = M3,
    H7 = H2,
    C7 = Rint,
    play_it_again(M7,H7,C7).
```

```
/* house-keeping rule */

   real_int(Re,In) :- Re = In.


/*                    end of program              */
```

Figure 12.3 shows a dialogue between the user and the program. The display of the dialogue between the computer and the user is made simple and clear so that the user can inspect the situation and decide what number to enter. The user can use his or her own winning strategy. The computer picks the number 1, 2, or 3 randomly; it uses no strategy other than luck. The user therefore has a greater chance of winning than does the computer.

```
┌──────────────────────────────────────────────────┐
│   ┌──────── Game of 23 Matches ────────┐          │
│   │ How many do you want to remove ?1   │          │
│   │ Now there are 6 match(es).          │          │
│   │                                     │          │
│   │ My turn.                            │          │
│   │ I am deciding !                     │          │
│   │ I removed 3.                        │          │
│   │ Now there is(are) 3 match(es).      │          │
│   │                                     │          │
│   │ Your turn.                          │          │
│   │ How many do you want to remove ?2   │          │
│   │ Now there are 1 match(es).          │          │
│   │                                     │          │
│   │ My turn.                            │          │
│   │ I am deciding !                     │          │
│   │ I removed 1.                        │          │
│   │ Now there is(are) 0 match(es).      │          │
│   │                                     │          │
│   │ You've won !                        │          │
│   │                                     │          │
│   │ Press the SPACE bar.                │          │
│   └─────────────────────────────────────┘          │
└──────────────────────────────────────────────────┘
```

Fig. 12.3. *A session with the Simple 23 Matches Game program.*

Exercises

12.5. Run the Simple 23 Matches program 10 times. How many times can you win?

12.6. Assume that you want to implement the four-pile version of the game. Write the steps to establish the procedure. (*Hint:* you need to start with four piles of matches, generate more random numbers, and update all the piles as the game progresses.)

12.7. Modify the program using the procedure you established in the preceding exercise. Run the program and observe the procedures of both the computer and the user.

An Intelligent 23 Matches Game Program

In the Simple 23 Matches Game, the computer as a player was programmed to choose at random the number of matches to remove. The computer was playing without a winning strategy. The Intelligent 23 Matches Game program shows you how to implement a winning strategy (or heuristic) for the computer.

In this game of 23 Matches, you will recall, each player tries to leave one match for the other player to remove. The initial number of matches is 23, the final target number is 1, and each player may remove 1, 2, or 3 matches. Thus you can see that the initial, intermediate, and final number of matches form a sequence with reference to each player.

To demonstrate the patterns of the sequence, two game sequences are shown in Table 12.2.

Table 12.2
23 Matches Game Sequences

Number removed by the user		Number left	Number removed by the computer	Number left	Remarks
Sequence	3	20	3	17	
No. 1	3	14	1	13	
	3	10	1	9	
	3	6	1	5	
	1	4	3	1	Computer wins
Sequence	1	22	1	21	
No. 2	2	19	2	17	
	3	14	1	13	
	2	11	2	9	
	1	8	3	5	
	2	3	2	1	Computer wins

In the first game, the sequences are as follows:

S = [23,20,17,14,13,10,9,6,5,4,1]

S = [23,17,13,9,5,1] left for the user

S = [20,14,10,6,4] left for the computer

In the second game, the sequences are

S = [23,22,21,19,17,14,13,9,8,5,3,2,1]

S = [23,21,17,13,9,5,1] left for the user

S = [22,19,14,11,8,3] left for the computer.

Analysis shows that certain numbers in the sequences are undesirable to have left for you. These numbers include 2, 3, 4, 6, 7,and 8. The numbers 1, 5, and 9, however, are considered safe.

In the sequences shown for the two games, notice that both of the user's sequences contain the "unsafe" numbers. The computer's first sequence contains 6 and 4, both of which are "safe" numbers.

The analysis reveals that each player tries to leave the "unsafe" numbers for the opponent. Therefore, it is interesting to find the relation between the number to be removed and the "unsafe" number to be left for the opponent. Game enthusiasts and theorists have studied this aspect of the game and offered various solutions to the problem.

A simplified version of a formulation is given here. If M is the number of matches left, remove C number of matches. The value of C is calculated by the formula:

$$C = (R + 3) - 4 * \text{integer} \, ((R + 3)/4)$$

where

$$R = M - (4 * \text{integer} \, (M/4))$$

Notice that the term "integer" implies an integer value of the expression in parentheses. Here are a few values of M and C. For example, if M = 8, then C = 3; and if M = 6, C = 1.

These rules can be transcribed into Turbo Prolog rules. The sequence of their transcription is as shown:

```
A_r = M2 / 4 - 0.45,
real_int(A_r, A_int),
A1_int = M2 - (4 * A_int),
A2_r = (A1_int + 3) / 4 - 0.45,
real_int(A2_r, A2_int),
A3_int = (A1_int +) - (4 * A2, int),
```

These subrules bind *A3_int* to the integer value of the number of matches to be removed. (The rule *real_int* is for conversion of a real number to an integer.)

The winning strategy outlined here can be used as a Turbo Prolog rule to replace the random-number strategy that was used in the Simple 23 Matches Game. The result is the Intelligent 23 Matches Game program, in listing 12.3.

```
/* Program: Intelligent 23 Matches Game    File:PROG1203.PRO */
/* Purpose: To demonstrate a game of 23 matches.           */
/*          A winning strategy is included.                */
/* Direction: Run the program. A goal is given.            */

predicates

    play_the_game
    do_windows
    play(integer,integer,integer)
    play_it_again(integer,integer,integer)
    real_int(real,integer)

goal

    play_the_game.

clauses

    /* goal as rule */

    play_the_game :-
            do_windows,
            play(23,0,0).

    /* rule to make windows */

    do_windows :-
        makewindow(1,7,7,"",0,0,25,80),
        makewindow(2,7,7," Game of 23 Matches ",1,5,22,40),
        makewindow(3,7,7," Observer ",1,50,10,20),
        cursor(2,2),
        write("RESULT UDATE"),
        gotowindow(2),
        nl, write(" Welcome to the game of 23 Matches."),
        M = 23,
```

```
      H = 0,
      C = 0,
      nl, write(" There are ",M," matches to begin."),
      nl, write(" Human removed ",H," match."),
      nl, write(" Computer removed ",C," match."), nl.

/* rule to play */

play(M,H,C) :-
   play_it_again(M,H,C).

/* rule to say human is the winner */

play_it_again(M,_,_) :-
   M <= 0,
   nl, write(" You the human won !"), nl,
   makewindow(4,7,7," Result ",13,50,10,15),
   nl, write("       YOU WON !"), nl, nl, nl,
   /* a tag for you */
   sound(4,392),
   sound(4,440),
   sound(4,494),
   sound(4,440),
   sound(4,494),
   sound(12,392),
   nl, write(" Press the SPACE bar."),
   readchar(_),
   clearwindow, !,
   exit.

/* rule to say computer is the winner */

play_it_again(M,_,_) :-
   M = 1,
   nl, write(" I the computer won !"), nl,
   makewindow(5,7,7," Result ",13,50,10,20),
   nl, write("       I WON !"), nl, nl, nl,
   /* a tag for you */
   sound(4,394),
   sound(4,440),
   sound(4,494),
   sound(4,440),
   sound(4,494),
```

```
        sound(12,392),
        nl, write(" Press SPACE bar."),
        readchar(_),
        clearwindow, !,
        exit.

/* rule to play repeatedly */

play_it_again(M,_,_) :-
    nl, write(" Your turn."),
    nl, write(" How many would you remove ? "),
    readint(Hn),
    M2 = M - Hn,
    H2 = Hn,
    write(" Now there is(are) ",M2," match(es)."),
    gotowindow(3),
    cursor(4,3),
    write(M2," match(es)   "),
    gotowindow(2),
    nl, nl, write(" My turn."),
    nl, write(" I am thinking !"),
    A_r = M2/4 - 0.45,
    real_int(A_r,A_int),
    A1_int = M2 - (4 * A_int),
    A2_r = (A1_int + 3)/4 - 0.45,
    real_int(A2_r,A2_int),
    A3_int = (A1_int + 3) - (4 * A2_int),
    M3 = M2 - A3_int,
    nl, write(" I removed ",A3_int,"."), nl,
    write(" Now there is(are) ",M3," match(es)."), nl,
    gotowindow(3),
    cursor(4,3), write(M3," match(es)   "),
    gotowindow(2),
    M7 = M3,
    H7 = H2,
    C7 = A3_int,
    play_it_again(M7,H7,C7).

/* rule to convert real into integer */

    real_int(Re,In) :- Re = In.

/*                  end of program                      */
```

The Intelligent 23 Matches Game program displays the number of matches in the pile. Then it accepts the user's input for the number of matches to be removed from the pile, updates the number of matches in the pile, and displays the updated number.

For the computer's turn, the program uses the winning-formula strategy to generate the number of matches to be removed from the pile. The program then updates the number of matches in the pile and displays the updated number.

Play is repeated until one of the players wins. Then the winner is declared and a musical tag is played.

Notice that this program provides two extra windows on the right side of the screen. The top one shows the updated number of matches after each play. The lower window displays the winner of the game.

Figure 12.4 shows a session of the Intelligent 23 Matches Game. Notice that the computer is the winner.

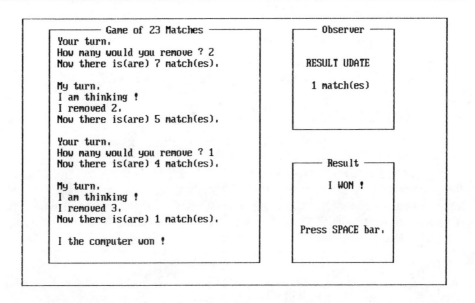

Fig. 12.4. *A session with the Intelligent 23 Matches Game program.*

————————————————— **Exercises** —————————————————

12.8. Run the Intelligent 23 Matches Game program and play 10 games. Did you win any? Did you try to use the same strategy or a different one?

12.9. Modify the winning strategy rule so that the human user has about a 40% chance to win. (*Hint:* you need to modify the formulae or invent your own winning strategy.)

12.10. Run the modified program and play several games.

The Monkey and Bananas Problem

The Monkey and Bananas problem is a classic AI problem that shows common-sense reasoning in Turbo Prolog programming. The problem can be stated as follows:

A monkey is enclosed in a room. In the room are a box on the floor and a bunch of bananas hanging from the ceiling, out of reach of the monkey. The solution to the problem is the sequence of actions that would allow the monkey to get the bananas.

The sequence can be stated as follows:

The monkey goes to the box and pushes the box to the spot under the bananas. Then the monkey climbs on top of the box and grasps the bananas.

Program Design Considerations

A program that solves the monkey and bananas problem must include some specific facts in the database. They are the monkey's position in the room, the box's position in the room, the position on the floor above which the bunch of bananas is hung, and whether the monkey is on the box or not. In this problem, the positions of the bananas, the box, and the monkey are variable. The monkey and the box, however, can be anywhere on the floor. These positions and box can be represented by variables. The preceding considerations lead to the following database facts:

The bananas are above a position from 1 to 10.

The box is initially at a position from 1 to 10.

The monkey is initially at a position from 1 to 10.

The monkey is not on the box.

The monkey does not have the bananas.

These facts describe the *initial state* of the problem. If the monkey is successful in its work, the *final state* of the problem will be described by the following facts:

The bananas are at the initial position.

The box is at the same position as the bananas.

The monkey is at the same position as the bananas.

The monkey is on the box.

The monkey grasps the bananas.

Next, you need to build rules to transform the initial state to the final state. Here are some plausible rule forms

```
move_to(box, position,position).
move_to(monkey, position,position).
go_to(position, position,position).
push_box(position, position,position).
climb_box.
grasp_bananas.
```

The first *move_to* rule is for moving the box to a new location, and the second *move_to* rule is for moving the monkey to a new location. The *go_to* rule is for logically transporting the box or the monkey from one position to another. The *push_box* rule is for the monkey's pushing of the box to another location. The *climb_box* rule is for the monkey's climbing on top of the box. The *grasp_bananas* rule is for grasping the bananas.

The Monkey and Bananas Program

Using the database and the rules indicated in the preceding section, you can write a Turbo Prolog program that solves the Monkey and Bananas problem. The structure chart for the program is shown in figure 12.5.

The main module in the structure chart is *solve_the_problem*. This module calls the submodules *request_positions*. The first module prompts the user to enter positions for the monkey, box, and bananas. These positions are bound to the variables *M*, *Bo*, and *B*. The module *monkey_works* calls four modules: *move_to(box,B,B1)*, *move_to(monkey,B,B1)*, *climb_box*, and *grasp_bananas*. The module *move_to(box,B)* calls the module *push_box(C,B)*, which in turn calls the module *move_to(monkey,B)*. This last module calls the module *go_to(C,B)* to perform the move from one position to another. The *climb_box* module provides the climbing action for the monkey and the *grasp_bananas* modules provides the grasping action for the monkey.

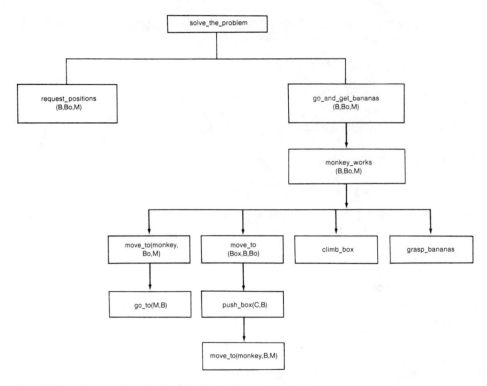

Fig. 12.5. *A structure chart for the Monkey and Bananas program.*

The Monkey and Bananas program, in listing 12.4, is an implementation of the design just described.

```
/* Program: Monkey and Bananas  File: PROG1204.PRO */
/* Purpose: To show a solution to the monkey and   */
/*          bananas puzzle.                         */

database

   is_at(symbol,integer)
   monkey_is_off_box
```

```
predicates

   solve_the_problem
      request_positions(integer,integer,integer)
      go_and_get_bananas(integer,integer,integer)
         monkey_works(integer,integer,integer)
            move_to(symbol,integer,integer)
            go_to(integer,integer)
            push_box(integer,integer)
            climb_box
            grasp_bananas

goal

   solve_the_problem.

clauses

   /* database */

      monkey_is_off_box.

      is_at(bananas,1).   is_at(bananas,2).
      is_at(bananas,3).   is_at(bananas,4).
      is_at(bananas,5).   is_at(bananas,6).
      is_at(bananas,7).   is_at(bananas,8).
      is_at(bananas,9).   is_at(bananas,10).

      is_at(box,1).       is_at(box,2).
      is_at(box,3).       is_at(box,4).
      is_at(box,5).       is_at(box,6).
      is_at(box,7).       is_at(box,8).
      is_at(box,9).       is_at(box,10).

      is_at(monkey,1).    is_at(monkey,2).
      is_at(monkey,3).    is_at(monkey,4).
      is_at(monkey,5).    is_at(monkey,6).
      is_at(monkey,7).    is_at(monkey,8).
      is_at(monkey,9).    is_at(monkey,10).

   /* rules to get bananas */
```

```
solve_the_problem :-

    makewindow(1,7,7,"",0,0,25,80),
    makewindow(2,7,7," MONKEY AND BANANAS ",
            1,10,23,50),

    request_positions(B,Bo,M),

    nl, write(" Monkey is thinking."),
    nl, write(" 'I want those bananas"),
        write(" hanging up there !'"), nl,

    go_and_get_bananas(B,Bo,M),

    write(" Monkey gets the bananas !"), nl, nl,
    write("    THREE CHEERS !!!"), nl, nl,
    write(" Press the SPACE BAR."),
    readchar(_).

request_positions(B,Bo,M) :-
    nl, nl,
    write(" Enter position of the bananas(1-10). "),
    readint(B),
    write(" Enter position of the box(1-10). "),
    readint(Bo),
    write(" Enter position of monkey(1-10). "),
    readint(M).

go_and_get_bananas(B,Bo,M) :-
    is_at(bananas,B),
    is_at(box,Bo),
    is_at(monkey,M),
    monkey_works(B,Bo,M).

monkey_works(B,Bo,M) :-
    nl, write(" Monkey looks around and spies the box."),
    move_to(monkey,Bo,M),
    nl, write(" Monkey goes from ",M," to ",Bo,"."),
    move_to(box,B,Bo),
    nl, write(" Monkey pushes the box from ",Bo," to ",B,"."), nl,
    climb_box,
    grasp_bananas.
```

```
move_to(monkey,B,M) :-
    is_at(monkey,B);
    is_at(monkey,M),
    go_to(M,B),
    fail.

move_to(box,B,M) :-
    is_at(box,B);
    is_at(box,C),
    push_box(C,B).

go_to(B,C) :-
    monkey_is_off_box,
    retract(is_at(monkey,B)),
    assert(is_at(monkey,C)),
    nl, write(" Monkey goes ",B," to ",C,".").

push_box(B,C) :-
    monkey_is_off_box,
    move_to(monkey,B,M),
    retract(is_at(monkey,B)),
    retract(is_at(box,B)),
    assert(is_at(monkey,C)),
    assert(is_at(box,C)).

climb_box :-
    monkey_is_off_box,
    retract(monkey_is_off_box),
    write(" Monkey climbs the box."), nl.

grasp_bananas :-
    write(" Monkey grasps the bananas."), nl.

/*              end of program              */
```

The database for the Monkey and Bananas program consists of these clauses:

```
monkey_is_off_box.

is_at(bananas,1).   is_at(bananas,2).
is_at(bananas,3).   is_at(bananas,4).
is_at(bananas,5).   is_at(bananas,6).
is_at(bananas,7).   is_at(bananas,8).
is_at(bananas,9).   is_at(bananas,10).
```

```
is_at(box,1).        is_at(box,2).
is_at(box,3).        is_at(box,4).
is_at(box,5).        is_at(box,6).
is_at(box,7).        is_at(box,8).
is_at(box,9).        is_at(box,10).

is_at(monkey,1).     is_at(monkey,2).
is_at(monkey,3).     is_at(monkey,4).
is_at(monkey,5).     is_at(monkey,6).
is_at(monkey,7).     is_at(monkey,8).
is_at(monkey,9).     is_at(monkey,10).
```

The first clause is a mere statement of the fact that the monkey is off the box. The other clauses indicate possible positions of the bananas, the monkey, and the box.

The goal module is

```
solve_the_problem :-

        makewindow(1,7,7,"",0,0,25,80),
        makewindow(2,7,7," MONKEY AND BANANAS ",
                    1,10,23,50),

        request_positions(B,Bo,M),

        nl, write(" Monkey is thinking."),
        nl, write(" 'I want those bananas"),
        write(" hanging up there !'"), nl,

        go_and_get_bananas(B,Bo,M),

        write(" Monkey gets the bananas !"), nl, nl,
        write("      THREE CHEERS !!!"), nl, nl,
        write(" Press the SPACE BAR."),
        readchar(_).
```

This module displays informative text in a window on the screen. Then it calls two sub-modules, *request_positions* and *go_and_get_bananas*. The second module proceeds to "get the bananas" by calling the *monkey_works* module. Then the main module displays some concluding text.

The *monkey_works* rule is implemented as shown:

```
monkey_works(B,Bo,M) :-
    nl, write(" Monkey looks around and spies the box."),
    move_to(monkey,Bo,M),
    nl, write(" Monkey goes from ",M," to ",Bo,"."),
    move_to(box,B,Bo),
    nl, write(" Monkey pushes the box from ",Bo," to ",B,"."), nl,
    climb_box,
    grasp_bananas.
```

In this module, the major task is broken down into a sequence of smaller tasks. The *move_to* and the *go_to* rules work together to move the monkey from one location to another:

```
move_to(monkey,B,M) :-
    is_at(monkey,B);
    is_at(monkey,M),
    go_to(M,B),
    fail.

move_to(box,B,M) :-
    is_at(box,B);
    is_at(box,C),
    push_box(C,B).

go_to(B,C) :-
    monkey_is_off_box,
    retract(is_at(monkey,B)),
    assert(is_at(monkey,C)),
    nl, write(" Monkey goes ",B," to ",C,".").
```

The *move-to* rule specifies that the position values instantiated to *B* and C be valid values. The *go_to* rule essentially *retracts* the monkey's old position and *asserts* the monkey's new position.

The rules *move_to* and *push_box* work together to move the box from one location to another:

```
move_to(box,B,M) :-
    is_at(box,B);
    is_at(box,C),
    push_box(C,B).
```

```
push_box(B,C) :-
    monkey_is_off_box,
    move_to(monkey,B,M),
    retract(is_at(monkey,B)),
    retract(is_at(box,B)),
    assert(is_at(monkey,C)),
    assert(is_at(box,C)).
```

The *move_to* rule specifies that the position values instantiated to B and C be valid values, and it passes those values (parameters) to the *push_box* rule. The *push_box* rule calls the rule *move_to(monkey,B,M)* to involve the monkey in pushing the box to another location. The *push_box* rule retracts the old positions of the monkey and the box and asserts new positions for them.

When the final position of the monkey and the box is attained, the *climb_box* and *grasp_bananas* rules cause the monkey to climb the box and grasp the bananas:

```
climb_box :-
    monkey_is_off_box,
    retract(monkey_is_off_box),
    write(" Monkey climbs the box."), nl.


grasp_bananas :-
    write(" Monkey grasps the bananas."), nl.
```

The body of the *climb_box* rule retracts the clause *monkey_is_off_box* so that, logically, the monkey climbs on top of the box. The *grasp_bananas* rule is a parameterless rule that simulates the monkey's grasping action.

Figure 12.6 shows a run session of the Monkey and Bananas program. The print shows the information on the initial positions of the box and the monkey and the position above which the bananas are hung. Then a short scenario text shows the monkey's progress as the rules work through the program.

The Monkey and Bananas problem is solved using a state-space representation. That is, the state of the system (monkey, box and bananas) is represented in terms of the positions of the monkey, the box, and the bananas. For this problem, a state is defined by five parameters:

state(B, Bo, M, C, G)

where *B* is the position of the bananas, *Bo* is the position of the box, *M* is the position of the monkey, *C* indicates whether the monkey is on or off the box , and *G* indicates whether the monkey has grasped the bananas (0 = no grasp, 1 = grasp). The initial state is

state(5, 10, 1, 0, 0)

```
┌─────────────────── MONKEY AND BANANAS ───────────────────┐
│                                                          │
│  Enter position of the bananas(1-10), 5                  │
│  Enter position of the box(1-10), 10                     │
│  Enter position of monkey(1-10), 1                       │
│                                                          │
│  Monkey is thinking,                                     │
│  'I want those bananas hanging up there !'               │
│                                                          │
│  Monkey looks around and spies the box,                  │
│  Monkey goes from 1 to 10,                               │
│  Monkey pushes the box from 10 to 5,                     │
│  Monkey climbs the box,                                  │
│  Monkey grasps the bananas,                              │
│  Monkey gets the bananas !                               │
│                                                          │
│       THREE CHEERS !!!                                   │
│                                                          │
│  Press the SPACE BAR,                                    │
│                                                          │
│                                                          │
└──────────────────────────────────────────────────────────┘
```

Fig. 12.6. *A session with the Monkey and Bananas program.*

and the final state is

state(5, 5, 5, 1, 1)

The Turbo Prolog rules are operators that act on the states to transform them into new states. In this problem, the initial state is operated on by the rules to arrive at the final state. Figure 12.7 shows a state-transition diagram for this problem.

The method used in the Monkey and Bananas program is an example of *backward chaining*. The program starts with the goal and works backward through the subgoals during the unification process. In Prolog, the left side of the rule (the rule-head) is the goal. The right side of the rule (the rule-body with subgoals) is used for matching the subgoals with data in the database. If the matching processes succeed, the left side of the rule succeeds. For this reason, backward chaining systems are known as *goal-driven systems*. The rule-based Dog Expert System you worked with in Chapter 10 is an example of a backward chaining expert system.

Exercise

12.11. Modify the Monkey and Bananas program so that the monkey also needs a stick to reach the bananas.

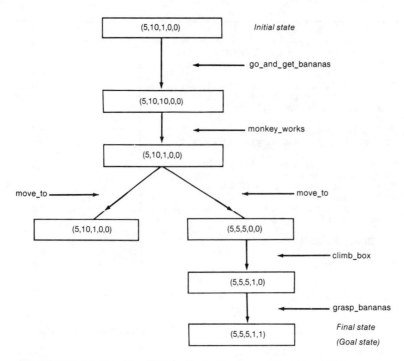

Fig. 12.7. *A state-transition diagram for the Monkey and Bananas problem.*

The Smith Family Reunion Puzzle

The last program in this chapter is one of those seemingly simple deductive logic problems where the player thinks the answer must be obvious. Of course, it isn't, simply
because the available data is a set of many related facts that must all be considered to
determine the solution. Turbo Prolog's powerful internal unification routines are the
major tools used in the Family Reunion Program.

Statement of the Problem

As a framework for the logic problem solver, think of a hypothetical family reunion. The
Smith family is getting together for the first time in several years. The four Smith sisters
have married. Through casual conversation, they discover that certain habits and interests might make it possible for two or more of the couples to spend an enjoyable vacation
together.

The categories of the couples' interests and habits are

1. Dietary customs and interests
2. Entertainment preferences
3. Vacation preferences
4. Morning rise-time habits

The facts about the couples' interests and habits, in addition to the names of the married couples, are stored in a database. The user is to identify two couples who have similar interests, based on the information given.

Designing the Logic Program

To solve the logic puzzle, you will need to create a database and a set of rules. In the design of the database, you may consider a unit in which the married couples are identified. A database predicate such as the one shown will be suitable for this purpose:

```
married(string,string)
```

The objects of each predicate are the names of the four Smith sisters and their husbands.

For the couples' habits and interests, the database predicates are

```
diet(string,string)
entertainment(string,string)
location(string,string)
rise_time(string,string)
```

The objects of each of these predicates are the names of the husband for each couple and the data as expressed in the conversations overheard. Cases where a couple expresses indifference to an interest or habit will result in two predicates. For example, the statement "[Ron] can eat any kind of food" gives rise to the following two predicates:

```
diet("Ron","vegetarian").
diet("Ron","non-vegetarian").
```

Both of these predicates can be used in the matching process.

To assist the player (user), the program contains a menu from which the player can view couples and their habits and interests. To write rules to view the couples and their interests, you will need a number of *process* rules. One rule, for example, can match the couples according to their dietary preferences. The basic rule-body should contain these predicates:

```
process(1) :-
    clearwindow,
    nl, write(" Turbo Prolog has searched "),
    nl, write(" the list of dietary preferences"),
```

```
nl, write(" and marriage matches."),
nl, write(" This search shows that "), nl,
married(X1,Y1),
diet(X1,D1),
nl, write(" ",X1," or ",Y1," or both "),
nl, write(" like ",D1," food."),
nl, write(" --Press the SPACE bar to continue."),
nl, readchar(_),
fail.
```

In this rule, *X1* and *Y1* are the variables for the couples' names, and *D1* is the variable for the couple's dietary preference. In the matching process, *X1* and *Y1* are bound to the values for the husband and wife in each *married* predicate, and *D1* is bound to the *diet* variable associated with the husband's name. The *write* predicates display the information on the screen for the player. Similar *process* rules are developed for the other interests and habits.

Next, a series of rules needs to be developed to match the couples according to their similar interests and habits. From a second menu, the player selects the category within which all the possible matches will be displayed. The rules to match the couples and their interests, called "process" rules, are written. The basic rule-body for any two matching couples and diet preferences contains these predicates:

```
process(1) :-
clearwindow,
nl,write(" Turbo Prolog has searched the list"),
nl,write(" of dietary preferences and found "),
nl, write(" a match. It has also searched the"),
nl, write(" list of married people and put "),
nl, write(" husbands and wives together."), nl,
nl, write(" The results are:  "),
married(X1,Y1),
diet(X1,D1),
married(X2,Y2),
X1 <> X2,
diet(X2,D2),
D1 = D2,
nl, write(" ",X1," and ",Y1,", and ",X2," and ",Y2),
nl, write(" are possible matching couples "),
nl, write(" eating ",D1," food."), nl,
nl, --Press the SPACE bar to continue."),
nl, readchar(_),
fail.
```

In this rule, *X1* and *1* are the variables for the first couple in the database, and *X2* and *Y2* are the variables for the second couple in the database. Note that $X1 <> X2$ is needed so that a couple is not matched with itself. To begin the matching process that is carried out here, *X1* and *Y1* are bound to the values "John" and "Mary", and *D1* is bound to the value "vegetarian". *X2* and *Y2* are bound to the values "Sam" and "Jane", and *D2* is bound to the value "non-vegetarian". Because "vegetarian" and "non-vegetarian" do not match, this rule fails.

Turbo Prolog returns to the database and binds *X2* and *Y2* to the next couple, "Ron" and "Amy" and then binds *D2* to the value "vegetarian", associated with "Ron" in the *diet* database predicate. Since "vegetarian" matches "vegetarian", the rule succeeds, and the three *write* lines display the match on the screen. The *readchar* predicate receives the user's input character and the rule backtracks the process until all possible matches have been made and displayed. Similar process rules are developed for the other interests and habits.

When the player has viewed all the initial data and the matching couples, he or she may choose to view the program solution—that is, the matching couples whose interests are most compatible. In this case, the process involves multiple pattern-matching. The rule-body is similar to the ones previously described, with the difference that the program determines whether there are two couples, *X1* and *Y1* and *X2* and *Y2*, who have all interests in common. That is,

$D1 = D2, E1 = E2, L1 = L2$ and $R1 = R2$,

where *D* represents the dietary habits, *E* the entertainment interests, *L* the vacation location preferences, and *R* the rise-time habits of the two couples.

When the program finds a match, the couples and the matching interests are displayed on the screen. The final predicate returns control to the first menu and the player exits from there.

The Family Reunion Program

The preceding considerations lead to a program with the structure chart shown in figure 12.8.

In the structure chart, the main module *do_the_job* calls the submodule *show_menu_1*, which in turn calls the submodules *process(1)* through *process(4)* to display the initial data. The submodule *process(6)* exits the program. The submodule *process(5)* calls the submodule *show_menu_2*, which in turn calls the six process modules to do the matching. With this structure chart, you could write a Turbo Prolog program that handles the logic of the puzzle quite well. The structure chart is specific, but its design is flexible and may be adapted for a wide variety of logic applications. The complete Family Reunion program is shown in listing 12.5.

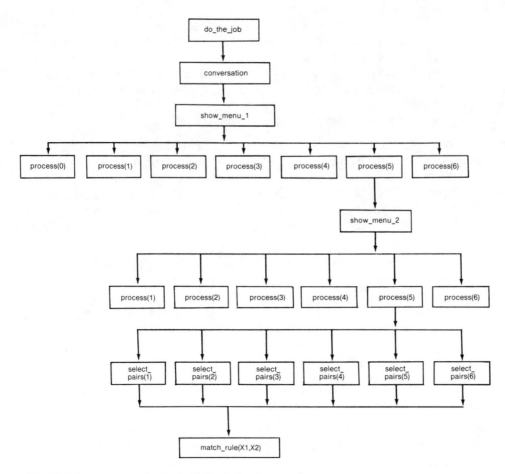

Fig. 12.8. *Structure chart for the Smith Family Reunion program.*

```
/* Program: Family Reunion        File: PROG1205.PRO */
/* Purpose: Puzzle solving in Turbo Prolog          */
/* Direction: Run the program. A goal is provided.  */

domains

   P, Q, R                    = integer

database

   married(string,string)
   diet(string,string)
```

```
        entertainment(string,string)
        location(string,string)
        rise_time(string,string)

predicates

    show_menu_1
    show_menu_2
    repeat
    process(P)
    proces(Q)
    do_the_job
    conversation
    select_pairs(R)
    match_rule(string,string).

goal

    do_the_job.

clauses

    /* database */

    /* declare married couples */

        married("John","Mary").
        married("Sam", "Jane").
        married("Ron", "Amy").
        married("Bill","Alice").

    /* establish diet information */

        diet("John","vegetarian").
        diet("Sam","non-vegetarian").
        diet("Ron","vegetarian").
        diet("Ron","non-vegetarian").
        diet("Bill","vegetarian").
        diet("Bill","non-vegetarian").
```

```
/* establish entertainment */

    entertainment("John","movies").
    entertainment("Sam", "movies").
    entertainment("Ron", "movies").
    entertainment("Ron", "dancing").
    entertainment("Bill","dancing").

/* establish preferred location */

    location("John","city").
    location("John","country").
    location("Sam", "country").
    location("Ron", "country").
    location("Bill","city").

/* establish personal habits */

    rise_time("John","early").
    rise_time("Sam", "late").
    rise_time("Ron", "early").
    rise_time("Bill","late").

/* rule to repeat */

    repeat.
    repeat :- repeat.

/* goal as a rule */

do_the_job :-
    makewindow(1,7,7," The Smith Family Reunion ",0,0,25,80),
    nl, write("  The four Smith sisters have all married. Returning to "),
    nl, write("  their parents' home for a family reunion, the four "),
    nl, write("  couples discovered that they have several interests and"),
    nl, write("  habits in common. In fact, the girls thought that perhaps"),
    nl, write("  two or more of the couples had enough in common that they"),
    nl, write("  could spend their summer vacation together."), nl,
    nl, write("  The married couples are: John and Mary; Sam and Jane"),
    nl, write("        Ron and Amy; and Bill and Alice."), nl,
    nl, write("        If you match the facts and interests each"),
    nl, write("        person reveals in casual conversation, you "),
    nl, write("        will know the couples that are best suited "),
```

```
          nl, write("       for a pleasant and rewarding vacation together. "),
          nl, write("       Each person speaks for both spouses as married "),
          nl, write("       people often do."),
          nl, nl, write("  The random snatches of conversation"),
             write(" overheard are shown next."),
          nl, write("  Then you will be able to view"),
             write(" the data and see the matches "),
          nl, write("  the conversation would imply. "),
          nl, write("  Finally, the matching couples will be shown."),
          nl, write("  --Press the SPACE BAR to continue."),
          readchar(_),
          clearwindow,
          conversation.

conversation:-
      makewindow(3,7,7," Conversation overheard ",2,4,20,68),
          nl, write("   These are the pertinent snatches of conversation "),
          nl, write("   that were overheard. "), nl,
          nl, write(" Mary prefers movies as entertainment;"),
             write(" she likes to rise early."),
          nl, write(" Sam likes to vacation in the country;"),
             write(" he really prefers "),
          nl, write(" vegetarian food."),
          nl, write(" Ron would be happy with either movies"),
             write(" or dancing. He can eat any"),
          nl, write(" kind of food."),
          nl, write(" Alice is happy eating any kind of food;"),
             write(" exploring a new city is"),
          nl, write(" her favorite vacation."),
          nl, write(" John is not a vegetarian and can be"),
             write(" happy vacationing in the"),
          nl, write(" city or in the country."),
          nl, write(" Jane likes movies as entertainment;"),
             write(" she is a late riser."),
          nl, write(" Amy rises early; she likes vacations"),
             write(" in the country."),
          nl, write(" Bill likes to go dancing frequently."),
             write(" He is a late riser."), nl,
          nl, write(" --Press the SPACE BAR to continue."),
          readchar(_),
          show_menu_1.
```

```
/* rule to show information window */

show_menu_1 :-
  repeat,
  makewindow(4,7,7," Information Window ",2,2,22,38),nl,
  write(" Enter one of the numbers shown"),nl,
  write(" to view the information below "), nl,nl,
  write(" 0. The Married Couples.   "),nl,
  write(" 1. Diet Interests.     "),nl,
  write(" 2. Entertainment Interests."),nl,
  write(" 3. Vacation Location Interests."),nl,
  write(" 4. Rising Habits.        "),nl,
  write(" 5. to go to the Matching Menu."), nl,
  write(" 6. to exit the program."), nl, nl,
  write(" Please enter your choice: (0-6) "),
  readint(P),
  P < 7,
  process(P),
  P >= 7, !.


/* show the married couples */

process(0) :-
   clearwindow,
   write("   Married Couples   "),nl,
   married(X1,Y1),
   nl, write("   ",X1," is married to ",Y1," ."),
   nl, write("   Press the SPACE bar to continue."),
   nl, readchar(_),
   fail.


/* rule to show diet habits */

process(1) :-
   clearwindow,
   nl, write(" Turbo Prolog has searched "),
   nl, write(" the list of dietary preferences"),
   nl, write(" and marriage matches."),
   nl, write(" This search shows that "), nl,
   married(X1,Y1),
   diet(X1,D1),
   nl, write(" ",X1," or ",Y1," or both "),
   nl, write(" like ",D1," food."),
```

```
      nl, write(" --Press the SPACE bar to continue."),
      nl, readchar(_),
      fail.

/* rule to show entertainment preferences */

process(2) :-
   clearwindow,
   nl, write(" Turbo Prolog has searched the list"),
   nl, write(" of entertainment preferences and marriage matches."), nl,
   nl, write(" This search shows that "),
   married(X1,Y1),
   entertainment(X1,E1),
   nl, write(" ",X1," or ",Y1, " or both "),
   nl, write(" ","enjoy ",E1," for entertainment."),
   nl, write(" --Press the SPACE bar to continue."),
   nl, readchar(_),
   fail.

/* rule to show vacation location preferences */

process(3) :-
   clearwindow,
   nl, write(" Turbo Prolog has searched the list"),
   nl, write(" of vacation location preferences"),
   nl, write(" and marriage matches."),nl,
   nl, write(" This search shows that "),
   married(X1,Y1),
   location(X1,L1),
   nl, write(" ",X1," or ",Y1, " or both like the"),
   nl, write(" ",L1," for a vacation location."),
   nl, write(" --Press the SPACE bar to continue."),
   nl, readchar(_),
   fail.

/* rule to show rise-time habits */

process(4) :-
   clearwindow,
   nl, write(" Turbo Prolog has searched the list"),
   nl, write(" of rising habits and "),
   nl, write(" marriage matches."),
   nl, write(" This search shows that "),nl,
```

```
        married(X1,Y1),
        rise_time(X1,R1),
        nl, write(" ",X1," or ",Y1, " or both "),
        nl, write(" like to rise ",R1,"."),
        nl, write(" --Press the SPACE bar to continue."),
        nl, readchar(_),
        fail.

process(5) :-
        show_menu_2.

process(6) :- exit.

show_menu_2 :-
        makewindow(1,7,7," Preference Matching ", 2,40,22,38),
        nl, write(" Enter one of the numbers below to "),
        nl, write(" View all the matches for a category"), nl, nl,
        nl, write("  1. Diet Matches."),
        nl, write("  2. Entertainment Matches."),
        nl, write("  3. Vacation Location Matches."),
        nl, write("  4. Rising Habit Matches.  "),
        nl, write("  5. You Match the Couples. "),
        nl, write("  6. The Most Compatible Couples."), nl,
        nl, write(" Enter your choice(1-6) "),
        readint(Q),
        Q <= 6,
        proces(Q),
        Q > 6, !.

    /* rule to match diet inforamtion */

    proces(1) :-
     clearwindow,
     nl, write(" Turbo Prolog has searched the list"),
     nl, write(" of dietary preferences and found "),
     nl, write(" a match. It has also searched the"),
     nl, write(" list of married people and put "),
     nl, write(" husbands and wives together."), nl,
     nl, write(" The results are:  "),
     married(X1,Y1),
     diet(X1,D1),
     married(X2,Y2),
     X1 <> X2,
```

```
        diet(X2,D2),
        D1 = D2,
        nl, write(" ",X1," and ",Y1,", and ",X2," and ",Y2),
        nl, write(" are possible matching couples "),
        nl, write(" because both couples are happy"),
        nl, write(" eating ",D1," food."), nl,
        nl, write(" --Press the SPACE bar to continue."),
        nl, readchar(_),
        fail.

/* rule to match entertainment */

    proces(2) :-
        clearwindow,
        nl, write(" Turbo Prolog has searched the list"),
        nl, write(" of entertainment preferences and"),
        nl, write(" found a match. It has also searched"),
        nl, write(" the list of married people and"),
        nl, write(" put husbands and wives together."),
        married(X1,Y1),
        entertainment(X1,E1),
        married(X2,Y2),
        X1 <> X2,
        entertainment(X2,E2),
        E1 = E2,
        nl, write(" ",X1," and ",Y1," , and ",X2," and ",Y2),
        nl, write(" are possible matching couples "),
        nl, write(" because both couples are happy "),
        nl, write(" with ",E1," for entertainment."), nl,
        nl, write(" --Press the SPACE bar to continue."),
        nl, readchar(_),
        fail.

/* rule to match locations */

proces(3) :-
        clearwindow,
        nl, write(" Turbo Prolog has searched the list"),
        nl, write(" of vacation preferences and found"),
        nl, write(" a match. It has also searched the"),
        nl, write(" list of married people and put"),
        nl, write(" husbands and wives together."), nl,
        married(X1,Y1),
```

```
      location(X1,L1),
      married(X2,Y2),
      X1 <> X2,
      location(X2,L2),
      L1 = L2,
      nl, write(" ",X1," and ",Y1," , and ",X2," and ",Y2),
      nl, write(" are possible matching couples "),
      nl, write(" because both couples like to "),
      nl, write(" vacation in the ",L1,"."), nl,
      nl, write(" --Press the SPACE bar to continue."),
      nl, readchar(_),
      fail.


/* rule to match rise times */

proces(4) :-
   clearwindow,
   nl, write(" Turbo Prolog has searched the list"),
   nl, write(" of rise-time preferences and found"),
   nl, write(" a match. It has also searched the"),
   nl, write(" list of married people and put"),
   nl, write(" husbands and wives together."), nl,
   married(X1,Y1),
   rise_time(X1,R1),
   married(X2,Y2),
   X1 <> X2,
   rise_time(X2,R2),
   R1 = R2,
   nl, write(" ",X1," and ",Y1," , and ",X2," and ",Y2),
   nl, write(" are possible matching couples "),
   nl, write(" because both couples like "),
   nl, write(" to rise ",R1,"."), nl,
   nl, write(" --Press the SPACE bar to continue."),
   nl, readchar(_),
   fail.


   /* rule to match two couples */

   proces(5) :-
    clearwindow,
    makewindow (14,7,7," You Match Couples ",0,0,25,80),
    nl, write(" Now, remember that the aim is to match the couples"),
    nl, write(" whose interests are most compatible. You may take as"),
```

```
    nl, write(" much time as you need. When you are ready, enter the"),
    nl, write(" number for the couples you think match best."),
    nl, write(" 1) John and Mary & Sam and Jane    "),
    nl, write(" 2) John and Mary & Ron and Amy     "),
    nl, write(" 3) John and Mary & Bill and Alice "),
    nl, write(" 4) Sam and Jane  & Ron and Amy     "),
    nl, write(" 5) Sam and Jane  & Bill and Alice "),
    nl, write(" 6) Ron and Amy   & Bill and Alice "),
    nl, write(" Enter the number for the couples and press ENTER."),
    readint(R),
    R < 7,
    select_pairs(R),
    R >= 7, !.

proces(6) :-
    clearwindow,
    makewindow(15,7,7," You Match Couples ",0,0,25,80),
    married(X1,Y1),
    diet(X1,D1),
    entertainment(X1,E1),
    location(X1,L1),
    rise_time(X1,R1),
    married(X2,Y2),
    X1 <> X2,
    diet(X2,D2),
    entertainment(X2,E2),
    location(X2,L2),
    rise_time(X2,R2),
    D1 = D2,
    E1 = E2,
    L1 = L2,
    R1 = R2,
    nl, nl,
    nl, write(" ",X1," and ",Y1,", and ",X2),
        write(" and ",Y2," would be happy on a"),
    nl, write(" vacation because"),
    nl, write(" both couples are happy eating "),
        write(" ",D1," food,"),
    nl, write(" both couples are happy with"),
        write(" ",E1," for entertainment,"),
    nl, write(" both couples like to"),
        write(" vacation in the ",L1," and"),
```

```
        nl, write(" both couples like to"),
            write(" rise ",R1,"."),
        !,
        nl, nl, write(" Press the SPACE bar."),
        readchar(_),
        clearwindow,
        show_menu_1.

select_pairs(1) :-
    X1 = "John", X2 = "Sam",
    match_rule(X1,X2).

select_pairs(1) :-
    nl, write(" Incomplete match results!"),
    nl, write(" Press the space bar."),
    readchar(_).

select_pairs(2) :-
    X1 = "John", X2 = "Ron",
    match_rule(X1,X2).

select_pairs(3) :-
    X1 = "John", X2 = "Bill",
    match_rule(X1,X2).

select_pairs(3) :-
    nl, write(" Incomplete match results!"),
    nl, write(" Press the space bar."),
    readchar(_).

select_pairs(4) :-
    X1 = "Sam", X2 = "Ron",
    match_rule(X1,X2).

select_pairs(4) :-
    nl, write(" Incomplete match results!"),
    nl, write(" Press the space bar."),
    readchar(_).

select_pairs(5) :-
    X1 = "Sam", X2 = "Bill",
    match_rule(X1,X2).
```

```
select_pairs(5) :-
   nl, write(" Incomplete match results!"),
   nl, write(" Press the space bar."),
   readchar(_).

select_pairs(6) :-
   X1 = "Ron", X2 = "Bill",
   match_rule(X1,X2).

select_pairs(6) :-
   nl, write(" Incomplete match results!"),
   nl, write(" Press the space bar."),
   readchar(_).

match_rule(X1,X2) :-
   married(X1,Y1),
   diet(X1,D1),
   entertainment(X1,E1),
   location(X1,L1),
   rise_time(X1,R1),
   married(X2,Y2),
   diet(X2,D2),
   entertainment(X2,E2),
   location(X2,L2),
   rise_time(X2,R2),
   D1 = D2,
   nl, nl, nl,
   nl, write(" ",X1," and ",Y1,", and ",X2),
       write(" and ",Y2," would be happy on a"),
   nl, write(" vacation to the extent that"),
   nl, write(" both couples are happy eating "),
       write(" ",D1," food."),
   E1 = E2,
   nl, write(" Both couples are happy with"),
       write(" ",E1," for entertainment."),
   L1 = L2,
   nl, write(" Both couples like to"),
       write(" vacation in the ",L1,"."),
   R1 = R2,
   nl, write(" Both couples like to"),
       write(" rise ",R1,"."),
```

```
!,
nl, nl, write(" Press the space bar."),
readchar(_).
```

```
/*                         end of program                      */
```

When the Family Reunion program is run, the opening text is presented. The reader is then prompted to press the space bar, and the conversational data lines are presented. The next stage of the program is menu-based, as the player selects the data to be viewed and the matches to be made. The final stage is also selected from the menu; that is, the multiple pattern-matching of the two couples with compatible interests and habits. The player is then prompted to return to the first menu, from which the exit option may be selected.

Turbo Prolog's capabilities to integrate graphics in the form of text and window integration, multiple menu options, and multiple pattern-matching are evident throughout the Smith Family Reunion program. A typical run-session dialogue, which illustrates these qualities, is shown in figure 12.9.

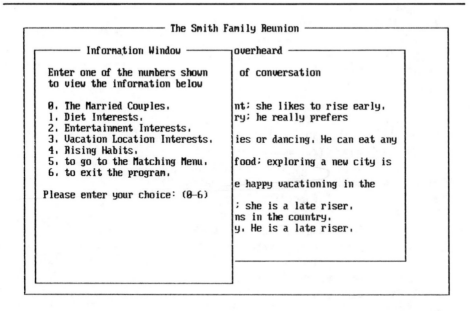

Fig. 12.9. *A dialogue with the Smith Family Reunion program.*

The Family Reunion program demonstrates interesting programming techniques in a format that is challenging to the player and attractive to the viewer. This program illustrates *forward chaining*. The matching couples are not known at the outset. But the facts in the database are known and are examined to arrive at the results of the matching process. In Turbo Prolog, the left side of the rule (the rule-head) specifies the combination of facts that is to be matched against facts in the data base. The matching process must not affect the existing data (although more data may be added as a result of applying the rule). If the matching of subgoals in the right side of the rule (the rule-body) succeeds, the variables in the rule-head (parameters) become instantiated to sets of data values. These sets may constitute additional information in the database. Thus forward chaining systems are known as *data-driven systems*.

The next section discusses the user-interface aspects of the Family Reunion program in some depth, as they are integral to the design and execution of the program.

The User Interface

The Family Reunion program has a user interface designed to make the user feel involved with the program. The user interface provides three distinct functions for interactions between the program and the user. The first function of the user interface, and the most evident to the user, is to provide a context in which the action will take place. This interface gives the user a sense of actuality regarding the story. You will see that this text framework is simply made up of the window that begins the story with the opening text, a kind of "Once upon a time."

In the program, the text windows are indicated by the *makewindow* predicates and the numerous *write* lines. As a further refinement, the text is often moved away from the left screen margin by a series of spaces within the quotation marks that enclose the text lines. The opening text is provided following *The Smith Family Story* predicate, as shown in Figure 12.10.

Additional context is provided for the user as the program proceeds. You will notice that when the second story segment is introduced, the new window "nests" inside the previous one. On the other hand, the windows that frame the several matching elements, habits and likes, occupy exactly the same space. This arrangement is shown in figure 12.11.

In designing an interface module such as this, you can take advantage of Turbo Prolog's capability of easily integrating graphics, text, and program commands in a single module.

The second purpose of the interface is to provide a friendly way for the user to interact with the database, which is the basis of the final solution by Turbo Prolog's internal unification routines. You, as the programmer, have a pretty good idea of what is going on. But the typical user cannot be assumed to have this data and is text- or screen-oriented. So the user interface sets out the database information in a logical and easily readable fashion.

```
┌──────────────────── The Smith Family Reunion ────────────────────┐
│                                                                   │
│  The four Smith sisters have all married. Returning to            │
│  their parents' home for a family reunion, the four               │
│  couples discovered that they have several interests and          │
│  habits in common. In fact, the girls thought that perhaps        │
│  two or more of the couples had enough in common that they        │
│  could spend their summer vacation together.                      │
│                                                                   │
│  The married couples are: John and Mary; Sam and Jane             │
│       Ron and Amy; and Bill and Alice.                            │
│                                                                   │
│       If you match the facts and interests each                   │
│       person reveals in casual conversation, you                  │
│       will know the couples that are best suited                  │
│       for a pleasant and rewarding vacation together.             │
│       Each person speaks for both spouses as married              │
│       people often do.                                            │
│                                                                   │
│  The random snatches of conversation overheard are shown next.    │
│  Then you will be able to view the data and see the matches       │
│  the conversation would imply.                                    │
│  Finally, the matching couples will be shown.                     │
│  --Press the SPACE BAR to continue.                               │
└───────────────────────────────────────────────────────────────────┘
```

Fig. 12.10. The beginning text of the Smith Family story.

```
┌─────────────────────── You Match Couples ────────────────────────┐
│  ┌──────── Information Window ────────┐                           │
│  │ the list of dietary preferences    │                           │
│  │ and marriage matches.              │                           │
│  │ This search shows that             │                           │
│  │                                    │                           │
│  │ John or Mary or both               │                           │
│  │ like vegetarian food.              │                           │
│  │ --Press the SPACE bar to continue. │                           │
│  │                                    │                           │
│  │ Sam or Jane or both                │                           │
│  │ like non-vegetarian food.          │                           │
│  │ --Press the SPACE bar to continue. │                           │
│  │                                    │                           │
│  │ Ron or Amy or both                 │                           │
│  │ like vegetarian food.              │                           │
│  │ --Press the SPACE bar to continue. │                           │
│  │                                    │                           │
│  │ Ron or Amy or both                 │                           │
│  │ like non-vegetarian food.          │                           │
│  │ --Press the SPACE bar to continue. │                           │
│  └────────────────────────────────────┘                           │
└───────────────────────────────────────────────────────────────────┘
```

Fig. 12.11. Overheard conversation is shown in a nested window.

For example, the dietary preferences of each couple are listed in the database in the form:

```
diet("John","vegetarian").
diet("Sam","non-vegetarian").
diet("Ron","vegetarian").
diet("Ron","non-vegetarian").
diet("Bill","vegetarian").
diet("Bill","non-vegetarian").
```

This portion of the database is then presented to the user in easily readable form, as shown in figure 12.12.

```
┌──────────────────────────── You Match Couples ────────────────────────────┐
│                                                                            │
│  John and Mary, and Ron and Amy would be happy on a                        │
│  vacation because                                                          │
│  both couples are happy eating  vegetarian food,                           │
│  both couples are happy with movies for entertainment,                     │
│  both couples like to vacation in the country, and                         │
│  both couples like to rise early.                                          │
│                                                                            │
│  Press the SPACE bar.                                                      │
│                                                                            │
│                                                                            │
│                                                                            │
│                                                                            │
└────────────────────────────────────────────────────────────────────────────┘
```

Fig. 12.12. *A portion of the Smith Family Program database.*

The third function is the most common in user interfaces: it provides a friendly way to move the program along. This is done by means of prompts, such as

```
--Press the SPACE BAR to continue.
```

These prompts allow the user as much time as he desires to read and absorb information presented on the screen. They also provide an effective way to move from module to module in larger programs where time is not a constraint or where user interaction or control of the program is a desirable characteristic. There is no doubt that

```
When you are ready, press the SPACE bar and you
will see the names of the pairs.
```

is much more readable than direct program commands such as

```
Match pairs ?              (_) .
```

Menu choices are another common, user-friendly control technique. You have used these in several of the previous programs, and in the Family Reunion program the menus provide an essential user interface. The menus allow the reader not only to progress through the program but also permit the reader to review information that may be vital. The two menus in the Smith Family Reunion program provide for both functions—viewing data in the first menu and viewing matches in the second menu. Both menus are shown in figure 12.13.

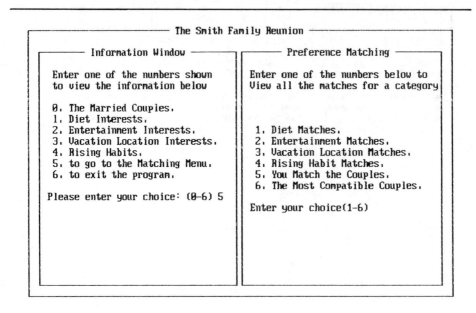

Fig. 12.13. *Menus for the Smith Family Reunion program.*

Bear in mind that the information presented in this gaming format may be essential in other applications of Turbo Prolog to enable the user to review information before proceeding to a decision. Turbo Prolog's menu construction makes this procedure easy to program and effective to use.

User-interface modules always make a program longer, but having good user interface modules is always worth the time and trouble. They make the program appear much more professional to the user and can often eliminate potential confusion in program execution. In many programs the user interface becomes crucial to the successful working of the program.

—————————————————— Exercises ——————————————————

12.12. Modify the Family Reunion program so that a different element is part of the matching process (smoking, for instance). You will need to construct an additional set of predicates, which should be mentioned in the overheard conversation. Remember to modify the *process(6)* module also. (You may also want to modify the *process(5)* module.) You may want to streamline this part for convenience in working. Remember that the matching will change if the data indicates different combinations.

12.13. Modify the Family Reunion program by adding a fifth couple to the family. You may want to make fewer areas of matching (eliminate the vacation location, for example). Again, the matching will give the result indicated by the data combinations (there may be no matches). Again, you may want to streamline the program by eliminating the *process(5)* module.

Chapter Review

In this chapter, you were introduced to the concepts of problem solving in AI. In this capstone chapter of the book, you saw how to use in complex programs many of the techniques presented throughout the book.

You were guided through the design and development of a number guessing game and two versions (simple and intelligent) of the 23 Matches game. In developing these game programs in Turbo Prolog, you saw that procedural oriented programming is also conveniently implemented. These programs required symbol-matching and strategy-development, which was implemented in Turbo Prolog.

You also were involved in the concepts and approach to solving logic problems. You learned the design and development of the classic Monkey and Bananas problem and the Smith Family Reunion program. You saw from the Self-Help Exercises how adaptable such programs can be. Throughout these programs you saw the power and flexibility of Turbo Prolog, which you are encouraged to apply to your specific needs and situations.

A

Using the Turbo Prolog Editor

The Turbo Prolog editor offers numerous functions that make writing Turbo Prolog programs faster and smoother. Even if you do not consider keyboard prowess your greatest skill, you will benefit from learning to use the more common editing functions. These basic functions are discussed in the first section of this appendix. Additional editing functions are covered in the second section.

You will probably find that learning a few basic editing commands works well. When you feel comfortable with these, pick out a couple more to incorporate as you program. Soon your editing toolkit will be well stocked.

Basic Editing Commands

The three most common editing operations are moving the cursor to a chosen position in the program file, deleting a word or a line, and inserting a word or a line. Learning these operations will allow you to make many Turbo Prolog program-writing changes comfortably.

Moving the Cursor

Placing the cursor at a certain position on the screen is done by moving the screen page up or down and adjusting the cursor within the screen. To move the page up or down, you can use either the PgUp and PgDn keys or the Ctrl-R and Ctrl-C key combinations. (To enter *Ctrl-C*, you hold down the Ctrl key while you press *C*. By convention, the alphabetic keys in such combinations are shown in uppercase. However, you can use either upper- or lowercase letters in Ctrl-key combinations.)

To position the cursor within the screen, use the arrow keys at the right of the keyboard. The cursor acts as a line-scrolling device when you move it at the upper or lower limits of the screen. You can also use the Ctrl-E and Ctrl-X key combinations to move the cursor up and down by one line.

The Ctrl-F or Ctrl-→ key combination moves the cursor one "word" to the right, and the Ctrl-D combination moves the cursor one space to the right. Ctrl-A or Ctrl-← moves the cursor one word to the left, and Ctrl-S moves the cursor one space to the left.

The Ctrl-Home key combination moves the cursor to the beginning of the screen text, and the Ctrl-End combination moves the cursor to the end of the text.

You can move the cursor to the beginning of the program file (rather than to the top of the screen) by using the Ctrl-QR key combination or Ctrl-PgUp. Likewise, you can move the cursor to the end of the file by using the Ctrl-QC combination or Ctrl-PgDn.

You will have noticed that the status line shows the current cursor position. You can move the cursor to any line within the program file by using the F2 function key. When you press F2, a line number is requested. When you enter the number and press F2 again, the cursor is placed at the beginning of the line indicated. If the line indicated is not on the screen, the display shifts so that the indicated line appears at the center of the screen.

Deleting Text

To delete a word, place the cursor at the beginning of the word and press Ctrl-T. To delete one character, press Ctrl-G. The Ctrl-G combination deletes one space or character above the cursor each time it is pressed. You can also use the Del (*delete*) key located at the lower right corner of the numeric keypad. The Del key erases one character at a time, moving to the left. To correct "exampled" to "example," position the cursor to the right of the "d" and press the delete key to eliminate the error.

To delete a line, place the cursor anywhere on the line and press either Ctrl-Y or Ctrl-Backspace. You should be aware that if you press Ctrl-Y when you mean to type an uppercase Y, you will inadvertently delete a line of your program.

Selecting Insert or Overwrite

The editor always has two text-entry modes: Insert and Overwrite. The word *Insert* or *Overwrite* on the status line of the Editor window indicates which mode is active. To toggle between Insert and Overwrite modes, press the Ins key on the numeric keypad or the Ctrl-V key combination. Figure A.1 shows the status line in Insert mode.

When Insert mode is active, anything you enter "bumps" the existing text or space. When Overwrite mode is active, anything you enter replaces the existing text.

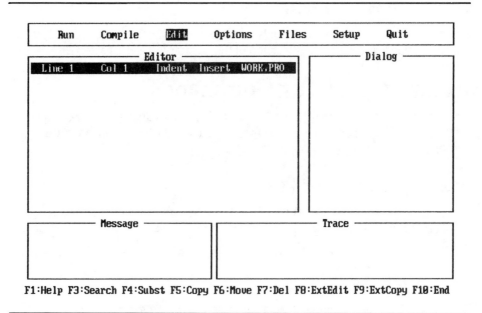

Fig. A.1. *The status line indicating Insert mode.*

Using Automatic Indentation

The automatic indentation feature provides automatic line indentation in your program file. That is, when you press the Enter key, the cursor moves to the next line and to the first column in which there was text in the previous line. If you move the cursor to a new starting position, this column will become the new indented position.

The default status of Auto Indent, active, is indicated as *Indent* on the status line of the edit screen. To deactivate automatic indentation, use the Ctrl-QI key combination. The *Indent* will disappear from the status line. You can reactivate the automatic indentation function with the same key combination.

When you edit an existing program file, the Auto Indent functions so long as Insert mode is active. Changing to Overwrite mode implies that you want to rewrite the program text, and thus the automatic indent function is not applicable.

Changing the Size of the Editor Window

While editing a program file, you can change the Editor window to full-screen size by pressing Ctrl-F10. Pressing Ctrl-F10 again returns the window to its original size.

Using the Help Facility

To get a full listing of editor commands and other useful information, press F1 while you are editing a file. For more discussion of the Help facility, see Chapter 1.

Additional Editing Commands

The editing commands that follow are of two types. Block commands mark a block of text and perform an operation on the entire block. The "search" commands simply find text or find text and replace it with other text.

Marking Blocks of Text

You can perform a number of useful editing operations with the block commands. These commands mark a section (or "block") of your program file for one of three purposes:

1. To move the block to another location in the program file
2. To copy the block
3. To delete the block

To practice using these commands on your screen, select *Editor* from the main menu. Make sure that any program you were working on has been properly saved. Now type the following lines on your screen so you'll have some material to work with:

```
Name:
Address:
City, State, ZIP:
Telephone:
Work Phone:
```

Now you will see how easy it is to mark these as a block. Position the cursor at the start of the *Name* line and enter the combination Ctrl-KB. (Hold down the *Ctrl* key while you press *K*, then press *B*; it makes no difference whether you continue to hold down the *Ctrl* key as you press *B*.) Now mark the end of the block by moving the cursor to the end of the *Work Phone* line and pressing the combination Ctrl-KK. The entire block you have defined will be highlighted. Depending on the kind of monitor you are using, the highlighting appears either as a contrasting color or as a change in the brightness of the text.

Now you can copy this block to another location in the file. First, press Enter a few times to make sure you have room to move around. (Otherwise, the copied text will "bump" the lines beyond the Editor window.) Then move the cursor down a couple of lines below the highlighted block and enter the combination Ctrl-KC. The entire block you have marked will be duplicated at the cursor position. Repeat the Ctrl-KC key combination to copy the block at least one more time. Notice that as you copy the block, the highlighting moves with it. Figure A.2 shows the screen with both the original block and a copied block.

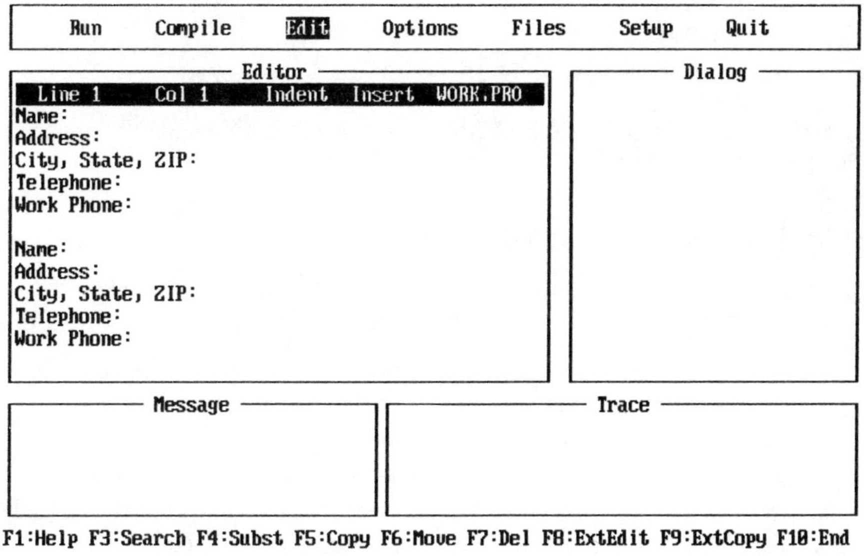

```
  Run        Compile      Edit      Options     Files     Setup     Quit

 ──────────── Editor ────────────         ──────── Dialog ────────
| Line 1      Col 1     Indent  Insert  WORK.PRO |                      |
|Name:                                            |                     |
|Address:                                         |                     |
|City, State, ZIP:                                |                     |
|Telephone:                                       |                     |
|Work Phone:                                      |                     |
|                                                 |                     |
|Name:                                            |                     |
|Address:                                         |                     |
|City, State, ZIP:                                |                     |
|Telephone:                                       |                     |
|Work Phone:                                      |                     |
|                                                 |                     |

 ──────── Message ────────         ──────── Trace ────────
|                         |        |                        |
|                         |        |                        |
|                         |        |                        |

 F1:Help F3:Search F4:Subst F5:Copy F6:Move F7:Del F8:ExtEdit F9:ExtCopy F10:End
```

Fig. A.2. *A copied block of text.*

To remove (or "hide") the highlighting, press Ctrl-KH. This command works regardless of the cursor position; the cursor does not need to be within the highlighted block.

Now you are ready to delete one of the address blocks. Move the cursor to the beginning of the *Name* line, and mark the beginning of the block with Ctrl-KB. Move the cursor to the beginning of the line after the *Work Phone:* line and use Ctrl-KK to mark the end of the block. To delete this block, enter Ctrl-KY.

You can also use three of the function keys to copy, move, or delete blocks of a program, as shown in table A.1. You begin each operation by moving the cursor to the beginning of the block and pressing the appropriate function key. Then you follow the commands that appear at the bottom of the screen. They will ask you in each case to mark the beginning and end of the block and tell you to press the function key again to perform the operation.

—————————— **Table A.1** ——————————
Issuing Block Commands with Function Keys

Operation	Control keys	Function keys
Copy a block	Ctrl-KC	F5
Move a block	Ctrl-KV	F6
Delete a block	Ctrl-KY	F7

You can also use the Shift-F5 key combination to repeat a copy command. Position the cursor at the next beginning point and press Shift-F5.

Using the Search Commands

The search commands are used to find a string of text within a program file. They can be used either to simply find a string or to find a string and replace it with another string.

To use these commands, you must first position the cursor somewhere before the string you wish to find. The beginning of the program is always a good place.

To search for a string without replacing it, press the F3 function key. Then, at the prompt that appears at the bottom of the screen, you enter the string you want to find, and press F3 again. Now the cursor moves to the first occurrence of the string you entered at the prompt. If the file has no occurrence of the string—or no occurrence "below" the current cursor position—the cursor does not move. To repeat the same search without having to reenter the search string, press Shift-F3.

You can see how this works by searching for *ZIP* in the text you have entered. First, press Ctrl-PgUp to move the cursor to the beginning of the file. Then press F3 and enter *ZIP* at the prompt. Figure A.3 shows how the screen looks at this point. Press F3 again to begin the search. Almost instantly, the cursor will move to the beginning of the first occurrence of *ZIP*.

The search-and-replace function enables you to find a string and replace it with another string. In your information block, for example, you might want to replace *Work Phone:* with *Work Extension:*. First, press F4. Now you are prompted to enter the string that is to be replaced. Enter and press F4 again. Another prompt now asks you for the replacement string; enter *Work Extension:* and press Enter. Figure A.4 shows the screen with the replacement prompt.

Now you are asked whether the replacement is to be global or local. If you press *G* to indicate a global search and replace, all occurrences of the search string will be replaced. If you press *L* for a local search and replace, only the first occurrence "below" the cursor is replaced. For this example, select a global search and replace. Now you are prompted to indicate whether you want to "approve" each replacement of the search string; figure

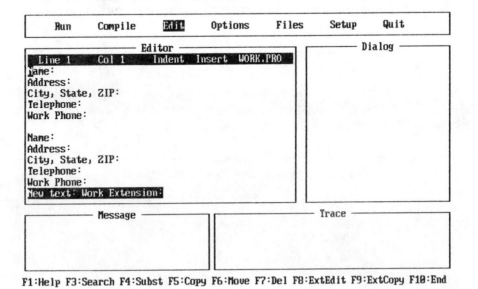

| Run | Compile | **Edit** | Options | Files | Setup | Quit |

┌─────────────────── Editor ───────────────────┐ ┌────── Dialog ──────┐
```
 Line 1     Col 1      Indent  Insert  WORK.PRO
Name:
Address:
City, State, ZIP:
Telephone:
Work Phone:

Name:
Address:
City, State, ZIP:
Telephone:
Work Phone:
F3: Search text, text: ZIP
```

┌────── Message ──────┐ ┌────── Trace ──────┐

F1:Help F3:Search F4:Subst F5:Copy F6:Move F7:Del F8:ExtEdit F9:ExtCopy F10:End

Fig. A.3. *Searching for the text* ZIP.

| Run | Compile | **Edit** | Options | Files | Setup | Quit |

┌─────────────────── Editor ───────────────────┐ ┌────── Dialog ──────┐
```
 Line 1     Col 1      Indent  Insert  WORK.PRO
Name:
Address:
City, State, ZIP:
Telephone:
Work Phone:

Name:
Address:
City, State, ZIP:
Telephone:
Work Phone:
New text: Work Extension:
```

┌────── Message ──────┐ ┌────── Trace ──────┐

F1:Help F3:Search F4:Subst F5:Copy F6:Move F7:Del F8:ExtEdit F9:ExtCopy F10:End

Fig. A.4. *Entering the replacement text.*

A.5 shows the screen at this point. If you press *Y*, then you will be prompted at each occurrence of the search string to indicate whether it should be replaced. For this example, press *N*. As soon as you enter your response, the Turbo Prolog editor replaces each occurrence of *Work Phone:* with *Work Extension:*.

```
┌──────────────────────────────────────────────────────────────────────────┐
│   Run      Compile     Edit     Options    Files    Setup    Quit          │
└──────────────────────────────────────────────────────────────────────────┘
┌──────────── Editor ────────────┐      ┌──────── Dialog ────────┐
│█ Line 1    Col 1    Indent  Insert  WORK.PRO █│      │                        │
│Name:                            │      │                        │
│Address:                         │      │                        │
│City, State, ZIP:                │      │                        │
│Telephone:                       │      │                        │
│Work Phone:                      │      │                        │
│                                 │      │                        │
│Name:                            │      │                        │
│Address:                         │      │                        │
│City, State, ZIP:                │      │                        │
│Telephone:                       │      │                        │
│Work Phone:                      │      │                        │
│█Prompt before replacing (y/n):█ │      │                        │
└─────────────────────────────────┘      └────────────────────────┘
┌──────── Message ────────┐      ┌──────── Trace ─────────┐
│                         │      │                        │
│                         │      │                        │
│                         │      │                        │
└─────────────────────────┘      └────────────────────────┘
F1:Help F3:Search F4:Subst F5:Copy F6:Move F7:Del F8:ExtEdit F9:ExtCopy F10:End
```

Fig. A.5. *The prompt for approving text replacements.*

Search or search-and-replace operations can also be performed using Ctrl key combinations. And both operations can be repeated using either the function keys or the Ctrl key combinations (see table A.2).

Table A.2
Search and Search-and-Replace Commands

Operation	Control keys	Function keys
Search	Ctrl-QF	F3
Search and replace	Ctrl-QA	F4
Repeat last search	Ctrl-L	Shift-F3
Repeat last search and replace	Ctrl-L	Shift-F4

It is often worth the trouble to approve changes on a case by case basis, as the global editor will also change all occurrences of the text you select for replacement. A replacement as harmless as changing "phone" to "telephone" for the sake of formality would also change "microphone" to "microtelephone" if you did a global search-and-replace operation and did not check the replacement each time.

Using the Auxiliary Editor

The F8 function key calls up the Turbo Prolog Auxiliary Editor. When you press this key, a window appears and you are prompted for the name of the file you want to edit, as shown in figure A.6. After you enter the file name, a separate window in which you can edit another file appears in the lower right corner of the editing screen. This capability is especially useful when you need to edit a file called by the program you are working on.

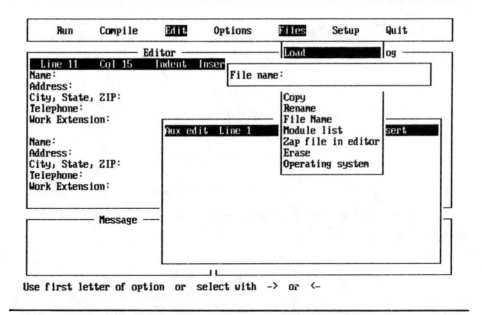

Fig. A.6. *Entering a file name for the Auxiliary Editor.*

All the editing commands can be used within the Auxiliary Editor. To leave the Auxiliary Editor, press the F10 function key. You can save the edited version of the file and return to your working program file.

Copying Text from Another File

Unlike most other editors, which only enable you to read an entire file into the file you are editing, the Turbo Prolog editor enables you to read a block from another file into your working file. To activate this feature, first move the cursor to the point at which you want to insert the block from the other file, then press F9. After you enter the name of the file from which you want to copy a block, the contents of that file appear in the Auxiliary Editor window, as shown in figure A.7.

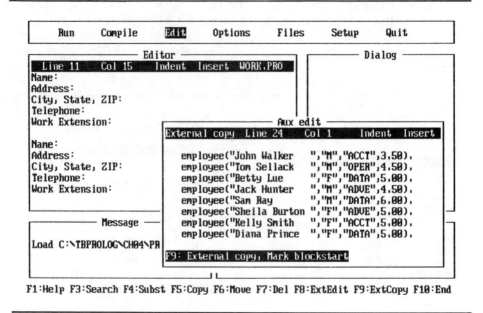

Fig. A.7. *Marking a text block in an external file.*

Using the normal cursor-movement commands, you now position the cursor at the beginning of the block and press F9. Then you move the cursor to the end of the block and press F9 again. The window disappears, and the marked block is copied to the working file.

B

More Features of
Turbo Prolog

The first section of this appendix describes Turbo Prolog's system options in some detail. The second section explains how to compile and link Turbo Prolog programs to create "stand-alone" files that you can run outside of the Turbo Prolog environment. The third section explains how to use Turbo Prolog's *trace* compiler directive to facilitate development and debugging of programs.

Turbo Prolog System Options

The Turbo Prolog environment is menu-driven. The main menu, displayed at the top of the screen, shows seven options: *Run*, *Compile*, *Edit*, *Options*, *Files*, *Setup*, and *Quit*. The main menu commands, *Run*, *Edit*, and *Quit*, and some subcommands of the main menu *Files* and *Setup* options are presented in Chapter 1. The rest of these commands are described in this section.

The Compile Command

The *Compile* command initiates the process of compiling a Turbo Prolog program. If the program contains an error, Turbo Prolog displays a short error message and places the cursor on the point in the program at which the error was recognized. You can then correct the error and press F10 to compile again. When your program is error-free, select the *Run* command and run the program.

By default, choosing *Compile* causes the program to be compiled into memory. However, you also have the option of compiling programs to disk; that option is discussed in the second section of this appendix.

The Edit Command

The *Edit* command activates the Turbo Prolog editor. When you select *Edit*, the cursor is placed in the Editor window and you can begin writing or editing your program. Appendix A of this book contains more information on using the Turbo Prolog editor.

The Options Command

The *Options* command is used to set the compiler options, which are *Memory*, *OBJ file*, and *EXE file (auto link)*. With the first option (the default), the program is compiled to memory. The other options enable you to create object files (for linking to other object files) and executable files. The currently active option is shown at the top of the submenu that appears when you select *Options*. For example, figure B.1 shows that the active option is *EXE file (auto link)*.

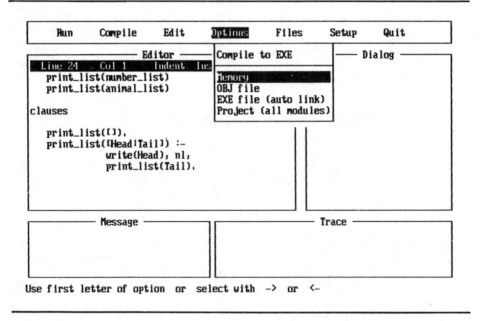

Fig. B.1. *The* Options *submenu.*

The Files Command

Selecting the *Files* option causes a submenu to appear, showing numerous suboptions. The suboptions are *Load*, *Save*, *Directory*, *Print*, *Copy*, *Rename*, *File Name*, *Module list*, *Zap file in editor*, *Erase*, and *Operating system*.

The *Save*, *Directory*, *Print*, and *Zap* options are discussed in Chapter 1. The rest of the options are described in this section.

The Copy Command

This command makes a copy of a disk file. When you select the *Copy* command, the system prompts you for the input file name and the output file name.

The Rename Command

The *Rename* command gives a new name to a disk file. When you select the *Rename* command, Turbo Prolog prompts you for the old file name and the new file name.

The File Name Command

The *File Name* command is used to give the work file in memory a new name.

The Erase Command

This command erases a selected disk file from a directory.

The Module List Command

This command is used to create a file containing the names of modules used for a project. Turbo Prolog enables you to break up a large programming project into modules that are edited and compiled separately, then linked together for a finished program. The names of the module files are listed in a project file. The *Module list* command is used to edit this project file.

The Operating System Command

This command temporarily transfers control to DOS. Use of the *Operating system* command is rarely necessary, however, because frequently used file-maintenance functions are already available in the Turbo Prolog environment. To return to Turbo Prolog from DOS, type *EXIT* at the DOS prompt.

The Setup Command

The options on the *Setup* menu are used to personalize the Turbo Prolog environment. When you select *Setup*, a submenu appears with the options *Colors*, *Window size*, *Directories*, *Miscellaneous settings*, *Load configuration*, and *Save configuration*. The options are described in the following sections.

Colors

To change the background or foreground colors of windows in the Turbo Prolog environment, select *Colors*. A submenu appears from which you can select the window you want to change. Suppose, for example, that you want to change the foreground and background colors for the Editor window. You select *Edit* from the submenu and press Enter. The pull-down menu disappears and a message is displayed at the bottom of the screen (see fig. B.2).

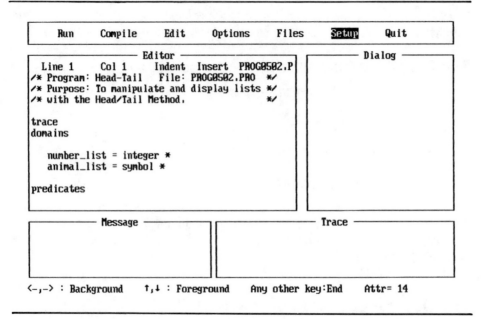

Fig. B.2. *Changing window colors.*

This message tells you to press the ← and → keys to select the background color and to press the ↑ or ↓ key to select the foreground color. Pressing any other key terminates the selection. The message *Attr* = indicates the number associated with the color attribute selected. If you have selected medium blue as the background color, for example, the bottom line shows *Attr = 18*. When you finish changing the colors, press Esc.

Window Size

The *Window size* command is useful for accommodating different programming situations. For example, you might want a large Editor window for editing programs and a large Dialog window for running the program. To change the Editor window size, follow these steps:

1. Select *Window size*.

2. When the second pull-down menu appears, select *Edit*. The pull-down menus now disappear and a message line appears at the bottom of the screen, as shown in figure B.3.

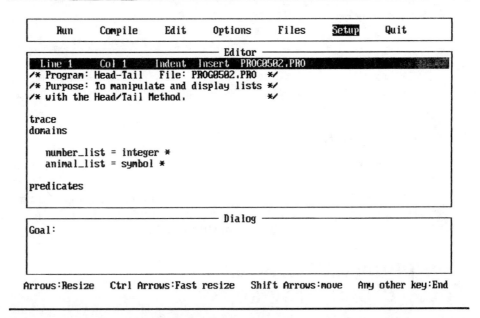

Fig. B.3. *Changing the size of the Edit window.*

3. Press the ← or → key to resize the window horizontally and the ↑ or ↓ key to resize the window vertically. These keys change the window sizes by one row or column at a time. To change the width by five columns, press Ctrl-→ or Ctrl-←. To move the window, press Shift and an arrow key. Pressing any other key terminates the process. Press Esc to return to the *Setup* menu.

Save Configuration

To save the new window configuration, select *Save configuration*. A one-line text window now appears on the screen, and you are prompted to enter a name for the configuration file. Enter a suitable configuration file name, such as EDWINDO1.SYS, and press

Enter. The new configuration file is saved in the .PRO directory unless you supply a different directory path. (If you enter the name PROLOG.SYS and save it to the directory containing the Turbo Prolog system files, the new configuration will become the default.)

Load Configuration

To load a window configuration file, select *Load configuration*; then enter the file name and press Enter. The configuration file is loaded by default from the .PRO directory. The selected window configuration appears on the screen, and you can press the space bar to move to the main menu.

Directories

The *Directories* command is used to select a default directory while you are working on the Turbo Prolog system. The options are *.PRO directory*, *.OBJ directory*, *.EXE directory*, *Turbo directory*, and *DOS directory*.

Miscellaneous Settings

The *Miscellaneous settings* command is for setting the IBM EGA adapter on or off and for setting stack size. The default stack size is 4000. The size can be between 600 and 4000. Turbo Prolog uses the stack to implement backtracking and recursion. Selecting the largest stack size that memory permits is advisable. This practice reduces the chance of stack overflow, which can result in program crashes and data loss.

Compiling and Linking a Turbo Prolog Program

A Turbo Prolog source code program consists of a series of ASCII characters. By convention, these files have the extension *.PRO*. Turbo Prolog programs in source code can be compiled to memory and run within the Turbo Prolog environment. To create an executable program file that can be run outside the Turbo Prolog environment, however, you must compile and link a source code file. Turbo Prolog's compiling and linking facilities are used to accomplish these tasks.

To create an executable file, Turbo Prolog creates object-code files with the extension *.OBJ*. These files are linked with code from the Turbo Prolog library to create an executable file with the file extension *.EXE*. If you select the *EXE file (auto link)* option from the *Options* menu, the linking is performed automatically.

To create an executable file, you follow these steps:

1. Load the source program into memory.

2. Select *Options* from the main menu, then select *.EXE file* from the submenu.

3. Select *Compile* from the main menu and press Enter. Turbo Prolog will start the compilation. As the compilation progresses, you will see compiler messages displayed in the message window. A successful compilation produces .OBJ files, .SYM files, .MAP files, and .EXE files.

Notice that the linker finishes the linking process and prompts you for executing the executable file. If you want to run the program, press *Y*; otherwise press *N*.

Using the Trace Facility

The Turbo Prolog system provides a trace facility, which gives a step-by-step report on execution of your program. To activate the trace facility, include the compiler directive *trace* in your program file, then compile the program to memory and run it. You must insert the *trace* before the *predicates* division. A good place to insert it is just before the *domains* division.

Including the *trace* directive causes program execution to pause after each attempt to satisfy a subgoal. The Trace window shows the values to which variables are bound and other information (see fig. B.4). To continue program execution, press the F10 key. In this way, you can follow the trace to the end of the program. If you want to terminate the program execution at any time, press Esc.

If you want to trace only selected predicates, follow the *trace* compiler directive with a list of those predicates you want to trace.

If you trace a program that has errors, the cursor in the Editor window will appear at the beginning of the predicate or rule where the error occurs, and the trace will show the corresponding trace of the predicate(s). In this way you can pinpoint where the error occurs. Trace is a convenient and powerful tool. You should use it whenever you need to debug a program or rule.

During step-by-step execution of a program, the Ctrl-T key combination can be used to toggle the *trace* predicate on and off as desired.

The *shorttrace* predicate, which can be used in the same manner as the *trace* predicate, results in less trace output in the Trace window.

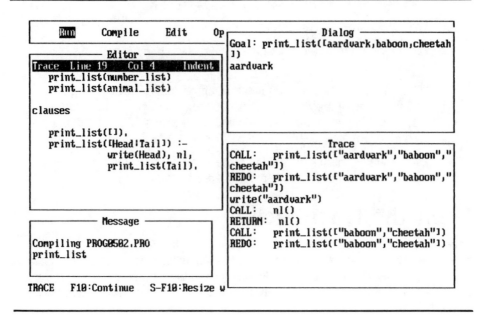

Fig. B.4. Using the trace facility.

C

Basic DOS Commands and Utilities

To work with Turbo Prolog, you need to know how to use several commands and utility programs of PC DOS (or MS-DOS, which is functionally equivalent). Those commands and utilities are described briefly in this appendix, and their purpose in relation to Turbo Prolog is explained. For detailed instructions on the use of these DOS commands and utilities, consult your DOS manual. You may also find Chris DeVoney's *Using PC DOS* (Que Corporation, 1986) a good book to consult for guidance and reference.

The operations and the commands explained in this appendix are listed in Table C.1. Some of the commands have both shorter forms and longer forms: for example, the command to make a directory can be entered as *MD* or as *MKDIR*. Both commands have the same effect. The examples in this appendix use the shorter forms, because those forms are preferred by most users of DOS.

Note: Commands marked with an asterisk (*) in table C.1 are known as "external commands." The term means that those commands are performed by separate programs. For example, the program that performs the PRINT command is called PRINT.COM. The programs for performing these external commands must be present on your DOS disk in order for you to use the commands.

DOS commands, file names, etc. can be entered either in upper- or in lowercase characters. In this appendix, they are shown in uppercase for purposes of clarity.

This appendix assumes that DOS is already "up and running" on your computer. The appearance on-screen of the DOS prompt (*A>* for floppy-disk machines or *C>* for hard-disk machines) indicates that DOS has been loaded and your computer is ready to execute the commands discussed in this appendix. For instructions on starting your computer and loading DOS, see Chapter 1.

—————————— **Table C.1** ——————————
DOS Operations and Commands

Operation	*DOS Command*
Formatting a disk	FORMAT*
Copying a disk	DISKCOPY*
Listing a directory	DIR
Making a directory	MD (or MKDIR)
Changing the default directory	CD
Removing a directory	RD (or RMDIR)
Using file masks ("wild cards")	* and ? (with COPY, DIR, and DEL)
Copying files	COPY
Deleting a file	DEL (or ERASE)
Renaming a file	REN (or RENAME)
Viewing the contents of a text file	TYPE
Printing the contents of a text file	PRINT*

The discussions of these commands assume that you are using a dual-floppy-disk system, and that the DOS disk is in drive A:, and another disk is in drive B:. (Remember to press Enter after each of the commands in these sections.) All of these commands are equally applicable to hard-disk machines.

Disk Commands

The commands discussed in this section apply to the disk as a whole. In addition to the commands discussed here, FORMAT and DISKCOPY, there is one more disk command you may want to learn about, especially when you have begun writing Turbo Prolog programs that read and write disk files. That command is CHKDSK (for *check disk*). CHKDSK has many uses, among them the recovery of disk space that becomes unusable if one of your programs "crashes" while writing a disk file. To learn about that command, consult your DOS manual or *Using PC DOS*.

Formatting a Disk (FORMAT)

Before a disk can be used for data storage, it must be formatted. Formatting involves preparing the disk medium for writing and reading of data. The PC DOS operating system includes a program file called FORMAT.COM, which is used to format blank disks.

To format a disk, place the blank disk in drive B and enter

    FORMAT B:

Then DOS will instruct you to place a new disk in drive B: and press a key. After doing so, you will probably hear whirring sounds while the FORMAT program prepares the disk. When the process is complete, the program displays a message saying that the process is complete and giving statistics concerning the disk that has been formatted. Then the FORMAT program asks whether you want to format another disk. If you do, press *Y*, then follow the instructions that appear.

A disk must contain special files known as *system files* if the disk is to be used for starting (or "booting") the computer. The easiest way to have PC DOS copy these files to a disk is to use a special option with the FORMAT command:

```
FORMAT B: /S
```

Then follow the procedure just given. The */S* option places a copy of the operating system files on your formatted disk.

Copying a Disk (DISKCOPY)

You will frequently want to make an exact copy of a disk. The DISKCOPY command is provided for that purpose. To use DISKCOPY, place your PC DOS system disk in drive A:, and enter

```
DISKCOPY A: B:
```

(Note that you *cannot* use DISKCOPY to copy the contents of a floppy disk to a hard disk. Use the COPY command, instead. However, you can use DISKCOPY on a hard-disk machine, even if the machine only has one floppy-disk drive. In executing the command *DISKCOPY A: B:* on such a machine, DOS regards the single physical drive as two logical drives. DISKCOPY therefore will prompt you to change disks as it copies one disk to another.)

After you enter the command, DISKCOPY displays these prompts:

```
Insert SOURCE diskette in drive A:

Insert TARGET diskette in drive B:

Press any key when ready . . .
```

The *SOURCE diskette* is the one you want to copy, and the *TARGET diskette* is the disk that will contain the copy of the target disk. The target disk need not be formatted; if DISKCOPY detects an unformatted target disk, the program formats the target disk as it copies the information from the source disk. Any data already on the target disk will be destroyed.

After you insert the disks and press a key, DISKCOPY proceeds to copy the target disk. When the program has finished, label your new disk in a way that distinguishes it from the original. Labels such as *Programs—Archive* and *Programs—April 1987* can help you distinguish the archival copies of your disks from the working copies.

Directory Commands

PC DOS supports *hierarchically structured directories*, which are also known as "tree-structured directories." Your files, whether they are Turbo Prolog programs or DOS utilities, should be stored in subdirectories that have some relation to the files' purpose or category, so that you can easily find a particular file when you need to use it. (Storing files in a logical manner is especially important if your system has a hard disk.) An example of a hierarchically structured directory is shown in figure C.1.

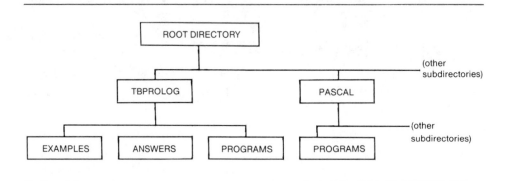

Fig. C.1. *A hierarchically structured directory.*

The topmost directory in figure C.1 is called the *root directory*. This is the main directory of the disk; the root directory is created when the disk is formatted. The figure shows two subdirectories created by you, the user. These subdirectories are TBPROLOG and PASCAL. TBPROLOG in turn has three subdirectories: EXAMPLES, ANSWERS, and PROGRAMS.

Notice that PASCAL also has a subdirectory named PROGRAMS, as well as other subdirectories that are not shown. Having two subdirectories with the same name poses no problem, because DOS identifies each subdirectory by means of its unique *path name*, which is explained in the next section. But if you tried to create another subdirectory named PROGRAMS below the subdirectory TBPROLOG, DOS would issue the message *Unable to create directory.*

Using Path Names

As you read about directory and file commands in this appendix, you'll notice that many of the commands use parameters consisting of one or more directory names; some parameters end with a file name. An example is

```
ERASE \TBPROLOG\PROGRAMS\TESTFILE.PRO
```

The parameter *\TBPROLOG\PROGRAMS\TESTFILE.PRO* is called a *path name*. It specifies the path along the hierarchical directory "tree" to the specified directory or file. In plain English, the preceding command means, "Erase the file named TESTFILE.PRO; this file is in the directory PROGRAMS, which is a subdirectory of the directory TBPROLOG below the root directory." Another translation is, "Search the directory TBPROLOG for the subdirectory PROGRAMS; in PROGRAMS, find the file TEST-FILE.PRO; erase that file."

If PROGRAMS does not contain the file TESTFILE.PRO, DOS issues the message *File not found*. If you specify a path name that does not exist—by entering *PROGRAM*, for example, instead of *PROGRAMS*—DOS issues the message *Invalid path or file name*.

Notice the use of the reverse slash or "backslash" character (\ ) as a prefix to the directory name. The backslash, sometimes called the *path character*, has two uses in specifying path names:

1. When the backslash appears at the beginning of a path name, the backslash means that the path begins at the root directory. (When the path name does *not* begin with a backslash, the path begins in the current or "default" directory.)

2. The backslash separates multiple elements of a path name.

This discussion assumes that the root directory is the current directory. For information on changing the current directory, see the section "Changing Directories."

In accordance with the first use of the backslash, then, the command *MD \TBPROLOG* means "Make a directory named *TBPROLOG* directly below the root directory." (The MD command is discussed elsewhere in this appendix.)

To understand the second use of the backslash, suppose that you are creating the subdirectory PROGRAMS below the TBPROLOG directory. The command you enter is

```
MD \TBPROLOG\PROGRAMS
```

The second backslash not only separates but also joins the two elements of the path name (TBPROLOG and PROGRAMS).

Actually, the first backslash (before TBPROLOG) is not necessary. We're assuming that the root directory is the current directory; the path therefore begins at the root directory. Consequently, you could just enter *MD TBPROLOG\PROGRAMS* to create the subdirectory name PROGRAMS below TBPROLOG.

However, many DOS users like to use the initial backslash even when it is not necessary, in order to eliminate errors. Suppose, for example, that you mistakenly think the root is the current directory, when in fact some subdirectory is current. Suppose also that you want to create a subdirectory named MISC below the root. If you enter *MD MISC*, your directory is created below whatever directory happens to be current; you may have difficulty finding the directory later. By entering *MD \MISC*, you ensure that the new directory is created where you want it to be, directly below the root directory.

Another optional part of the path name is the drive indicator, which, when used, appears at the beginning of the path name. If your path name does not include a drive indicator, DOS commands refer to the *current drive*. (See the next section for more information about the meaning of *current drive*.) When A: is the current drive, the command *MD TBPROLOG* causes the directory TBPROLOG to be created on the disk in drive A:. To create the directory TBPROLOG on the disk in drive B:, you enter *MD B:TBPROLOG* (or *MD B:\TBPROLOG*).

Changing the Default Drive

The disk drive used to boot DOS becomes the current drive when DOS is up and running. On floppy-disk systems, the default drive at startup is A:, and on hard-disk systems, the default drive usually is C:. The default drive is indicated by the letter appearing in the DOS prompt, such as

A>

or

C>

Unless you indicate a drive, DOS commands refer to the default drive. When A: is the default drive, for example, the command *DIR* causes DOS to show a directory listing of files on the disk in drive A:. To get a directory listing of files on the disk in drive B:, you enter *DIR B:*.

To change the default drive, you simply enter the letter of the drive followed by a colon. To make B: the default drive, for example, enter

B:

(Do not enter a space or any other character between the letter and the colon.)

Listing a Directory (DIR)

To see a listing of the files in a directory, you use the command *DIR*. If you enter this command without specifying the drive, you will see a directory listing for the current drive and subdirectory. If the current drive is A: and you want to see the directory of files in the disk in drive B:, you enter

    DIR B:

The resulting display is shown in figure C.2. Notice that besides showing information about files, the listing also shows subdirectories of the current directory. These are identified with *<DIR>*. (The directory structure of this disk differs from the structure depicted in figure C.1. If it were the same, the line *Directory of B:* in figure C.2 would read *Directory of B:\TBPROLOG.*)

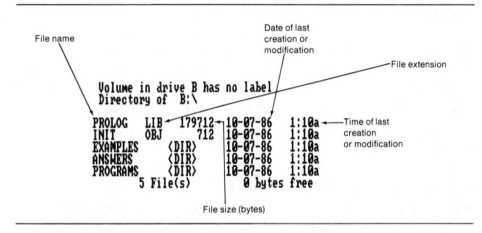

Fig. C.2. *A directory listing.*

Making a Directory (MD or MKDIR)

To create a directory or a sub-directory, use the command *MKDIR* (or the shorter form, *MD*) followed by the name of the directory you want to create. The command for creating the directory TBPROLOG, for example, is

    MD \TBPROLOG

The directory name can have a maximum of eight characters.

Like many other DOS commands, MD supports the use of path names. If you have already created the directory TBPROLOG, you can create the subdirectory PROGRAMS by entering *MD TBPROLOG\PROGRAMS.*

Changing the Default Directory (CD or CHDIR)

When you start your computer, the default directory is the root directory of the drive used to boot the operating system. Your commands and file references are assumed to refer to this directory. This directory to which you are "logged on" is called the *default directory*. Once you have begun to work, the default directory is whatever directory you are currently working in. For example, consider the following command:

```
COPY TESTFILE.PRO FILETEST.PRO
```

This command will be executed successfully if the file TESTFILE.PRO is in the default directory. If TESTFILE.PRO is in some other directory, however, the copy operation fails, and DOS issues the error message `File not found`.

When the source file and the destination file are in different directories, you can use path names to override the default directory setting. For example, to copy the file TEST-FILE.PRO from EXAMPLES to PROGRAMS, and assign the name FILETEST.PRO to the new file, you enter

```
COPY \TBPROLOG\EXAMPLES\TESTFILE.PRO \TBPROLOG\PROGRAMS\FILETEST.PRO
```

If you change the default directory, however, you can make your commands shorter and less susceptible to typing errors. One way is first to change the default directory to the destination subdirectory PROGRAMS with the command

```
CD \TBPROLOG\PROGRAMS
```

Now, unless you use a path name, DOS will interpret your commands as referring to this directory, which is the new default directory. Now you can enter the command

```
COPY \TBPROLOG\EXAMPLES\TESTFILE.PRO FILETEST.PRO
```

The file TESTFILE.PRO will be copied to the PROGRAMS subdirectory and given the new name FILETEST.PRO.

Because both EXAMPLES and PROGRAMS are below the directory TBPROLOG, you could instead make TBPROLOG the default directory. Then you could copy your file by entering *COPY EXAMPLES\TESTFILE.PRO PROGRAMS\FILETEST.PRO.*

Another use of the CD command is to "go up" through the subdirectory structure. The command

```
CD \
```

makes the root directory the default. The command

```
CD ..
```

changes the default directory to the "parent" of the directory that is current when you issue the command. If you are logged on to the subdirectory EXAMPLES, entering

    CD ..

makes TBPROLOG the new default directory. Repeated execution of this command will take you to the root directory of your disk.

You can go down the hierarchy of directories by specifying each directory with the CD command. Thus to change from the TBPROLOG directory to the EXAMPLES directory you would give the command

    CD EXAMPLES

You can also use the CD command to go directly from one directory to another:

    CD \TBPROLOG\EXAMPLES

Removing a Directory (RD or RMDIR)

Reorganization of a program or a set of files can entail removing a directory. The RMDIR command is used for that purpose. If, for example, the ANSWERS subdirectory contains a subdirectory called DEMO that you want to remove, the complete command to accomplish this task is

    RD B:\TBPROLOG\ANSWERS\DEMO

As you can see, the path name includes references to the drive, to the directory TBPROLOG, and to the subdirectory ANSWERS, which contains the subdirectory you want to remove. (If the directory you want to remove is on the current drive, then the drive reference is optional.)

A subdirectory cannot be removed if it contains any files. The commands for deleting files are discussed elsewhere in this appendix.

File Commands

Now that you have learned about directories, path names, and the commands for "moving around" in the DOS directory structure, you are ready to learn about commands that apply to individual files and groups of files. You'll find these commands most useful in your work with Turbo Prolog.

Using File Names

A DOS file specification has two parts: the file name and a file extension. The name and the extension are separated by a dot (.):

    <file name>.<extension>

The file name can be any combination of one to eight characters chosen from letters A to Z, the numbers 0 to 9, and the special characters and punctuation symbols:

! @ # $ % ^ & ( ) – _ { } ´ ~ '

The extension can be any combination of one to three characters chosen from the same set of characters.

The following names are all valid file specifications:

TEST.PRO	TEST.123	123.123
_TEST.&&&	–THIS.FIL	–THATX.DAT
MYLIFE.TXT	12345678.123	__NEXT.LIN
LOOK3.PXY	$$$$$.$$$	

Of course, some of these file names are not very informative. You'll want to choose file names and extensions that give information as to the contents and functions of the files. Extensions are commonly descriptive of file functions. The extension .DAT, for example, often identifies a data file, .TXT or .DOC a document file, .HLP a help file, and .EXE an executable program file. File names often describe of the contents of the file: MEMO12, MYLIFE, or PROGRAM6.

Using Wild-Card Characters

Like some other operating systems, DOS enables you to refer to files by means of "wild cards." If you examine again the list of permissible characters for file specifications, you will notice that the list does not contain the asterisk (*) or the question mark (?). These characters are reserved by DOS for use as wild-card characters.

The character "*" is used to refer to any number of characters in a directory, file name or extension. The following examples will show you how to use this convenient special character.

To refer to all files with the extension .PRO, you use the file specification *.*PRO*. For example, the command

    DIR *.PRO

causes DOS to show all files in the current directory with the extension *.PRO*. Similarly, to see a listing of all files with the name PRESIDENT, regardless of the extension, the command is

    DIR PRESIDENT.*

To see the listing of all files with names whose first 4 characters are TEST and whose extension is PRO, the command is

    DIR TEST*.PRO

This command causes DOS to display directory information on files with names such as *TEST1.PRO*, *TESTPRED.PRO*, and even *TEST.PRO*. (The asterisk wild-card character can stand for any character or for no character.)

Thus if you want to refer to all files in the current directory, regardless of their file names or extensions, the reference is *∗.∗*. For example, the command

```
DEL *.*
```

causes DOS to erase all files in the current directory. See the section "Deleting Files" for important warnings on the use of wild-card characters with the DEL command (or its equivalent, ERASE).

Note that the ∗ wild-card character always stands for all characters from the position of ∗ to the end of the file name or extension. Suppose, for example, that your disk contains files named PGM12OLD.PRO, PGM13OLD.PRO, and PGM14OLD.PRO, as well as files named PGM13NEW.PRO, PGM14NEW.PRO, and PGM15NEW.PRO. You want to copy the "OLD" files from the disk in drive A: to the disk in drive B:, but you do not want to copy the "NEW" files. You could not use the command

```
COPY A:PROG*OLD.PRO B:
```

because DOS would "ignore" all characters following the ∗ in the file name; the "NEW" files would be copied along with the "OLD" files. The effect would be the same as if you had entered *COPY A:PROG∗.PRO B:*. However, the *?* wild-card character enables you make this kind of selective reference to your files.

The wild-card *?* functions in the same manner as the ∗, except that it stands for any single character in the same place in the file specification. For example, to copy the files PGM12OLD.PRO, PGM13OLD.PRO, and PGM14OLD.PRO, without copying the files named PGM13NEW.PRO, PGM14NEW.PRO, and PGM15NEW.PRO, you would enter

```
COPY A:PROG??OLD.PRO B:
```

Note, however, that this command would not copy the files PROG1OLD.PRO and PROG2OLD.PRO, because the because each occurrence of the *?* stands for only one character in the file specification.

Wild-card characters are most useful. Feel free to experiment with them by using the DIR command along with various file specifications containing wild cards.

Copying Files (COPY)

You will often want to copy a file from one disk to another. To copy a file called TEST-FILE.PRO, for example, you place in drive A: (the source drive) the disk containing TESTFILE.PRO. Place a formatted disk in drive B: (the target drive), and enter

```
COPY A:TESTFILE.PRO B:
```

Note that the file name must immediately follow the drive identifier, with no intervening spaces.

Your command means, "Copy the file TESTFILE.PRO from the disk in drive A: to the disk in drive B:." The option switch /V (for *verify*) tells DOS to "double-check" the data as it is copied to the target disk.

Used in this way, the COPY command assigns the name of the file on the source-drive disk to the file on the target-drive disk. If you want the copy to have a different name from that of the original file, enter the name of the new file along with the drive identifier:

```
COPY A:TESTFILE.PRO B:NEWFILE.PRO
```

Again, no spaces can be between the drive identifier and the file name.

You need to exercise some care in copying files from one directory or disk to another. If an existing file in the target directory has the same name as the new file you are copying to the target, then the new file overwrites the existing file; DOS gives no warning beforehand.

Of course, pathnames can be used with the COPY command. To copy the file TEST-FILE.PRO from the subdirectory EXAMPLES to the subdirectory PROGRAMS and to assign the name NEWFILE.PRO to the copy, you could enter

```
COPY \TBPROLOG\EXAMPLES\TESTFILE.PRO \TBPROLOG\PROGRAMS\NEWFILE.PRO
```

If you do not want to assign a different name to the copy, you enter

```
COPY \TBPROLOG\EXAMPLES\TESTFILE.PRO \TBPROLOG\PROGRAMS
```

This command creates a new copy of TESTFILE.PRO in the directory PROGRAMS; the copy has the same name as the original.

No doubt you've noticed that these path names are lengthy. Review the section "Changing Directories" to learn how to save keystrokes by changing directories before using commands that require specification of file names.

Deleting a File (DEL or ERASE)

If you need to remove a file to make more space on a disk, or if you have produced variants of a file and no longer need them, then you will want to use the DEL command. To delete TESTFILE.PRO, for example, you might place the disk containing the file in drive B: and enter

```
DEL B:TESTFILE.PRO
```

When the deletion process is complete, the system will again display the DOS prompt.

Be careful in using the DEL (or ERASE) command. If you enter *DEL* along with a path name that ends with the name of a subdirectory, DOS will erase all files in the subdirectory. For example,

```
DEL \TBPROLOG\EXAMPLES
```

causes DOS to erase all files in the subdirectory EXAMPLES. Before erasing all files, DOS requests verification with the prompt

```
Are you sure (Y/N)?
```

If you press *N*, the command is cancelled.

However, DOS issues no warning when you use a "partial" wild-card file specification such as *.PRO*, even if that file specification applies to all files in the directory. If all files in the directory have the extension *.PRO*, the command *DEL *.PRO* causes all files to be erased—and DOS will give no warning. Be careful.

Renaming a File (REN or RENAME)

Sometimes you will want to rename a file; for instance, a data file called TESTFILE.PRO might be more useful named FILETEST.PRO. If the file is in the directory PROGRAMS on the disk in drive B:, the command to rename the file is

```
REN B:\TBPROLOG\TESTFILE.PRO FILETEST.PRO
```

Notice that the path name is not used with the new file name.

Viewing the Contents of a Text File (TYPE)

Occasionally you will want to inspect the contents of a text file. The TYPE command is used for this purpose. Suppose, for example, that you want to display on-screen the contents of the file TESTFILE.PRO. To do so, you place the disk containing the file in drive B: and enter

```
TYPE B:TESTFILE.PRO
```

Note that the TYPE command is not useful with binary files, that is, files having the extensions .OBJ, .EXE, and .COM.

Printing the Contents of a Text File (PRINT)

Often you will want to create a hardcopy (printed) listing of one of your text files to double-check your Turbo Prolog program source code. To produce the hardcopy output, place the disk containing your file in drive B: and enter the PRINT command:

```
PRINT B:TESTFILE.PRO
```

Be sure you have turned on the printer. At the prompt

```
Name of list device [PRN:]
```

press Enter. Like the TYPE command, this command is only effective with text files.

D

A Glossary of Terms

Action predicate   A predicate declared for the purpose of making a rule or goal. Compare with *database predicate*.

Anonymous variable   A variable used in place of a variable name in a clause whose specific value is of no interest. An underscore (_) symbolizes the anonymous variable.

Artificial Intelligence (AI)   The area of computer science concerned with designing computer systems that exhibit characteristics associated with intelligence in human behavior.

Backward chaining   A control procedure that starts with a goal to be achieved and recursively attempts to satisfy each unresolved subgoal until either a solution is found or all subgoals have been expanded into their simplest components.

Backtrack After Fail (BAF) method   A Prolog method that uses the *fail* predicate to backtrack in a database so that all the possible clauses are visited and examined for the intended purposes.

Backtracking   A built-in mechanism in Prolog. When an evaluation of a given subgoal is complete, Prolog returns to the previous goal and attempts to satisfy the goal in a different way.

Binding   An assignment of a variable name to a value, usually in a clause. The variable is then known as a *bound variable*.

Call   A procedure call that stands for invoking a task assigned to a built-in predicate.

Complex domain   A Turbo Prolog domain that is built from basic domains, usually involving functor(s).

Context-free grammar   A model of making a sentence where the meaning of the sentence is interpreted without reference to the context in which each constituent word is used.

Cut and Fail (CAF) method   A Prolog method which uses the *cut* predicate to stop backtracking in a database when a predefined condition is met.

Data-flow diagram (DFD)   A graphical diagram that shows the flow of data or control in a module or program; a tool used in the structured design of a program.

Database   A collection of clauses that contain data (facts). The facts are alterable by rules and predicates that act on the database.

Database predicate   A predicate declared for the purpose of storing facts in the database. Compare with *Action predicate*.

Definite clause grammar   A generalization of context-free grammar that is executable and that constitutes a notational variant of a class of Prolog programs.

Deterministic predicate   A predicate in which the internal unification process is controlled so that only a single solution is found. The opposite is *non-deterministic*.

Domain   A range and type of values defined for a basic data type. In Turbo Prolog, the basic data types are *char, integer, real, string* and *symbol*.

Dynamic database   A database in which facts can be added, altered, or deleted. It can be memory-based or disk-based.

Expert system   A computer program that emulates in a narrow domain the expertise of a human expert. It has the facility to manipulate data and infer conclusions from facts.

Expert system shell   A shell with the facility to make an expert system that usually has a database as an integral part.

External goal   A goal entered by the user when a Turbo Prolog program is running.

Forward chaining   A control procedure that starts with initial knowledge and applies rules to generate knowledge until one of the rules satisfies a goal or until no further inferences can be made.

Free variable   A variable that is not currently bound to any value.

Functor   A name for a compound object. In Turbo Prolog, functors are declared in the *predicates* division of a program.

General Recursive Rule (GRR) method   A Prolog method in which a rule is built as a recursive rule.

Goal   A collection of subgoals that Turbo Prolog attempts to satisfy. A goal may be internal or external.

Head-Tail method   A Prolog method in which the elements of a non-empty list are accessed by treating the list as a head-tail combination.

Inference engine   The part of an expert system that performs inferencing. It consists of operating rules and principles. The inference engine uses the knowledge base to reach conclusions.

Instantiation   The act of replacing a variable in a pattern or formula with a possible constant, usually as a result of searching and pattern matching.

Intelligent database   A database with the facility to accept queries written in human-oriented language (as in natural language interfaces) and in which data can be added to, modified, or deleted.

Internal goal   A goal that is presented from within a Turbo Prolog program.

Keyword analysis   A method of analyzing verbal text by using selected words as keys to perform predetermined functions.

Knowledge base   A dynamic database, usually manipulated and maintained in an expert system.

Lexical analysis   A method of analyzing text wherein the program accesses a lexicon containing symbolic definitions of the words and phrases in the text.

Logic-based expert system   An expert system in which the knowledge base is constructed as a dynamic clausal database, as in Prolog.

Module   A body of rules and predicates that perform a defined task within a Turbo Prolog program.

Natural-language processing   A branch of AI in which natural languages are modeled so that defined processes may be performed utilizing them.

Object   The name of an individual element in Turbo Prolog program construction.

Parsing   A method of separating a sentence or command string into its component parts.

Pattern matching   A matching process that compares a set of patterns embodied in rules against patterns in data, which is usually contained in a database.

Predicate   A statement of relation among objects, declared by stating its name and the domains of its arguments. An example is *likes(domain1,domain2)*, where *likes* is the predicate name and *domain1* and *domain2* are names of object domains.

Predicate logic   The study of relationships of implications between assumptions and conclusions.

Production rule   A rule in the body of a rule-based expert system that determines whether or not an entity fits the description specified by the rule.

Prolog   A programming language whose name is derived from "*Pro*gramming in *Log*ic." The language structure is based on predicate logic.

Query   An inquiry, usually in the form of a sentence or command, used to access information in a database.

Recursion   A property or structure of a rule that calls itself one or more times.

Rule   A statement of relationship between one fact and other facts. In Prolog, rules take the form $A \leftarrow B1,B2 \ldots ,Bn$, where A is the *head* of the rule and the components $B1, B2, \ldots$ are its *body*. In Turbo Prolog, rules take the form A *if* $B1,B2 \ldots Bn$.

Rule-based expert system   An expert system in which rules produce inferences; the rules are often called production rules.

Structure chart (SC)   A chart that describes a program in terms of a hierarchical structure of modules.

Syntactic analysis   A method of analyzing text in terms of sentence syntax. This method usually requires parsing of the sentence.

Token   A name, an unsigned number, or a character.

Top-down modular design (TDMD)   A program-design method in which the task of the program is divided into smaller tasks, forming a hierarchical structure of modules (tasks).

Unification   A process that attempts to match a goal with a clause. It usually includes searching, pattern-matching, and instantiation.

User-defined repeat (UDR) method   A method of making a repeat rule in which a subrule is recursive.

User interface system   The portion of a program that handles interaction with the user; it may take the form of a natural language process system, as in intelligent database systems and expert systems.

Variable   An object name beginning with a capital letter or the underscore character. See also *anonymous variable* and *free variable*.

E

Suggestions for Further Reading

Clark, K. L., and S. A. Tarnlund. *Logic Programming*. New York: Academic Press, Inc., 1982.

> A collection of papers that make up an introductory text for logic programming. Of special interest are the papers by Kowalski, Colmerauer, Bruynooghe, Mellish and Clark, *et al*.

Clocksin, W. F., and C. S. Mellish. *Programming in Prolog*. New York: Springer-Verlag, 1981.

> Prolog implementations that follow the Prolog described in Clocksin and Mellish's book are known as "C & M Prologs." This classic book presents and explains "common" C & M Prolog predicates and rules. Turbo Prolog implements many of the features described in Clocksin and Mellish.

Colmerauer, Alain. "Prolog in 10 Figures," in *Communications of ACM*, Vol. 28, No. 12, December, 1985.

> The leader of the Prolog developers explains here the working of Prolog in graphical terms. This work provides special insight on unification and tree data structures.

Date, C. J. *Database: A Primer*. Reading, Mass.: Addison-Wesley Publishing Co., 1983.

> This book describes the structure and organization of databases at the introductory level. Special attention is paid to relational databases. The book is commendable for being quite readable.

Hayes-Roth, F., D. A. Waterman and D. B. Lenat. *Building Expert Systems*. Reading, Mass.: Addison-Wesley Publishing Co., 1983.

A classic on expert systems, this work contains numerous examples from actual expert systems. Methods and techniques for rule-based systems are treated in depth.

Hogger, C. J. *Introduction to Logic Programming*. New York: Academic Press, Inc., 1984.

A major contribution to logic programming with Prolog as a primary language. This work covers derivations of logic programs and implementations in Prolog for novice and expert alike.

Jackson, Peter. *Introduction to Expert Systems*. Reading, Mass.: Addison-Wesley Publishing Co., 1986.

An introductory text on expert systems and artificial intelligence. Structures and organization of expert systems are described. Examples are provided from both rule-based and logic-based classic expert systems.

Kluznick, F., and S. Szpakowicz. *Prolog for Programmers*. New York: Academic Press, Inc., 1985.

Fundamentals of Prolog rule building with emphasis on practical applications, especially relational databases. A Toy-Prolog written in Pascal is included.

Kowalski, R. A. *Logic for Problem Solving*. New York: Elsevier Holland, 1979.

This classic book presents, clearly and patiently, the fundamentals of predicate logic. First-order logic, Horn clauses, and Robinson's unification theorem are well presented. Kowalski's book is a complete, professional work on predicate logic.

Li, Deyi. *A Prolog Database System*. Letchworth, Hertfordshire, England: Research Studies Press Ltd., 1984.

This work uses Prolog to construct relational databases, especially to write rules to make database queries. Appendix 2 of *Programming in PROLOG* is a short summary of C & M Prolog and gives many example rules.

Nilsson, N. J. *Problem-Solving Methods in Artificial Intelligence*. New York: McGraw-Hill Book Co., 1971.

This book deals with resolution-based theorem proving in predicate calculus and its application to problem solving. It gives specific details for solutions of games and puzzles in particular. There are no programming details and no programs. The classic "Monkey and Bananas" problem-solving program in *Using Turbo Prolog* is an implementation based on state representation as discussed in this book.

Pereira, F. C. N., and D. H. D. Warren. "Definite Clause Grammar for Language Analysis," in *Readings in Natural Language Processing*. Edited by Barbara J. Grosz *et al.* Los Altos, Calif.: Morgan Kaufmann Publisher, Inc., 1986.

A readable, yet comprehensive description of context-free grammar and definite-clause grammar. Techniques for sentence analysis are described in detail. This work is fundamental for natural language programming.

Rubin, Darryl. "Turbo Prolog: A Prolog Compiler for the PC Programmer," in *AI EXPERT*, Vol.1, No.1 (Premier Issue), 1986.

A review article on the features of Turbo Prolog written shortly after Version 1.0 appeared on the market. Its features for programmers and users alike are described, with special attention paid to the Geobase program as illustrative of "some interesting AI programming techniques."

Wah, B., and G.-J. Li, Editors. *Computers for Artificial Intelligence Applications*. IEEE Computer Society, The Institute of Electrical and Electronics Engineers, Inc., 1986.

This is a collection of classic papers in AI and applications. For Prolog programming, Chapter 3, "Artificial Intelligence Languages and Programming," and Chapter 7.A, "Logic Programs," are of special relevance.

Winograd, T. "A Procedural Model of Language Understanding," in *Readings in Natural Language Processing*. Edited by Barbara J. Grosz *et al.* Los Altos, Calif.: Morgan Kaufmann Publisher, Inc., 1986.

This classic paper explores the interconnection between different types of knowledge required for language understanding, using English as the topic language. It further describes the design of a program to understand sentence structures.

Winston, P. H. *Artificial Intelligence*, 2nd edition. Reading, Mass.: Addison-Wesley Publishing Co., 1984.

This work covers many research areas of AI. Of special interest are Chapter 6, "Problem-Solving Paradigms," which is useful in building rule-based expert systems and Chapter 9, "Language Understanding for Natural Language Processing."

Turbo Prolog Standard Predicates

Turbo Prolog's standard predicates are the backbone of the language. The first section of this appendix groups the predicates by function. The second section lists them in alphabetical order in the following format:

predicate(argument list) (domain types):(flowpatterns)

This listing is followed by a functional description which is the outcome of a call to the predicate for the flowpatterns.

Predicates Grouped by Function

System-Level Predicates

beep, bios, comline, date, keyword, membyte, memword, portbyte, ptr_dword, sound, storage, system, time, trace

Language Predicates

bound, exit, fail, findall, free, not

File-System Predicates

closefile, consult, deletefile, dir, disk, eof, existfile, filemode, filepos, file_str, flush, openappend, openmodify, openread, openwrite, readdevice, renamefile, save, writedevice

Reading Predicates

readchar, readint, readln, readreal, readterm

Writing Predicates

nl, write, writedevice, writef

Screen-Handling Predicates

attribute, back, clearwindow, cursor, cursorform, display, dot, edit, editmsg, field_attr, field_str, forward, gotowindow, graphics, line, makewindow, pen-color, pendown, penpos, penup, removewindow, scr_attr, scr_char, scroll, shift window, text, window_attr, window_str

Database Predicates

asserta, assertz, consult, retract, save

String-Handling Predicates

concat, frontchar, frontstr, fronttoken, isname, str_len

Type-Conversion Predicates

char_int, str_char, str_int, str_real, upper_lower

Alphabetical List of Predicates

asserta(<fact>)   (dbasedom):(i)

Inserts a fact at the beginning of a memory-resident database. (The *dbasedom* domain is automatically declared for each database predicate.)

assertz(<fact>)   (dbasedom):(i),(o)

Inserts a fact at the end of a memory-resident database.

attribute(Attr)   (integer):(i),(o)

(i): Sets screen position attribute values.
(o): Binds *Attr* to screen position default attribute value.

back(Step)   (integer):(i)

Moves the turtle cursor backward the number of steps represented by the value of *Step*. If the resultant position is beyond the edge of the screen, the predicate fails.

beep   (i)

Causes the computer to produce a high-pitched sound.

bios(InterruptNo,RegsIn,RegsOut)   (integer,regdom,regdom):(i,i,o)

Requests the operating system's interrupt services. *InterruptNo* represents a valid interrupt number, *RegsIn* is the input register list, and *RegsOut* is the output register list. The *regdom* type is predefined in Turbo Prolog. The definition is

regdom = reg(integer,integer,integer,integer,
                    integer,integer,integer,integer)

The *integer* components correspond to the microprocessor's AX, BX, CX, DX, SI, DI, DS and ES registers, respectively.

bound(Variable)   (<Any valid variable>):(o)

If *Variable* is bound, this predicate succeeds.

char_int(CharParam,IntParam)   (char,integer):(i,o),(o,i),(i,i)

(i,o): Binds *IntParam* to the ASCII value of *CharParam*.
(o,i): Binds *CharParam* to the value of *IntParam*.
(i,i): If *IntParam* is bound to the value of *CharParam*, this predicate succeeds.

clearwindow

Fills the currently active text window with its background color, thus clearing it.

closefile(SymbolicFileName)   (file):(i)

Closes the physical disk file associated the logical file *SymbolicFileName*. This predicate succeeds even if the named file is closed.

comline(Line)   (String):(o)

Permits the reading of command-line parameters for a program you have written.

concat(String1,String2,String3)
(string,string,string):(i,i,o),(o,i,i),(i,o,i),(i,i,i)

(i,i,o): Builds *String3* by concatenating *String1* and *String2*.
(o,i,i): Causes *String1* to be bound to the string "left over" from *String3* when *String2* is bound to part of *String3*.
(i,o,i): Causes *String2* to be bound to the string "left over" from *String3* when *String1* is bound to part of *String3*.
(i,i,i): Causes all parameters to be bound; if *String3* is a concatenation of *String1* and *String2*, this predicate succeeds.

consult(DOS_FileName)   (string):(i)

Loads the database file *DOS_FileName* (a text file) into the working memory.

cursor(Row,Column)   (integer,integer):(i,i),(o,o)

(i,i): Places the cursor in the position identified by the input values for *Row* and *Column*.

(o,o): Binds *Row* and *Column* to numbers identifying the cursor position.

cursorform(Startline,Endline)   (integer,integer):(i,i)

Specifies the cursor height and vertical placement within the 14 scan line display area of its position (the values can range from 1 to 14).

date(Year,Month,Day)   (integer,integer,integer):(i,i,i),(o,o,o)

(i,i,i): Sets the system date to the values bound to *Year*, *Month*, and *Day*.
(o,o,o): Retrieves the system date from the internal clock of the computer.

deletefile(DOS_FileName)   (string):(i)

Deletes the file *DOS_FileName* from the default directory.

dir(Pathname,FileSpecString,DOS_FileName)   (string,string,string):(i,i,o)

Invokes the Turbo Prolog file directory service. The input variables *Pathname* and *FileSpecString* determine what files appear in the directory window. The output variable *DOS_FileName* is bound to the name of the file selected by the user.

disk(DOS_Path)   (string):(i),(o)

(i): Specifies the current default drive and path. When the input value is a valid drive or directory name, this predicate succeeds.
(o): Binds *DOS_Path* to the current default drive and path.

display(String)   (string):(i)

Displays the value bound to *String* in the currently active window.

dot(Row,Column,Color)   (integer,integer,integer):(i,i,i),(i,i,o)

(i,i,i): "Paints" a dot (a lit pixel) on the video screen at the position specified by *Row* and *Column* in the specified *Color* when the display is in graphics mode.
(i,i,o): Binds *Color* to the number representing the color of the pixel at *Row* and *Column*.

edit(InputString,OutputString)   (string,string):(i,o)

Invokes the Turbo Prolog editor. The variable *InputString* can be edited to produce *OutputString*.

editmsg(InStr,OutStr,LeftHeader,RightHeader,Message,HelpFileName, Position,Code)
(string,string,string,string,string,string,string, integer,integer):(i,o,i,i,i,i,i,o)

Invokes the Turbo Prolog editor. An input string *InputString* can be edited to produce an output string *OutputString*. *LeftHeader* and *RightHeader* hold texts. *Position* indicates the cursor location. *HelpFileName* indicates the name of the file loaded when the Help key (F1) is pressed. *Code* signals the way in which editing was terminated (0 = function key F10; 1 = Escape key).

eof(SymbolicFileName)   (file):(i)

Succeeds if the file pointer is at the end of the file *SymbolicFileName*.

existfile(DOS_FileName)   (string):(i)

Succeeds if the *DOS_FileName* file exists in the currently active disk directory.

exit

Terminates a running program and transfers control to the Turbo Prolog system, if the program is running within the Turbo Prolog environment, or to DOS, if the program is not running within the Turbo Prolog environment.

fail

Causes backtracking by assuring that the current predicate does not succeed.

field_attr(Row,Column,Length,Attr)
(integer,integer,integer,integer):(i,i,i,i),(i,i,i,o)

(i,i,i,i): Creates a field *Length* characters long and having the attribute *Attr* starting at the position *Row*, *Column* within the current window. (The window must accommodate the defined field length and position.)

(i,i,i,o): Binds *Attr* to the value of the attribute of the field *Length* characters long starting at the position specified by *Row* and *Column*. (The window must accommodate the defined field length and position.)

field_str(Row,Column,Length,String)
(integer,integer,integer,string):(i,i,i,i),(i,i,i,o)

(i,i,i,i): Writes as many characters of *String* as will fit in a field *Length* characters long at position *Row*, *Column* in the active window.

(i,i,i,o): Binds *String* to *Length* number of characters starting at the position specified by *Row* and *Column*. (The field specified must be accommodated inside the currently active window.)

filemode(SymbolicFileName,FileMode)   (file,integer):(i,i),(i,o)

(i,i): Permits binary files to be accessed by specifying the SymbolicFileName and the FileMode (0 = text mode; 1 = binary mode).

(i,o): Returns the *FileMode* for the input *SymbolicFileName*.

filepos(SymbolicFileName,FilePosition,Mode)
(file,real,integer):(i,i,i),(i,o,i)

(i,i,i): Determines the position in the file *SymbolicFileName* at which a value will be written or read. (*Mode* = 0 indicates position relative to the beginning of the file; *Mode* = 1 indicates position relative to the current position; *Mode* = 2 indicates position relative to the end of the file.)

(i,o,i): Binds *FilePosition* to the position in *SymbolicFileName* at which the next value will be written or read. This position is relative to the beginning of the file.

file_str(DOS_FileName,StringVariable)
(string,string):(i,i),(i,o)

(i,i): Writes the characters of *StringVariable* (64K maximum) to the file *DOS_FileName*.

(i,o): Binds *StringVariable* to the characters contained in the file *DOS_FileName* (64K maximum).

findall(Variable,<atom>,ListVariable)

Stores the values of *Variable* in the list *ListVariable* list. <atom> is a predicate having Variable as one of its arguments.

flush(SymbolicFileName)   (file):(i)

Causes the contents of a file buffer in memory to be written to the current *writedevice*.

forward(Step)   (integer):(i)

In graphics mode, *forward* causes the turtle cursor to move forward by the number of steps specified by *Step*.

free(Variable)   (<variable>):(o)

Succeeds if Variable is not bound.

frontchar(String,FrontChar,RestString)
(string,char,string):(i,o,o),(i,i,o),(i,o,i),(i,i,i),(o,i,i)

(i,o,o): Binds the front character of *String* to *FrontChar* and binds the rest of String to *RestString*.
Other flow patterns are possible, so long as either *String* is bound or *FrontChar* and *RestString* are both bound.

fronstr(NumberOfChars,String1,StartStr,String2)
(integer,string,string,string):(i,i,o,o)

Binds *StartStr* to the front *NumberOfChars* from *String1*; the rest of the characters from *String1* are bound to String2.

fronttoken(String,Token,RestString)
(string,string,string):(i,o,o),(i,i,o),(i,o,i),(i,i,i,),(o,i,i)

(o,i,i): Concatenates *Token* with *RestString* to form *String*. *Token* is a group of characters constituting a Turbo Prolog <name>, or constituting a valid string representation of a Turbo Prolog integer or real number; or *Token* is a single character other than the space character.
Other flow patterns are possible, so long as at least two of the parameters are bound.

gotowindow(WindowNo)   (integer):(i)

Permits very fast shifts between windows that do not overlap. Can also be used to shift to a window behind the currently active window.

graphics(ModeParam,Palette,Background)
(integer,integer,integer):(i,i,i)

Invokes the graphics facility and sets the values for the parameters ModeParam, *Palette*, and Background.

isname(StringParam)   (string):(i)

Succeeds when the name input as *StringParam* is a Turbo Prolog name.

keypressed

Succeeds if a key has been pressed.

line(Row1,Col1,Row2,Col2,Color)
(integer,integer,integer,integer,integer):(i,i,i,i,i)

Draws a *Color* line as specified by *Row1*, *Col1*, *Row2*, and *Col2* when the display is in graphics mode.

makewindow(WindowNo,ScrAtt,FrameAttr,Header,Row,Col,Height,Width)
(integer,integer,integer,string,integer,integer,integer,integer):
(i,i,i,i,i,i,i,i),(o,o,o,o,o,o,o,o)

Creates a window identified by *WindowNo*. The window as specified by *Row*, *Col*, *Height* and *Width* must fit the screen. A border is drawn around the window when *FrameAttr* is not 0; and *Header* provides a title.

membyte(Segment,Offset,Btye)
(integer,integer,integer):(i,i,i),(i,i,o)

(i,i,i): Stores the value of *Byte* at the address in memory specified by *Segment* and *Offset*.
(i,i,o): Binds *Byte* to the value at the address in memory specified by *Segment* and *Offset*.
In both cases, the address is calculated as Segment * 16 + Offset.

memword(Segment,Offset,Word)
(integer,integer,integer):(i,i,i),(i,i,o)

(i,i,i): Stores the value of *Word* at the address in memory specified by *Segment* and *Offset*.
(i,i,o): Reads the value of Word at the address in memory specified by Segment and Offset.
In both cases, the address is calculated as Segment * 16 + Offset.

nl

Sends a carriage-return, line-feed sequence to the current *ritedevice*.

not(<atom>)

Succeeds if <atom> represents a goal that fails on evaluation.

openappend(SymbolicFileName,DOS_FileName)
(file,string):(i,i)

Opens the file *DOS_FileName* file for appending and attaches the *Symbolic-FileName* to the file.

openmodify(SymbolicFileName,DOS_FileName)   (file,string):(i,i)

Opens the file *DOS_FileName* for reading or writing and attaches *Symbolic-FileName* to the file.

openread(SymbolicFileName,DOS_FileName)   (file,string):(i,i)

Opens the file *DOS_FileName* for reading and attaches the *SymbolicFileName* to the file.

openwrite(SymbolicFileName,DOS_FileName)   (file,string):(i,i)

Opens the file *DOS_FileName* for writing and attaches the *SymbolicFileName* to the file.

pencolor(Color)   (integer):(i)

Specifies the *Color* of lines drawn by the turtle graphics pen. The display must be in graphics mode.

pendown

Causes the pen to draw lines according to the *forward* and *back* predicates.

penpos(Row,Column,Direction)
(integer,integer,integer):(i,i,i),(o,o,o)

(i,i,i): Places the graphics turtle at the position specified by *Row* and *Column* and orients the turtle to the direction specified by *Direction*.
(o,o,o): Binds the current position of the turtle to *Row* and *Column* and binds *Direction* to the heading of the turtle cursor.

penup

Causes the turtle graphics pen to stop drawing (see *pendown*).

portbyte(PortNo,Value)   (integer,integer):(i,i)(i,o)

(i,i): Causes the *Value* to be sent to the I/O port specified by *PortNo*.
(i,o): Binds *Value* to the decimal equivalent of the byte value at the I/O port specified by *PortNo*.

ptr_dword(StringVar,Segment,Offset)
(string,integer,integer): (i,o,o),(o,i,i)

(i,o,o): Returns the internal Segment and Offset address of the *StringVar* which is bound.

(o,i,i): Returns the contents of *StringVar* at the address specified by *Segment* and *Offset*. The address is calculated as Segment * 16 + Offset. The end of the string is indicated by a null byte.

readchar(CharVariable) (char):(o)

Reads a single character from the current *readdevice*.

readdevice(SymbolicFileName) (symbol):(i),(o)

(i): Selects *SymbolicFileName* for reading.

(o): Binds *SymbolicFileName* to the current *readdevice*.

readint(IntVariable) (integer):(o)

Permits an integer to be read from the current *readdevice*.

readln(StringVariable) (string):(o)

Permits a character string to be read from the current *readdevice*.

readreal(RealVariable) (read):(o)

Permits a real number to be read from the current *readdevice*.

readterm(Domain,Term) (<name>,<variable>):(i,o)

Permits any object that can be written by the *write* predicate to be read from an open file. Binds *Term* to the object so long as the object conforms with the domain declaration of *Term*.

removewindow

Removes the current window.

renamefile(OldDOS_FileName,NewDOS_FileName)
(string,string):(i,i)

Renames *OldDOS_FileName* with the value bound to *NewDOS_FileName*.

retract(<fact>) (dbasedom):(i)

Deletes the first <fact> in a database that matches the given <fact>.

save(DOS_FileName)   (String):(i)

Stores clauses for database predicates in the text file specified by *DOS_FileName*.

scr_attr(Row,Col,Attr)   (integer,integer,integer):(i,i,i),(i,i,o)

(i,i,i): The character at screen position *Row*, *Col* is given the attribute specified by *Attr*.

(i,i,o): Gives the value of Attr at screen position Row, Col.

scr_char(Row,Column,Char)   (integer,integer,char):(i,i,i),(i,i,o)

(i,i,i): Writes *Char* at the screen position specified by *Row*, *Col*.

(i,i,o): Reads the character at screen position *Row*, *Col*.

scroll(NoOfRows,NoOfCols)   (integer,integer):(i,i)

Scrolls the current window up or down by the number of rows specified in *NoOfRows*; scrolls right or left by the number of columns specified by *NoOfCols*. Scrolling is up or left for positive numbers and down or right for negative numbers.

shiftwindow(WindowNo)   (integer):(i),(o)

(i): Activates the window referred to by *WindowNo*; also stores the contents of the currently active window.

(o): Binds *WindowNo* to the number of the currently active window.

sound(Duration,Frequency)   (integer,integer):(i,i)

Causes the computer to produce a note specified by *Frequency* for *Duration* hundredths of a second.

storage(StackSize,HeapSize,TrailSize)   (real,real,real):(o,o,o)

Gives the available memory in KBytes for the three run-time memory areas.

str_char(StringParam,CharParam)   (string,char):(i,o),(o,i),(i,i)

(i,o): Binds *CharParam* to the character specified by *StringParam*.

(o,i): Binds *StringParam* to the character specified by *CharParam*.

(i,i): Succeeds if *CharParam* and *StringParam* are both bound to representations of the same character.

str_int(StringParam,IntParam)   (string,integer):(i,o),(o,i),(i,i)

(i,o): Binds *IntParam* to the binary equivalent of the decimal integer string to which *StringParam* is bound.

(o,i): Binds *StringParam* to a string of decimal digits representing the value to which *IntParam* is bound.

(i,i): Succeeds if *IntParam* is bound to the binary representation of the decimal integer to which *StringParam* is bound.

str_len(String,Length)   (string,integer):(i,i),(i,o)

(i,i): Succeeds if *Length* characters are in *String*.

(i,o): Binds *Length* to the number of characters in *String*.

str_real(StringParam,RealParam)   (string,real):(i,o),(o,i),(i,i)

(i,o): Binds *RealParam* to the binary equivalent of the real number string to which *StringParam* is bound.

(o,i): Binds *StringParam* to a string of decimal digits representing the value to which *RealParam* is bound.

(i,i): Succeeds if *RealParam* is bound to the binary representation of the decimal real number represented by the string to which *StringParam* is bound.

system(DOS_CommandString)   (string):(i)

Causes *DOS_CommandString* to be sent to DOS for execution.

text

Returns the screen to text mode from graphics mode.

time(Hours,Minutes,Seconds,Hundredths)
(integer,integer,integer,integer):(i,i,i,i),(o,o,o,o)

(i,i,i,i): Sets the system clock to the time represented by the values bound to *Hours*, *Minutes*, *Seconds*, and *Hundredths*.

(o,o,o,o): Binds *Hours*, *Minutes*, *Seconds*, and *Hundredths* to the values returned by the system clock.

trace(Status)   (symbol):(i),(o)

(i): Follows system execution in step-by-step tracing to assist in efficient development of a program when *trace(on)* is at the top of a program. *trace(off)* causes the tracing to be turned off. The variant *shorttrace* functions in the same manner, and results in less information in the Trace window.

(o): Binds *Status* to be bound to *on* or *off*, indicating the status of the tracing function.

upper_lower(StringInUpperCase,StringInLowerCase)
(string,string):(i,o),(o,i),(i,i)

- (i,o): Binds *StringInLowerCase* to the lowercase equivalent of the string bound to *StringInUpperCase*.
- (o,i): Binds *StringInUpperCase* to the uppercase equivalent of the string bound to *StringInLowerCase*.
- (i,i): Succeeds if *StringInLowerCase* and *StringInUpperCase* are bound to lowercase and uppercase versions of a string.

window_attr(Attr)   (integer):(i)

Sets attributes of the currently active window to the value to which *Attr* is bound.

window_str(ScreenString)   (string):(i),(o)

- (i): Displays the value bound to *ScreenString* in the currently active window.
- (o): Binds *ScreenString* to the string displayed in the currently active window.

write(e1,e2,e3, . . . ,eN)   ((i)*)

Causes constants or values in the currently active window to be written to the current *writedevice*. The number of arguments is optional; they can be constants or variables which are bound to values of the standard domain types.

writedevice(SymbolicFileName)   (symbol):(i),(o)

- (i): If the file *SymbolicFileName* has been opened, this predicate causes the current *writedevice* to be reassigned to this file.
- (o): Binds *SymbolicFileName* to the name of the current *writedevice*.

writef(FormatString,Arg1,Arg2,Arg3 . . .)   (i,(i)*)

Produces output in the format indicated by *FormatString*, which contains ordinary text and the marker % indicating the position of the arguments. The optional format specifiers –, m, and p, f, e, and g can be used. The hyphen causes left justification, and integer values for m and p indicate the number of digits displayed to the left and right, respectively, of the decimal point. The specifiers f and e specify fixed-point decimal notation and exponential notation, respectively. The specifier g causes the shortest form to be used.

INDEX

C

D

More Computer Knowledge from Que

Que Order Line: **1-800-428-5331** All prices subject to change without notice.

MORE COMPUTER KNOWLEDGE FROM QUE

C Programming Guide, 2nd Edition
by Jack Purdum, Ph.D.

The *C Programming Guide,* 2nd Edition, expands and updates the reader's knowledge of the applications introduced in the first edition. The second edition of the *C Programming Guide* gives numerous examples and illustrations to help you learn how to program in C. You won't want to miss the second edition of one of the best-selling C programming tutorials on the market.

> For a serious treatment of C at the tradebook level, *C Programming Guide,* 2nd Edition, is hard to beat.
> —*Computer Book Review*

1-2-3 Tips, Tricks, and Traps, 2nd Edition
By Dick Andersen and Douglas Cobb

The expanded 2nd Edition includes information on Lotus's most recent enhancements for 1-2-3: expanded memory capability, larger worksheet size, new @ functions, and new database and macro commands. For both beginning and advanced users, this quick reference offers hundreds of practical power-packed tips and helps you avoid problems when developing spreadsheets, producing graphs, using macros, and much more. Learn techniques for creating special 1-2-3 applications, such as setting up data-entry forms and validating data entered into a database. If you use 1-2-3, *Tips, Tricks, and Traps,* 2nd Edition, is a must.

dBASE III Plus Advanced Programming, 2nd Edition
by Joseph-David Carrabis

dBASE III Plus Advanced Programming, 2nd Edition, is for experienced programmers who thrive on challenge. Stretch your programming skills as you tackle sophisticated and proven techniques for writing tighter, faster, more efficient dBASE programs. Learn what good programming is by examining examples of code, as well as underlying theories and concepts. A special section shows you what add-on packages such as Nantucket's Clipper, C Tools, dBRUN, RunTime+, and dBASE Programmer's Utilities can do. Also featured is a discussion of Plus' networking capabilities and a handy Command Reference appendix.

Using Paradox
by George T. Chou, Ph.D.

A powerful database program, Paradox is capable of managing large amounts of data quickly and easily. *Using Paradox* emphasizes this program's free-form database style to develop useful business applications. Examples of Paradox's program logic and illustrations help show how Paradox can be used in everyday business situations. *Using Paradox* is easily understood and will become a desk reference for both beginning and advanced users.

Mail to: Que Corporation • P. O. Box 50507 • Indianapolis, IN 46250

Item	Title	Price	Quantity	Extension
188	C Programming Guide, 2nd Edition	$19.95		
62	1-2-3 Tips, Tricks, and Traps, 2nd Edition	$19.95		
79	dBASE III Plus Advanced Programming, 2nd Edition	$22.95		
191	Using Paradox	$21.95		
		Book Subtotal		
		Shipping & Handling ($2.50 per item)		
		Indiana Residents Add 5% Sales Tax		
		GRAND TOTAL		

Method of Payment:

☐ Check   ☐ VISA   ☐ MasterCard   ☐ American Express

Card Number _____ Exp. Date _____

Cardholder's Name _____

Ship to _____

Address _____

City _____ State _____ ZIP _____

If you can't wait, call **1-800-428-5331** and order TODAY.

All prices subject to change without notice.

FOLD HERE

Place
Stamp
Here

Que Corporation
P. O. Box 50507
Indianapolis, IN 46250

SAVE VALUABLE TIME!

Gain immediate access to all the programs listed in this book and the data files for the programs that require them with the

Using Turbo Prolog Disk
Only $29.95

Available in IBM PC format, this handy, ready-to-run disk is worth the small investment. Order your disk **TODAY** and save yourself the time and trouble of manual entry.

Mail to: Que Corporation • P.O. Box 50507 • Indianapolis, IN 46250

Please send _____ copy(ies) of *Using Turbo Prolog* disk(s), #279, at $29.95 each.

Subtotal	$ _____
Shipping & handling ($2.50 per item)	$ _____
Indiana residents add 5% sales tax	$ _____
TOTAL	$ _____

Method of Payment:

☐ Check ☐ VISA ☐ MasterCard ☐ American Express

Card Number _____ Expiration Date _____

Cardholder's Name _____

Ship to _____

Address _____

City _____ State _____ ZIP _____

In a hurry? Call **1-800-428-5331** and order TODAY.

All prices subject to change without notice.

UTP-875

FOLD HERE

_____

_____

_____

_____

Que Corporation
P. O. Box 50507
Indianapolis, IN 46250

FOLD HERE

Que Corporation
P. O. Box 50507
Indianapolis, IN 46250